From Mental Imagery to Spatial Cognition and Language

The nature of mental images and their relation to language has caused controversy amongst psychologists for years, and the so-called "imagery debate" is still unresolved. Fresh light is now being shed on this topic using recent findings in neuroscience and the development of behavioural studies.

Reviewing state-of-the-art research in the field of imagery, visuo-spatial memory, spatial representation and language, with special emphasis on their interactions, this volume shows how, and to what extent, findings from studies on imagery can positively influence and enrich other psychological areas, such as:

- Working memory
- Space and time representation
- Language and embodiment

Chapter 9, written by Michel Denis, to whom this book is dedicated, analyses more than three decades of research and outlines the shared scientific journey of friendship and discovery that has developed across various cognitive topics, all of which are linked to, and inspired by, imagery conceptualization.

This is the only book to present a critical outline of research on these topics in a single volume and, as such, will be invaluable to advanced undergraduates, postgraduates and researchers in such fields as cognitive psychology, neuroscience, computer science and neuropsychology.

Valérie Gyselinck is Professor of Psychology at the University of Paris Descartes, France. Her main research interest is visuo-spatial working memory in the construction of spatial representations.

Francesca Pazzaglia is Professor of Psychology at the University of Padua, Italy. Her research interests are individual differences in spatial cognition.

From Mental Imagery to Spatial Cognition and Language

Essays in Honour of Michel Denis

Edited by Valérie Gyselinck and Francesca Pazzaglia

Psychology Press
Taylor & Francis Group

LONDON AND NEW YORK

First published 2012
by Psychology Press
27 Church Road, Hove, East Sussex BN3 2FA

Simultaneously published in the USA and Canada
by Psychology Press
711 Third Avenue, New York NY 10017

[www.psypress.com]

Psychology Press is an imprint of the Taylor & Francis Group, an informa business

© 2012 Psychology Press

British Library Cataloguing in Publication Data
A catalogue record for this book is available from the British Library

Library of Congress Cataloging-in-Publication Data
From mental imagery to spatial cognition and language: essays in
honour of Michel Denis / edited by Valérie Gyselinck and
Francesca Pazzaglia.
     p. cm.
  Includes bibliographical references and index.
  ISBN 978–1–84872–049–7 (hb)
  1. Imagery (Psychology)   2. Cognition.   3. Language acquisition.
  I. Denis, Michel, 1943-   II. Gyselinck, Valérie.   III. Pazzaglia,
  Francesca.   IV. Title.
  BF367.F766 2012
  153.3′2—dc23

                                                              2011032321

ISBN: 978–1–84872–049–7 (hbk)

Typeset in Times New Roman
by RefineCatch Ltd, Bungay, Suffolk

Cover design by Hybert Design

Printed and bound in Great Britain by
TJ International Ltd, Padstow, Cornwall

Contents

Acknowledgments   vii
List of contributors   viii
Foreword   ix
CESARE CORNOLDI AND ROSSANA DE BENI

Introduction   xi

PART I
Events and representations   1

1 **Telling tales, or journeys**   3
   BARBARA TVERSKY

PART II
Visual imagery and imagery processes   17

2 **Scanning visual mental images: some structural
   implications, revisited**   19
   GRÉGOIRE BORST AND STEPHEN M. KOSSLYN

3 **Visual imagery in the brain: modality-specific and spatial,
   but perhaps without space**   43
   HUBERT D. ZIMMER

PART III
Working memory and imagery   75

4 **Working memory: an ensemble of functions in
   on-line cognition**   77
   ROBERT H. LOGIE AND ELAINE H. NIVEN

5   Theories and debate in visuo-spatial working memory:
    the questions of access and rehearsal   106
    J. GERRY QUINN

PART IV
Language, space, and action   125

6   Individual differences in spatial text processing   127
    FRANCESCA PAZZAGLIA, VALÉRIE GYSELINCK, CESARE CORNOLDI,
    AND ROSSANA DE BENI

7   Language of space: a comparison between blind and
    sighted individuals   162
    MATTHIJS L. NOORDZIJ AND ALBERT POSTMA

8   Language and action: an approach to embodied cognition   177
    MANUEL DE VEGA

PART V
Interconnections   201

9   Decades of images: reminiscences of a shared scientific journey 203
    MICHEL DENIS

    Name index   255

    Subject index   265

Acknowledgments

We are indebted to many friends and colleagues who helped us in many ways to allow this book to exist; our thanks for their scientific advice and personal support.

First of all, we would like to thank the chapter authors for the enthusiasm they demonstrated in adhering to this project and for the very uncommon timeliness they demonstrated in respecting deadlines. As leading scholars in their specific topics, they gave their best not only in providing in-depth analyses of their research topic, but also in underlining the potential connections among the different areas. It was a pleasure and an honor for us to collaborate with them in the completion of this book.

Then, we would like to thank some eminent scientists we solicited to review some of the chapters, and who accepted very gently and enthusiastically. They have obviously contributed to enhancing the quality of the book. Thanks to Grégoire Borst, Cesare Cornoldi, Tad Brunyé, Tina Iachini, Maria Kozevhnikov, David Pearson, Trevor Harley, Gerry Quinn, John T. E. Richardson, Holly Taylor, and an anonymous reviewer.

Thanks also to Cesare Cornoldi and Rossana De Beni, for their support to us in the present project and for their important role in our professional growth. They are esteemed colleagues and sincere friends.

Finally, our thoughts and gratitude go to Michel Denis. He is an eminent scientist who has given us a lot, from both a professional and personal point of view. We cannot forget the insightful discussions on scientific topics and the friendly meetings with him and Maryvonne Carfantan in Paris, Venice, Padua, and in many other beautiful places where our common research brought us. Thank you Michel. We wish you many years of professional and personal achievements.

This book originated from the International Workshop on Mental Imagery, Spatial Cognition, and Language (MICL 2009), in honour of Michel Denis, which was held in Padua and Venice (Italy) on 12–13 June 2009. We are indebted to Francesco Del Prete and David Giofrè for their help in the organization. We also gratefully acknowledge all the colleagues who attended the workshop and thank the Department of General Psychology, the University of Padua, ADESCO, AIRIPA, and ESCOP for their financial support.

Contributors

Grégoire Borst: University Paris Descartes, Sorbonne Paris Cité, GINDEV–CNRS, Paris, France.

Cesare Cornoldi: University of Padova, Italy.

Rossana De Beni: University of Padova, Italy.

Michel Denis: LIMSI-CNRS, Orsay, France.

Manuel de Vega: University of La Laguna, Spain.

Stephen M. Kosslyn: Center for Advanced Study in the Behavioral Sciences, and Department of Psychology, Stanford University, Stanford, CA, USA.

Robert H. Logie: Human Cognitive Neuroscience, University of Edinburgh, UK.

Elaine H. Niven: Human Cognitive Neuroscience, University of Edinburgh, UK.

Matthijs L. Noordzij: Department of Cognitive Psychology and Ergonomics, University of Twente, The Netherlands.

Albert Postma: Experimental Psychology, Helmholtz Institute, Utrecht University, The Netherlands; Department of Neurology, University Medical Centre Utrecht, The Netherlands.

J. Gerry Quinn: University of St Andrews, UK.

Barbara Tversky: Columbia Teachers College and Stanford University, USA.

Hubert D. Zimmer: Department of Psychology, Brain & Cognition Unit, Saarland University, Germany.

Foreword

Cesare Cornoldi and Rossana De Beni

The study of mental imagery underwent a tumultuous growth in the second part of the twentieth century, when the ostracism was finally removed. During that time, researchers in the field were involved in showing the legitimacy of the area and in examining the various facets of human mental images. Mental images have been mainly, although not completely, considered in their visuospatial form, and it is not surprising that one of the most important developments of the research in this area has concerned spatial cognition. In fact, spatial cognition is based on spatial representations, which can be considered one of the most important examples of mental images. Therefore, a book that collects essays by some of the most prominent researchers in the areas of mental imagery and spatial processes well represents the interface between the two areas.

But what about language? Language has been always considered as the area opposed to that of mental imagery. Sometimes the definition of mental imagery has itself been based on the exclusion of verbal (or propositional) processes. Why, then, does the book also include language? There are two reasons. The first resides in the fact that language has many forms of interaction with imaginal processes. The generation of mental images may be primed by verbal instructions; mental images can be evoked for a deeper encoding of verbal material and can be described with the help of language. In particular, linguistic descriptions of spatial layouts can be adequately processed only on the basis of imaginal spatial representations. The present book is interested in language only to the extent that there are implications for mental imagery. The second reason is that the area represented by the overlap between mental imagery, space, and language can be identified as the core scientific interest of Michel Denis, to whom this book is dedicated.

Michel Denis has gained an outstanding international reputation for a series of different roles and contributions, but we like to remember him for the fact that he was one of the protagonists of the Mental Imagery Renaissance, which gave rise to new interest in the area and led to the development of a European Network on Mental Imagery (which is still active), creating the premises for the development of a series of research lines that have characterized the research in the field. Many of the authors of the chapters of the present volume have assiduously attended the biennial meetings organized within the Imagery and Cognition network. At the same time, Denis has maintained strict contact with some of the research leaders in America, as eyewitnessed by their presence in the book.

When we were informed that Michel was close to retirement, we decided, together with Valérie Gyselinck and Francesca Pazzaglia, in agreement with friends and colleagues, to organize a workshop that could include the topics he had developed on imagery, space, and language and could also offer a coherent and updated view of the research in this area. The workshop was held on 12 June 2009 at our University of Padua and had a continuation the following day in Venice, a city that Michel has always loved and that is associated with one of the most popular studies he ran. The workshop was intense and rich of stimulations and is at the origins of the present book. However, we did not want the book to be simply considered as a text of circumstance or a nostalgic review of old lines of researches. The precious efforts of the editors have created a compact text in which the authors have been able to show how fresh ideas and data can be used for renovating the classic lines of research in mental imagery, space, and language. We are grateful to Michel for having in many ways inspired the research, but we are also grateful to him for inspiring this book. Without his influential contacts, we would have not been able to bring together a group of such important researchers!

Introduction

The cognitive revolution of the 1950s marked the end of behaviorism and the rise of cognitive psychology. In this context, research on mental imagery began to reemerge with the pioneering work of Alan Paivio (see Paivio, 1971), which led to the development of objective methods to study the properties of the mental representations that underlie imagery. Very soon, studies on imagery proved their fruitfulness in many cognitive fields, bringing evidence that imagery was involved in fundamental cognitive functions such as learning (e.g., Paivio, 1971), memory (e.g., Schacter, 1996), and reasoning (e.g., Kosslyn, 1983).

The present book offers a clear example of how, and to what extent, findings from mental imagery studies (chapters 2 and 3) can provide useful information on other psychological dominions, such as working memory (chapters 4 and 5), spatial cognition and spatial language (chapters 6 and 7), reflection on space and time representation (chapter 1), and language and embodiment (chapter 8). Chapter 9, written by Michel Denis, to whom this book is dedicated, looks at over more than three "decades of images", presenting the many productive interconnections of a "shared scientific journey", which has put together friendship and scientific discoveries in different cognitive topics, all linked to, and inspired by, imagery conceptualization.

The encoding, maintenance, and processing of visual and spatial information are important components of the human cognitive system and have been fruitful fields of investigation in the recent decades. In editing the present book, our intention has been to offer an updated review of the studies on imagery, spatial representation, and language, with a particular emphasis on their interactions. With a broad vista from cognitive models to the neural underpinning of particular cognitive processes, the various chapters review and discuss critical issues and influential models in the fields of cognition concerned with mental imagery, with a theoretical emphasis on the perceptual-like nature of visual mental images, visuospatial working memory (VSWM), spatial mental models, spatial cognition and blindness, and spatial language and action. Particular attention is also devoted to individual differences and cognitive styles in spatial representation and imagery. However, the range of topics goes above and beyond those of typical books on spatial cognition, language, and imagery. For example, chapter 1 is concerned with the role of visuospatial processes in segmenting events in comics and graphic novels, which opens new theoretical and applied opportunities for research in media communication.

The visual imagery debate

In spite of almost fifty years of empirical research, understanding visual imagery remains a challenge. Many authors considered that visual imagery processes were modality-specific and analogue and were fundamentally different from verbal processes, which were seen as propositional. However, the question of the nature of mental images, their format of representation, and their relation to language – the so-called imagery debate – has been strongly discussed for years and is still unresolved. Two opposite accounts of visual imagery have been formulated: one asserts that representations that underlie the experience of mental imagery are the same as those used in language (e.g., Pylyshyn, 1981, 2003); the other (e.g., Kosslyn, 1980, 1994), that mental representations underlining imagery "serve to depict, not describe, objects" (Kosslyn, 2005, p. 333). The terms of the debate changed over time, even though the focus still remained the format of imagery representations. During the last two decades, neurocognitive research has brought indisputably new evidence in favor of the depictive format of visual mental images, but it has not closed the controversy (Kosslyn, 2005; Pylyshyn, 2003). Not all research has focused on the debate per se. In parallel, some mental imagery studies addressed other issues and have contributed to shedding light on how the cognitive system works in general and on the relations between imagery and language, imagery and visuospatial memory, and imagery and spatial representations. In this book, the format of imagery representations will be considered (see chapters 2 and 3), but we intend to provide a broader overview of imagery by presenting studies in which the imagery construct has been used to inform other cognitive domains, such as memory, spatial language, and spatial representation.

The outline of the book

The opening chapter of the book is a conceptual journey into depictions and event representation, in relation to Michel Denis's work. Part II is devoted to visual imagery and imagery processes; Part III is devoted to working memory (WM) and images; and Part IV opens the door to the language of space. The closing chapter is written by Michel Denis, who proposes another journey in the history of his research in relation to the history of research in imagery and its connections to language and spatial cognition.

In each chapter, the authors provide a short review of the research area and discuss major points and controversies of the various theoretical models, along with relevant experimental evidence and future research directions. By doing so, the hope is to provide readers with a complete, updated, and critical overview of this field of research.

Part I: Events and representations

The opening chapter is presented as a conceptual journey that Barbara Tversky proposes we should follow. She offers a wide review of the literature on spatial language and figural representation, with historical examples and a special focus on the cognitive characteristics of figural language.

The starting point is a review of Tversky's and her collaborators' studies on cognitive maps and the characteristics of them with regard to the specificities of the environment to be represented. Tversky also analyzes the vehicle (language or depictions) used for the construction of such a representation and how it influences the representation itself: "We were interested in how people described environments they learned from maps and how people understood those descriptions. We found that people's spontaneous descriptions took one of two perspectives: either one from above, a survey perspective, or one from within, a route perspective" (chapter 1, p. 4). Another example of spatial language – route directions – is then examined, with a comparison between route sketches and route descriptions. Investigation of route directions is extended to different forms of directions: from directions to get from here to there to directions for putting something together, with final indications of a number of cognitive design principles. The comparison between verbal and pictorial instructions allows the reader to look for the parallels in semantics and syntax that would suggest the same underlying mental representation.

Finally, the chapter focuses on the analysis of visual narratives: "What intrigued us is that like verbal narratives, visual narratives are highly structured and convey rich and layered meanings" (chapter 1, p. 9), with a deep examination of the cognitive mechanisms underlining the use and comprehension of a set of visual devices, such as frames and arrows, that are frequently used in visual narratives and carry shared meanings.

Part II: Visual imagery and imagery processes

To determine the closest route between two points or whether a window was left open in an apartment, people often report having visualized the scene. The study of the format of this type of visual mental images, and the way these representations are generated and manipulated, are developed in Part II. To this end, imagery processes and their neurocognitive basis are considered and discussed in chapters 2 and 3. An examination of past and more recent behavioral and neuroimaging studies on image generation and inspection will allow readers to establish what assumptions are definitely supported by research and, further, what issues are still open to debate.

Chapter 2 focuses on the studies on image scanning, defined as a systematic shifting of attention over an object or scene in a mental image. Studies of image scanning are of great interest not only because of what they can tell us about the mechanisms of visual cognition per se, but also because of what they can tell us about the structural properties of the representations. The rationale of image scanning studies is that if mental images are in some sense pictorial, then space in the representation should embody actual space, resulting in an increase of scanning time with increasing distance between objects. In this chapter, Grégoire Borst and Stephen Kosslyn first review previous research on image scanning and the way it illuminates the properties of the underlying representations. They then describe experiments conducted to examine whether the structure of spatial images created from information stored in long-term memory is similar to the structure of iconic images with degraded spatial structure. Finally, they discuss the distinction between functional and structural equivalence of imagery and perception and argue that the two are not dissociable.

Chapter 3 discusses the possibility for neuroscientific methods to improve our understanding of imagery – more specifically, the format of images in our mind and the existence of "picture-like" representations. The discussion, made mainly in reference to Kosslyn's view, goes beyond a simple review of literature and instead proposes a (new) controversy. Hubert Zimmer presents in chapter 3 a selection of results on imagery and its neurocognitive basis in order to revisit the imagery debate, and asks about the functional role of the visual buffer. He analyzes which assumptions can be considered as well supported and which are still awaiting a resolution. The conclusion is mixed. On the one hand, at a global level, neuroscientific data provide clear evidence for the existence of specific imagery processes that are different from verbal ones. On the other hand, however, some of these processes seem to be less holistic than originally assumed. For example, object processing is highly fragmented. Most importantly, some central questions are still open – the data do not yet tell us whether a visual buffer really exists, where it is located in the brain, and how it provides the analogue processes that are considered as the origin of a conscious image. Understanding visual imagery therefore remains a challenge even after two decades of neurocognitive research.

Part III: Working memory and imagery

The two fields of research on working memory (WM) and imagery share a number of common benchmarks. For example, in the first paragraph of chapter 9, Michel Denis very clearly illustrates the mutual support (other than the theoretical divergences) between constructs derived from the study of WM and imagery. The original formulation of the visuospatial sketchpad (VSSP; see, e.g., Baddeley, 1986) as a WM component designed for the encoding, maintenance, and manipulation of visuospatial information made it a privileged cognitive structure involved in visual mental images activation, storage, and processing. In the same step, there are affinities between the VSSP and the visual buffer (Kosslyn, 1980), a structure thought to hold images either generated from long-term memory or coded from perceptual inputs or verbal descriptions. Several studies (Logie & Salway, 1990; Pearson, Logie, & Gilhooly, 1999; Pearson, Logie, & Green, 1996) demonstrated that visuospatial WM (VSWM; Logie, 1995) plays a role in the manipulation of mental images – such as during mental rotation and mental synthesis. Chapters 4 and 5 of this book are devoted to WM, with a particular emphasis on the issue of considering separate systems for verbal and for visual and spatial memory, and the analysis of theoretical consequences in WM architecture.

In chapter 4, Robert Logie and Elaine Niven propose a very closely argued refutation of the way individual differences data have been used to support a view of WM as activated long-term memory rather than the classical long-standing view issued from Baddeley and Hitch's (1974) initial model. In this last view, WM is rather considered as an ensemble of domain-specific functions. Studies based on the individual differences approach and complex span methodology are critically reviewed by the authors to shed light on our understanding of the cognitive functions of WM. Although many of the experiments reported deal with verbal WM, an examination of VSWM studies is also proposed, which has to be considered to complement the debate.

In chapter 5, Gerry Quinn, in line with the view defended by Logie and Niven, investigates visuospatial fractionation within the VSWM component. The chapter questions the adequacy of a number of techniques used to study visuospatial memory. Over recent years, the Corsi block test has been shown to involve a number of codes, including spatial-sequential and executive codes. More recently, the visual patterns test, a popular technique adopted to investigate specifically visual coding, has also been shown to involve a number of codes over and above the visual, again including executive ones. Experiments are presented further raising the issue of visual empirical techniques and suggesting that separation of the visual and the spatial, rather than their integration, may lead to an improved understanding of "visuospatial" processes.

Part IV: Language, space, and action

Spatial information can be obtained from various input channels – vision, locomotion, proprioception – and even by means of more abstract, linguistic descriptions. Imagery and WM play an important role in the construction, maintenance, and reactivation of mental models derived from spatial language. Chapters 6 and 7 use the theoretical backgrounds presented in the preceding chapters and extends them to very recent research fields that connect space representation to language and action. Sensorimotor components in cognition and action are central in the current debate on the embodied cognition approach and are discussed in chapter 8.

In chapter 6, Francesca Pazzaglia, Valérie Gyselinck, Cesare Cornoldi, and Rossana De Beni review the studies on spatial text processing and demonstrate that spatial abilities and VSWM are specifically involved in spatial text processing. Spatial text processing is described as the coordinated work of distinct cognitive components: verbal and spatial abilities, verbal, visual, and spatial WM components. In the first part of the chapter, the most relevant text comprehension models related to this topic are reviewed. Then, spatial mental models derived from spatial descriptions are analyzed, with a particular emphasis on the contribution of mental images, imaginative strategies, and VSWM in the construction of an "accurate" spatial representation. Finally, the study of individual differences in spatial text processing is presented to emphasize the importance of such analyses in order to get more information on the cognitive mechanisms involved in everyday complex tasks.

The examination of the cognitive components of spatial language continues in chapter 7, where Matthijs Noordzij and Albert Postma review studies comparing blind and sighted people. The chapter focuses on whether and how blind and sighted people generate spatial representations from language and haptic inputs. The role of text perspective and of metric encoding is specifically examined. Evidence is provided that blind people have a preference for spatial descriptions from a route perspective, whereas sighted individuals express preference for text from a survey perspective. Interestingly, in both groups the mental representations created possess an intrinsic "metric" even though this information was not explicitly provided in the verbal descriptions. A number of quantitative and qualitative differences between groups of blind and sighted people in haptic learning of a spatial array are presented.

Chapter 8 considers the particular case of language where not only spatial information but also actions are represented. Very recently, a field of studies has developed within the renewed theoretical background of embodied cognition. The issue examined by Manuel de Vega is whether action verbs are processed in a peculiar, not abstract, way that requires the involvement of brain motor areas. The conclusion, which supports the embodiment approach, is that action language indeed has a special cognitive status and involves the activation of motor simulation areas in the brain.

The author presents an updated, well-argued, and convincing case in favor of an embodied view of language. In particular, strengths and limits of evidence supporting the motor simulation basis of linguistic processes are discussed. Evidence showing the crucial relevance of action simulation for language comprehension is presented. The author brings support to the existence of motor system activation and discusses the apparent ambiguity of experimental data showing that the motor system may yield both facilitation and interference. Abstraction is the challenge faced by the embodied cognition view, and this point is discussed by showing that an embodied approach may satisfactorily respond to the challenges of a symbolic approach. Recognizing that some unclear aspects of an embodied interpretation have to be clarified, the author opens new opportunities for research.

Part V: Interconnections

Chapter 9 is the ideal closing chapter and conclusion to this volume. Its author, Michel Denis, illustrates and examines from a critical point of view the many productive interconnections between imagery conceptualization and the domains of cognitive psychology addressed throughout the other chapters.

In the first section of the chapter, the concept of imagery is presented in association with the discussions that led to the differentiation of the subsystems of WM, with particular consideration to the visuospatial sketchpad subsystem (Baddeley, 1986) and the subsequent VSWM model (Logie, 1995). Then, the role of imagery is considered with reference to the conceptualization of mental models, and within the field of spatial cognition. The role of imagery in the construction of mental representations of routes and environments is acknowledged. Moreover, the chapter illustrates how the investigation of the properties of images constructed from language contributed to the study of the mental representations of blind people. Michel Denis concludes his chapter affirming that even though some questions remain unsolved, it is remarkable for a cognitive construct like imagery to have broadened the perspectives of research in human cognition and to have disseminated profitably to other domains of psychological knowledge. We agree with this latter optimistic view of Michel Denis, and we think that the book offers a concrete overview of how imagery research has developed and influenced the study of cognitive processes.

Valérie Gyselinck and Francesca Pazzaglia

References

Baddeley, A. D. (1986). *Working memory*. Oxford, UK: Clarendon Press.

Baddeley, A. D., & Hitch, G. J. (1974). Working memory. In G. H. Bower (Ed.), *The psychology of learning and motivation: Advances in research and theory* (Vol. 8, pp. 47–89). New York: Academic Press.

Kosslyn, S. M. (1980). *Image and mind*. Cambridge, MA: Harvard University Press.

Kosslyn, S. M. (1983). Mental representation. In J. R. Anderson & S. M. Kosslyn (Eds.), *Tutorials in learning and memory: Essays in honor of Gordon Bower*. San Francisco, CA: W. H. Freeman.

Kosslyn, S. M. (1994). *Image and brain*. Cambridge, MA: Harvard University Press.

Kosslyn, S. M. (2005). Mental images and the brain. *Cognitive Neuropsychology, 22*, 333–347.

Logie, R. H. (1995). *Visuo-spatial working memory*. Hove, UK: Lawrence Erlbaum Associates.

Logie, R. H., & Salway, A. F. S. (1990). Working memory and modes of thinking: A secondary task approach. In K. J. Gilhooly, M. T. Keane, R. H. Logie, & G. E. Erdos (Eds.), *Lines of thinking: Reflections on the psychology of thought* (Vol. 2, pp. 99–113). Chichester, UK: Wiley.

Paivio, A. (1971). *Imagery and verbal processes*. New York: Holt, Rinehart and Winston.

Pearson, D. G., Logie, R. H., & Gilhooly, K. J. (1999). Verbal representations and spatial manipulation during mental synthesis. *European Journal of Cognitive Psychology, 11*, 295–314.

Pearson, D. G., Logie, R. H., & Green, C. (1996). Mental manipulation, visual working memory, and executive processes. *Psychologische Beiträge, 38*, 324–342.

Pylyshyn, Z. W. (1981). The imagery debate: Analogue media versus tacit knowledge. *Psychological Review, 87*, 16–45.

Pylyshyn, Z. W. (2003). Return of the mental image: Are there really pictures in the brain? *Trends in Cognitive Science, 7*, 113–118.

Schacter, D. L. (1996). *Searching for memory: The brain, the mind, and the past*. New York: Basic Books.

Part I

Events and representations

1 Telling tales, or journeys

Barbara Tversky

Years ago, Michel Denis gave us the secret of life. Life, after all, is a journey. And Michel gave us the instruction manual for a journey, the Denis Plan. According to the Denis Plan, the trick is to break it into steps, into segments, into parts. Segmenting is so crucial that it applies not just to space, but to time; not just to each alone, but to both together; after all, that's what a journey is. Indeed, this key step applies equally to any knowledge domain. But this is only the beginning. Each major segment can be further segmented, and the segments are not mere slices, they are integral parts, wholes at a finer level. For a journey: first a Start Point, then a Reorientation, then an Action, with progression along its path, and finally an End Point. Repeat until destination is reached. As he, Francesca Pazzaglia, Cesare Cornoldi, and Laura Bertolo have shown, this instruction manual is so good it even works in Venice (Denis, Pazzaglia, Cornoldi, & Bertolo, 1999). And, as should be evident by now, this is an instruction manual for life: Start somewhere. Reorient. Take an action. Arrive somewhere. Repeat.

Michel's life has included many journeys. Some have been to pursue research in imagery and spatial cognition, some have been to promote cognitive psychology in France and Europe, some have been to advance scientific psychology in the world. He has been an exemplary leader in each of those journeys, forging the way, seeking others to accompany him, encouraging them, coalescing communities, and finding resources to nurture them. I was fortunate to get picked up on one of his earliest journeys, into imagery and spatial cognition. His visits to Stanford and invitations to Paris allowed his work to inspire mine, and perhaps vice versa. He involved me in his efforts on behalf of the International Union of Psychological Sciences, first the inspiring International Congresses, and then the governance, where he served elegantly as Chair. What follows is a selective view of our work and his, the many places where our separate routes through cognitive psychology have intersected, and some where they diverged.

Cognitive maps

When I first met Michel, among other things, he had been working on scanning mental maps, using a paradigm of Steve Kosslyn (for a description of this paradigm, see chapters 2 and 9, this volume), another scholar whom he had picked up on his virtual and real travels. Somewhat later, Holly Taylor and I began a different way to study maps and mental maps. We were interested in how people described environments they learned from maps and how people understood those descriptions. We found that people's spontaneous descriptions took one of two perspectives: either one from above, a survey perspective, or one from within, a route perspective. In a survey perspective, people describe landmarks relative to one another in terms of north, south, east, and west – for example, "The Eiffel Tower is west of the Louvre". In a route perspective, people describe landmarks relative to a moving traveler, "you," in terms of left, right, front, and back – for example, "As you travel up the Seine, you will see the Louvre on your right and, later, the Eiffel Tower on your left" (Taylor & Tversky, 1992, 1996). Despite claims that perspective should be consistent, half our participants mixed perspectives, often mid-sentence, rarely – if ever – signaling the switch. Rather than depending on some fixed mental representation, choice of perspective in descriptions depended on features of the environments; environments with landmarks on several size scales and with multiple routes received relatively more survey descriptions. Perspective is not just survey (or exocentric, the term favored by environmental psychologists, or absolute, the term favored by some linguists) or route (or egocentric or intrinsic or embedded). An embedded perspective can be yours or mine. In an interactive situation, we found that choice of perspective also depended on the relative cognitive loads of speaker and listener (Mainwaring, Tversky, Ohgishi, & Schiano, 2003). Participants were asked to describe the location of one object – say, a cache of gems – to a purported partner in espionage with a different perspective on the scene. Speakers spontaneously adopted the listener's perspective when the cognitive load of the listener was greater than that of the speaker, but speakers took their own perspective when their cognitive load was greater.

More surprisingly, we have found that people often spontaneously adopt another's perspective rather than their own even in a noninteractive situation (Tversky & Hard, 2009). Students sharing the same perspective as an experimenter were shown a photograph of a man seated at a table with a bottle to his left, reaching for a book on his right, and they were asked, "In relation to the bottle, where did he put the book?" More students answered from the perspective of the man in the photo, "on the right," than from their own and the experimenter's perspective. That one's own perspective does not necessarily have primacy and that perspective-taking is flexible and consequently responsive to the circumstances suggests that mental representations of well-learned environments may be perspective-free. That this is the case is corroborated by companion research showing that spatial mental models of well-learned environments were more abstract than any specific perspective (Taylor & Tversky, 1992). In those experiments, students studied descriptions of a small town or a zoo or a convention center, each with 11–13 landmarks. Half studied descriptions with a route perspective and half studied descriptions with a survey perspective. Later, students verified true–false statements about the environments, taken verbatim from the descriptions or requiring inferences from the descriptions. Half the statements used a route perspective and half used a survey perspective. Students responded as quickly and accurately to inference statements from the perspective they had read as from the other perspective. This suggests that their mental models of the environments were perspective-free and allowed taking either perspective with equal ease. Evidence from neuroscience also shows that the experienced world is encoded in multiple perspectives simultaneously (e.g., O'Keefe & Nadel, 1978; Tipper & Behrmann, 1996).

Routes

Shortly thereafter, Michel became interested in route directions. Route directions are different from route descriptions, although both typically take an egocentric perspective. Route directions are meant to take someone from one place to another rather than describing an environment. Michel stopped dozens of people in the streets and asked them for directions from here to there. He painstakingly analyzed what they told him. He found that despite differences in style, accuracy, length, detail, and more, route instructions reduced to the structure described earlier – iterations of units consisting of start points, reorientations, progressions on a path, and end points (Denis, 1997). With others, he went on further forays and explorations of what makes route directions effective (e.g., Denis et al., 1999). I was so excited by Michel's analysis that I translated an earlier version of his 1997 paper into English for my students. Paul Lee and I then went out into the field and collected and compared route sketches to route descriptions (Tversky & Lee, 1998, 1999). We asked hungry students outside their dormitory if they knew how to get to a popular fast-food restaurant; if they did, we asked them to either sketch a route map or write directions to get there. We found the same four-step structure or syntax in route sketches as Michel had found in route directions as well as the same semantics. This meant that, despite external differences, besides differences in modality, the same mental model was used to generate both route sketches and route directions. Other research examining the order of sketching the maps indicated that the mental representations were organized hierarchically and that the hierarchy depended on specifics of the environments – for example, geographic features like mountains and rivers, or architectural features like entrances and paths (Taylor & Tversky, 1992). Despite similarities of semantics and even syntax, there were intriguing differences in the pragmatics of depictions and descriptions, in how the semantics and syntax of routes are used in one medium or the other. Descriptions could and did elide; they could and often did omit one or more of the segments that depictions of routes could not. For example, because the next start point is the previous end point, only one need be mentioned: the other can be inferred. By contrast, drawing a route requires continuity of end and start points for each segment. Indeed, it would be awkward to segment a route map, to draw separate sketches for each segment, and effortless to make it continuous.

Somewhat later, after a hiatus, we returned to route directions, combining two of Michel's interests: route directions and imagery. This was no mere coincidence; it was at the instigation of one of Michel's graduate students, Ariane Tom, whom he graciously sent to me for postdoctoral research. Ariane and Michel had found that when people recalled route directions, they remembered landmarks better than streets (Tom & Denis, 2004). In reexamining that work carefully, Ariane and I realized that the landmarks in the route directions were vivid (e.g., *church* rather than *building*), while the street names were rather bland (e.g., *Williams St.* rather than street *lined with ornate gas lamps*). We wondered if the superiority of landmarks was due to their vividness and distinctiveness rather than their status as a component of a route, and, indeed, it was (Tom & Tversky, in press). In one experiment, we reversed the effects, showing that streets were better remembered than landmarks when the streets were vivid and distinctive and the landmarks were bland. In a second study, we found that when both the streets and the landmarks in the route directions were vivid and distinctive, the directions were remembered better than when the streets and landmarks were nondistinctive. In addition, we found that people higher in imagery abilities both read the descriptions faster and remembered them better. We interpreted the findings as showing that mental model construction has two aspects: a spatial structure, in this case, the connectivity of streets and landmarks, and associative relations, the specific content of the streets and landmarks. Vividness seems to support both creating the associative relations and creating and remembering the spatial structure.

Assembly

We took a turn here, from one kind of directions to another, from directions to get from here to there, to directions for putting something together. Both tasks are familiar, and sometimes frustrating. Both have depictive and descriptive possibilities. We selected assembly of a TV cart because it is representative not only of other assembly tasks but also of a large class of learning tasks. That class includes any task where there are separate parts and relationships among them – for example, learning how things work or how to operate things or learning how characters interact in space and time in stories (Heiser & Tversky, 2010 submitted; Tversky, Agrawala et al., 2007). Putting together a TV cart was convenient because students could figure out how to do it and do it in a relatively short time. The task was simple: students were presented with the parts to be assembled and the picture of the assembled TV cart on the box. They were first asked to assemble the cart. After students assembled the TV cart, they were asked to produce instructions that would enable others to assemble it accurately and efficiently. Some were simply asked to produce instructions, so they could use a combination of words and sketches as they chose. Others were asked to create instructions by only using sketches or only using language; still others explained to a video camera, so they could and did use gestures.

As with route directions, we wanted to compare verbal and pictorial instructions to look for the parallels in semantics and syntax that would suggest the same underlying mental representation. But we had other interests as well: we wanted to characterize the nature of the depictions and descriptions, and we wanted to extract cognitive design principles for creating effective visual instructions. We were working with a group of whizzes in computer graphics who would instantiate the cognitive design principles in a program that generated assembly instructions from models of the objects to be assembled (Agrawala et al., 2003). Just as we were beginning this project, another of Michel's wonderful students arrived as a visiting researcher, Marie-Paule Daniel (we are back-tracking here, so common in narrative; Marie-Paule actually preceded Ariane; we are sacrificing a temporal path for a conceptual one). Marie-Paule had also worked on route directions with Michel. They had found that when participants were asked to give concise directions, participants retained the essential information, the information about actions, and omitted the less essential, more descriptive, information (Daniel & Denis, 2003). It seemed natural to add the same manipulation to our new experiments (Daniel, Tversky, & Heiser, 2010). Asking people to be concise would have the added advantage of informing us what information about assembly participants thought was critical.

The findings were rich. To begin with, spatial ability – as indexed by a common measure, the Vandenberg mental rotations task (Vandenberg & Kuse, 1978) – affected performance. Those high in spatial ability both assembled the TV cart faster and produced better pictorial instructions. We know their instructions were better because a new group of students rated them higher, and they helped yet another group of students to assemble the TV cart more efficiently. What made pictorial instructions effective? First, they were segmented into steps, where each new step corresponded to a new part to be attached. The steps were action–object pairs, analogous to turns at landmarks. Next, the highly rated instructions used perspective and showed the perspective of action. Finally, they used extra-pictorial devices, arrows, and guidelines. Arrows showed the actions that assemblers should take and were generally used for large parts; guidelines showed how parts fit together and were generally used for smaller parts. By contrast, those low in mental rotation skills made more errors assembling the TV cart and produced less effective diagrams. Often, those low in spatial ability only depicted menus of the parts, and they used words to describe assembly actions. When they showed assembly, their depictions were typically flat and imprecise. They rarely made perspective drawings and rarely showed action. The analyses of language corroborated the importance of conveying action in assembly instructions. That was the information that participants regarded as critical, and retained, even when asked to be concise. High spatial ability was expressed in language as well as in the visual instructions. Those high in mental rotation ability included more action information in their language than did those low in mental rotation ability. The key to instructions – whether to reach a destination or to assemble an object – are actions.

Cognitive design principles

Three major cognitive design principles for effective assembly instructions emerged from this project: proceed step-by-step, where each step is the addition of a part; depict the perspective of action; use arrows and guidelines to show actions. These were incorporated into the computer algorithm, and the resulting instructions enabled a new group of students to assemble the TV cart more efficiently and accurately than the instructions that came with the TV cart.

In fact, the earlier work on route maps had also yielded cognitive design principles. The route sketch maps that people produced ignored exact angle of turn, exact shape of road, and exact distances. Most turns were drawn as right angles, irrespective of actual angle; most roads were drawn as either straight or slightly curved; and small distances with many turns were exaggerated, whereas long distances without turns were minimized. These principles were instantiated into an algorithm that produces route maps on demand and almost instantly (Agrawala & Stolte, 2001).

Together, the projects suggest that cognitive design principles for effective visual instructions and explanations can be derived systematically from users' productions of verbal and visual instructions or explanations (Tversky, Agrawala, et al., 2007). The program for revealing cognitive design principles has several elements: production, preference, and performance. In the best cases, and routes and assembly were such cases, these converge.

Visual explanations

The depictive instructions, both for routes and for assembly, are examples of visual explanations. Diagrams of how something works or how to work something are also examples of visual explanations. The superior route and assembly depictive instructions, as well as the verbal instructions, had a narrative structure. They opened with a beginning: for depictions, typically a pictorial list of parts, much like the ingredients of a recipe. For descriptions, the beginnings were frequently the overall goal of the task. They had middles, a step-by-step progression of actions. Typically steps were marked. In the highly rated depictions, each step was a new drawing of the TV cart, with the new part added. Often the steps were numbered, and sometimes there were arrows leading from one step to another. In the verbal instructions, the next step was typically introduced by an adverb, like "then," or explicitly numbered. Finally, the instructions had endings. For the highly rated depictions, the last picture was of the completed cart, often with sparkly lines all around it. For the verbal instructions, there was often a verbal indication of completion, such as, "you're done". Importantly, the depictive narratives added noniconic elements, such as guidelines, arrows, and sparkly lines, features that users noticed and appreciated. These are simple visual elements that do not resemble what they represent but nevertheless carry meaning. We were intrigued by these visual devices, which can be termed *glyphs*, and turned in their direction.

Visual narratives

At this point, our paths separated somewhat. Although Michel continued on the path of route directions and navigation, leading to current projects on sound and virtual reality, we continued on a path from visual explanations to visual narratives. What intrigued us is that like verbal narratives, visual narratives are highly structured and convey rich and layered meanings. They carefully select depictions that carry meaning through resemblance, but they also use a set of visual devices, termed *glyphs*, like frames and arrows that carry shared meanings through their gestalt or geometric properties rather than through resemblance.

Glyphs

Following the Denis Plan, we went in steps. The first step was to show that certain simple visual forms – for example, lines, boxes, and arrows – are readily understood in context as a consequence of their Gestalt or geometric properties (Tversky, Zacks, Lee, & Heiser, 2000). These visual forms are common in common visual communications – maps, graphs, diagrams, charts, and comics. The general technique we adopted to verify shared meanings is pairs of complementary experiments, one in which participants interpret visual forms and the other in which they produce visual forms. Convergence is an indication of shared meanings. This technique is borrowed from a common procedure for verifying equivalences of meaning across languages: translate from language A to language B and back again. Meanings, of course, are context-bound. One context we examined was graphs, in particular, lines and bars. Lines connect, like paths in the world. Lines indicate that there is a relationship between the variables connected by the lines, they share an underlying dimension. Bars contain and separate; they indicate that there are a bunch of things contained in each bar, but what's in each bar is different. As a consequence, people should interpret lines in graphs as trends and should interpret bars as discrete comparisons. We found that to be the case even when the content of the relationships conflicted with the visual representations of them – for example, lines to represent the height of men and women or bars to represent heights of 10- and 12-year-olds. Similarly, when people were asked to produce a graph for a description of a trend, they tended to produce lines, but when they were asked to produce a graph for a description of a discrete comparison, they tended to produce bars (Zacks & Tversky, 1999). Continuing our forays into nonresembling visual forms, we turned from lines to arrows. Arrows are asymmetric lines and should convey asymmetric relations. We asked students to describe diagrams of mechanical systems, such as a car brake or bicycle pump, that either had arrows or did not have arrows. The arrows followed the flow of action in the mechanical system. When asked to interpret diagrams of mechanical systems without arrows, participants gave structural descriptions, the parts and their spatial configuration. When asked to interpret diagrams with arrows, participants gave behavioral, causal descriptions, recounting the step-by-step actions of the system. For example, for the bicycle pump: "When you push on the handle, it forces air into the cylinder. That opens the valve, forcing air into the tire". Conversely, when given structural descriptions and asked to produce diagrams, participants tended to label parts but did not add arrows. When given functional descriptions and asked to produce diagrams, participants drew arrows but tended not to label parts (Heiser & Tversky, 2006). Like lines, arrows have multiple meanings. Arrows, for example, can point: they can indicate a temporal sequence, they can indicate a causal sequence, they can indicate motion, manner of motion, direction of motion, they represent invisible forces, and more.

Arrows, of course, are common in route directions and on routes in the world. Michel, too, became fascinated with arrows and has been collecting examples of confusing ones, perhaps because they are so frequent on the road. The world can be regarded as a diagram. People have built paths connecting places and have placed arrows and other signs to direct them along the paths.

These visual forms – lines, boxes, and arrows – are communicative in many of the same ways that spatial words are communicative. Spatial words, like "relationship," "field," "area," "connection," "direction," have ambiguities like those of nondepictive visual devices such as lines, boxes, and arrows. Is it a romantic relationship or a mathematical one? Is the direction in the real world or some conceptual one? As for verbal language, so for depictive language: context helps to disambiguate. A well-crafted diagram, like a well-crafted sentence, will disambiguate the ambiguities, but, sadly, many do not, including many diagrams in textbooks of science and engineering (Tversky et al., 2007).

These are just some of the examples of glyphs, and glyphs are instances of a larger class of visual devices to structure narratives and provide meaning. Position in the space of a page as well as marks on the space of a page also conveys meanings. Think of the spaces between written words; they indicate that one set of letters belongs to one meaning and another set to another meaning. Consider indentation for paragraphs; they separate one idea from another. The place on a page, notably, up or down, but also middle, left, and right, also affects meanings (e.g., Tversky, 2011).

Comics and graphic novels

To find even richer sources of both depictive and nondepictive spatiovisual devices used in visual narratives, we appeared to veer even farther from Michel's work and turned to comics and graphic novels. This work has been in collaboration with Jonathan Bresman, a graduate student with a passion for and great insights into comics, having been, among other things involving visual narratives, an editor at *MAD* magazine. Much of our inspiration and many ideas have come from talks by and conversations with Francoise Mouly and Art Spiegelman, as well as insightful analyses of Eisner (1985), McCloud (1994), and others, plus many happy hours of looking at comics, at graphic novels, at websites, at children's books, at *New Yorker* covers, and at art.

Film

The path to comics/graphic novels is not as remote from Michel's journey as it may seem. Before Michel became a serious academic, he indulged a passion for film, with notable publications that included a biography of Buster Keaton. Some of the analysis to come of cognitive-science underpinnings of visual storytelling holds for films. Films have cuts, and, like cuts, frames, pages, and chapters in comics/graphic novels, they segment action. How action is cut and how continuity is maintained are parts of the arts of film and of comics. Because both are visual, and typically about people, they change spatial place and perspective and, as for action, need to maintain continuity in the face of changes in space.

Segmenting events

Journeys take place in space and also in time. Although space is primary for route directions, space incidentally conveys time qualitatively, as a sequence, because the segments of routes are segments of time as well as of space. Let us go now from route maps, which are primarily spatial, to events, which are primarily temporal. Although life is continuous through time, we segment it in many alternative ways: the events of a day into morning, noon, and night, or into home and work, the events of life into childhood, adulthood, and old age (e.g., Barker & Wright, 1955; Newtson, 1973; Newtson & Engquist, 1976; Tversky, Zacks, & Hard, 2008; Zacks & Tversky, 2001; Zacks, Tversky, & Iyer, 2001). Kinds of events, for example, visits to restaurants or doctors, also have a temporal structure of parts and subparts (e.g., Abbott, Black, & Smith, 1985). Events, in fact, are segmented as they happen. How this happens has been brought into the laboratory. In a typical task, people watch videos of ordinary events like making a bed or doing the dishes. They press a button whenever they think one event segment has ended and another has begun. There is considerable consensus both within and between observers on event boundaries, called breakpoints. Like the visual explanations for assembly, new event segments are identified when there is a new object or object part or a new action on an object. More abstractly, breakpoints are identified at local maxima of physical change in the input (Tversky, Zacks, & Hard, 2008). In the larger world, observing people going about their lives, segments are identified when there is a change in sphere of behavior, a change of scene, or a change in the direction or tempo (e.g., Barker & Wright, 1955).

Depicting events

The next step in our journey was from the perception of events to the telling of events in depictions. Of course, some of this had been done in developing assembly instructions. In depicting explanations and stories, time is primary and is one-dimensional. Just as routes are organized in a sequence that is spatial, comics are organized in a sequence that is typically temporal; when there is backtracking, it is usually explicit. In comics and graphic novels, segmentation is explicit, by frames. Frames, like boxes, contain and separate; for comics and other forms of visual narratives, they indicate that everything contained in one box is relevant to one segment and everything contained in another box is relevant to a different moment or episode. Framing episodes has a long history – Roman frescoes and stained-glass windows are examples. Yet segmentation of episodes can occur without explicit frames or boxes, using simpler visual devices – for example, grouping by proximity, putting the elements of one episode closer to one another and separating them from the elements of other episodes, another ancient device, apparent, for example, in Greek vases and reliefs. Normally, the stories in comics are told in reading order – that is, the arrangement of frames or panels proceeds, in Western languages, from top to bottom and left to right.

There are intriguing parallels between use of space in route sketch maps and the use of time in frames of comics. Remember that people's sketch maps enlarged space where there were many turns and minimized it when there were few or none. That is, space in sketch maps was proportional to action, not to distance. A similar stretching and contracting occurs with time both in event segmentation and, even more so, in event portrayal. These changes that segment the stream of action are analogous to turns in routes, and, like turns, they keep rhythm with the action, not with time. Similarly, the segmentation of events in visual narratives by frames does not correspond to equal temporal units. Frames in comics control readers' attention, readers stop and contemplate each frame in turn, and authors can use that segmentation and those pauses to pace reading and for effect. Suspense, for example, can be created by slowing down the action, by breaking it into small parts, requiring the reader to examine each. Film directors stretch time in similar ways to create suspense.

Each frame of a visual narrative freezes a moment in time. In observing events, those moments, the transitions from one segment to another, have been called breakpoints. Which moments are chosen? Not only are breakpoints signaled by changes in setting, action, object, and the like, more generally they are moments of greatest change in sheer physical aspects of the visual stream (e.g., Tversky, Zacks, & Hard, 2008). Scrambled slides made at breakpoints are more accurately sequenced than scrambled slides made from intermediate slides; breakpoint slides are described more accurately and rated as more intelligible than ordinary moments (Newtson & Engquist, 1976). Films of events with ordinary moments removed but breakpoint moments retained are remembered better than films with breakpoint moments removed (Schwan & Garsoffky, 2004).

Frames separate episodes. Each frame is a clip of the action, and readers need to infer what happens between the clips; the expression is "in the gutter" (McCloud, 1994). The frames must be linked to make the narrative coherent. How can artists provide visual continuity? In language, continuity is assured by overlaps of topic. Here, for example, the first sentence raised the issue of separation, of segmentation; the second elaborated and extended that idea. The third came to a conclusion based on the first two. Similarly, in visual narratives, connectedness is often established by preserving one or more visual elements from one frame into the next. Sometimes, authors want to disconnect: there is a new chapter, a new place, a new set of characters. This is easily accomplished in visual narratives by changing visual elements – in particular, the setting or the characters. Just as the frames freeze episodes in time, they also freeze perspectives in space. By rapidly switching perspective, authors can create an impression of fast action. The rapid perspective-switching also requires more attention from the reader to figure out what is happening, exactly the kind of confusion that observers might have in watching a fast-moving event. Again, film uses a similar device to similar effect.

There is far more to say on segmenting events and connecting them, and the role of frames. Groensteen (2007) analyzes the organization of frames in depth, including the embedding and organization of speech balloons, showing many ways that the organization and pattern of frames create and reflect meaning. Authors often break frames and frame convention for effect – for example, when characters burst out of frames, or frames bleed into one another. Often these are means of connecting frames, but they can be used to create more sophisticated meanings. In a comic story of the physicist Richard Feynman, he is shown in one panel with a letter in his hand, his arm reaching out across another panel into a panel depicting his girlfriend, handing her the letter. A clever retelling of *The Three Pigs* (Wiesner, 2001) uses popping out of the frame to tell a meta-story. The first pig the wolf has attacked peeks out of the frame, talking to the reader (or the second pig inside the adjacent frame), saying "it's safe out here". These are some of the insightful ways that the interplay of frames and depictions convey subtle meanings. They do this purely visually, readily accessible even to young readers. And the subtle meanings would take buckets of words to express.

Establishing meaning: depictions and figures of depiction

Visual narratives make subtle use of the depictions in the frames to create meanings as well, again, meanings that are readily understood but would take many words to convey. Facial expressions, gaze direction, body posture, proximity to others or to objects – the myriad ways that humans express thoughts and feelings through their bodies and the relationships of their bodies to other things – are frozen in comics' frames, as are depictions of backgrounds, settings, scenes. But comics go beyond this and, like poetry, use metaphor, analogy, alliteration, and other figures of depictions to enhance their stories. One wonderful Winsor McKay story shows Little Sammy sneezing in slow motion, increasing suspense. When the sneeze finally comes, it shatters the frame. In another imaginative page from George Herriman's *Krazy Kat*, a fast-moving chase has the frames arranged at parallel diagonals, conveying the reckless speed directly. In yet another Winsor McKay, Little Nemo is sleeping. As he begins to dream, the bed grows legs and transports him to dreamland. Dreams always seem to end abruptly, and at the end of his dream Nemo's bed suddenly dumps him out. Bresman and I have collected hundreds of these examples of visual poetry – but that is another journey for another time.

End point

This is an end point, not an arrival. It is another in the many segments that comprise our journeys, apart and separate. It has been an honor and a pleasure to be part of Michel's journeys, and I look forward to more. Given that he has become involved in virtual reality and I in augmented reality, both for navigation, surely there will be more intersections in our journeys.

References

Abbott, V., Black, J. H., & Smith, E. E. (1985). The representation of scripts in memory. *Journal of Memory and Language, 24*, 179–199.

Agrawala, M., Phan, D., Heiser, J., Haymaker, J. Klingner, J., Hanrahan, P., & Tversky, B. (2003). Designing effective step-by-step assembly instructions. *Proceedings of SIGGRAPH 2003*, 929–937.

Agrawala, M., & Stolte, C. (2001). Rendering effective route maps: Improving usability through generalization. *Proceedings of SIGGRAPH 2001*, 241–250.

Barker, R. G., & Wright, H. F. (1955). *Midwest and its children*. Evanston, IL: Row, Peterson and Co.

Daniel, M.-P., & Denis, M. (2003): The production of route directions: Investigating conditions that favor concise spatial discourse. *Applied Cognitive Psychology, 18*, 57–75.

Daniel, M.-P., Tversky, B., & Heiser, J. (2010). *How to put things together*. Manuscript submitted for publication.

Denis, M. (1997). The descriptions of routes: A cognitive approach to the production of spatial discourse. *Current Psychology of Cognition, 16*, 409–458.

Denis, M., Pazzaglia, F., Cornoldi, C., & Bertolo, L. (1999). Spatial discourse and navigation: An analysis of route directions in the city of Venice. *Applied Cognitive Psychology, 13*, 145–174.

Eisner, W. (1985). *Comics and sequential art*. Tamarac, FL: Poorhouse Press.

Groensteen, T. (2007). *The system of comics*. Jackson, MS: University Press of Mississippi.

Heiser, J., & Tversky, B. (2006). Arrows in comprehending and producing mechanical diagrams. *Cognitive Science, 30*, 581–592.

Heiser, J., & Tversky, B. (2010). *Mental models of complex systems: Structure and function*. Manuscript submitted for publication.

Mainwaring, S. D., Tversky, B., Ohgishi, M., & Schiano, D. J. (2003). Descriptions of simple spatial scenes in English and Japanese. *Spatial Cognition and Computation, 3*, 3–42.

McCloud, S. (1994). *Understanding comics*. New York: HarperCollins.

Newtson, D. (1973). Attribution and the unit of perception of ongoing behavior. *Journal of Personality and Social Psychology, 28*, 28–38.

Newtson, D., & Engquist, G. (1976). The perceptual organization of ongoing behavior. *Journal of Experimental Social Psychology, 12*, 436–450.

O'Keefe, J., & Nadel, L. (1978). *The hippocampus as a cognitive map*. New York: Oxford University Press.

Schwan, S., & Garsoffky, B. (2004). The cognitive representation of filmic event summaries. *Applied Cognitive Psychology, 18*, 37–55.

Taylor, H. A., & Tversky, B. (1992). Descriptions and depictions of environments. *Memory and Cognition, 20*, 483–496.

Taylor, H. A., & Tversky, B. (1996). Perspective in spatial descriptions. *Journal of Memory and Language, 35*, 371–391.

Tipper, S. P., & Behrmann, M. (1996). Object-centered not scene-based visual neglect. *Journal of Experimental Psychology: Human Perception and Performance, 22*, 1261–1278.

Tom, A., & Denis, M. (2004). Referring to landmark or street information in route directions: What difference does it make? *Applied Cognitive Psychology, 18*, 1213–1230.

Tom, A., & Tversky, B. (in press). Remembering routes: Streets and landmarks. *Applied Cognitive Psychology*.

Tversky, B. (2011). Visualizations of thought. *Topics in Cognitive Science, 3*, 499–535.

Tversky, B., Agrawala, M., Heiser, J., Lee, P. U., Hanrahan, P., Phan, D., et al. (2007). Cognitive design principles for generating visualizations. In G. Allen (Ed.), *Applied spatial cognition: From research to cognitive technology* (pp. 53–73). Mahwah, NJ: Lawrence Erlbaum Associates.

Tversky, B., & Hard, B. M. (2009). Embodied and disembodied cognition: Spatial perspective taking. *Cognition, 110*, 124–129.

Tversky, B., Heiser, J., Lozano, S., MacKenzie, R., & Morrison, J. (2007). Enriching animations. In R. Lowe & W. Schnotz (Eds.), *Learning with animation* (pp. 263–285). Cambridge: Cambridge University Press.

Tversky, B., & Lee, P. U. (1998). How space structures language. In C. Freksa, C. Habel, & K. F. Wender (Eds.), *Spatial cognition: An interdisciplinary approach to representation and processing of spatial knowledge* (pp. 157–175). Berlin: Springer-Verlag.

Tversky, B., & Lee, P. U. (1999). Pictorial and verbal tools for conveying routes. In C. Freksa & D. M. Mark (Eds.), *Spatial information theory: Cognitive and computational foundations of geographic information science* (pp. 51–64.) Berlin: Springer.

Tversky, B., Zacks, J. M., & Hard, B. M. (2008). The structure of experience. In T. Shipley & J. M. Zacks (Eds.), *Understanding events* (pp. 436–464). Oxford: Oxford University Press.

Tversky, B., Zacks, J., Lee, P. U., & Heiser, J. (2000). Lines, blobs, crosses, and arrows: Diagrammatic communication with schematic figures. In M. Anderson, P. Cheng, & V. Haarslev (Eds.), *Theory and application of diagrams* (pp. 221–230). Berlin: Springer.

Vandenberg, S. G., & Kuse, A. R. (1978). Mental rotations: A group test of three-dimensional spatial visualization. *Perceptual Motor Skills, 47*, 599–604.

Wiesner, D. (2001). *The three pigs.* New York: Houghton-Mifflin.

Zacks, J., & Tversky, B. (1999). Bars and lines: A study of graphic communication. *Memory and Cognition, 27*, 1073–1079.

Zacks, J., & Tversky, B. (2001). Event structure in perception and conception. *Psychological Bulletin, 127*, 3–21.

Zacks, J., Tversky, B., & Iyer, G. (2001). Perceiving, remembering and communicating structure in events. *Journal of Experimental Psychology: General, 136*, 29–58.

Part II

Visual imagery and imagery processes

2 Scanning visual mental images

Some structural implications, revisited

Grégoire Borst and Stephen M. Kosslyn

Mental imagery has arguably become one of the best understood cognitive functions, despite having been banished for more than 40 years as an object of study by behaviorists. Behaviorists such as John B. Watson (1913) stated that psychology should focus solely on observable stimuli and the responses to these stimuli; according to this view, thinking occurs via subtle movements of the vocal apparatus. Thus, given that mental imagery was accessible only via introspection, the behaviorists rejected it as a suitable subject of scientific study. Mental imagery became a legitimate object of study only after the cognitive revolution of the 1950s and began to re-emerge with the work of Alan Paivio and his students, who showed that imagery can help people to learn verbal material (for an overview, see Paivio, 1971).

Studying mental imagery became respectable not only because researchers demonstrated that it is involved in fundamental cognitive functions such as learning (e.g., Paivio, 1971), memory (e.g., Schacter, 1996), and reasoning (e.g., Kosslyn, 1983), but also because researchers developed objective methods to study the properties of the mental representations that underlie imagery. Some of this work focused on showing that the representations and processes used in mental imagery are comparable to those used in same-modality perception. In addition, some of this work focused on delineating the characteristics of the representations themselves.

In this chapter, we first briefly review key findings that demonstrate functional equivalence between imagery and like-modality perception. We then consider characteristics of imagery representations and focus in particular on ways that image scanning paradigms can illuminate such characteristics. Following this, we build on the previous sections to consider the structural equivalence between representations used in spatial mental imagery and in visual perception. Finally, we extend this discussion to consider how such work informs us about the spatial resolution of spatial mental images. In this last section, we present new data that show that mental images formed on the basis of information stored in long-term memory are in some ways comparable to relatively precise iconic images.

Functional equivalence between imagery and like-modality perception

Considerable research has focused on demonstrating functional equivalence between visual mental imagery and visual perception, without regard for properties of the representation. Such functional equivalence occurs when objects in images mimic actual objects in perception. Such findings are often taken to show that similar mechanisms are used in the two functions (e.g., Finke, 1985; Shepard, 1984). For example, Podgorny and Shepard (1978) used a dot localization task to study similarities in imagery and perception. In this task, participants either visualized or viewed a block letter within a grid and decided whether the dot fell on or off the letter (real or visualized). Crucially, the pattern of response times (RTs) was essentially the same when the letter was imagined and when it was displayed visually. In addition, many researchers have demonstrated that imagery and perception in the same modality interfere with each other, which has been taken to show that they both rely on the same underlying mechanisms (e.g., Craver-Lemley & Reeves, 1992; Perky, 1910; Segal & Fusella, 1970). However, being focused only on functional equivalence, such findings say nothing about the nature of the representations or processes used either in imagery or perception.

Consistent with these findings, many studies have documented functional similarities between visual mental imagery and visual perception when comparing behavior (e.g., Denis, 1989; Finke, 1985; Kosslyn, 1980; Paivio, 1986; Shepard & Cooper, 1982), evaluating effects of brain damage on these two functions (e.g., Basso, Bisiach, & Luzzatti, 1980; Bisiach & Luzzatti, 1978; Farah, 1984; Farah, Levine, & Calvanio, 1988), and comparing patterns of activation in the brain while participants engage in the two types of tasks (e.g., Ganis, Thompson, & Kosslyn, 2004; Ghaëm et al., 1997; Ishai, Ungerleider, & Haxby, 2000; Kosslyn & Thompson, 2003; Kosslyn, Thompson, & Alpert, 1997; Mellet et al., 2000; O'Craven & Kanwisher, 2000).

From a neurocognitive perspective, in order to demonstrate functional equivalence between the two kinds of mental activities, one needs to show that common neural circuitry is engaged by them. For example, some researchers focused on whether similar patterns of activation are found in the temporal cortex when pictures of objects are presented visually and when pictures of the same objects are visualized. In fact, a growing body of evidence documents that the lateral fusiform gyrus responds more strongly when participants view pictures of faces than when they view other categories of objects, whereas the medial fusiform gyrus and the parahippocampal gyri respond more strongly when participants view pictures of buildings than when they view other categories of objects (e.g., Downing, Chan, Peelen, Dodds, & Kanwisher, 2006; Haxby et al., 2001; Kanwisher & Yovel, 2006). Moreover, comparable results are found in perception and imagery: for instance, in a functional magnetic resonance imaging (fMRI) study, O'Craven and Kanwisher (2000) showed that faces and buildings evoked the expected spatial segregation of activation in the ventrotemporal cortex, and they found the same pattern of activation when the stimuli were visualized – with the fusiform face areas (FFA) being activated when faces were visualized and the parahippocampal place areas (PPA) being activated when buildings were visualized. The similarity between vision and mental imagery was further demonstrated by the fact that more than 84% of the voxels activated in the mental imagery condition were activated in the perceptual condition.

Ishai, Ungerleider, and Haxby (2000) replicated these results. In their study, participants either passively viewed pictures of three types of objects (faces, houses, chairs), of scrambled versions of these pictures (perceptual control condition), or of a gray background (imagery control condition) or visualized the pictures while looking at the gray background (imagery condition). Different regions in the ventral stream were activated by faces (FFA), houses (PPA), and chairs (inferior temporal gyrus) in the perceptual condition; moreover, more than 88% of the voxels in these three ventral stream regions were activated comparably in the mental imagery condition.

However, functional equivalence between visual mental imagery and visual perception is not always reported. For example, Behrmann, Moscovitch, and Winocur (1994) found that patient CK – who had a left homonymous hemianopia and a possible bilateral thinning of the occipital lobes – was impaired at recognizing objects but had relatively intact visual mental imagery. For instance, CK was able to draw objects from memory but could not identify objects presented visually. A similar dissociation was observed in Madame D. (Bartolomeo et al., 1998). Following bilateral brain lesions to the extrastriate visual areas (i.e., Brodmann Areas 18, 19 bilaterally and 37 in the right hemisphere), Madame D. developed severe alexia, agnosia, prosopagnosia, and achromatia. Her ability to recognize objects presented visually was severely impaired. In sharp contrast, she could draw objects from memory and performed well on mental imagery tests. In addition, other studies have reported the reverse pattern of dissociation: preserved visual perception associated with deficits in visual mental imagery (e.g., Goldenberg, 1992; Guariglia, Padovani, Pantano, & Pizzamiglio, 1993; Jackobson, Pearson, & Robertson, 2008).

To account for such dissociations between imagery and perception, Denis and Kosslyn (1999) and others (Ganis, Thompson, & Kosslyn, 2004; Kosslyn, 1994) hypothesized that visual perception relies on bottom-up organizational processes that are not required in visual mental imagery, whereas forming an image relies on top-down processes that are not always necessary in visual perception. And, in fact, not all of the same brain areas are activated during visual mental imagery and visual perception (Ganis, Thompson, & Kosslyn, 2004; Kosslyn, Thompson, & Alpert, 1997). Furthermore, the specific disparities in which brain areas were and were not activated during the two activities are consistent with the hypothesized differences in functions. For example, Ganis, Thompson, and Kosslyn (2004) found less overlap in activation during imagery and perception in the occipital and temporal lobes than in the frontal and parietal lobes, which they interpreted as indicating that perception relies in part on bottom-up organizational processes that are not used as extensively in imagery.

Characteristics of imagery representations

Functional equivalence in imagery and perception tells us that information is processed in comparable ways, but it says nothing about the nature of the representations that are used in common. However, some experimental paradigms offer the opportunity to study possible *structural* overlap between the representations used in visual mental imagery and visual perception. These paradigms use chronometric data to reveal properties of the underlying representations. Among the earliest examples of such techniques was image scanning.

Image scanning has allowed researchers to investigate whether visual mental imagery and visual perception represent the spatial layout of surfaces in the same way. Specifically, the image scanning paradigm was originally developed to determine whether mental images – like visual percepts – rely on depictive representations. In depictive representations, each part of the representation corresponds to a part of the object represented, and the relative distances among parts of the objects are preserved by the distances among the corresponding parts of the representation (see Kosslyn, 1980; Kosslyn, Thompson, & Ganis, 2006). Depictive representations must occur in a representational space that embodies actual space. The logic of the original image scanning studies is straightforward: If visual mental images rely on such a representation, then the time to scan from one point to another on a mental image should reflect the distance between the points on the depicted object: as the distances between the points increase, scanning times should increase.

Kosslyn (1973) developed the first image scanning paradigm. In this study, participants closed their eyes, visualized elongated objects, focused their attention on one end of the object, and then scanned the image – that is, shifted their attention – to "look" for a named property of this object. As predicted, RTs increased with increasing distance to scan from the initial point of focus to the named part. This finding suggested that the representation did indeed embody distance. In order to overcome the limitations of the first image scanning study (i.e., the confound between distance and the number of intervening properties), Kosslyn, Ball, and Reiser (1978) devised a series of new scanning paradigms in which the number of intervening items was controlled. In one of the experiments (i.e., Expt. 2), participants first memorized a map of an island with seven landmarks (e.g., a tree, a hut), and then visualized the map, and scanned between pairs of landmarks upon hearing their names. Landmarks were positioned in such a way that the 21 distances between each pair of landmarks were different. As expected, the time to scan increased linearly with the distance between landmarks.

Image scanning is not restricted to visual mental images of two-dimensional objects. For example, Pinker and Kosslyn (1978) found a linear increase in RTs with increasing distance when participants visualized a box with various small objects hanging from strings, and mentally scanned between pairs of objects. The scanning times were more closely related to the three-dimensional distances than to the distances in a two-dimensional planar projection.

Many researchers interpreted the mental image scanning effect as demonstrating that visual mental imagery relies on representations that have a structural isomorphism to the corresponding objects. In other words, the scanning effect was obtained because mental images depict – they incorporate the metric information present in the original object. The data collected in the scanning studies challenged the claim made by some researchers (Anderson & Bower, 1973; Pylyshyn, 1973) that the underlying representations used in mental imagery are the same as those involved in processing language.

However, not all researchers agree that the image scanning paradigm provides a way to determine the structural properties of the underlying representations. These researchers have opined that the results merely reflect: (1) task demands, which correspond to instructions that lead participants to try to mimic what they think would happen in the corresponding perceptual situation (Mitchell & Richman, 1980; Pylyshyn, 1981; Richman, Mitchell, & Reznick, 1979); and, (2) experimenter expectancy effects, which occur when experimenters prompt participants on how to respond (Intons-Peterson, 1983).

Finke and Pinker (1982) were the first to design an image scanning paradigm that circumvented both objections; this paradigm does not rely on instructions that could have induced either sort of demand characteristics. In their paradigm, on each trial a set of four dots is presented, with each dot at a different location. The pattern of dots is then removed, and after 2 s – in order to avoid afterimages of the dots – an arrow appears at an unexpected location. The participants are asked to determine whether the arrow points to a location previously occupied by one of the dots. The distance between the tip of the arrow and the dots is varied. Many studies have now shown that the time taken to make the judgments increases linearly with the distance from the arrow to the nearest dot (on trials on which the arrow points to one of the locations previously occupied by a dot). Moreover, not only do the instructions and procedure circumvent possible influences of demand characteristics, but the task also prevents participants from explicitly encoding inter-point distances when learning the pattern and then intentionally (even if unconsciously) using this information to delay their responses by an amount proportional to the distance.

In follow-up experiments, Pinker, Choate, and Finke (1984) showed that the time between the presentation of the dots and the appearance of the arrow has no effect on the relationship between distance and scanning times. In addition, Pinker, Choate, and Finke showed that participants could scan visual mental images created on the basis of information stored in long-term memory.

Structural equivalence between visuospatial imagery and visual perception

When the mental image scanning paradigm was first developed, researchers thought of visual mental imagery as a single kind of representation. Since then, researchers in cognitive neuroscience have shown that we must distinguish between two broad classes of visual representations, those that specify object properties (such as shape, color, and texture) and those that specify spatial properties (such as size and orientation; see Ungerleider & Mishkin, 1982). This distinction has also been shown to apply to visual mental imagery (e.g., Levine, Warach, & Farah, 1985; Kozhevnikov, Kosslyn, & Shephard, 2005). The Finke and Pinker (1982) scanning paradigm primarily taps spatial imagery. In fact, in the Finke and Pinker paradigm, one needs to visualize the exact locations of the dots in order to perform the task. On the other hand, visualizing the shape or the color of the dots is not critical in this task. In the following section, we review evidence of a structural equivalence specifically between visuospatial mental imagery and spatial vision.

Surprisingly, the underlying assumption of all image scanning studies – that the same, relatively low-level, type of representation is used in imagery and perception (cf. Finke, 1985) – was not initially studied systematically or in depth. Using the scanning paradigm first introduced by Finke and Pinker (1982) and later refined by Borst, Kosslyn, and Denis (2006), Borst and Kosslyn (2008) studied whether visuospatial mental imagery and spatial vision rely on the same type of representation of the spatial layout of surface. The hypothesis that visual mental imagery and visual perception rely on the same spatial representation is plausible, given that certain cortical areas in the visual system, notably those processing spatial properties of objects, are topographically organized – the spatial layout of cortical activation represents the spatial layout of the object or scene (e.g., Tootell, Hadjikani, Mendola, Marrett, & Dale, 1998).

In Borst and Kosslyn (2008), we reasoned that if the same representations are processed in spatial mental imagery and spatial vision, then similar results should be observed when participants scan an object in an image and when they scan the same object during perception. In the first experiment, the same group of participants was asked to scan (1) mental images created on the basis of a just-seen display, (2) visual percepts, and (3) iconic images (see Figure 2.1). In all three conditions, participants were instructed to determine whether an arrow was pointing at a dot (or a location previously occupied by a dot).

In the mental imagery condition, the paradigm was similar to the one used in the original Finke and Pinker (1982) paradigm. In the visual perception condition, arrows were displayed on the pattern of dots, and participants were allowed to move their eyes to make their decision. In the iconic image condition, a pattern of dots and an arrow were presented very briefly on the computer screen, and participants relied on an iconic image to make their judgments. Sperling (1960) and others (e.g., Avons & Phillips, 1980; Francis, 1996; Wede & Francis, 2006) have demonstrated that the brain has the capacity to store for a limited time (up to 1 s) a large amount of precise visual information in the form of an iconic image. Our iconic image condition was novel, and critically important. First, given that iconic image representations arise at a low-level of processing in the visual system, this task allowed us to consider whether mental image scanning draws on mechanisms used in low-level visual processing. In addition, given that the first cortical areas that process visual input are topographically organized (e.g., see Tootell, Silverman, Switkes, & De Valois, 1982), if data in the iconic image condition were very

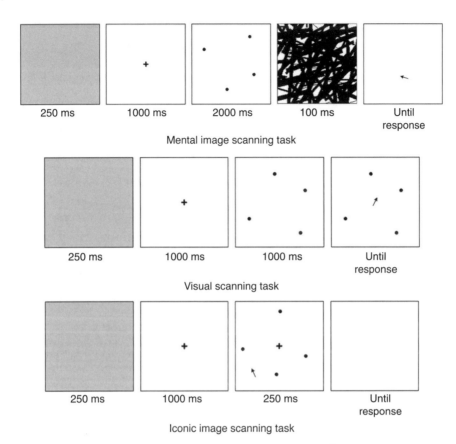

Figure 2.1 The procedure used in the three scanning tasks of Experiment 1 in Borst and Kosslyn (2008). (From G. Borst & S. M. Kosslyn, 2008. Visual mental imagery and perception: Structural equivalence revealed by scanning processes. *Memory & Cognition, 36*, 849–862. Reprinted with permission.)

similar to data in the mental imagery condition, this would demonstrate that mental images rely on representations that depict information – representations qualitatively different from the sorts of descriptive representations that underlie language (e.g., Pylyshyn, 1973, 2002, 2003; for a review, see Kosslyn, Thompson, & Ganis, 2006).

As expected, in all three conditions participants took longer to determine that the arrow was pointing at a dot when the distance between the tip of the arrow and the dot increased (see Figure 2.2). In addition, the speed with which participants scanned (as revealed by the slopes of the best-fitting lines) did not differ, and scanning speeds in the different conditions were highly correlated. Taken together, these results support the inference that the same process is used to scan spatial percepts, spatial iconic images, and spatial mental images. Moreover, because a

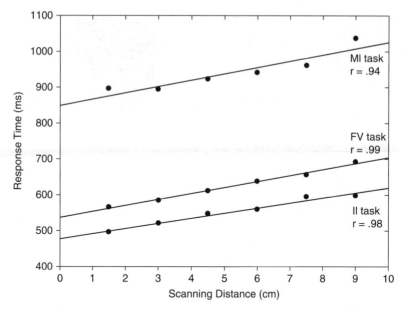

Figure 2.2 The time to scan increasing distances in the three scanning tasks used in Experiment 1 of Borst and Kosslyn (2008). (From G. Borst & S. M. Kosslyn, 2008. Visual mental imagery and perception: Structural equivalence revealed by scanning processes. *Memory & Cognition, 36,* 849–862. Reprinted with permission.) MI = Mental Imagery; FV = Free Vision; II = Iconic Imagery.

specific cognitive process is only appropriate for representations that have compatible characteristics, these results indicate that the representations processed in the three cases shared the same spatial structure. Furthermore, the highly similar results in the iconic image and the mental imagery tasks supported the hypothesis that spatial mental images rely on relatively low-level representations – given that iconic images are created within the primary visual cortex (V1) (e.g., Engel, 1970; Super, Spekreijse, & Lamme, 2001).

In Experiment 2 of Borst and Kosslyn (2008), participants scanned spatial mental images created on the basis of information stored in long-term memory (LTM) – by learning the positions of the dots prior to the experiment. Thus, as opposed to Experiment 1, the dots were no longer presented during the experimental trials. In this case, their image scanning speed (revealed by the steepness of the slopes) was slower than in the iconic image task (see Figure 2.3). However, scanning abilities remained strongly correlated between the mental imagery and iconic image tasks, which supports the idea that the same processes – and thus similar representations – were drawn upon in both tasks.

Finally, mental images were more difficult to scan when generated from information stored in LTM (Experiment 2) than when generated on the basis of a just-seen display (Experiment 1). This led us to suggest that spatial information specified in mental images generated on the basis of information stored in LTM

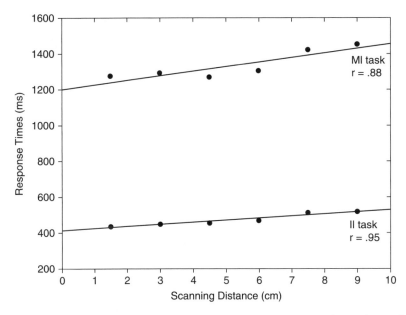

Figure 2.3 The time to scan increasing distances in the two scanning tasks used in Experiment 2 of Borst and Kosslyn (2008). (From G. Borst & S. M. Kosslyn, 2008. Visual mental imagery and perception: Structural equivalence revealed by scanning processes. *Memory & Cognition, 36*, 849–862. Reprinted with permission.) MI = Mental Imagery; II = Iconic Imagery.

could be degraded as compared to the spatial information specified in iconic images. In the following section, we report two new unpublished experiments designed to address this hypothesis.

Spatial resolution of mental images

In our study, we developed a procedure to assess the structural properties of representations used in spatial mental imagery. We focused specifically on the spatial structure—the layout of parts of the image in space (as opposed to color, texture, or other properties associated with shapes). The logic of our approach rested on the fact that iconic images represent the exact locations of objects in space, given that they are sensory traces of visual scenes and elicit activation within V1 – a topographically organized visual area. We reasoned that one way to "externalize" the precision of spatial mental images (created on the basis of information in LTM) is to determine how much their spatial resolution is degraded (i.e., less accurate) than the spatial resolution of iconic images of the same scene. Following this logic, we varied the degree of precision that needed to be specified in order to perform scanning tasks.

Specifically, we reasoned that if locations in spatial mental images generated from LTM are specified less precisely than are locations in iconic images of the same scenes, then participants should require more time to locate dots in spatial mental images than in iconic images. By definition, if spatial mental images are less precise, then there will be greater uncertainty about where the dots are located. The trick of the study is that we compared behavioral performance between the two scanning tasks when the locations of the dots needed to be specified either very precisely or less precisely in order to locate the dots easily. By comparing the effects of how precisely the dots must be specified in the two conditions, we could discover how precisely locations in an iconic image must be specified in order to mimic how precisely they are represented in a mental image. This comparison would establish the degree to which spatial mental images are degraded (i.e., less precise) than iconic images.

Each participant performed two scanning tasks. In the iconic image (II) scanning task, a pattern of dots was presented on the screen for 125 ms and immediately replaced by an arrow that was shown for 125 ms (see Figure 2.4). The task was to decide whether the arrow pointed directly at any of the dots. To prevent participants from memorizing the pattern of dots, a different pattern was presented on each trial. In the spatial mental image (MI) scanning task, participants memorized a pattern of dots prior to the task. The task required the participants to visualize this pattern of dots and then to decide whether an arrow would have pointed at one of them, if they were on the screen as they appeared when memorized (see Figure 2.4); this procedure ensured that participants did not rely on an iconic image to perform the task.

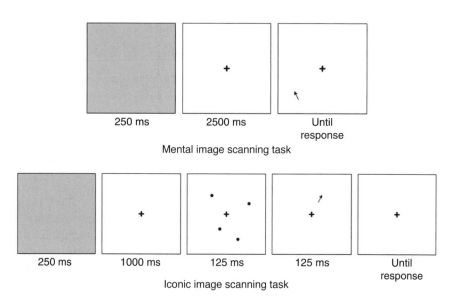

Figure 2.4 The procedure used in the spatial mental imagery and the iconic image scanning tasks.

In both tasks, we presented a series of conditions that differed in how precisely the locations of the dots had to be specified in order to perform the task correctly. We defined the degree of precision of the spatial information as an *area of uncertainty* (AoU) surrounding each dot. As the radius of the AoU decreased, the location of the dots needed to be more precise to perform the task correctly. The AoU affected only the way we designed the No arrows (those that did not point at a dot): for a given AoU, we placed the No arrows on one of the tangents of a circle defined by the AoU. For each task, we used four different AoUs (see Figure 2.5), which defined four different levels of precision needed in order to perform the task correctly. Because we expected the MI task to be harder than the II task, the

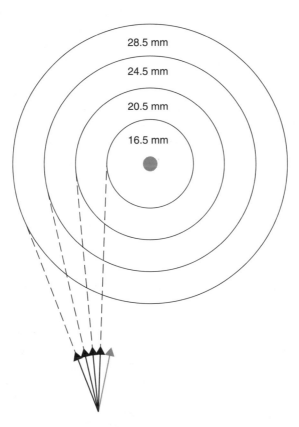

Figure 2.5 Experiment 1: Principles of construction of the areas of uncertainty (AoU). The location of the dot is represented in gray. The gray arrow represents an arrow that points at a dot; black arrows represent the arrows that miss the dot. Each circle represents a different radius of the AoU. Dashed lines represent the tangent of each circle on which a No arrow is aligned. Note that the angle with which arrows miss the dot increases as the AoU radius increases (From G. Borst & S. M. Kosslyn, 2010, Individual differences in spatial mental imagery. *Quarterly Journal of Experimental Psychology, 63*, 2031–2050. Reprinted with permission.)

range of the AoU levels differed in the two tasks; the AoU levels ranged respectively from 16.5 mm to 28.5 mm for the MI task and from 8.5 mm to 20.5 mm for the II task, with 4-mm increments of difference in radius (hereafter referred as Levels 1 to 4). We designed these ranges to ensure that two of the levels were comparable in the two tasks (i.e., Level 1 in the MI task vs. Level 3 in the II task and Level 2 in the MI task vs. Level 4 in the II task). We expected that as the radius of the AoU increased, scanning would be faster.

The key idea driving the design of the study was as follows: If the spatial information represented in spatial mental images is systematically degraded (i.e., less precise), compared to the information represented in iconic images, we should be able to identify the AoU in a spatial mental image that produces the same results as a smaller AoU in an iconic image (good performance with smaller AoUs requires more precise representations). And the difference in the radii of the two AoUs reflects the amount that the spatial information in the spatial mental image is degraded, relative to the spatial information specified in the iconic image.

As shown in Figure 2.6, at all levels of AoU in both tasks, the time to scan increased linearly when the distance between the arrow and the dots increased, on the trials where arrows were actually pointing at target dots. We interpreted this result as reflecting the time to scan over a spatial representation. This finding shows that the underlying representation incorporates metric properties. This is important because the goal of this experiment was to estimate the extent to which

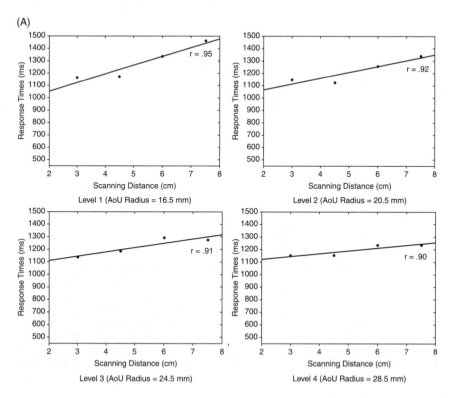

(A)

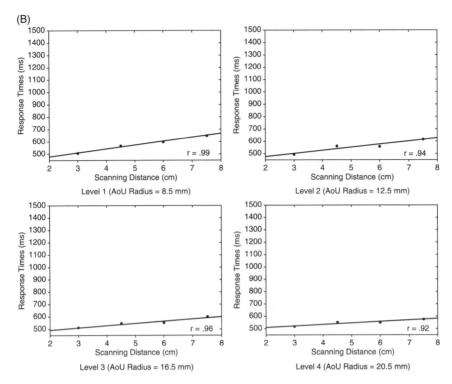

Figure 2.6 Experiment 1: The time to scan increasing distances in (A) the mental imagery (MI) task (Borst & Kossslyn, 2010, Expt. 1) and (B) the iconic image (II) task for different levels of the area of uncertainty (AoU). (From G. Borst & S. M. Kosslyn, 2010, Individual differences in spatial mental imagery. *Quarterly Journal of Experimental Psychology, 63*, 2031–2050. Reprinted with permission.)

spatial locations in a mental image are degraded, compared to those in an iconic image, and our method rests on the assumption that the underlying representation depicts spatial properties.

Our manipulation of AoU had the expected effects. For example, on trials in which arrows were not pointing at a dot, RTs were highly correlated with distance only for the levels of AoU with the smaller radius (with $r = .99$, $p < .01$); RTs were not significantly correlated with distance in the condition with the largest AoU. As the radius of the AoU decreased, participants scanned in the direction indicated by the arrow up to the region of the nearest dots, as Finke and Pinker (1982, 1983) demonstrated; however, with the largest AoU (i.e., with the largest radius), the discrimination was easy enough that participants did not necessarily need to scan to make their decision. That is, with a large AoU, it was easy to distinguish between Yes and No trials, and participants might have used a fast attentional process that did not require scanning (see Borst & Kosslyn, 2008). In addition, as shown in Table 2.1, participants typically slowed their rate of scanning and

Table 2.1 Experiment 1: Mean slopes and error rates (ER) for different levels of area of uncertainty (AoU) for the two scanning tasks

	MI task				II task			
	Level 1	*Level 2*	*Level 3*	*Level 4*	*Level 1*	*Level 2*	*Level 3*	*Level 4*
Slopes	71 (37)	47 (42.1)	35 (22.4)	22 (15.5)	31 (12.6)	24 (6.9)	18 (8.7)	12 (6.2)
ER	29.6 (8.7)	27.6 (9.9)	24 (9.8)	20.5 (9.9)	39 (7.2)	34.9 (6.7)	26.8 (6.4)	18.2 (6.7)

Note: MI task: the mental image scanning task; II task: the iconic image scanning task. Standard deviations in parentheses. (From G. Borst & S. M. Kosslyn, 2010. Individual differences in spatial mental imagery. *Quarterly Journal of Experimental Psychology, 63*, 2031–2050. Reprinted with permission.)

committed more errors when the task required having a more precise representation of the positions of the dots (i.e., when the radius of the AoU decreased).

As expected, participants scanned spatial mental images more slowly than iconic images, and they committed more errors when scanning such mental images (i.e., Level 1 in MI task vs. Level 3 in II task and Level 2 in MI task vs. Level 4 in II task; see Table 2.1). When we compared the slopes between the two scanning tasks at the different levels of AoU, we found no difference in slopes when we compared adjacent levels of the AoU (i.e., Level 1 vs. Level 2, for example) between the MI task and the II task. These comparisons reflected a 12-mm increase of the radius of the AoU from the II task to the MI task. In short, a 12-mm increase of the radius of the AoU from the II task to the MI task led to comparable scanning rates. Under the present conditions in the present tasks, the precision of spatial mental images is comparable to the precision of iconic images that have 12 mm larger regions of uncertainty.

To summarize, we varied the spatial resolution needed to decide whether an arrow pointed at one of the locations previously occupied by a dot. Not surprisingly, we found that the greater the precision required, the slower the rate of scanning. This was true both for iconic images and for spatial mental images. If we assume that spatial information represented in a spatial mental image is degraded compared to the spatial information specified in an iconic image, we can directly compare the scanning slopes and thereby establish the conditions in mental imagery that would produce the corresponding slope in an iconic image. Relying on this logic, we can infer that the spatial structure of spatial mental images is degraded, relative to iconic images, by somewhere between an 8- and a 12-mm radius surrounding each dot – which, in the conditions in which we tested participants here, translates into .61 to .92 degrees of visual angle. That is, spatial mental images are like iconic images where the locations are less precise by this amount.

However, one could argue that the design of our tasks does not allow us to draw such inferences about the underlying spatial structure of the spatial imagery representation. First, the No arrows were positioned at the same four possible distances as the Yes arrows, thus when the radius of the AoU decreased, the angle with which No arrows missed the dots decreased as well. Consequently, participants' scanning rates could have been slower for the smaller AoU levels not because of the radius length (which defined the AoU) but, rather, because of a "discrimination effect" (i.e., the angle with which No arrows were missing the dots). Second, within each level of the AoU, the farther the No arrows were positioned from the nearest possible target dot, the smaller was the angle with which No arrows missed the dots. Thus, one could argue that the increased RTs with greater distance for the Yes trials is an indirect result of the "discrimination effect" on the No arrows. If so, then the slopes of the best-fitting lines do not reflect positional uncertainty in the representation. Third, in the MI task, participants scanned the same pattern of dots for all four levels of AoU, which could have affected the differences in slopes among the levels of AoU.

In a second experiment, we revised the procedures in both tasks to address these issues. First, for all levels of AoU we kept constant the angle with which the No arrows missed the dots; by doing so, we could determine whether the level of AoU alone was the factor responsible for the findings in the first experiment. Consequently, the No arrows were positioned closer to the nearest possible target dot as the radius of the AoU became smaller. Second, within each level, because all No arrows were positioned at the same distance from the nearest possible target dot, if a linear increase of the RTs with distance was to be found on the Yes trials, it could not be attributed to a "discrimination effect." Third, in the MI task, participants memorized a new pattern of dots for each of the levels of AoU. Finally, we used the results of Experiment 1 to guide us in more precisely defining the levels of AoU, and we now included only three levels in each of the two scanning tasks.

In these versions of the tasks, we used three sizes of AoU, ranging respectively from a 14.5-mm to a 26.5-mm radius for the MI task and from an 8.5-mm to a 20.5-mm radius for the II task, with 6-mm increments of differences in radius (hereafter referred as Levels 1 to 3). Because we designed the No arrows to miss the dots by 20° at all three levels, the distance between the tip of the No arrows and the nearest possible target dot increased as the radius of the AoU increased (see Figure 2.7). Thus, this design precluded a "discrimination effect" on the No trials, which could have then influenced scanning on the Yes trials.

As in Experiment 1, RTs increased linearly with distance in both tasks, and RTs were highly correlated with distance (with rs ranging from .96 to .99, $p < .05$ in all cases; see Figure 2.8). The data suggest that in the MI task, participants created a spatial mental image of the pattern of dots and scanned the distance between the tip of the arrows and the dot to decide whether the arrows pointed at one of the dots; the data also indicate that in the II task, participants scanned the distances between the tip of the arrows and the dots in their iconic images to make their decision.

As in Experiment 1, in both tasks participants scanned at a slower rate and made more errors as the radius of the AoU decreased (see Table 2.2). Moreover, participants scanned at comparable rates in the two tasks when the AoU in the II task was 12 mm larger than that in the MI task (between Level 1 in the II task and Level 2 in the MI task, or between Level 2 in the II task and Level 3 in the MI

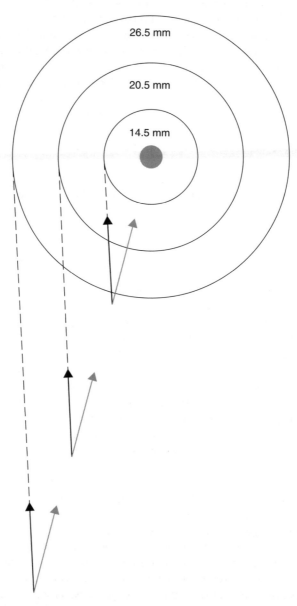

Figure 2.7 Experiment 2: Principles of construction of the areas of uncertainty (AoU). The
location of the dot is represented in gray. The gray arrows represent arrows that
point at a dot; black arrows represent the arrows that miss the dot. Each circle
represents a different radius of the AoU. Dashed lines represent the tangent of
each circle on which a No arrow is aligned. Note that the angle with which the
black arrows miss the dot is kept constant (From G. Borst & S. M. Kosslyn,
2010. Individual differences in spatial mental imagery. *Quarterly Journal of
Experimental Psychology, 63,* 2031–2050. Reprinted with permission.)

task). These results are consistent with what we found in Experiment 1, and they suggest that the underlying structure of spatial mental images resembles an iconic image in which the spatial structure is degraded (i.e., is less precise). It is unlikely that a speed–accuracy trade-off could explain the differences observed on the rate of scanning (i.e., revealed by the steepness of the slopes of the best-fitting lines) because: (1) for four out of six of the comparisons, we observed no difference on the ERs at similar AoUs; (2) for the two comparisons that were significant, participants made more errors in the task in which they scanned at a lower rate.

As in Experiment 1, the time to scan increased linearly as the distance between the tip of the arrows and the dots increased. The fact that we observed this effect is important because – as opposed to Experiment 1 – a "discrimination effect" could not occur on the No trials. Thus, it is of interest that we replicated and extended the findings of Experiment 1. First, we again found that AoU affected both the rate of scanning and accuracy. Second, by keeping constant the angle with which the No arrows missed the dots over the different levels of AoU, we demonstrated that the different scanning rates at the different levels should be attributed to the variation of the sizes of the AoU per se. Finally, given that we provided evidence that a speed–accuracy trade-off could not account for the

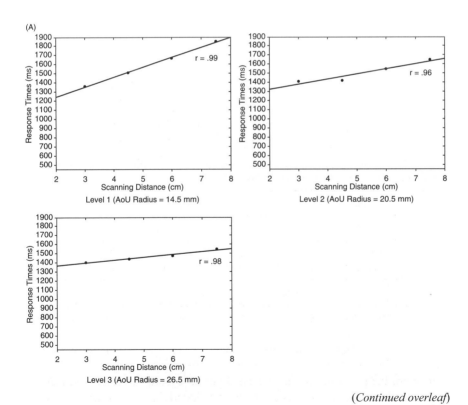

(Continued overleaf)

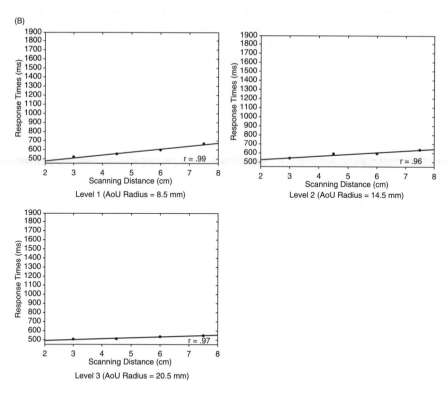

Figure 2.8 Experiment 2: The time to scan increasing distances in (A) the mental imagery (MI) task (Borst & Kosslyn, 2010, Expt. 2) and in (B) the iconic image (II) task for different levels of the area of uncertainty (AoU). (From G. Borst & S. M. Kosslyn, 2010. Individual differences in spatial mental imagery. *Quarterly Journal of Experimental Psychology, 63*, 2031–2050. Reprinted with permission.)

Table 2.2 Experiment 2: Mean slopes and error rates (ER) for different levels of area of uncertainty (AoU) for the two scanning tasks

	MI task			II task		
	Level 1	*Level 2*	*Level 3*	*Level 1*	*Level 2*	*Level 3*
Slopes	108 (51.5)	56 (31)	31 (21.1)	33 (15.7)	20 (8.3)	10 (4.2)
ER	33.4 (9.6)	28.5 (7.6)	22.6 (7.5)	41.3 (5)	30.7 (5.8)	21.7 (4.7)

Note: MI task: the mental image scanning task; II task: the iconic image scanning task. Standard deviations in parentheses. (From G. Borst & S. M. Kosslyn, 2010. Individual differences in spatial mental imagery. *Quarterly Journal of Experimental Psychology, 63*, 2031–2050. Reprinted with permission.)

difference in scanning rates within or between the tasks, we are confident that this paradigm offered a window on the structure of the representations scanned.

In short, the pattern of results validated our procedure and confirmed that the slopes of the best-fitting lines could reveal the underlying spatial structure of the representation involved in the scanning tasks. Thus, we can reasonably argue that spatial mental images are akin to iconic images that have greater positional uncertainty (see Figure 2.9).

In all conditions in both tasks, RT increased as the distance to scan increased, which suggests that depictive representations were processed. This finding was a prerequisite for drawing inferences about the effects of the AoU on the precision of spatial mental imagery. The logic of these studies rests on the idea that points in the image are represented in a coordinate space, such that we could estimate the spatial error surrounding each point. Specifically, we used the effects of AoU in an iconic image to anchor the corresponding effect in spatial mental imagery, allowing us to liken spatial mental images to iconic images that have a certain level of spatial precision.

The two experiments summarized here converged in showing that participants generally scanned patterns of points in mental images more slowly than they scanned comparable patterns in iconic images. This finding is consistent with the idea that spatial mental images are like iconic images where the positions of the points are less precisely specified. To observe similar rates of scanning in such mental images and iconic images, the radius of the AoU of the exact position of the dots had to be increased by about 12 mm in the MI task (as compared to the AoU radius in the II task). In addition, even when we kept constant the size of the angle with which the No arrows missed the dots, similar results were found – which allowed us to rule out explanations based on the difficulty of discriminating between targets and distractors.

The present results are of interest from the point of view of both theory and method. First, there is no question that iconic images are represented depictively. Thus, showing similarities between iconic images and spatial mental images is another piece of evidence that mental images are depictive. Second, we observed individual differences both on the RT slopes and on the ERs in each of the two tasks – and hence the scanning task could be used as an objective way to assess the quality of a person's spatial mental imagery. That is, the quality of the coordinate

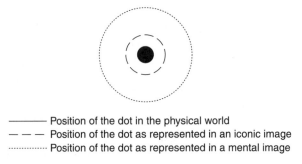

————— Position of the dot in the physical world
— — — Position of the dot as represented in an iconic image
················ Position of the dot as represented in a mental image

Figure 2.9 Illustration of the position of the dots in the physical world, in an iconic image, and in a mental image. Dashed circular regions surrounding the dot denote the range of errors in the remembered dot location.

locations incorporated in a particular person's spatial representations could be determined by observing the effect of the variation of the AoU on the scanning slope and on the number of errors. The logic is that as the radius of the AoU decreased, participants with the least accurate representation of the coordinate locations of the dots should make increasingly greater numbers of errors. And in fact, in a recent study using this method, we demonstrated that this measure has good convergent validity (Borst & Kosslyn, 2010): we showed that it is related to scores on the Paper Folding test, on the Paper Form Board test, and on the visuo-spatial items on Raven's Advanced Progressive Matrices. We also showed that this measure has good divergent validity, as witnessed by the fact that it is not corre-lated with scores on questionnaires measuring object-based mental imagery.

Conclusions

One strand of research on mental imagery has pushed beyond providing demon-strations that mental images can function like percepts and that objects in mental images can function like the corresponding actual objects. This strand of research focuses on characterizing the nature of the underlying representations used in imagery. For the most part (although not exclusively; e.g., see Stevens & Coupe, 1978), this type of research has focused on the question of whether mental images rely on depictive representations. The mental imagery scanning paradigm has proven useful in this effort, in large part because it is can reveal the spatial layout of representations – and using space to represent space is a key property of depictions.

The first focus of image scanning studies was simply to demonstrate that visual mental images embody space, that they use space to represent space. Image scan-ning studies have demonstrated that spatial mental images have a spatial structure much like that of representations arising from direct input from the retina during perception. Such findings reveal that mental images do rely on depictive represen-tations and incorporate metric information about the objects or scene they represent.

In addition, the scanning paradigm can (as we showed in this chapter) be used to reveal the spatial resolution of spatial mental images. This paradigm offers a way to externalize a mental representation – at least its spatial structure.

Finally, the scanning paradigm is evolving into a useful tool to assess objec-tively individual differences in at least one type of mental imagery, namely spatial mental imagery. However, there is still a need to develop objective ways to measure individual differences in object mental imagery – that is, mental imagery that deals with the color, texture, and shape of objects.

In closing, we note a number of questions that remain unanswered in order to achieve a full understanding of spatial mental imagery and image scanning processes. In particular, we need to understand the actual mechanisms in the brain that underlie image scanning – which, among other insights, will illuminate the relation between image scanning and other forms of the control of attention. Although a great deal of work has been done to specify the neural mechanisms involved in shifting attention in a scanning task that involves voluntarily shifting attention over an imagined map (e.g., Mellet, Tzourio, Denis, & Mazoyer, 1995), no study to date has investigated the neural underpinning of the scanning processes involved in the Finke and Pinker (1982) paradigm. This would not be a trivial investigation, given that scanning processes involved in these two paradigms have been shown to be distinct (Borst, Kosslyn, & Denis, 2006).

References

Anderson, J. R., & Bower, G. H. (1973). *Human associative memory.* Washington, DC: Winston.

Avons, S. E., & Phillips, W. A. (1980). Visualization and memorization as a function of display time and post-stimulus processing time. *Journal of Experimental Psychology: Human Learning and Memory, 6,* 407–420.

Bartolomeo, P., Bachoud-Levi, A. C., De Gelder, B., Denes, G., Dalla Barba, G., Brugieres, P., et al. (1998). Multiple-domain dissociation between impaired visual perception and preserved mental imagery in a patient with bilateral extrastriate lesions. *Neuropsychologia, 36,* 239–249.

Basso, A., Bisiach, E., & Luzzati, C. (1980). Loss of mental imagery: A case study. *Neuropsychologia, 18,* 435–442.

Behrmann, M., Moscovitch, M., & Winocur, G. (1994). Intact visual imagery and impaired visual perception in a patient with visual agnosia. *Journal of Experimental Psychology: Human Perception and Performance, 20,* 1068–1087.

Bisiach, E., & Luzzatti, C. (1978). Unilateral neglect of representational space. *Cortex, 14,* 129–133.

Borst, G., & Kosslyn, S. M. (2008). Visual mental imagery and perception: Structural equivalence revealed by scanning processes. *Memory and Cognition, 36,* 849–862.

Borst, G., & Kosslyn, S. M. (2010). Individual differences in spatial mental imagery. *Quarterly Journal of Experimental Psychology, 63,* 2031–2050.

Borst, G., Kosslyn, S. M., & Denis, M. (2006). Different cognitive processes in two image-scanning paradigms. *Memory and Cognition, 34,* 475–490.

Craver-Lemley, C., & Reeves, A. (1992). How visual imagery interferes with vision. *Psychological Review, 99,* 633–649.

Denis, M. (1989). *Image et cognition.* Paris: Presses Universitaires de France.

Denis, M., & Kosslyn, S. M. (1999). Scanning visual mental images: A window on the mind. *Current Psychology of Cognition, 18,* 409–465.

Downing, P. E., Chan, A. W., Peelen, M. V., Dodds, C. M., & Kanwisher, N. (2006). Domain specificity in visual cortex. *Cerebral Cortex, 16,* 1453–1461.

Engel, G. R. (1970). An investigation of visual response to brief stereoscopic stimuli. *Quarterly Journal of Experimental Psychology, 22,* 148–166.

Farah, M. J. (1984). The neurological basis of mental imagery: A componential analysis. *Cognition, 18,* 245–272.

Farah, M. J., Levine, D. N., & Calvanio, R. (1988). A case study of mental imagery deficit. *Brain and Cognition, 8,* 147–164.

Finke, R. A. (1985). Theories relating mental imagery to perception. *Psychological Bulletin, 98,* 236–259.

Finke, R. A., & Pinker, S. (1982). Spontaneous imagery scanning in mental extrapolation. *Journal of Experimental Psychology: Learning, Memory and Cognition, 8,* 142–147.

Finke, R. A., & Pinker, S. (1983). Directional scanning of remembered visual patterns. *Journal of Experimental Psychology: Learning, Memory and Cognition, 9*, 398–410.

Francis, G. (1996). Cortical dynamics of visual persistence and temporal integration. *Perception and Psychophysics, 58*, 1203–1212.

Ganis, G., Thompson, W. L., & Kosslyn, S. M. (2004). Brain areas underlying visual mental imagery and visual perception: An fMRI study. *Cognitive Brain Research, 20*, 226–241.

Ghaëm, O., Mellet, E., Crivello, F., Tzourio, N., Mazoyer, B., Berthoz, A., & Denis, M. (1997). Mental navigation along memorized routes activates the hippocampus, precuneus, and insula. *NeuroReport, 8*, 739–744.

Goldenberg, G. (1992). Loss of visual imagery and loss of visual knowledge – a case study. *Neuropsychologia, 30*, 1081–1099.

Guariglia, C., Padovani, A., Pantano, P., & Pizzamiglio, L. (1993). Unilateral neglect restricted to visual imagery. *Nature, 364*, 235–237.

Haxby, J. V., Gobbini, M. I., Furey, M. L., Ishai, A., Schouten, J. L., & Pietrini, P. (2001). Distributed and overlapping representations of faces and objects in ventral temporal cortex. *Science, 293*, 2425–2430.

Intons-Peterson, M. J. (1983). Imagery paradigms: How vulnerable are they to experimenters' expectations? *Journal of Experimental Psychology: Human Perception and Performance, 9*, 394–412.

Ishai, A., Ungerleider, L. G., & Haxby, J. V. (2000). Distributed neural systems for the generation of visual images. *Neuron, 28*, 979–990.

Jakobson, L. S., Pearson, P. M., & Robertson, B. (2008). Hue-specific color memory impairment in an individual with intact color perception and color naming. *Neuropsychologia, 46*, 22–36.

Kanwisher, N., & Yovel, G. (2006). The fusiform face area: A cortical region specialized for the perception of faces. *Philosophical Transactions of the Royal Society London. Series B, Biological Sciences, 361*, 2109–2128.

Kosslyn, S. M. (1973). Scanning visual images: Some structural implications. *Perception and Psychophysics, 14*, 90–94.

Kosslyn, S. M. (1980). *Image and mind*. Cambridge, MA: Harvard University Press.

Kosslyn, S. M. (1983). Mental representation. In J. R. Anderson & S. M. Kosslyn (Eds.), *Tutorials in learning and memory: Essays in honor of Gordon Bower*. San Francisco, CA: W. H. Freeman.

Kosslyn, S. M. (1994). *Image and brain*. Cambridge, MA: Harvard University Press.

Kosslyn, S. M., Ball, T. M., & Reiser, B. J. (1978). Visual images preserve metric spatial information: Evidence from studies of image scanning. *Journal of Experimental Psychology: Human Perception and Performance, 4*, 47–60.

Kosslyn, S. M., & Thompson, W. L. (2003). When is early visual cortex activated during visual mental imagery? *Psychological Bulletin, 129*, 723–746.

Kosslyn, S. M., Thompson, W. L., & Alpert, N. M. (1997). Neural systems shared by visual imagery and visual perception: A positron emission tomography study. *NeuroImage, 6*, 320–334.

Kosslyn, S. M., Thompson, W. L., & Ganis, G. (2006). *The case for mental imagery*. New York: Oxford University Press.

Kozhevnikov, M., Kosslyn, S. M., & Shephard, J. M. (2005). Spatial versus object visualizers: A new characterization of visual cognitive style. *Memory and Cognition, 33*, 710–726.

Levine, D. N., Warach, J., & Farah, M. J. (1985). Two visual systems in mental imagery: Dissociation of 'what' and 'where' in imagery disorders due to bilateral posterior cerebral lesions. *Neurology, 35*, 1010–1018.

Mellet, E., Briscogne, S., Tzourio-Mazoyer, N., Ghaëm, O., Petit, L., Zago, L., et al. (2000). Neural correlates of topographic mental exploration: The impact of route versus survey perspective learning. *NeuroImage, 12*, 588–600.

Mellet, E., Tzourio, N., Denis, M., & Mazoyer, B. (1995). A positron emission tomography study of visual and mental spatial exploration. *Journal of Cognitive Neuroscience, 4*, 433–445.

Mitchell, D. B., & Richman, C. L. (1980). Confirmed reservations: Mental travel. *Journal of Experimental Psychology: Human Perception and Performance, 6*, 58–66.

O'Craven, K. M., & Kanwisher, N. (2000). Mental imagery of faces and places activates corresponding stimulus-specific brain regions. *Journal of Cognitive Neuroscience, 12*, 1013–1023.

Paivio, A. (1971). *Imagery and verbal processes.* New York: Holt, Rinehart and Winston.

Paivio, A. (1986). *Mental representations: A dual coding approach.* New York: Oxford University Press.

Perky, C. (1910). An experimental study of imagination. *American Journal of Psychology, 21*, 422–452.

Pinker, S., Choate, P. A., & Finke, R. A. (1984). Mental extrapolation in patterns constructed from memory. *Memory and Cognition, 12*, 207–218.

Pinker, S., & Kosslyn, S. M. (1978). The representation and manipulation of three-dimensional space in mental images. *Journal of Mental Imagery, 2*, 69–83.

Podgorny, P., & Shepard, R. N. (1978). Functional representations common to visual perception and imagination. *Journal of Experimental Psychology: Human Perception and Performance, 9*, 21–35.

Pylyshyn, Z. W. (1973). What the mind's eye tells the mind's brain: A critique of mental imagery. *Psychological Bulletin, 80*, 1–24.

Pylyshyn, Z. W. (1981). The imagery debate: Analogue media versus tacit knowledge. *Psychological Review, 87*, 16–45.

Pylyshyn, Z. W. (2002). Mental imagery: In search of a theory. *Behavioral and Brain Sciences, 25*, 157–238.

Pylyshyn, Z. W. (2003). Return of the mental image: Are there pictures in the brain? *Trends in Cognitive Sciences, 7*, 113–118.

Richman, C. L., & Mitchell, D. B., & Reznick, J. S. (1979). Mental travel: Some reservations. *Journal of Experimental Psychology: Human Perception and Performance, 5*, 13–18.

Schacter, D. L. (1996). *Searching for memory: The brain, the mind, and the past.* New York: Basic Books.

Segal, S. J., & Fusella, V. (1970). Influence of imaged pictures and sounds on detection of visual and auditory signals. *Journal of Experimental Psychology, 83*, 458–464.

Shepard, R. N. (1984). Kinematics of perceiving, imagining, thinking, and dreaming. *Psychological Review, 91*, 417–447.

Shepard, R. N., & Cooper, L. A. (1982). *Mental images and their transformations.* Cambridge, MA: MIT Press.

Sperling, G. (1960). The information available in brief visual presentations, *Psychological Monographs: General and Applied, 74*, 1–24.

Stevens, A., & Coupe, P. (1978). Distortions in judged spatial relations. *Cognitive Psychology, 10*, 422–437.

Super, H., Spekreijse, H., & Lamme, H. (2001). A neural correlate of working memory in the monkey primary visual cortex. *Science, 293*, 120–124.

Tootell, R. B., Hadjikani, N. K., Mendola, J. D., Marrett, S., & Dale, A. M. (1998). From retinotopy to recognition: fMRI in human visual cortex. *Trends in Cognitive Science, 2*, 174–183.

Tootell, R. B., Silverman, M. S., Switkes, E., & De Valois, R. L. (1982). Deoxyglucose analysis of retinotopic organization in primate striate cortex. *Science, 218*, 902–904.

Ungerleider, L. G., & Mishkin, M. (1982). Two cortical visual systems. In D. J. Ingle, M. A. Goodale, & R. J. W. Mansfield (Eds.), *Analysis of visual behavior* (pp. 549–586). Cambridge, MA: MIT Press.

Watson, J. B. (1913). Psychology as the behaviorist views it. *Psychological Review, 20*, 158–177.

Wede, J., & Francis, G. (2006). The time course of visual afterimages: Data and theory. *Perception, 35*, 1155–1170.

3 Visual imagery in the brain

Modality-specific and spatial, but perhaps without space

Hubert D. Zimmer

Whereas in everyday life imagination is commonly accepted as a specific mental state, postulating a mental and a corresponding neural faculty for provision of this competence is controversial in psychological science. This is even more the case if a specific format of mental representation (e.g., a depiction instead of a description – see below) is postulated. One reason for this is the fact that imagery is exclusively a personal experience. Any report on the qualities of a mental image is therefore ultimately grounded in introspective data that cannot be approached via direct empirical observation. It is therefore quite understandable that one looked to neuroscientific methods to increasingly disclose the state of imagery, as these promised a better understanding of imagery and perhaps a proof of the existence of such a neural faculty and the depictive format. However, as I show in the following, this is still – at least partially – an unfulfilled desire.

Kosslyn and colleagues recently specified what imagery should be:

> Mental imagery occurs when perceptual information is accessed from memory, giving rise to the experience of "seeing with the mind's eye", "hearing with the mind's ear", and so on. In contrast, perception occurs when information is registered directly from the senses. Mental images need not be simply the recall of previously perceived objects or events; they can also be created by combining and modifying stored perceptual information in novel ways.
>
> (Kosslyn, Thompson, & Ganis, 2006, p. 195)

Consequently, visual imagery – I will restrict my discussion to visual images – can be specified as a mental state that is *experienced* as "perceiving" a self-generated visual representation in mind – for example, a mental image of a picture. Most people would agree that this metaphor correctly describes the experience of a person who is imagining something visual. What is debatable, however, is what is meant by a visual mental representation being experienced. In principle, it can refer to three different levels of description. (1) It may simply mean that the person's experience feels like a percept. In general, imagery processes are considered as modality-specific because they are similar to perceiving a stimulus in a specific modality (they have, so to speak, the qualia of a specific sensation). (2) It means that having a visual image has the consequence that this representation shares physical constraints with the picture that is imagined. For example, one may postulate that a visual image of an object has color and spatial extent, that all spatial relations between subparts, including distances to each other, are preserved, and that the relations between them correspond to a Euclidian metric. (3) Beyond this, speaking of visual mental images may even mean that not only are these constraints effective at the informational level, but they exist already at the neural level, so that they are a necessary consequence of the structures – and processes – that represent the spatial and perceptual qualities of visual mental images. This chapter is about these different levels of interpretation and the arguments that were put forward in favor of and against a neural causation of the spatial and perceptual qualities of imagery.

Visual imagery representations were characterized as depictive, and this quality was contrasted with a propositional representation. Propositions are predicate argument structures like *red (ball)*, which make qualities of a percept explicit; in the example, the perceived (imagined) object is a ball, and it is red. In contrast, if images depict something, no explicit relation exists, and the red ball is represented as a drawing that is an analogue of the physical entity it represents. Accordingly, the mental image of a picture should be represented in a spatial medium. In Kosslyn's model (e.g., 1980, 1981)[1] the medium was called the "visual buffer". This buffer was assumed have a spatial, matrix-like structure, which is why one referred to this approach also as "the array theory of imagery". This postulate was the origin of the so-called imagery debate, a controversy that persisted for years. Later, neuroscientific data caused Kosslyn (1994) to claim the "resolution" of this debate. In the main, two arguments were put forward. First, brain imaging studies showed that neural structures that are involved in perception are also active during imagery; and, second, some of these visual structures show a retinotopic organization: that is, they preserve the spatial structure of the retinal image by spatial neighborhood. However, this claim again met with opposition (Pylyshyn, 2003).

In the following I want to revisit this controversy. I present a selection of results on imagery and its neurocognitive basis, and, taking stock, I analyze which assumptions can be considered as well supported and which are still awaiting resolution. The final count will show a stand-off. On the one hand, we have clear evidence for the involvement of dedicated neural structures that provide modality-specific processes (for a recent review see, e.g., Zimmer, 2008), but on the other hand, even these neurocognitive data do not yet tell us anything about the organization of the visual buffer and its spatial structure. They do not show that these structures provide the postulated visual buffer, nor that a buffer is necessary for experiencing visual images, and they also do not prove that the retinotopic topography of the visual network that should provide the buffer is functional. In order to show this, I present a critical evaluation of the imagery debate. Having briefly introduced the historical background, I then treat three topics: (1) The modality specificity of imagery, (2) the spatial quality of visual images, and (3) the functional role of the spatial structure of visual processing domains at the neural level. Finally, I pose the question as to whether these results should cause us to re-evaluate the debate.

A brief history of imagery research and the imagery debate

Today, several neural networks are known that are organized according to the modality of input and are used to retrieve modality-specific information (Meyer & Damasio, 2009). It is sometimes suggested that all (world) knowledge is grounded in perceptual and motor systems (Barsalou, Simmons, Barbey, & Wilson, 2003), and evidence is presented suggesting mental simulation of perceptual or physical processes – in the absence of external stimuli – as the basis of thinking about the world (Barsalou, 2008). Hence, today, postulating cognitive processes that are not based on verbal, propositional, or conceptual units seems to be the rule rather than the exception. This has not always been the case. For a long time, mental images that can be accessed only via introspection were banished from scientific reasoning. "Picture-like representations" in the head were less conceivable than propositions in the head, even though the latter were also abstract hypothetical constructs that nobody had "seen".

Nevertheless, in the 1960s several experiments were conducted in an effort to contrast performances in a mental imagery condition with verbal encoding. In this context, it was shown that the instruction to generate a mental image modifies behavior – for example, it often strongly increases memory (e.g., Bower, 1970; Denis, 1975) – and this was ascribed to "visual" processing causing pictorial memory traces. Most of these studies were run in the context of the dual code theory (Paivio, 1971, 1986), in which an analogue, picture-like representation was postulated alongside a verbal one. In Europe, Michel Denis (e.g., 1976) and John Richardson (1980) were early followers of this approach. Most of these experiments had shown that imagery instructions change memory, even though they did not prove that this is due to a picture-like representation. A further observation was that processes operating on mental images as inspecting (e.g., Kosslyn, 1973) or scanning (Kosslyn, Ball, & Reiser, 1978) and mental rotation (Shepard & Metzler, 1971) behave as if they were running in real physical space. These spatial qualities caused researchers to assume that imagery processes happen in analogue spatial representations.

A shortcoming of Paivio's model was that he had not clearly specified what "analogue" really means. His was mainly a theory about nonverbal content; he stated only that the nonverbal code is picture-like, spatial, and continuous. These qualities were formulated more precisely by Kosslyn (e.g., 1980). The representation was specified as a "depiction" of an object (of its appearance), which is a quasi-pictorial surface representation within a visual buffer – a "surface" because it might be generated from a differently represented long-term memory entry (Kosslyn, 1981). The buffer was considered to be a functional space that behaves like a Euclidean medium with a specified resolution. Importantly, in the 1980 model it was not a physical space – as is actually assumed (e.g., Kosslyn, Thompson, & Ganis, 2006, p. 141) – but only a functional one: a structure that *behaves* like a physical space. Importantly, it is assumed that these spatial characteristics are intrinsic to the medium (i.e., to the buffer). The medium behaves in this way, and it cannot behave differently. Hence, the spatial qualities of the visual buffer can be considered as the functional component that explains imagery effects.

In later versions of the theory (e.g., Kosslyn, 1994), the visual buffer was specified more precisely at the neural level: "the present conception is that the visual buffer corresponds to a set of topographically mapped visual areas in cortex, . . . resolution is greatest in the center and decreases toward the periphery . . . images are represented at different spatial scales within this structure" (Kosslyn, 1994, p. 388). Anatomically, it was located within early visual processing structures (V1 to V4) in the occipital cortex. In its latest version the parietal cortex was included, and different types of images were introduced (Kosslyn, Thompson, & Ganis, 2006). I will later come back to this issue. Visual imagery as a depiction has, therefore, three characteristic features: (1) it uses modality-specific representations in neural structures used also in perception; (2) it is spatial in nature (which has to be differentiated); and (3) this spatial quality is brought about by the spatial structure of the visual buffer located in early visual processing structures.

Imagery as a modality-specific process within modality-specific brain structures

The modality specificity of images

Because mental imagery was defined as "perceiving with the mind's eye or ear", imagery must in some way be modality-specific because the imagined *content* stems from a specific modality. We imagine, for example, a specific picture we have seen or a melody we have heard before. From this perspective, imagery is a specific form of memory. More precisely, it is a reactivated memory entry or a transformation thereof based on perceptual experience. In the case of visual imagery, it would consist of the retrieval of modality-specific visual information. It is, as it were, re-experiencing a concrete event, including modality-specific visual attributes like the specific color of a flower or the appearance of the landscape. From this perspective, "modality specificity" represents a conscious experience of a previously encountered sensory content within a specific modality.

Nowadays it is assumed that such memory is provided by a reinstatement of representations within structures that were active during encoding (e.g., Rugg, Johnson, Park, & Uncapher, 2008). This is called the reinstatement hypothesis, and this model predicts that the previously encountered visual event is reinstantiated in the visual neural networks involved in perception. For memory, this has been frequently shown. For example, it was found that if pictures are remembered, it is "visual" structures within the fusiform and occipital cortex (extending to extrastriate regions, BA 19) that are more active (Slotnick & Schacter, 2006; Wheeler, Petersen, & Buckner, 2000), whereas for sounds it is the superior temporal cortex (Nyberg, Habib, McIntosh, & Tulving, 2000; Wheeler, Petersen, & Buckner, 2000). If imagery follows similar principles, imagining a specific content should activate modality-specific brain structures involved in the processing of the specific information during perception and action. We should see activity in specific occipital, lateral, and inferior temporal areas for visual images according to the feature focused on: mid-frontal activity for actions and superior temporal activity for auditory images. These predictions were confirmed. It was found that visual perception and visual imagery have much neural activity in common (Kosslyn, Thompson, & Alpert, 1997). Activation of the visual association cortex (BA 37 and BA 19) was reported for imaging words' referents (D'Esposito et al., 1997; Mechelli, Price, Friston, & Ishai, 2004; Mellet, Tzourio, Denis, & Mazoyer, 1998). When faces or places were imagined, activity was found either in the fusiform face area or the para-hippocampal place area, respectively (O'Craven & Kanwisher, 2000). Motion-specific activities were reported for middle temporal areas in the context of dynamic images (Goebel, Khorram-Sefat, Muckli, Hacker, & Singer, 1998; Kourtzi & Kanwisher, 2000; Podzebenko, Egan, & Watson, 2005). In contrast, when auditory images (melodies) were generated, activity in associative auditory cortex (BA 21/22) was observed (Zatorre & Halpern, 2005); during tactile imagery, activity occurred in somatosensory cortical areas (Yoo, Freeman, McCarthy, & Jolesz, 2003), and when actions were imagined, it was in the supplementary motor area and premotor cortex (Decety & Grèzes, 1999; Dechent, Merboldt, & Frahm, 2004; Porro et al., 1996). These data are in close agreement with the prediction that modality-specific areas are activated when the corresponding content is imagined.

However, in the absence of perceptual stimulation, activity in modality-specific brain structures is not restricted to imagery. It has even been seen when people did not imagine a specific content but only retrieved knowledge of specific attributes, such as the color of a denoted object, the specific sound associated with an object, or the size of the object (Kellenbach, Brett, & Patterson, 2001; Kiefer, Sim, Herrnberger, Grothe, & Hoenig, 2008; Martin, Haxby, Lalonde, Wiggs, & Ungerleider, 1995). One interpretation of this result is that retrieval of modality-specific knowledge and imagery processes (partially) share neural structures. Even though the tasks are different, the accessed representations may be the same. Repetition priming between these two tasks provides direct evidence for this (Zimmer, 1988). For this study we selected object names such that a unique perceptual feature could be generated for each item, but the feature and the object were not verbally associated – for example, "burgee/triangular", "porthole/round", or "cigarette/columnar". We did this because we assumed that for such items participants have to access a visual representation of the word's referent in order to retrieve the perceptual feature (a figurative component – Denis, 1982). In one condition, participants had to verify predicates about the perceptual features of the objects; in another condition they generated images of the objects. In both tasks we measured participants' response times. Each item was presented twice – once in each task – and the sequence of presentation was counterbalanced. Both tasks resulted in reciprocal repetition priming (~200 ms), and the response times in both tasks correlated highly across items ($r = .70$). Finally, if the verification task was performed with an additional visual memory load, response times were clearly slower (by about 190 ms). For a control condition, we selected items with a verbal association between the object and the feature so that an access to a visual representation was not obligatory. For these items, all effects were much smaller (only half as large). I took these results as support for the assumption that visual imagery and retrieval of visual knowledge use the same structures. Hence, modality-specific processing is not a unique characteristic of imagery. Many mental processes that make use of specific sensory information seem to access neural structures that are also used for perception. The interesting and currently unanswered question is which level these down-stream processes proceed towards – it may be higher visual processing areas such as the lateral occipital and fusiform cortex or lower levels such as V1 and V2 – and whether these different levels are experienced as different mental states.

Obviously imagery uses to some extent the same modality-specific brain structures that are also found active during perception. However, other cognitive tasks that access sensory features do so as well; hence this is not a unique feature of imagery. Probably all tasks that make specific perceptual information available access modality-specific networks that process – and represent – this information during perception. Perceptual information is, in my view, made available in working memory in this way, and for this reason I have postulated that even though access to these networks is different, imagery and visual working memory use the same neural networks (cf. Zimmer, 2008). Not all researchers share this opinion. For example, Pearson (2001) and Logie and van der Meulen (2009) consider the visual buffer used in imagery and the visual cache used in working memory to be different. On the other hand, Kosslyn and colleagues seem not to make this distinction: "mental imagery is a good example of the kind or representation used in working memory" (Kosslyn, Thompson, & Ganis, 2006, p. 22), or, more explicitly, "imagery processes must draw on retrieved episodic information to generate explicit, accessible representations in working memory" (Moulton & Kosslyn, 2009, p. 1274). Given the behavioral and neural evidence, I consider it therefore as likely that the sensory representations in imagery tasks, in perception, and in working memory are provided by the same neural networks (see Zimmer, 2008, for a more extended discussion). However, processing this content in these different tasks results in different conscious experiences.

Evidence for a contribution to imagery by modality-specific early neural structures

Progress in neuroscientific methods has recently made it possible to provide more direct evidence for a contribution of perceptual processing networks to imagery. For example, Daselaar, Porat, Huijbers, and Pennartz (2010) have directly compared visual and auditory imagery and perception in an event-related fMRI study. The authors presented words together with a cue that indicated a visual or auditory perceptual or an imagining trial. In the perceptual condition, a picture was seen or a sound was heard for 3 s. In the imagery condition, participants were to imagine the corresponding picture or sound during the 3-s pause. In order to identify imagery-specific but modality-independent brain structures, it was determined which brain structures were more active in *both* imagery conditions than in the corresponding perceptual conditions (conjunction). In this analysis active clusters were found in the posterior cingulate (BA 31) extending into retrosplenial cortex (BA 29/30), the left and right ventral parietal cortex (BA 39), and medial prefrontal cortex (BA 10). In all these clusters signal change was correlated with imagery quality independent of modality. In a second analysis the authors identified modality-specific visual activities by searching for common activity (conjunction) in the contrasts between visual as against auditory imagery and visual as against auditory perception, and vice versa for auditory modality by contrasting auditory with visual processing. In this analysis, increased activity in the visual association cortex – the lateral occipital cortex (LOC) – was found for visual images and in the respective auditory association cortex – posterior superior temporal gyrus (STG) – for auditory images. Signal change correlated with imagery quality only in the corresponding modality, i.e., visual images in LOC and auditory images in STG (see Figure 3.1a).

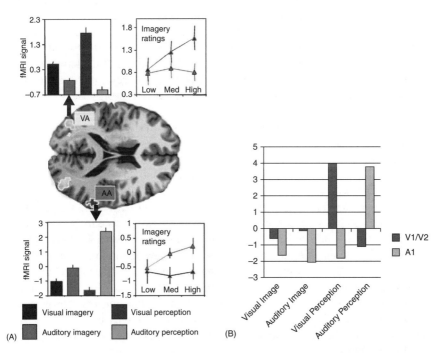

Figure 3.1 (A) An illustration of the modality-specific neural activity observed during auditory and visual imagery (VA indicates the visual, AA the auditory association cortex). To enhance the contrast, the borders of the activity clusters are accentuated in the grayscale transformation of Figure 3 of Daselaar et al. (2010). (From S. M. Daselaar, Y. Porat, W. Huijbers, & C. M. A. Pennartz, 2010. Modality-specific and modality-independent components of the human imagery system. *Neuroimage, 52*(2), 677–685. © Elsevier, Amsterdam. Reprinted with permission.) (B) An indication of the suppression of the primary visual and auditory cortices in the imagery conditions. The bars depict mean cluster activity in V1/2 and A1 in the four different conditions. (Data from Daselaar et al., 2010, Fig. 4.)

The modality-independent structures that were reported in this study belong to the so-called default mode network, which seems to be involved in any kind of imagery or simulation (Buckner, Andrews-Hanna, & Schacter, 2008). Additionally, the corresponding sensory association cortices were found to be active when a respective stimulus was imagined. This is the expected modality-specific neural activity. In contrast, the primary visual (V1/V2) and auditory cortices (A1) showed reduced activity (suppression) if an image in the corresponding modality was generated. In the latter analysis, visual processing regions were first identified by contrasting visual perception with auditory perception; it was then ascertained where, within this region, activity during visual imagery is lower than during auditory imagery. A parallel procedure was applied to auditory imagery and perception. In both modalities early sensory structures were clearly activated when physical stimuli were presented, but they were significantly suppressed during imagery in the specific modality (cf. Figure 3.1b). Daselaar et al. (2010) consider this to be an integral part of imagery because it "helps the processing of internally-generated images or sounds by shielding the associative sensory regions from external perceptual input processed by primary regions" (p. 684). This assumption is the opposite of the one made in the tradition of depictive imagery representations. The authors, however, admit that high-resolution images may differ and additionally activate these early sensory networks. In the closing section I revisit this result.

The most direct evidence for shared modality-specific neural structures is population-specific activity during imagery and perception. Brain scientists wanted to show that during perception and imagery the pattern of neural activity in sensory brain structures partially overlaps if the same content is processed. Thirion and colleagues (2006) presented different patterns in a visual and imagery condition and tried to predict from brain activity which pattern each participant was watching at the time. For this purpose they first solved the forward problem – which pattern of activity in retinotopically organized early brain structures (BA 17 and BA 18) corresponds to a specific seen pattern – and then they applied this knowledge to the inverse problem – which pattern was presented if a specific activity was observed. In perceptual conditions this procedure was successful. About 80% of classifications were correct (on a trial-by-trial basis). For imagery, however, the procedure was much less successful: It worked only for only 6 of the 16 participants, and even for them it was correct only in about 60% of the trials (chance level was about 17%).

Pattern analysis was used to predict the specifically processed content from neural activity in two further studies. Stokes, Thompson, Cusack, and Duncan (2009) contrasted two stimulus conditions. In the perceptual condition, they presented their participants with either an X or an O. In the imagery condition, they presented cues (high or low tone) and requested their participants to imagine either an X or O corresponding to the tone. When they contrasted these two conditions with baseline, activation of the visual cortex was observed in both, including calcarine sulcus, cuneus, and lingual gyrus, and this activity was extending into the inferior/middle occipital gyrus. In the imagery condition the activity in the visual cortex was even greater than in the perceptual condition, whereas the opposite pattern was observed for activation in temporal cortex. The authors then selected two regions in the extrastriate cortex that had shown category-specific activity in other studies (anterior and posterior regions in the lateral occipital cortex, LOC). For these subregions they trained a neural classifier (multivoxel pattern analysis) to identify the processed content. Using the pattern of the neural activity in the anterior or posterior LOC, the authors were able to identify the cognitive state with about 70% accuracy in the imagery condition. In the perceptual condition this was significant only for patterns in the posterior LOC. Importantly, the perceptual classifier in the left LOC could also successfully identify the state of the imagery condition. This demonstrates that during visual imagery via top-activation highly specific population codes were accessed in the perceptual cortex.

Reddy, Tsuchiya, and Serre (2010) used a similar approach. In the visual condition they presented pictures of objects (fruits and vegetables, tools, faces, buildings) and in the imagery condition their spoken names, together with the instruction to visualize each referent. They then identified object-responsive voxels for these categories by searching for clusters that were more active when a picture from the specific category was processed than when a scrambled picture was presented. As expected, enhanced activity was found in the fusiform face area, the parahippocampal place area, and the lateral occipital cortex. Within these regions a pattern classification techniques was applied to predict which content was being processed, given a specific activity pattern in these voxels. Using the perceptual classifier, they were able to categorize 67% of the perceptual trials (chance 25%); in the imagery condition, the same held true for generated images (50% correct). Importantly, even if the classifiers were crossed (trained with visual input and applied to imagery and vice versa) the classifier's prediction was in about 50% of the trials correct. In contrast, when retinotopic voxels in the primary visual cortex were used, only the perceptual but not the imagery condition could successfully be predicted by classifiers trained with visual input. The authors concluded "that actual viewing and mental imagery shared the same representations at the level of fine-grained multivoxel activation patterns in object-responsive ventral–temporal cortex (Reddy, Tsuchiya, & Serre, 2010, p. 824).

The modality specificity of processing visual images

Another assumption about modality-specific characteristics goes beyond shared modality-specific representations. Not only should the same structures be active during imagery and perception of physical events, but the mental processes running on these images (or performed with these images) should also be analogues of the real processes in the corresponding modality. This is relevant for the functional role of imagery. An important computational function of mental imagery is making predictions of events in the physical world (Moulton & Kosslyn, 2009). One function of imagery is generating tentative worlds that might become real in the future (Schacter, Addis, & Buckner, 2007) or running a mental simulation providing "imaginative constructions of hypothetical events or scenarios" (Buckner, Andrews-Hanna, & Schacter, 2008, p. 20). We imagine what it would look like if we were to arrange furniture in a specific way; we imagine a specific object in its place in order to test whether it would fit the space; and we imagine a specific action in order to check its feasibility. For that purpose imagery simulates parts of the physical world within a specific modality in order to anticipate a specific event or scenario before it has happened. In accordance with the idea of imagery as simulation, cognitive processes are today frequently considered as "embodied" (e.g., Aziz-Zadeh & Damasio, 2008), which is the customary way of speaking about modality-specific representations and processes that simulate perception and action.

The objective of simulation has several consequences. First, a simulation is functional only if it follows the same constraints in respect of the goal-relevant features as the simulated world. For example, in order for a visual image to be useful for making a spatial prediction it necessarily must represent space and it must keep the spatial constraints, otherwise the prediction would be useless. Second, simulating additional features of a physical process is frequently advantageous, even though these features are not directly task-relevant. For example, if one mentally moves from A to B, "traversing" intermediate locations might be a useful feature in many task contexts (these locations may be dangerous, or difficult to reach, etc.). Finally, because simulations make use of previous experiences – that is, memory – they also make use of memory of former physical processes. If memory of these events and actions is used, components that are bound in this memory trace are reactivated, which may or may not be necessary for the mental task. For example, if one wants to rotate a figure mentally, one might remember a physical action of rotating objects. A reactivation of this motor program, together with the forward model of its outcome, can be used to mentally simulate rotating a figure (Kosslyn, Thompson, Wraga, & Alpert, 2001). However, the action has happened in the real world, and therefore physical constraints determined enactment and, with this, the content of the memory trace. Consequently, the reactivated memory follows the same constraints. Because of the variety of these possibilities, it is difficult to say what causes the analogy between a mental and a physical process. The process may be habitually simulated because it was experienced that way or is implemented in the same (modality-specific) way.

According to this, imagery is a kind of simulation with "implemented constraints". Imagery has therefore been called an *emulative simulation* (Moulton & Kosslyn, 2009). The authors distinguish between an instrumental and an emulative version of simulating events. The main difference between these is the way in which transformations are implemented. Common to both is that they represent the relevant information and the sequence of states: ". . . the steps of the simulation mimic the corresponding steps of the represented situation. Mental simulations are 'run' such that intermediate steps in the process correspond to intermediate states in the event being simulated" (Moulton & Kosslyn, 2009, p. 1276) – even though the correspondence is not necessarily one-to-one. Critically, the sequence of steps is functional, not epiphenomenal. A step makes intermediate information accessible, and the specific information constrains the succeeding step. If a mental simulation has these characteristics, it is instrumental, and this is independent of the way these processes are simulated. An *emulative* simulation has the additional characteristic that it not only provides the intermediate states but also *imitates the process* that changes the content. Emulations "rely on algorithms that mimic the processes that transform successive states of that [simulated] event" (Moulton & Kosslyn, 2009, p. 1276). In the case of mental rotation, for example, providing information on the orientation of a stimulus at intermediate steps would not be sufficient for emulation; an emulative simulation must additionally mimic the physical rotation itself. Demonstrating this would be important because ". . . all imagery is mental emulation" (Moulton & Kosslyn, 2009, p. 1276).

When we take this seriously and we want to support the fact that processing an image – for example, mentally rotating the image – is an analogue process, it is necessary to demonstrate that intermediate steps are passed and that these steps are functional. This is what has been done in many studies on mental rotation (see Finke & Shepard, 1986). However, this is not sufficient evidence for characterizing mental rotation as emulative. For this purpose it is critical to demonstrate that the process of mental transformation imitates the represented physical transformation process. In the case of mental rotation, for example, this would be satisfied if images are represented in a spatial medium and they are rotated by incremental shifts of the represented shape within the spatial medium. In this case a direct structural similarity would be established between the physical and the mental processes. A spatially organized visual buffer would be suitable, for example, to implement mental rotation in this way. Alternatively, mental rotation may be provided by a process that also passes intermediate states and this process cannot be performed without taking these intermediate steps – as physical rotation does – but it does not happen within a spatial medium. Consequently, passing intermediate steps has no physical causation and, although it does necessarily happen during rotation – because the algorithm is implemented in that way – it only simulates the movement in space. Is this an emulative representation? The answer depends on the "depth of mimicry" that is demanded. Both versions are functionally equivalent if the same dependence on spatial information is represented. From the behavioral outcome, these two alternatives are indistinguishable. The difference is in the way the spatial information comes into effect: whether it is in the medium or in the simulation.

It is not always clear which explanation is favored and what kind of evidence is available in favor of one or the other version of these interpretations. For example, Kosslyn, Thompson, and Ganis (2006) wrote about mental rotation:

> this image transformation relies on incrementally modulating the mapping function from the object-properties-processing subsystem to the visual buffer. This process would alter the orientation of the pattern in the visual buffer itself . . . this is accomplished by shifting the parts [of a figure] along arcs around the central axis while rotating them so that they continue to be aligned the same way, relative to the central axis.
>
> (p. 149)

However, on the basis of these assumptions, the analogue spatial mental rotation is implemented in a way such that physical space causes the intermediate steps only if one assumes that the mapping function itself is implemented in a spatial medium. Kosslyn, Thompson, and Ganis (2006) discuss the fact that "the brain also uses depictive representations to specify information about the locations of objects in space" (p. 18). These structures are assumed to be located in the posterior parietal cortex. If these structures provide the mapping function and if they do this in a spatial manner, one would have good evidence of emulation. There is much evidence that the parietal cortex contributes to mental rotation (see Zimmer, 2008). However, contrary to the retinotopic structures in the occipital cortex, as discussed above, the current evidence in favor of a topographical organization of the parietal cortex (e.g., Sereno, Pitzalis, & Martinez, 2001) is spatially not yet fine-scaled enough to allow any inference about a depictive representation.

Spatial information and visual mental imagery

Spatial effects while processing visual images

When people make use of imagery, it is commonly observed that behavioral performances show spatial effects. For example, the time for mental scanning is often a linear function of the distance between the start and the landing position. In these experiments, participants usually learn a spatial layout (or it is pre-experimentally known to them). Then a start location "A" is specified, and participants are required to scan the mental image from A to a target location "B". They are asked to push a button the moment they "arrive" at B. In these studies, scanning time linearly increased with the distance between the points (Kosslyn, Ball, & Reiser, 1978), and these distances followed the Euclidean rules (for an overview, see Denis & Kosslyn, 1999). Similarly, the time required to mentally shift the focus of attention between different parts of an imagined object while answering questions is a function of the spatial distance between these loci (Kosslyn, 1973). The same result was observed even if participants were not explicitly instructed to scan an image. When asked to keep a spatial layout of dots in memory and then required to judge whether a presented arrow points to a distant target location (or has minimally missed it), the response time is a linear function of the spatial distance between the arrow and the target (Finke & Pinker, 1982). Because participants were not explicitly instructed to imagine the layout, either the task is solved by spatial imagery or spatial distance effects are a general characteristic of processing spatial information in visual working memory. However, please note that although both tasks show spatial distance effects, it has been observed that the slopes of the linear functions of scanning imagined versus memorized layouts can be different (Borst, Kosslyn, & Denis, 2006). Recently, however, Borst and Kosslyn (2008) have directly compared visual scanning, mental scanning of a perceived layout held in memory, and mental scanning of the image of the layout generated from memory. The authors observed similar slopes (correlations between .59 and .70). They concluded that a perceived stimulus held in memory and a mental image are similarly represented and processed (see also chapter 2 Borst and Kosslyn, this volume).

Spatial effects were also observed in other types of imagery tasks. For example, mental images seem to have a spatial resolution. Judging a perceptual detail of an imagined object is inversely related to the size of the image (Kosslyn, 1975, 1976). Another well-supported "spatial" phenomenon is the already mentioned mental rotation effect (for a review, see Finke & Shepard, 1986). The time mentally to rotate a figure is a – roughly linear – function of the angle by which the figure has to be rotated (e.g., Shepard & Metzler, 1971). Usually in these tasks participants are not explicitly instructed mentally to rotate the figure, thus simulating a rotation. Their task is only to judge whether two figures can be matched by rotation without flipping it in the third dimension or whether the two figures presented with an angular disparity are identical or mirror images of each other. The mental rotation task also provides the most compelling evidence for the functional relevance of the intermediate steps of a simulation. If participants see the reference figure followed by a cue indicating the orientation of the later presented target figure, the response time is no longer dependent on the angle of rotation. This is to be expected because participants can rotate the figure in advance. However, if the given advance time is not sufficient to finish the rotation, the response time is a function of the angle between the estimated orientation into which the figure could be rotated within the given time and the angle of the target – that is, it is a function of the remaining to-be-rotated angle (Cooper & Shepard, 1973). Similar effects were obtained when the participants were instructed to rotate a stimulus at a specified speed (Cooper & Shepard, 1984).

Another probably frequent use of spatial imagery is spatial navigation. People have spatial knowledge of their environment, and they generate something like a mental map or a spatial mental model (Taylor & Tversky, 1992). These maps partly preserve spatial information, and they can be used to infer spatial relations, such as shortcuts that have never been used before. When participants process such maps, modality-specific brain-structures are reactivated; these are, however, different from those found during object imagery. For example, in the study of Mellet and colleagues (2000), participants acquired spatial knowledge from actual navigation or from a map, and afterwards they mentally explored the environment. Brain activity was measured during the mental spatial exploration. During both tasks the hippocampus was active, and, after learning by navigation, the parahippocampus was as well. Additionally, superior and middle frontal structures and the intraparietal sulcus were active in both tasks. The authors consider these structures a spatial mental imagery network. Interestingly, in these tasks it is mainly the parietal cortex that is active, not the early visual network. Imagery seems therefore not to be a unique process. On the contrary, the type of task determines whether the ventral or dorsal network is active. It is therefore not always the early extrastriate visual cortex that contributes to imagery, but sometimes the parietal cortex that houses images (Mellet, Petit, Mazoyer, Denis, & Tzourio, 1998). We will later come back to this difference, which refers to visual and spatial images, respectively.

Generating spatial mental models

From the perspective of imagery and its functional role for spatial processing, a further observation is particularly important. Spatial effects were observed even when the mental image to be scanned was generated not from a visual input but from a description of the visual layout. Several of these studies were conducted in the laboratory of Michel Denis or in cooperation with him. In such experiments the maps were not overly complex, so that they could be learned from a verbal description alone, even though no map of the island was presented (see Figure 3.2a for illustration). An example of a verbal description is the following "The island is circular in shape. Six features are situated at its periphery. At 11 o'clock, there is a harbor. At 1.00, there is a lighthouse. At 2.00, there is a creek. Equidistant from 2.00 and 3.00 there is a hut. At 4.00, there is a beach. At 7.00, there is a cave" (example from Expt. 2 in Denis & Zimmer, 1992). Once participants had learned the spatial layout, a mental scanning task followed. Again, scanning times were a function of the Euclidian distances between the landmarks, even though the map was generated from a description and had never been seen in physical space (Cocude & Denis, 1988).

The same results were also observed by Denis and Zimmer (1992, Expt. 2). Additionally, they demonstrated spatial effects when participants were not explicitly

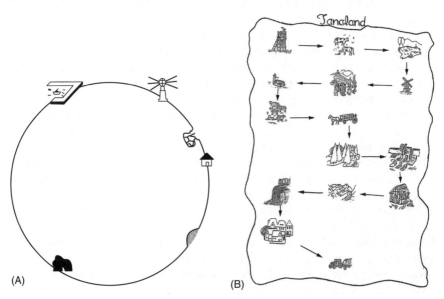

(A)   (B)

Figure 3.2 An illustration of islands used in imagery tasks. (A) The island used in the scanning experiment, (B) the island used in the priming experiment. The arrows were not visible; they only indicate the sequence of spatial relations that were explicitly expressed in the sentences. (Examples taken from M. Denis & H. D. Zimmer, 1992. Analog properties of cognitive maps constructed from verbal descriptions. *Psychological Research, 54,* 286–298. © Springer, Berlin. Reprinted with permission.)

instructed to simulate spatial processing but only to access mental representations that were generated in a spatial task (Expt. 1). For that purpose we gave a verbal description of the arrangement of landmarks that constituted a grid-like structure (cf. Figure 3.2b), and we later asked for the presence or absence of a landmark in a recognition test. In the learning phase we first presented an empty map of the outline of the island on which every possible location of each landmark was indicated by a small cross (the cells of a 3 × 7 matrix). The real locations of the landmarks were given in a text – for example: *In the extreme north-west there is a raised hide. East of the raised hide there is grazing land. East of the grazing land, there is a lake. South of the lake you will find a windmill. West of the windmill a vineyard is located . . .*" Two different types of spatial relations were realized. Explicit relations directly provided information about the spatial neighborhood in the text. In this case the sentences were arranged so that the relations between landmarks were explicitly mentioned in a sentence (e.g., fountain/grazing land). In the implicit condition, the spatial vicinity was not mentioned, and the names of the landmarks were never presented together (e.g., grazing land/vineyard). Consequently, a close spatial relation between two landmarks existed only within a correct spatial (mental) model; it was never physically presented. If the spatial model is not built, the landmarks are not related. We tested memory for the landmarks in a primed recognition paradigm. Critically, the target was preceded by another landmark that was either spatially near it or far from it. Response times were shorter after presentation of spatially near than of distant primes, and this was the case even if the spatial prime target relation was not explicitly given in the text but only implicitly by the spatial constraints of the virtual grid. The priming effect was smaller for large than for small distances. Such an effect would be expected if participants process a spatial mental model during memory retrieval – that is, they focus attention on the prime and then shift attention to target within a spatial image.

Similarly, in a direction judgment task spatial effects were observed even though mental scanning was not explicitly requested. We asked our participants to learn the spatial layout of an island either from a verbal description or a real physical map (Zimmer, 2004). After study, we presented the name of a city located on this island, followed by an arrow pointing in a specific direction, and then the name of a target city was shown – this paradigm was adopted from the already mentioned experiment of Finke and Pinker (1982). We requested our participants to decide whether, seen from the viewpoint of the reference city, the arrow was pointing towards the target. In nonmatching trials it pointed slightly to one side of it. We observed similar spatial distance effects in the visual and the verbal condition. Additionally, we created two different visual conditions, one in which a complete map was shown and another in which a sequence of pictures – each presenting a subset of the map elements – was shown; the latter would provide the complete map if the part maps were overlaid. Both visual conditions yielded equivalent results, and the two physical map conditions (complete and piecemeal map) were better than the verbal condition (sentence). This demonstrates that a pictorial input supports the generation of a spatial mental representation, but that the usually observed pictorial advantage is not caused by the fact that all possible spatial relations are simultaneously available in the picture. On the contrary, because the piecemeal presentation in some way simulates sequential encoding and performances were comparable in the complete and piecemeal conditions, the spatial mental model may generally be the result of a sequential encoding process. Participants encode spatial information about the locations of landmarks and their spatial relations, and they use these pieces of information to generate a consistent spatial image or spatial model at the time of testing. Obviously, this representation is not a reactivation of a "snapshot" of the whole physical map.

Taken together, these results suggest that participants use a spatially consistent mental model of the spatial layout when they make inferences about spatial relations in the environment. Mentally, this model is a spatial image. Participants are able to generate such a model not only after processing real physical two-dimensional inputs, but also if they process a verbal description and even without an explicit instruction to generate images. Introducing a task with spatial demands was sufficient to induce a behavior that corresponds to Euclidean spatial qualities. Minimal spatial cues seem to be sufficient to implement such spatial processing. Even the presentation of narrative texts in which the protagonists move in a spatial surrounding can show spatial distance effects (de Vega, 1994; Zimmer & de Vega, 1996). From an imagery perspective, these data are taken as evidence that partici-pants had constructed a spatially consistent mental image of the layout, and retrieval of information operates on this spatial image. The image provides the spatial relations and the Euclidean spatial qualities. In light of these results, encoding of a spatial description may be best described as the generation of a mental image of the map (Denis, 1986).

The parietal cortex and (spatial) imagery

In contrast to the case with visual images, in the spatial tasks the parietal cortex (the dorsal route), the parahippocampus, and the hippocampus were primarily found to be active, not the primary or secondary visual cortex (Mellet et al., 1996). This does not fit what we had said before about the locus of the visual buffer and the reported retinotopically organized neural structures. Rather, it suggests the existence of a further structure in the parietal cortex that provides spatial images. Consequently, in the 2006 version of the imagery model, Kosslyn and colleagues suggested two structures as locus of the visual buffer.

> We group the topographically organized areas in the occipital lobe into a single functional structure, which we refer to as the *visual buffer* . . . the brain also uses depictive representations to specify information about the locations of objects in space. These representations are primarily in the posterior pari-etal lobes . . . we will distinguish between *object images*, which represent shape (and related properties such as color and texture), versus *spatial images*, which represent relative locations in space.
>
> (Kosslyn, Thompson, & Ganis, 2006, p. 18)

Other researchers considered the parietal cortex as generally more important for the higher processing of spatial information and imagery than early visual brain structures. Burgess (2008) reviewed the literature on human spatial processing and highlighted that a variety of representations with different reference frames contribute to spatial processing. Two different spatial systems – an egocentric and an allocentric one – are mainly used in parallel (Burgess, 2006).

Egocentric representations make explicit the location of objects relative to the viewer. These locations are automatically updated when the viewer is moving in the environment. As with other types of spatial processes, this updating is efficiently possible if participants are only imagining moving in the environment (Wraga, 2003). The egocentric representation is probably the kind of information that is used in many spatial tasks including working memory tasks, and this spatial representation is supramodal. It is not restricted to a visual input. Recent results from our lab provide support for this view. We designed visual and auditory spatial location tasks. In the visual condition, participants had to indicate from memory the locations of previously seen objects; in the auditory condition this was the locations of previously heard objects (the source of a sound that was not visible). Both tasks caused comparable memory performances in modality-pure and modality-mixed lists, leading us to the conclusion that both tasks loaded the same memory component (Lehnert & Zimmer, 2006) (see Figure 3.3a). In a similar task we recorded scalp potentials during maintenance, and we calculated the slow-wave potentials during maintenance. In both modalities we observed increasing slow-wave potentials over the posterior cortex, and these potentials were similar for both types of information (Lehnert & Zimmer, 2008) (see Figure 3.3b for an example).

Further support for the idea of a parietal contribution to spatial imagery can be seen in the posterior parietal activity that was found – together with premotor activity – in tasks of imagined egocentric rotation during spatial updating (Creem et al., 2001). When object rotations and egocentric self-rotations were directly compared (Wraga, Shephard, Church, Inati, & Kosslyn, 2005), strong activations were found in the posterior parietal lobe in both tasks, but the object location task additionally activated the primary motor cortex, whereas in the self-rotation task the supplementary motor area was active. Additionally, several other smaller clusters were active, but no early visual brain structures. These data support the assumption of an egocentric spatial representation within the posterior parietal cortex.

Other spatial representations are allocentric. In this case, locations are represented relative to environmental landmarks. Different types of cells were found that show the strongest activity for a specific type of spatial relation. "Place cells" in the hippocampus show the strongest activity if the animal is at a specific location in the environment, head direction cells have the highest firing rate if the landmark and the head are in the preferred angular orientation for these specific cells, and grid cells fire maximally if three neighboring landmarks' locations form a regular triangle (the resulting firing pattern of these cells shows maxima at the crossings of a grid) (see Burgess, 2008, for more information).

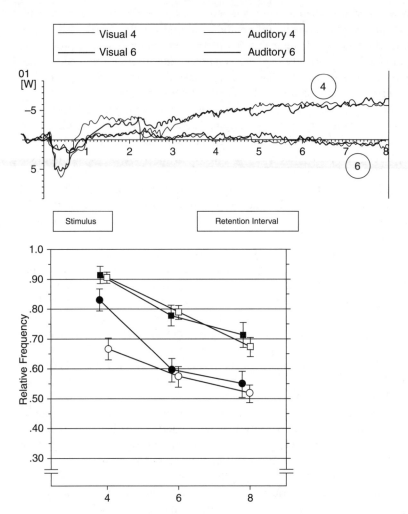

Figure 3.3 (A) Memory performances in a visual (squares) and auditory (circles) spatial
working memory task in which 4, 6, or 8 items were presented that were
all from the same modality (open symbols) or equally distributed to both
modalities (closed symbols), e.g., 3 pictures and 3 sounds for set size 6. The
higher memory performance with 2 sounds presented with 2 pictures is due to
a guessing advantage (see the discussion in the original article of Lehnert &
Zimmer, 2006). (From G. Lehnert & H. D. Zimmer, 2006. Auditory and visual
spatial working memory. *Memory & Cognition*, 1080–1090. © Psychonomic
Society. Reprinted with permission.) (B) An illustration of the slow-wave
potentials at an occipital electrode for 4 (upper curves) and 6 (lower curves)
items presented in the visual (pictures of objects) and auditory (sounds)
modality during the retention interval of a short-term memory task of locations.
"Stimulus" indicates the time window (0–2 s) in which the item was presented.
The time scale is 0–8 s.

Based on these results, Burgess and colleagues suggested a temporo-parietal model of spatial memory (Byrne, Becker, & Burgess, 2007), and this should also be a model of imagery. According to this model, three main components can be distinguished. The parietal window provides an egocentric representation that is the exclusive access into long-term spatial memory used in mental imagery, planning, and navigation. Allocentric representations are located in the medial temporal lobes (the parahippocampal region and hippocampal place cells), which provide long-term spatial memories. Finally, circuits involving the retrosplenial cortex and the parieto-occipito sulcus provide the interface (transformation) between the parietal window and the allocentrically stored spatial representations in the medial temporal lobe. "Both short-term spatial memory and imagery are modeled as egocentric representations of locations in the precuneus, which can be driven by perception or by reconstruction from long-term memory" (Byrne, Becker, & Burgess, 2007, p. 344). In this model, spatial imagery is used to "inspect" the result of the spatial reconstructive process, and this image is provided by the parietal window. Spatial information is retrieved from long-term memory, and "these products of retrieval are then capable of being put into a head-centered representation for imagery in medial parietal areas via (re)constructive mechanisms in retrosplenial/parieto-occipital and posterior parietal areas" (Burgess, 2008, p. 91). In this model, the parietal window is the structure that represents egocentric representations driven by perception, retrieval, and also imagery.

Treating space with caution: the difference between the representation of features, features of a representation, and features of the representing neural structures

Given what I have presented so far, which kinds of spatial representations exist, and how is imagery related to them? Or, more precisely, what aspect of a spatial representation causes the observed behavioral spatial effect? The conceptions of Burgess and colleagues on the one hand and of Kosslyn and colleagues on the other hand show some similarities, but they also differ. An uncontroversial constraint seems to be that mental "space" preserves a number of spatial features in order to be an analogue to physical space, and transformations are a function of the amount of change on the transformed physical dimension, such as the angle of rotation or the distance traversed. Some of these effects were presented; many others can be found in in-depth reviews (see, e.g., Kosslyn, 1994; Kosslyn, Thompson, & Ganis, 2006). It is therefore generally accepted that even in absence of real physical input when using spatial images, people behave – to some extent – as if they are operating in a physical space. However, it is controversial where this behavior originates from.

The visual buffer as spatial structure

Kosslyn (1980) published the first detailed processing model of mental imagery, and one of its central assumptions was that imagery is based on depictions within a visual buffer (Kosslyn, 1980, pp. 31–35). The model was later modified (as we will discuss), but in my view one of the core features of imagery (depictive representations) was laid down in this publication, and these assumptions are still valid. A depiction represents as a drawing does. It has no distinctive relation or argument, it is concrete, and it occurs in a spatial medium. This medium has two qualities: an abstract spatial and an abstract surface-property isomorphism. Abstract spatial isomorphism means that the spatial qualities of the physical image are preserved. Each portion of the representation corresponds to a portion of what is represented, and the represented distances among the portions correspond to the distances between the portions of the represented object. This is a consequence of the fact that images occur in a spatial medium that is functionally equivalent to a coordinate space. It is only functional because the medium behaves like a physical space (as I discuss later, this was changed in the 2006 model). It is sufficient that the array behaves like physical space; it need not be physical. A simulated array structure in a digital computer on which transformation processes are operating that interpret and transform the cell entries and the represented spatial relations in accordance with Euclidean metrics is consistent with this assumption, even though it has no physical space. In depictive representations, images are represented by altering local regions in portions of the spatial medium, so that each portion represents a portion of the physical object and the spatial neighborhood is preserved (the image is, so to speak, drawn on the array). "The visual buffer, in essence, is the canvas upon which images are painted . . ." (Kosslyn, Thompson, & Ganis, 2006, p. 18). The mental image depicts information not only about spatial content but also about the appearance of surface properties (this assumption was later restricted to visual images), and these properties also "simulate" the qualities of the physical properties, such as intensity relations. The latter is the abstract surface property isomorphism. A consequence thereof is that a representation necessarily has part/whole relations, it has size and orientation, and surface qualities do not exist without the surface of which they are a property – for example, a color cannot be imagined without representing some shape on which it is painted.

> Such mechanisms rely in part on depictive representations, where configurations of densely arranged points (with size, intensity and colour) in a coordinate space are arranged so that the pattern "resembles" the appearance of the referent. . . . In object-based visual imagery, for instance, depictive representations make available the full set of visual information (i.e., size, intensity and colour values of each point).
>
> (Moulton & Kosslyn, 2009, p. 1274)

However, please note that this is a quality of the surface representation of an image that is constructed from more abstract and distributed underlying subsystems that do not have these constraints. Therefore, these pieces of information – belonging to the perceived object – can be independently lost: if they were not encoded or have been forgotten, for example.

An inverse position was held by Pylyshyn (e.g., 1981). According to him people have tacit knowledge about the physical world. They have learned how physical objects behave and what the world looks like from specific points of view. When they process the respective information, they apply the corresponding knowledge and they simulate the physical world (note that this simulation is not necessarily conscious) (Pylyshyn, 2003). From Pylyshyn's perspective no spatial medium is necessary, and it is arbitrary how this knowledge is represented; what is relevant is that only the physical qualities are simulated. One argument put forward against this tacit knowledge explanation was demonstrating accurate physical constraints even though people have misleading assumptions about the physical rules. This has been shown, for example, for mental scanning. Scanning times were a linear function of the scanned distances even though participants had false beliefs about the relationship between scanning times and distances (Goldston, Hinrichs, & Richman, 1985). However, this is only a counterargument against the intentional use of explicit knowledge, which means that people explicitly follow an assumed rule. It is still possible for people to have false explicit beliefs but nevertheless for the unconsciously performed simulation to be physically correct. In other contexts it has also been observed that what people verbalize is different from that what people do. For many mental processes it is assumed that they are cognitively impenetrable (Fodor, 1983). Introspectively one cannot "see" how such a process works, and one also has no access to it in order to change its parameter. If mental scanning and mental rotation are of this kind, then the simulation and the belief may be divergent. The independence of the scanning times from the explicit beliefs is therefore not yet a final argument against a spatial medium and, vice versa, neither is the spatial effect an argument in favor of it. Accordingly, more direct evidence was sought.

Before I come to these studies, however, I want to discuss another counterargument. Pylyshyn argued that the medium cannot be spatial because in some conditions mental scanning violates the space–distance law (Pylyshyn, 2003). He asked participants to learn a map that had, at each landmark, lights that could be switched on or off. Critically, if a specific light was turned off, the light at another landmark immediately went on. After memorizing the map, participants were asked by the authors to imagine the map and to focus a landmark. Now they should imagine that the light has been switched off and indicate when they mentally "see" the second landmark where the light has gone on. The time for this judgment was independent of distance. Similarly, when participants judged the orientation of a landmark relative to a reference, distance between the landmarks had no effect. Only if participants inspected a real map were distance effects observed. This is a strong argument that distance effects are not ubiquitous, as they should be if the spatial map is represented within a spatial medium and if this representation is the only one. However, this result can easily be explained if one assumes that mental processes simulate physical experience only if it is task-relevant, but not always. In contrast, if the assumption of a spatial representation within a spatial medium is to be kept, one has to postulate an additional representation without spatial qualities that can be used alternatively. Spatial information is then not obligatorily processed within a spatially organized visual buffer.

If such a spatial buffer is postulated, how does it provide this information, and where is it located? In the 1980s Kosslyn spoke of an abstract isomorphism; it was not specified how it is realized at the neural level. Later a spatial analogy also at the neural level was postulated. Kosslyn, Thompson, and Ganis (2006) claimed that "depictive representations make explicit and accessible all aspects of shape and the relations between shape and other perceptual qualities (such as color and texture), as well as spatial relations among each point. . . . Depictive representations of shape must also incidentally specify size and orientation . . ." (p. 14) and "there is good evidence that the brain depicts representations literally, using space on the cortex to represent space in the world" (p. 15) . . . "a functional space is sufficient as a depictive form of representation only if the geometric properties of the representation emerge because there are fixed, hard-wired processes that interpret the representation as if it were a space" (p.15). A population code is not considered as sufficient. "Because these representations do not use space to represent space . . . they cannot be considered to depict" (p. 137). Correspondingly, the studies of Stokes et al. (2009) and Reddy, Tsuchiya, and Serre (2010) do not give support to a depictive representation even though they demonstrate an overlap of perceptual and imagery representations at the neural level. If one holds such a position, one needs empirical arguments for physical spatial representations in the brain, and, correspondingly, one searches for evidence that spatially organized brain structures are active during mental imagery. Candidates for this are the early retinotopically organized structures of the visual cortex (V1, V2).

The visual buffer as a physical space at the neural level

It could be shown via radioactive markers that within the occipital cortex of monkeys (V1) a geometric pattern is represented keeping the topographic structure of the pattern (Tootell, Silverman, Switkes, & De Valois, 1982; Tootell, Switkes, Silverman, & Hamilton, 1988) – even though it is spatially distorted due to the cortical magnification of the fovea. Similarly, human V1 is topographically organized (Tootell, Hadjikhani, Mendola, Marrett, & Dale, 1998). Accordingly, this structure would be the ideal medium for a depictive representation. Consequently, Kosslyn and colleagues searched for evidence for the involvement of this structure in imagery. They could show, for example, that the extent of activity within the primary visual cortex (V1) varied with the size of the image (Kosslyn et al., 1993; Kosslyn, Thompson, Kim, & Alpert, 1995). In later positron emission tomography (PET) studies, they asked their participants questions about detailed visual properties of imagined patterns. Again they could show that during visualizing activity in V1 was enhanced (Kosslyn et al., 1999; Thompson, Kosslyn, Sukel, & Alpert, 2001). At around the same time, Chen and colleagues reported an fMRI study in which participants were to imagine walking in their hometown or a flashing light pattern that they had seen earlier, with eyes closed. Again V1 and even earlier structures (the lateral geniculate nucleus) were activated during visual imagery without external visual input (Chen, Kato, Zhu, Ogawa, Tank, & Ugurbil, 1998). These and similar results were taken as evidence that the visual buffer used in imagery is located in the retinotopically organized early visual brain structures.

Klein and colleagues also provided evidence for neural activity in retinotopic brain areas during mental imagery (mostly the calcarine sulcus) (Klein et al., 2004). They compared a visual and an imagery condition. In the visual condition, they presented, in a horizontal or a vertical orientation, a bow-tie shape that was flickering at 8 Hz. The two orientations were each associated with a different tone. In the imagery condition only the tones were presented, and participants were required to imagine the corresponding shape with eyes closed. For each participant the activation pattern associated with the actually seen stimulus was compared with the pattern of the imagined stimulus. They observed no clear topographic organization and no activation at the group level when the imagery condition was compared to baseline, although in five out of six participants small activation clusters were found also in V1, but with a high interindividual variability. In contrast, the visual condition showed clear topographically organized activity along the horizontal and vertical meridians. When horizontal images were directly compared with vertical ones or vice versa, V1 activity in the imagery condition partially matched those in the perceptual condition, and this was orientation-selective. About 70 voxels showed spatial correspondence when the orientations were the same, whereas it was fewer than five if the orientations were different.

In a later study Slotnick, Thompson, and Kosslyn (2005) contrasted real perception and imagery using an overt criterion task. They devised a perceptual condition and an imagery condition. In the perceptual condition they presented really rotating stimuli (wedges similar to the bow-tie shapes of the previous experiment and also flickering at 8 Hz). In the imagery condition only the outer edges of the wedges were visible, and participants had to imagine the remaining part of the shape. At various points in time a small red square was flashed that was either on the shape or alongside it. Participants were requested to decide whether the square was on or off the real or imagined figure. Additionally, in an attention condition, designed for control, participants saw the edges of the shapes as in the imagery condition but had to judge only whether the red square was on the left or the right side of the screen. When the neural activity that covaried with the angle of rotation of the flickering shape or image was analyzed, a correlation was found between the visual and the imagery but not the attention condition. Importantly, this activity was found in retinotopically organized early visual areas. In a conjunction analysis between the imagery and the perception conditions, neural activity was found in the parietal lobe (BA 7), temporal cortex (BA 37), and the extrastriate cortex. Interestingly, the inferior temporal sulcus (hMT+) was included, which is a structure that is involved in processing motion information. This activity was even higher in the imagery condition than during perception. However, again, only half of the participants showed this effect. The authors interpreted their results as "compelling support for the claim that depictive representations are used in visual imagery" (Slotnick, Thompson, & Kosslyn, 2005, p. 1582).

Is the neural spatial structure functional?

Obviously in these studies activity in the early, retinotopically organized visual cortex was observed during imagery. Is this activity really proof of the functional role of the spatiotopic representation in imagery – that is, of the functional role of a depictive representation at the neural level? I am skeptical about that. This spatial organization can have other reasons that have no relation to the computational function of these neurons. For example, at the retina physical spatial relations necessarily exist, and it is possible that they are kept for a while on their way into the brain without any representational function. We know that some neural representations show a spatial organization – for example, in the auditory cortex – even though neural space has nothing to do with a representation of physical space. Hence, the spatial structure of a neural network may be arbitrary, and it may not be necessary. Furthermore, if activity was found in early visual cortices at the group level, a considerable proportion of participants did not show the effect. Admittedly, these are always null effects and therefore the nonsignificant results might be due to a test power that was too low or a suboptimal design that masked V1 activity. However, activity of the to-be-expected effect size was generally detected in higher visual brain areas, and it is therefore not plausible that activity in V1 should not have been detected. Again, these results support that a visual image does not depend on activity in early visual structures.

The study of Reddy, Tsuchiya, and Serre (2010) also points to that possibility. In the imagery condition, it was not possible efficiently to train a pattern classifier on the basis of the neural activity in V1. The authors concluded that V1 may be activated during imagery but that this is not a necessary condition for processing images. I agree with this conclusion. The early visual activation acts more as a surplus of imagery on me than as a necessary precondition. As counterargument against this interpretation TMS effects were put forward. Performances in imagery tasks were impaired under TMS stimulation over V1 (e.g., Kosslyn et al., 1999). However, even this is not compelling. V1 provides input into the visual processing stream, and changing neural activity at V1 can therefore influence any stage of visual processing. Remember that Daselaar and colleagues even observed a deactivation of V1 when a visual image was generated. They concluded

> that suppression of primary sensory regions represents an integral part of constructing internal representations in the brain. We propose that this suppression helps the processing of internally-generated images or sounds by shielding the associative sensory regions from external perceptual input processed by primary regions.
>
> (Daselaar, et al., 2010, p. 684)

As a solution for this discrepancy, Kosslyn and colleagues suggested that the detail or resolution of the requested visual image is critical. Early visual activity should be observed when a visual image of sufficient detail was generated (Kosslyn & Thompson, 2003). However, when the requested resolution was directly manipulated, it did not influence the amount of activation in V1 (in this study it was always active) (Thompson et al., 2001). Later, Kosslyn and colleagues used a step-wise logistic regression approach with a large set of studies to analyze the conditions that caused activity in V1 (Kosslyn, Thompson, & Ganis, 2006). Conditions that enhanced the likelihood of finding such an effect were, in descending order, that the task demands high-resolution details, the images are nonspatial (properties of shapes and not spatial relations), and the technique has a sufficiently high sensitivity (e.g., more than 3T fMRI). Formulating it differently, this activity can be detected if the methods are sensitive enough to find small effects. However, given the central relevance of the buffer for image generation, this early activity should not be a weak effect, and it should correlate with imagery ratings. This speaks more in favor of a surplus than of a functional role of this activation.

However, even when we assume that under high-resolution conditions V1 is regularly active, what does this activity mean, and is the spatial organization of this structure functional? In virtually all imagery studies other visual areas were active too. In object imagery the fusiform and lateral occipital cortex was frequently found to be active. In a study by Slotnick, Thompson, and Kosslyn (2005), strong activity in hMT+ was also found during the generation of rotating images. Activity in the intra-parietal sulcus or the posterior parietal cortex has also frequently been reported. Remember that the parietal window representing egocentric spatial information was discussed as a structure in which spatial images are processed and transformed (Byrne, Becker, & Burgess, 2007). It is therefore equally possible that these higher structures, together with other – for example, prefrontal – areas provide spatial transformations as mental scanning and mental rotation, and that these transformations cause the spatial effects and not the topographically organized primary visual cortex. In the latest version of the model this possibility was considered, and the parietal cortex was declared a part of the visual buffer (Kosslyn, Thompson, & Ganis, 2006). However, the conflict still remains. The spatial structure of the early visual cortices is, then, no longer functional for spatial imagery provided in the parietal cortex.

Extending the visual buffer to other structures is even a problem for the consistency of the model. The spatial structure of V1 was considered a canvas on which the images are depicted, and its spatial organization as the origin of the spatial effects. However, V1 was most likely to be found active in nonspatial (!) object tasks. In object imagery, space is not a dominant feature, and space is more or less only used to represent a shape. In contrast, spatial representations are assumed to be provided by the parietal cortex. However, if V1 is not active in spatial tasks, then the spatial quality of a depiction within V1 cannot be responsible for spatial effects. A solution would be that the parietal cortex also depicts, but then it has to be shown that physical space at the neural level is functional here, too. To my knowledge, the studies reporting a topographical organization of parietal brain structures do not provide a sufficiently high spatial resolution to allow this conclusion (see, e.g., Sereno, Pitzalis, & Martinez, 2001; Silver & Kastner, 2009). It is a rather coarse topographical map.

Finally, claiming a functional role of physical space at the neural level has a further general weakness. It is always the structure–process combination that is considered to be relevant, not physical space of the structure alone. Even though real space in the visual cortex is assumed be the critical representational feature, it comes to effect only indirectly. "Keep in mind what is important is not how the area looks to an external observer but how it is interpreted by the processes that operate on it in the brain" (Kosslyn, Thompson, & Ganis, 2006, p. 104). Such an assumption is necessary because the representation in the early visual cortex, even if it is topographically organized, is not a one-for-one copy of a two-dimensional uniform physical space. For example, the fovea is enlarged at the expense of more peripheral regions (see, e.g., Grill-Spector & Malach, 2004), and spatial processing must compensate for this during spatial transformations, otherwise linear distance effects would not occur. However, if the space–process combination is relevant, then the spatial organization of the neural structure is nearly unimportant for the explanation. Any arbitrary organization can be mapped onto the physical space as long as it represents the spatial information. This would be possible even for a population code, and I do not see that such a representation would cause any problems for an imagery theory. Taking seriously that the physical (!) spatial arrangement is really functional, we can only know if a spatial rearrangement of the neural structure were to change the observed spatial effect. This, however, is virtually impossible. We therefore still do not know whether or not the spatial structure of V1 (or of any other network) per se is functional because we only see the results of processing, which is always the consequence of a combination of structure and process.

Conclusion

In closing, I want to summarize the discussion. There is much evidence that imagery is a specific mental state and that not all information is represented as explicit propositional relations. We know that low-level sensory information of the appearance of a stimulus is represented and also memorized. Furthermore, this information can be reactivated and used in imagery (and also transformed). These processes happen in modality-specific structures. Imagery is therefore modality-specific. However, we still do not know how the information is represented at the neural level. The activation can go down towards primary sensory networks. However, the activity at the primary sensory level seems not to be a precondition for image generation. On the contrary, visual images of objects can be generated at different levels of abstraction (resolution), and they are provided by different neural structures, depending on the content. Similarly, different spatial representations and processes exist. It is assumed that spatial images are provided by the parietal cortex. V1 should therefore play no role in these spatial processes. Consequently, the topographical organization of the primary visual cortex is not relevant when we want to explain the different spatial effects that are observed while processing spatial images. Finally, even if V1 is active, as it was sometimes found in object imagery, we cannot be sure that the physical spatial organization of the neural network has any functional role. Shape must be represented, but even if it is a depiction, the topographical spatial organization of V1 may not be relevant.

Pylyshyn's (1981) warning about the confusion between two different interpretations of an "image of object X with property *P*" is therefore still valid. It can be read as "[image of object X] with property P" or as "image of [object X with property P]". All that we know is that a specific property is preserved when an image of object X is generated. At present, as the neuroscientific results do not tell us that the image has a specific property, we still can only say that (object X with property P) is represented, imagined, or simulated. I therefore suggest toning down the postulation of a spatial neural medium that represents images as depictions and that is the canvas on which images are drawn. At this level, the imagery debate is not resolved, and it may not even be possible to resolve it even in the century of cognitive neuroscience. I therefore suggest keeping the idea of mental imagery as a specific mental state with specific processes, but downscaling the spatial analogy of the depiction and the weight given to topographically organized neural networks. I believe that less "physical realism" is not negative. Giving up postulating a direct relationship between spatial qualities of images and the spatial organization of early visual brain structures will not narrow the utility of the imagery approach.

Note

1 A note is advisable in order to avoid misinterpretations of this chapter. Even though I often refer to the work of Kosslyn and colleagues, this chapter should not provide a critical evaluation of the most recent version of Kosslyn's model. I selected his work only because this group is most active and most influential in the field of imagery. As is to be expected, their view has changed during the course of the past thirty years in accordance with new empirical results. Nevertheless, I quote specific work, and I also refer to older work, even though some of these positions have changed over the years. Consequently, one should not take this as reference to the current version of the theory. Such references should only provide examples of papers where the discussed stand was taken. Sometimes I explicitly indicate changes in the theoretical perspective – especially when it is strong one. However, I do not do it in any case, mainly because it is not clear which of the former positions have really been given up and which are still assumed to be valid. One should therefore not interpret my discussion as a specific statement about Kosslyn's present thinking about imagery; it is about imagery models in general. What I would like to do is to discuss different variants of an imagery approach and possible assumptions about the spatial qualities of images and their neural underpinnings, independently of any specific model. However, the arguments put forward in this chapter do, of course, also apply to Kosslyn's interpretation of the spatial qualities of the representing neural structures.

References

Aziz-Zadeh, L., & Damasio, A. (2008). Embodied semantics for actions: Findings from functional brain imaging. *Journal of Physiology*, *102*, 35–39.

Barsalou, L. W. (2008). Grounded cognition. *Annual Review of Psychology*, *59*, 617–645.

Barsalou, L. W., Simmons, W. K., Barbey, A. K., & Wilson, C. D. (2003). Grounding conceptual knowledge in modality-specific systems. *Trends in Cognitive Sciences*, *7*, 84–91.

Borst, G., & Kosslyn, S. M. (2008). Visual mental imagery and visual perception: Structural equivalence revealed by scanning processes. *Memory and Cognition, 36*, 849–862.

Borst, G., Kosslyn, S. M., & Denis, M. (2006). Different cognitive processes in two image-scanning paradigms. *Memory and Cognition, 34*, 475–490.

Bower, G. H. (1970). Imagery as a relational organizer in associative learning. *Journal of Verbal Learning and Verbal Behavior, 9*, 529–533.

Buckner, R. L., Andrews-Hanna, J. R., & Schacter, D. L. (2008). The brain's default network: Anatomy, function, and relevance to disease. *Annals of the New York Academy of Sciences, 1124*, 1–38.

Burgess, N. (2006). Spatial memory: How egocentric and allocentric combine. *Trends in Cognitive Sciences, 10*, 551–557.

Burgess, N. (2008). Spatial cognition and the brain. *Annals of the New York Academy of Sciences, 1124*, 77–97.

Byrne, P., Becker, S., & Burgess, N. (2007). Remembering the past and imagining the future: A neural model of spatial memory and imagery. *Psychological Review, 114*, 340–375.

Chen, W., Kato, T., Zhu, X. H., Ogawa, S., Tank, D. W., & Ugurbil, K. (1998). Human primary visual cortex and lateral geniculate nucleus activation during visual imagery. *Neuroreport, 9*, 3669–3674.

Cocude, M., & Denis, M. (1988). Measuring the temporal characteristics of visual images. *Journal of Mental Imagery, 12*, 89–102.

Cooper, L. A., & Shepard, R. N. (1973). The time required to prepare for a rotated stimulus. *Memory & Cognition, 1*, 246–250.

Cooper, L. A., & Shepard, R. N. (1984). Turning something over in the mind. *Scientific American, 251*, 106–114.

Creem, S. H., Downs, T. H., Wraga, M., Harrington, G. S., Proffitt, D. R., & Downs, J. H. (2001). An fMRI study of imagined self-rotation. *Cognitive, Affective & Behavioral Neuroscience, 1*, 239–249.

Daselaar, S. M., Porat, Y., Huijbers, W., & Pennartz, C. M. A. (2010). Modality-specific and modality-independent components of the human imagery system. *NeuroImage, 52*, 677–685.

Decety, J., & Grèzes, J. (1999). Neural mechanisms subserving the perception of human actions. *Trends in Cognitive Sciences, 3*, 172–178.

Dechent, P., Merboldt, K.-D., & Frahm, J. (2004). Is the human primary motor cortex involved in motor imagery? *Cognitive Brain Research, 19*, 138–144.

Denis, M. (1975). Free recall of mental images. *Psychologie Française, 20*, 165–174.

Denis, M. (1976). The concept of mental imagery: Its place in recent theories of representation. *Bulletin de Psychologie (Special Issue)*, 125–130.

Denis, M. (1982). On figurative components of mental representations. In F. Klix, J. Hoffmann, & E. van der Meer (Eds.), *Cognitive research in pychology*. Berlin: VEB Deutscher Verlag der Wissenschaften.

Denis, M. (1986). Visual imagery: Effects or role in prose processing? In F. Klix & H. Hagendorf (Eds.), *Human memory and cognitive capabilities* (pp. 237–244). Amsterdam: Elsevier.

Denis, M., & Kosslyn, S. M. (1999). Scanning visual mental images: A window on the mind. *Cahiers de Psychologie Cognitive/Current Psychology of Cognition, 18*, 409–465.

Denis, M., & Zimmer, H. D. (1992). Analog properties of cognitive maps constructed from verbal descriptions. *Psychological Research, 54*, 286–298.

D'Esposito, M., Detre, J. A., Aguirre, G. K., Stallcup, M., Alsop, D. C., Tippet, L. J., et al. (1997). A functional MRI study of mental image generation. *Neuropsychologia, 35*, 725–730.

de Vega, M. (1994). Characters and their perspectives in narratives describing spatial environments. *Psychological Research, 56*, 116–126.

Finke, R. A., & Pinker, S. (1982). Spontaneous imagery scanning in mental extrapolation. *Journal of Experimental Psychology: Learning, Memory, and Cognition, 8*, 142–147.

Finke, R. A., & Shepard, R. N. (1986). Visual functions of mental imagery. In K. R. Boff, I. Kaufman, & J. Thomas (Eds.), *Handbook of perception and human performance* (Vol. 2, pp. 37.31–37.55). New York: Wiley.

Fodor, A. (1983). *The modularity of mind*. Cambridge, MA: MIT Press.

Goebel, R., Khorram-Sefat, D., Muckli, L., Hacker, H., & Singer, W. (1998). The constructive nature of vision: Direct evidence from functional magnetic resonance imaging studies of apparent motion and motion imagery. *European Journal of Neuroscience, 10*, 1563–1573.

Goldston, D. B., Hinrichs, J. V., & Richman, C. L. (1985). Subjects' expectations, individual variability, and the scanning of mental images. *Memory & Cognition, 13*, 365–370.

Grill-Spector, K., & Malach, R. (2004). The human visual cortex. *Annual Review of Neuroscience, 27*, 649–677.

Kellenbach, M. L., Brett, M., & Patterson, K. (2001). Large, colorful, or noisy? Attribute- and modality-specific activations during retrieval of perceptual attribute knowledge. *Cognitive, Affective, & Behavioral Neuroscience, 1*, 207–221.

Kiefer, M., Sim, E.-J., Herrnberger, B., Grothe, J., & Hoenig, K. (2008). The sound of concepts: Four markers for a link between auditory and conceptual brain systems. *Journal of Neuroscience, 28*, 12224–12230.

Klein, I., Dubois, J., Mangin, J.-F., Kherif, F., Flandin, G., Poline, J.-B., et al. (2004). Retinotopic organization of visual mental images as revealed by functional magnetic resonance imaging. *Cognitive Brain Research, 22*, 26–31.

Kosslyn, S. M. (1973). Scanning visual images: Some structural implications. *Perception and Psychophysics, 14*, 90–94.

Kosslyn, S. M. (1975). Information representation in visual images. *Cognitive Psychology, 7*, 341–370.

Kosslyn, S. M. (1976). Can imagery be distinguished from other forms of internal representation? Evidence from studies of information retrieval times. *Memory & Cognition, 4*, 291–297.

Kosslyn, S. M. (1980). *Image and mind*. Cambridge, MA: Harvard University Press.

Kosslyn, S. M. (1981). The medium and the message in mental imagery: A theory. *Psychological Review, 88*, 46–66.

Kosslyn, S. M. (1994). *Image and brain: The resolution of the imagery debate*. Cambridge, MA: MIT Press.

Kosslyn, S. M., Alpert, N. M., Thompson, W. L., Maljkovic, V., Weise, S. B., Chabris, C. F., & et al. (1993). Visual mental imagery activates topographically organized visual cortex: PET investigations. *Journal of Cognitive Neuroscience, 5*, 263–287.

Kosslyn, S. M., Ball, T. M., & Reiser, B. J. (1978). Visual images preserve metric spatial information: Evidence from studies of image scanning. *Journal of Experimental Psychology: Human Perception and Performance, 4*, 47–60.

Kosslyn, S. M., Pascual-Leone, A., Felician, O., Camposano, S., Keenan, J. P., Thompson, W. L., et al. (1999). The role of area 17 in visual imagery: Convergent evidence from PET and rTMS. *Science, 284*, 167–170.

Kosslyn, S. M., & Thompson, W. L. (2003). When is early visual cortex activated during visual mental imagery? *Psychological Bulletin, 129,* 723–746.

Kosslyn, S. M., Thompson, W. L., & Alpert, N. M. (1997). Neural systems shared by visual imagery and visual perception: A positron emission tomography study. *NeuroImage, 6,* 320–334.

Kosslyn, S. M., Thompson, W. L., & Ganis, G. (2006). *The case of mental imagery.* New York: Oxford University Press.

Kosslyn, S. M., Thompson, W. L., Kim, I. J., & Alpert, N. M. (1995). Topographical representations of mental images in primary visual cortex. *Nature, 378,* 496–498.

Kosslyn, S. M., Thompson, W. L., Wraga, M., & Alpert, N. M. (2001). Imagining rotation by endogenous versus exogenous forces: Distinct neural mechanisms. *Neuroreport, 12,* 2519–2525.

Kourtzi, Z., & Kanwisher, N. (2000). Activation in human MT/MST by static images with implied motion. *Jounal of Cognitive Neuroscience, 12,* 48–55.

Lehnert, G., & Zimmer, H. D. (2006). Auditory and visual spatial working memory. *Memory & Cognition,* 1080–1090.

Lehnert, G., & Zimmer, H. D. (2008). Common coding of auditory and visual spatial information in working memory. *Brain Research, 1230,* 158–167.

Logie, R. H., & van der Meulen, M. (2009). Fragmenting and integrating visuospatial working memory. In J. R. Brockmole (Ed.), *The visual world in memory* (pp. 1–32). Hove, UK: Psychology Press.

Martin, A., Haxby, J. V., Lalonde, F. M., Wiggs, C. L., & Ungerleider, L. G. (1995). Discrete cortical regions associated with knowledge of color and knowledge of action. *Science, 270,* 102–105.

Mechelli, A., Price, C. J., Friston, K. J., & Ishai, A. (2004). Where bottom-up meets top-down: Neuronal interactions during perception and imagery. *Cerebral Cortex, 14,* 1256–1265.

Mellet, E., Briscogne, S., Tzourio-Mazoyer, N., Ghaëm, O., Petit, L., Zago, L., et al. (2000). Neural correlates of topographic mental exploration: The impact of route versus survey perspective learning. *NeuroImage, 12,* 588–600.

Mellet, E., Petit, L., Mazoyer, B., Denis, M., & Tzourio, N. (1998). Reopening the mental imagery debate: Lessons from functional anatomy. *NeuroImage, 8,* 129–139.

Mellet, E., Tzourio, N., Crivello, F., Joliot, M., Denis, M., & Mazoyer, B. (1996). Functional anatomy of spatial mental imagery generated from verbal instructions. *Journal of Neuroscience, 16,* 6504–6512.

Mellet, E., Tzourio, N., Denis, M., & Mazoyer, B. (1998). Cortical anatomy of mental imagery of concrete nouns based on their dictionary definition. *Neuroreport, 9,* 803–808.

Meyer, K., & Damasio, A. (2009). Convergence and divergence in a neural architecture for recognition and memory. *Trends in Neurosciences, 32,* 376–382.

Moulton, S. T., & Kosslyn, S. M. (2009). Imagining predictions: Mental imagery as mental emulation. *Philosophical Transactions of the Royal Society B: Biological Sciences, 364,* 1273–1280.

Nyberg, L., Habib, R., McIntosh, A. R., & Tulving, E. (2000). Reactivation of encoding-related brain activity during memory retrieval. *Proceedings of the National Academy of Sciences of the United States of America, 97,* 11120–11124.

O'Craven, K. M., & Kanwisher, N. (2000). Mental imagery of faces and places activates corresponding stimulus-specific brain regions. *Journal of Cognitive Neuroscience, 12,* 1013–1023.

Paivio, A. (1971). *Imagery and verbal processes*. New York: Holt, Rinehard & Winston.

Paivio, A. (1986). *Mental representations: A dual coding approach*. New York: Oxford University Press.

Pearson, D. G. (2001). Imagery and the visuo-spatial sketchpad. In J. Andrade (Ed.), *Working memory in perspective* (pp. 33–59). Hove, UK: Psychology Press.

Podzebenko, K., Egan, G. F., & Watson, J. D. G. (2005). Real and imaginary rotary motion processing: Functional parcellation of the human parietal lobe revealed by fMRI. *Journal of Cognitive Neuroscience, 17*, 24–36.

Porro, C. A., Francescato, M. P., Cettolo, V., Diamond, M. E., Baraldi, P., Zuiani, C., et al. (1996). Primary motor and sensory cortex activation during motor performance and motor imagery: A functional magnetic resonance imaging study. *Journal of Neuroscience, 16*, 7688–7698.

Pylyshyn, Z. W. (1981). The imagery debate: Analogue media versus tacit knowledge. *Psychological Review, 88*, 16–45.

Pylyshyn, Z. W. (2003). Return of the mental image: Are there really pictures in the brain? *Trends in Cognitive Sciences, 7*, 113–118.

Reddy, L., Tsuchiya, N., & Serre, T. (2010). Reading the mind's eye: Decoding category information during mental imagery. *NeuroImage, 50*, 818–825.

Richardson, J. T. E. (1980). *Mental imagery and human memory*. New York: St. Martin's Press.

Rugg, M. D., Johnson, J. D., Park, H., & Uncapher, M. R. (2008). Encoding-retrieval overlap in human episodic memory: A functional neuroimaging perspective. *Progress in Brain Research, 169*, 339–352.

Schacter, D. L., Addis, D. R., & Buckner, R. L. (2007). Remembering the past to imagine the future: The prospective brain. *Nature Reviews. Neuroscience, 8*, 657–661.

Sereno, M. I., Pitzalis, S., & Martinez, A. (2001). Mapping of contralateral space in retinotopic coordinates by a parietal cortical area in humans. *Science, 294*, 1350–1354.

Shepard, R. N., & Metzler, J. (1971). Mental rotation of three-dimensional objects. *Science, 171*, 701–703.

Silver, M. A., & Kastner, S. (2009). Topographic maps in human frontal and parietal cortex. *Trends in Cognitive Sciences, 13*, 488–495.

Slotnick, S. D., & Schacter, D. L. (2006). The nature of memory related activity in early visual areas. *Neuropsychologia, 44*, 2874–2886.

Slotnick, S. D., Thompson, W. L., & Kosslyn, S. M. (2005). Visual mental imagery induces retinotopically organized activation of early visual areas. *Cerebral Cortex, 15*, 1570–1583.

Stokes, M., Thompson, R., Cusack, R., & Duncan, J. (2009). Top-down activation of shape-specific population codes in visual cortex during mental imagery. *Journal of Neuroscience, 29*, 1565–1572.

Taylor, H. A., & Tversky, B. (1992). Spatial mental models derived from survey and route descriptions. *Journal of Memory and Language, 31*, 261–292.

Thirion, B., Duchesnay, E., Hubbard, E., Dubois, J., Poline, J. B., Lebihan, D., et al. (2006). Inverse retinotopy: Inferring the visual content of images from brain activation patterns. *NeuroImage, 33*, 1104–1116.

Thompson, W. L., Kosslyn, S. M., Sukel, K. E., & Alpert, N. M. (2001). Mental imagery of high- and low-resolution gratings activates area 17. *NeuroImage, 14*, 454–464.

Tootell, R. B. H., Hadjikhani, N. K., Mendola, J. D., Marrett, S., & Dale, A. M. (1998). From retinotopy to recognition: fMRI in human visual cortex. *Trends in Cognitive Sciences, 2*, 174–183.

Tootell, R. B. H., Silverman, M. S., Switkes, E., & De Valois, R. L. (1982). Deoxyglucose analysis of retinotopic organization in primate striate cortex. *Science, 218*, 902–904.

Tootell, R. B. H., Switkes, E., Silverman, M. S., & Hamilton, S. L. (1988). Functional anatomy of macaque striate cortex. II. Retinotopic organization. *Journal of Neuroscience, 8*, 1531–1568.

Wheeler, M. E., Petersen, S. E., & Buckner, R. L. (2000). Memory's echo: Vivid remembering reactivates sensory-specific cortex. *Proceedings of the National Academy of Sciences of the United States of America, 97*, 11125–11129.

Wraga, M. (2003). Thinking outside the body: An advantage for spatial updating during imagined versus physical self-rotation. *Journal of Experimental Psychology: Learning, Memory, and Cognition, 29*, 993–1005.

Wraga, M., Shephard, J. M., Church, J. A., Inati, S., & Kosslyn, S. M. (2005). Imagined rotations of self versus objects: An fMRI study. *Neuropsychologia, 43*, 1351–1361.

Yoo, S. S., Freeman, D. K., McCarthy III, J. J., & Jolesz, F. A. (2003). Neural substrates of tactile imagery: A functional MRI study. *Neuroreport, 14*, 581–585.

Zatorre, R. J., & Halpern, A. R. (2005). Mental concerts: Musical imagery and auditory cortex. *Neuron, 47*, 9–12.

Zimmer, H. D. (1988). Formkonzepte und Bildmarken: Zwei verschiedene Repräsentationen für visuell-sensorische Merkmale? *Sprache und Kognition, 7*, 40–50.

Zimmer, H. D. (2004). The construction of mental maps based on a fragmentary view of physical maps. *Journal of Educational Psychology, 96*, 603–610.

Zimmer, H. D. (2008). Visual and spatial working memory: From boxes to networks. *Neuroscience and Biobehavioral Reviews, 32*, 1372–1395.

Zimmer, H. D., & de Vega, M. (1996). The medium and the message in spatial communication. In T. Ensink & C. Sauer (Eds.), *Researching technical documents* (pp. 153–180). Groningen, The Netherlands: University of Groningen.

Part III

Working memory and imagery

4 Working memory

An ensemble of functions in on-line cognition

Robert H. Logie and Elaine H. Niven

Introduction

Ever since the concept of working memory was first described by John Locke (1690) as "contemplation" (see discussion in Logie, 1996), the understanding of temporary memory and on-line cognition has undergone a range of transformations. The Edinburgh philosopher David Hume (1748/1955) described it as "perceptions of the mind"; William James (1890/1902) alluded to the "specious present" or primary memory; George Stout (1898) described the concept of ideation, while Frederick Bartlett (1958) explored it as the vehicle for thinking. More contemporary theoreticians have referred to short-term memory (Atkinson & Shiffrin, 1968), working memory (Baddeley, 1986, 2007; Baddeley & Hitch, 1974; Osaka, Logie, & D'Esposito, 2007), and links with consciousness (Baars, 1997; Logie, 1995, 2009). With the change of name and increased research activity on the topic has come increased complexity and increased debate, along with use of the same term to refer to related but different concepts. In this chapter we focus on one contemporary approach to the study of working memory that considers primarily the impact of differences between individuals in their working memory capacity, and what might underlie those differences. We will contrast two different theoretical perspectives, one of which considers working memory as an ensemble of domain-specific functions, the other of which views working memory primarily as activated long-term memory coupled with controlled attention. We note that some differences are more apparent than real; others echo long-standing debates thought to be resolved by previous generations of researchers; whereas key contrasts arise simply because researchers are asking fundamentally different questions.

Working memory as an ensemble of multiple, domain-specific resources

The ensemble view has grown from studies of memory function. It considers working memory (WM) as a number of domain-specific cognitive functions that act together in different combinations in the service of moment-to-moment cognition (e.g., Baddeley, 1986, 2007; Baddeley & Logie, 1999; Logie, 1995; Logie &

van der Meulen, 2009). Specific functions have been identified for temporary phonological storage and subvocal rehearsal thought to support immediate memory for short verbal sequences. Other functions have been identified for temporary storage of visual appearance of single stimuli or stimulus arrays, and of sequences of movements to targets or pathways. Still other functions are thought to activate and retain current representations of stored knowledge on a temporary basis – for example, as visual images (van der Meulen, Logie, & Della Sala, 2009). Finally, a range of executive functions (originally termed "the central executive" – Baddeley & Hitch, 1974) act to coordinate dual-task performance (Logie, Cocchini, Della Sala, & Baddeley, 2004), to inhibit irrelevant material, switch between tasks, and update the contents of immediate memory (e.g., Emerson & Miyake, 2003; Miyake et al., 2000). The focus in this kind of theoretical framework has been to explore how different domain-specific cognitive functions are used to carry out different kinds of cognitive tasks, and to account for selective impairment of specific cognitive functions following focal or diffuse brain damage. Extensive reviews of the ensemble, or multiple-component, view are given elsewhere (see reviews in Baddeley, 2007; Baddeley & Logie, 1999; Logie, 2011a, 2011b).

The same, multiple-component view of WM has been used to explore performance of complex tasks that require multiple cognitive functions acting in a coordinated fashion rather than in isolation (Logie, Baddeley, Mane, Donchin, & Sheptak, 1989; Logie, Trawley, & Law, 2011; Phillips, Gilhooly, Logie, Della Sala, & Wynn, 2003). Applications of this view of WM have been diverse, and include the forming of mental maps of the world (e.g., Denis, 1996; Deyzac, Logie, & Denis, 2006), immediate verbal short-term memory (Baddeley, Lewis, & Vallar, 1984; Larsen & Baddeley, 2003), impairments of verbal (Vallar & Shallice, 1990) and visuo-spatial (Logie & Della Sala, 2005) short-term retention, acquiring novel vocabulary (Gathercole & Baddeley, 1989, 1993), limiting aspects of children's learning (Alloway & Gathercole, 2006), accounting for accuracy in counting and mental arithmetic (Logie & Baddeley, 1987; Logie, Gilhooly, & Wynn, 1994), and a breakdown in dual-task performance with Alzheimer's disease (Logie et al., 2004). Indeed the power and utility of this multiple-component framework lies in its success in accounting for a substantial number of laboratory phenomena, specific cognitive deficits following brain damage, and much of everyday on-line cognition.

Working memory as control of attention

A contrasting conception has come from studies of visual and auditory attention and views WM as a limited-capacity attentional focus coupled with currently activated material derived from memories of previous experiences and acquired skills (e.g., Anderson, Fincham, Qin, & Stoccoet, 2008; Anderson et al., 2004; Cowan, 2005). In particular, Cowan (1995, 2005) views the content of WM as currently activated material from long-term memory (LTM), with a limited-capacity focus of attention that can be directed flexibly and rapidly to different subsets of that activated material. Loss of contents from WM arises from decay of activation, lack of rehearsal, or displacement by new material being activated. Engle, Kane, and Tuholski (1999) refer to a related concept as WM comprising controlled attention coupled with temporary storage. The focus of this approach has been to consider the extent to which individual differences in the capacity of WM correlate with other measures of more general cognitive ability such as language comprehension (Baddeley, Logie, Nimmo-Smith, & Brereton, 1985; Caplan & Waters, 1999; Daneman & Carpenter, 1980; Daneman & Hannon, 2007; Just, Carpenter, & Keller, 1996), control of attention and inhibition of attentional capture (Hasher & Zacks, 1988; Kane, Conway, Hambrick, & Engle, 2008; Stoltzfus, Hasher, & Zacks, 1996), and general intelligence (Kane & Engle, 2002). There has been much less consideration within this approach of accounting for specific cognitive impairments following brain damage or in exploring nonverbal processing. We shall return to the latter topic later in this chapter.

According to Engle, Kane, and Tuholski (1999), controlled attention (or executive attention – Kane, Poole, Tuholski, & Engle, 2006) comprises the crucial link between WM capacity and higher cognitive abilities. Executive or controlled attention in WM is thought to activate memory representations, maintain information, inhibit irrelevant information, and suppress unnecessary or detrimental response tendencies (Heitz, Unsworth, & Engle, 2005). It has been likened (Engle, Kane, & Tuholski, 1999) to the focus of attention (Cowan, 1995) and the central executive (Baddeley & Hitch, 1974) or executive resources in other prominent models of WM, and it is inherently domain free, flexibly deployed, and capacity limited. The content of short-term memory (STM) comprises LTM representations that are activated above some threshold, again akin to Cowan's (1995, 2005) view. Activation of representations can be lost due to both decay over time and interference resulting from information similarity or can be gained due to allocation of controlled attention.

The central and essential role of controlled attention in WM is stressed when the capacity of the system as a whole is considered, referred to as working memory capacity (WMC): "capacity" is not concerned with storage or memory per se, but with the "capacity for controlled, sustained attention in the face of interference or distraction" (Engle, Kane, & Tuholski, 1999, p. 104). WMC typically is measured by requiring some form of cognitive processing, such as reading a series of sentences or carrying out a series of simple arithmetic sums, coupled with remembering the final words of the sentences, the arithmetic totals, or unrelated words (e.g., Baddeley et al., 1985; Daneman & Carpenter, 1980; Duff & Logie, 2001; Turner & Engle, 1989). The most common measure of capacity comprises the maximum number of items that can be recalled, and this measure correlates more highly with other measures of complex cognition than do measures of simple memory span such as digit span or word span in the absence of the processing task.

Conway, Cowan, and Bunting (2001) demonstrated that individuals with a relatively high WMC were more adept at inhibiting nontarget information in a dichotic-listening task than were individuals with a low WMC. Kane and

Engle (2003) found that high- and low-WMC participants differed significantly in performing a color-word Stroop task, and Kane, Bleckley, Conway, and Engle (2001) found that low-WMC individuals performed poorly in an anti-saccade task in comparison to high-span individuals. In this last task, participants are required to move their eyes away from a lateral target that appears on a screen. This is thought to require inhibition of the natural tendency to look towards a new target when it appears.

The contrast between simple span tasks (memory only) and complex span tasks (memory in the context of processing) was revisited by Unsworth and Engle (2007a), who noted that patterns of errors in the two tasks were similar with longer lists of words. Specifically, both tasks showed a decrease in the proportion of words recalled in correct serial order as list length increased, even though there was an increase in the total number of items recalled with the longer lists. Both simple span and complex span as a measure of WMC were found to be affected by the length of the words for recall, the phonological similarity of the items within the list, and the requirement to repeat aloud an irrelevant word (articulatory suppression). Similar findings were reported by Lobley, Baddeley, and Gathercole (2005), who found better recall of phonologically dissimilar words than of similar words in complex span tasks. The presence of a phonological similarity effect suggests the use of the domain-specific phonological loop component of the multicomponent model, which has been demonstrated in a large number of simple span experiments (for a review see Baddeley, 2007). However, when the different tasks have been compared, the effects were larger in simple than in complex span performance, suggesting that subvocal rehearsal is required for both forms of memory tasks but is more important for simple than for complex spans. Nevertheless, it is clear that simple span and complex span rely more on common cognitive functions than had been previously assumed.

While investigating list lengths, Unsworth and Engle (2006) found that although correlations between WMC and higher cognition remained stable across list lengths, the correlations between simple span and higher cognition increased as list length increased, eventually reaching a level similar to those found for complex span. Unsworth and Engle (2007a) reported a meta-analysis of 22 previously published studies and found to their surprise that simple and complex span tasks displayed comparable correlations with measures of higher order cognition. They found also that in a structural equation model based on a reanalysis of previously reported data (Engle, Tuholski, Laughlin, & Conway, 1999), WMC and simple span latent variables were highly correlated, and it was the common variance between the two memory measures that was predictive of their measure of general fluid intelligence. It was concluded that WMC and the capacity of STM are one construct.

On the basis of these observations, Unsworth and Engle (2006, 2007b) proposed a framework comprising two states of activated representation, namely items currently activated above threshold and items that are at different levels of activation below threshold. For these two, Unsworth and Engle adopted the terms originally proposed by William James (1890/1902): respectively primary memory and secondary memory. Representations in secondary memory are brought to higher levels of activation by retrieval through a "cue-dependent search process". It is proposed that primary memory has a small capacity limit, echoing the views of Locke (1690) and others mentioned earlier, as well as James (1902), Cowan (2005), and Broadbent (1958). Like those earlier views, in the Unsworth and Engle framework incoming items will displace information from primary memory into secondary memory. Removal of attention will also displace items from primary memory. Thus, during complex span tasks, the intervening processing is thought to displace items held in Primary Memory, and in simple span tasks items later in the list displace items already in Primary Memory from earlier in the list. Recall of items from primary memory is thought to be an easy "unloading" of information, while retrieval from secondary memory is a much more effortful process requiring discrimination of appropriate retrieval cues among competitors. One important point of divergence from previous views of controlled attention is the focus on cue-dependent retrieval and the rejection of decay-based explanations of forgetting (Unsworth & Engle, 2007b). As pointed out in Kane et al. (2008), a buildup of proactive interference over trials leads to a reduction in ability to discriminate retrieval cues; active maintenance of representations in Primary Memory is, however, challenged by additional processing demands and so, therefore, is the encoding of memory representation. Active maintenance and retrieval discrimination processes are thought to vary in efficiency between individuals and to be the primary limiting factors reflected in the individual differences in WMC.

A recent study by Healey and Miyake (2009) explored the Unsworth and Engle (2007b) view that active maintenance and long-term retrieval are key drivers for individual differences in memory performance on WMC tasks. Participants were required to perform recall in a standard WMC task (operation span task) and in a modified task, while at the same time executing secondary tasks designated as easy or hard. The modified task required all processing components to be performed before the memory storage element of the task began. This effectively turned the storage element into a simple span task. Dividing attention at recall between the WMC tasks and a secondary task was shown to affect accuracy and delayed the initiation of recall to a much greater extent in the operation span task than in the "modified" (simple) task. It was suggested that complex span storage measures may involve attention and other executive resources that are required in retrieval from long-term, or Secondary, memory. Healey and Miyake (2009) suggested that there are many levels of activity at which a representation may lie, and when active maintenance is prevented (e.g., due to executive attention being used to complete processing requirements, or because the number of items exceeds active maintenance capabilities) activity of a representation declines due to either decay or interference. In contrast, Unsworth and Engle see no role for decay. Healey and Miyake state that retrieval of "long term memory representations" is necessary for representations at a very low level of activity. A number of relevant executive resources are suggested, such as generation and elaboration of cues, search for cue matching representations, and blocking of irrelevant information; the recall requirements of WMC tasks are thus proposed to require more effortful processing than previously assumed. The suggestion that active maintenance and LTM retrieval contribute to complex span performance is described as an "emerging view" in the literature (see also Unsworth, Brewer, & Spillers, 2009).

Processing and storage measures in complex span performance: evidence for independent resources

Much of the literature on WMC has drawn conclusions on the functioning of the WM system solely through measuring recall performance and has assumed that the processing requirement draws on the same limited-capacity attention system as does the memory load. However, rarely has performance on the processing component of the task been recorded. One of the few exceptions was a study by Waters and Caplan (1996), who adopted a task originally described by Baddeley et al. (1985) in which participants verified a series of simple sentences and were asked to remember the final word of each sentence. Crucially, Waters and Caplan measured performance on the verification (processing) element of the task as well as recall performance. If processing and memory both rely on the same limited-capacity resource, we would expect large negative correlations between processing and memory performance for list lengths that are close to maximum WMC. In contrast, they found low to moderate positive correlations between processing and storage measures at all list lengths, not all of which were significant. When they generated a composite score that included both processing and memory performance, this yielded a correlation with other measures of high-level cognition that was nearly double that obtained from the memory score alone. A similar pattern of results was reported by Daneman and Hannon (2007), indicating that processing and memory make independent contributions to the variance that overlaps with general cognitive ability, suggesting that processing and memory reflect independent, not interdependent, cognitive functions.

Duff and Logie (1999) further demonstrated that processing and memory performance on complex span tasks does not fit predictions from a common limited-capacity view. They first measured capacity for a simple processing task with no memory load, then measured memory capacity with no processing load, and finally measured processing capacity and memory capacity when both were required. For the processing task, participants were shown a series of squares in unpredictable locations on a computer screen, and they had to use the mouse to click on these as each square appeared. Capacity for this visuo-spatial tracking task was assessed by gradually increasing the number of squares in the series and decreasing the amount of time available to click on a square before the next one appeared. This continued until a given participant could no longer "keep up" his or her speed of clicking with the speed of stimulus presentation. For the memory task, simple abstract line forms appeared embedded within each of the presented squares. Participants simply had to view each line form and then reproduce (draw) all of the forms after the complete series had been presented. The length of the series gradually increased with a fixed rate of presentation until participants were no longer able to reproduce all of the presented forms. For the processing plus memory task, participants were asked to click on the squares as they appeared and to remember the line form embedded within each square. The number of squares (and hence number of forms) in the series gradually increased, while the time available to click on each square and encode each form gradually decreased until performance on both clicking accuracy and reproduction accuracy failed. Recall performance was not significantly different when completed alone and when completed along with visuo-spatial tracking as part of a complex span task. Tracking performance decreased by less than 3% between tracking alone and tracking plus memory. Such a preserved processing and memory capacity in a complex span task is consistent with the view that the processing task and the memory task draw on independent capacities that can operate in parallel. The results directly conflict with an account that assumes that the same limited-capacity attention system is used for both. A second experiment repeated the same procedure but required participants to suppress articulation (repeat aloud an irrel-evant word) throughout, so as to prevent the use of verbal encoding and rehearsal of possible names for the abstract line forms. The results were similar to those of the first experiment, indicating that the unchanged performance levels between simple and complex processing and memory could not be attributed to use of supplementary verbal coding for the memory component.

Duff and Logie (2001; Logie & Duff, 2007) replicated their findings using verbal stimuli. Participants performed either sentence verification (based on Baddeley et al., 1985) or arithmetic verification, in both cases with no load on memory. The number of sentences or sums to verify was gradually increased while allowing progressively less time to verify each one. So, participants first were given three items to verify within 10 s, allowing 3.3 s for each. If they were successful, they were then given four items in 10 s, allowing 2.5 s for each; then five items allowing 2 s for each; and so on. This procedure stopped when partici-pants could no longer accurately respond to all of the sentences or sums in the time available for each one. This yielded a measure of processing capacity for each participant. Simple memory span was measured by giving participants progressively longer lists of words or numbers for serial ordered recall, with a fixed rate of presentation, but with no processing requirement. Then the processing and memory tasks were combined, with the number of items to be verified within a 10-s period gradually increased, coupled with a requirement to recall the last word of each sentence or the total for each sum. When asked to verify sentences/sums and recall the final word/number for each, maximum accurate processing speed and maximum list length for accurate recall were very similar to those observed for processing alone or memory alone. Overall performance in the complex task as a combined average of percentage change in processing and in storage was between 94% and 98% of single-task performance. That is, combining processing and memory has little or no effect on the capacity for memory alone or for processing alone.

A study by Bayliss, Jarrold, Gunn, and Baddeley (2003) provided further evidence that was inconsistent with a single pool of resources underlying both processing and storage components of complex span performance. Bayliss et al.

tested 8-year-old children on four different versions of a complex span task. These WMC tasks were the product of combining two different (verbal and visuo-spatial) processing requirements with two different (verbal and visuo-spatial) storage components. Storage and processing tasks were also performed in single task conditions. Verbal processing required matching colored squares from a grid to an item usually associated with the same color. Verbal memory involved ordered recall of digits presented after each processing item in the complex span task and presented as a sequence of digits in the simple span task. Visuo-spatial processing required finding a target with a distinctive characteristic in a displayed array, and visuo-spatial memory required remembering the location of each target. Simple visuo-spatial memory required remembering a sequence of locations highlighted within the display but with no memory load. From complex span performance, only a recall measure was taken.

In a series of hierarchical regression analyses it was found that for all complex span measures, domain-specific simple storage performance accounted for variance that was independent of the processing measures. In a factor analysis, three factors were identified: a processing factor incorporating visuo-spatial and verbal processing, a verbal storage factor, and a visuo-spatial storage factor. Bayliss et al. (2003) concluded that span performance is determined by a combination of domain-specific storage and domain-general processing efficiency. When a suitably adapted version of these procedures was used with adult participants, the factor analysis again produced three factors: visuo-spatial storage, verbal storage, and processing. A follow-up study by Bayliss, Jarrold, Baddeley, and Gunn (2005) with young children yielded a very similar pattern of results.

Unsworth, Redick, Heitz, Broadway, and Engle (2009) further explored the possible independent contributions from processing and storage using a latent variable approach based on measures of processing accuracy, reaction time, and recall data. The relationship of these various measures of complex span to each other and their shared or independent relationships to higher order cognition were assessed. Three complex span measures from three different domains were employed in the study: numerical, verbal, and visuo-spatial. An operation span (Turner & Engle, 1989) task required verification of sums, combined with memory for a series of letters; a modified reading span task (Daneman & Carpenter, 1980) required "sense" judgments of statements, combined with memory for a series of letters; and a symmetry span task (Kane et al., 2004) required judgment as to the symmetry present or not in half-filled matrices, combined with memory for a series of locations presented in matrices. All processing accuracy, reaction-time data, and recall measures were taken from complex span performance rather than obtaining processing or storage measures from a component task performed by itself. A number of different measures, covering numerical, verbal, and spatial domains, were taken to index higher order cognition. Taken together, the resulting latent variable using these measures was believed to represent general fluid intelligence (Gf). Processing accuracy and storage measures were highly related, and this relationship was comparable across domains. Processing time correlated negatively with both recall and accuracy measures, and processing time correlations were equivalent across domains. Confirmatory factor analysis found a three-factor model – representing recall, accuracy, and processing time – offered the best fit to the data. The latent variables of recall, accuracy, and processing time in the best-fit model were each shown to correlate highly with the Gf variable; this was taken as further evidence that each measure of complex span performance represents "slightly different processes" (Unsworth et al., 2009, p. 646), which represents a change of theoretical direction from the assumption that a single pool of resources underlies performance in complex span tasks.

Structural equation modeling revealed that both processing measures (reaction time and accuracy) mediated the relationship between recall performance and their measure of Gf. Processing accuracy, reaction time, and recall measures each made independent contributions to explaining the variance found in the latent variable representing Gf. It is notable that all three recorded measures of complex span performance had independent predictive utility for higher order cognition. Unsworth et al. (2009) argued that there is currently no theoretical account of complex span performance that would adequately predict all the revealed relationships between complex span measures and their relation to measures of cognitive ability. However, their pattern of results is only problematic if a single, general-purpose attentional resource is assumed. In fact, there is a theoretical model not considered by Unsworth et al. that can explain the results, as described earlier in this chapter. The multiple-component model of WM assumes independent domain-specific resources for storage and a domain-general resource for processing. These separate resources then act in a coordinated fashion to maximize performance on complex span tasks.

Interpretation of complex span performance within the multiple-component model

Duff and Logie (1999, 2001; Logie & Duff, 2007) proposed that complex span task performance – specifically the mounting evidence for separable resources underlying performance – is best explained by the multiple-component model (Baddeley & Logie, 1999). Duff and Logie (2001) argued that the central executive was responsible for performing the processing aspect of the span task and the phonological loop system supported maintenance of final words for recall, employing subvocal rehearsal. Duff and Logie (2001) interpreted the very small drop in performance found when combining a processing and a storage component at span level, as the cost of a WM system coordinating the concurrent operation of two specific resources supporting performance on each of the two tasks. This coordination ability was attributed to the central executive. However, they posited that this cost of coordination could manifest both in processing and also in storage performance, due to the possible requirement of executive processes in encoding or retrieval of the stored information.

Further evidence against a domain-general model of resources was also reported by Duff and Logie (1999), who demonstrated that the requirement to undertake articulatory suppression in addition to performing a visuo-spatial complex span did not lead to an appreciable decrement in performance; this is not compatible with a domain-general model of shared resources that would consider articulatory suppression to be a third cognitive load (in addition to processing and storage) competing for finite resources. The multiple-component model accounts for the observed finding by assigning the effects of articulatory suppression to the phonological loop whose resources are distinct from those of the visuo-spatial system. The multiple-component model would thus make the prediction that visuo-spatial complex span performance requires domain-specific storage that should not be affected by a concurrent verbal suppression task, and this is what was found in the Duff and Logie (1999) study.

As indicated in the previous section, the multiple-component model also can account for the Unsworth and Engle (2007a) finding that recall measures of complex and simple span tasks are equally predictive of higher order cognition. It can also account for the observation that complex and simple span are affected in a similar way by a number of experimental manipulations and for the conclusion from latent variable analyses that these two recall measures reflect one rather than separate constructs. These observations all indicate a common rehearsal and storage mechanism similar to the concept of the phonological loop. It is also compatible with the above evidence that the separate measures of complex span tasks, namely processing time and recall accuracy, show independent predictive utility for higher order cognition, suggesting dissociable resources for processing and for storage.

Bayliss et al. (2003) concluded that their findings were compatible with the model of Baddeley and Logie (1999), and they proposed the same interpretation as Duff and Logie (1999, 2001) of complex span performance, namely that storage is provided by domain-specific temporary memory stores and that processing recruits domain-general resources. However, although simple and complex span recall measures were equally predictive of cognitive abilities, the residual variance in verbal complex span recall was still predictive of higher order cognition, after variance shared with verbal simple span was removed. The authors suggested that the presence of independent predictive value of complex span recall indicates that simple and complex tasks may use a common storage system, but that complex span requires additional domain-general processing resources as well as the domain-specific memory store.

Decay and interference in complex span

In some earlier studies, Turner and Engle (1989; see also La Pointe & Engle, 1990) found that manipulating the difficulty of the processing task in a WMC task affected its correlation with a measure of language comprehension. They suggested that the increased difficulty of the ongoing processing lessened the likelihood of rehearsal and so was a more accurate measure of the ability to maintain items in the face of possible interference from the ongoing processing task. This ability was proposed as the link between complex span performance and higher order cognition.

Towse, Hitch, and Hutton (1998, 2000) noted that an alternative crucial feature of complex span is that the ongoing processing task occupies time and therefore constitutes a filled delay between the items to be recalled. They demonstrated that recall performance on three complex span tasks (counting span, operation span, and reading span) could be reduced by increasing the amount of time spent on the intervening processing between presentation of memory items. Like Turner and Engle (1989), Towse, Hitch, and Hutton (1998, 2000, 2002) proposed that when participants are undertaking the processing task, then they are not rehearsing the memory items, but they return to memory rehearsal after each instance of processing. However, unlike Turner and Engle (1989) and later work by Unsworth and Engle (2007a, 2007b), Towse, Hitch, and Hutton (1998, 2000, 2002) argued that the delay while processing leads to decay of the memory trace for the items to be recalled, and that trace decay, not only interference from the processing task items, underlies complex span performance: longer processing tasks lead to longer delays, thereby increasing the chance of time-based decay of the items for recall. Therefore, the Turner and Engle (1989) observation of a decrease in span performance with increased processing difficulty could be reinterpreted by suggesting that more time is needed to process the items in the more difficult processing task. Miyake (2001) pointed out that the Towse, Hitch, and Hutton interpretation of complex span performance leads to an indirect relationship between separate processing and storage components of a complex span task.

Turley-Ames and Whitfield (2003; see also McNamara & Scott, 2001) demonstrated that strategies such as rehearsal of to-be-recalled items between processing episodes can be deployed in complex span tasks, and that use of a rehearsal strategy increases span performance. Similar effects of spontaneous use of different strategies by participants have been reported for simple span tasks (Logie, Della Sala, Laiacona, Chalmers, & Wynn, 1996). Turley-Ames and Whitfield (2003) also showed that when participants consistently all used the same strategy for complex span tasks, then the correlations with higher order cognition were higher than when strategy use was less homogeneous. Therefore, variation in strategy use by participants in many complex span tasks may limit the correlation found between span performance and cognitive ability measures. This contrasts with the assumption that complex span recall scores reflect consistent use of a specific WM system as proposed by Turner and Engle (1989) and La Pointe and Engle (1990). Performance could be contaminated by differences in the way in which the task is performed by different participants. Indeed, as argued by Logie et al. (1996) for simple span, different strategies most likely engage different cognitive systems to undertake the same complex span task.

Saito and Miyake (2004) suggested that Towse and colleagues had confounded the amount of processing to be completed with the time over which this processing was to be carried out, so it was unclear as to whether forgetting resulted from decay or from interference. Saito and Miyake (2004) systematically varied the number of items for processing while maintaining a fixed amount of time for processing, and they found that there was poorer memory performance with the higher processing load. They also systematically altered the time for processing while keeping the number of processing items fixed, and they found no difference in memory performance as a result of the delay between presentation of memory items. Saito and Miyake (2004) suggested that complex span performance is driven more by interference with the memory representations from the amount of processing required rather than decay of the memory trace while the processing is taking place. Representation-based interference would, however, be somewhat difficult to reconcile with the Duff and Logie (1999, 2001; Logie & Duff, 2007) results showing that increasing the number of processing items while keeping time constant leads to little or no drop in memory performance compared with simple span. One important feature of the Duff and Logie experiments is that simple processing span (no memory load) was assessed as well as simple memory span (no processing load), and performance of both the processing task and the memory task as a complex span task was compared with the simple spans for each individual participant. This comparison of both processing and memory performance with demand adjusted for the span of each participant may be a crucial difference from studies in which the demands are set at the same level for all participants, regardless of their span. A similar argument has been made with respect to dual-task performance in studies of cognitive ageing (Logie, Della Sala, MacPherson, & Cooper, 2007; Logie et al., 2004). It is also worth noting that the debate as to whether forgetting in memory arises from decay or interference has a very long history, dating back to McGeoch (1932; for reviews see Della Sala, 2010). As an aside, this raises concerns about just how much progress has been made in resolving that debate during the intervening eight decades of research.

A variation of the decay-based theory of WMC that eschews the role of interference has been proposed by Barrouillet and colleagues. For example, Barrouillet and Camos (2001) assessed children (age 8–11 years) on counting span (Case, Kurland, & Goldberg, 1982). This required participants to count out loud the number of items in a processing episode and to remember letters presented with each. Time required to count was recorded, and in a follow-up procedure participants had to spend the same amount of time articulating aloud an irrelevant word, interspersed with presentation of letters for recall. Participants could recall the same number of items whether the letters for recall were separated by the counting task or by overt articulation at their counting rate. In older children (age 9–11 years) a similar experiment showed that recall was poorer when there was a more complex processing task compared with articulatory suppression, keeping the total time for processing fixed. These findings were interpreted as suggesting both time-based decay, consistent with the Towse, Hitch, and Hutton (1998, 2000) argument, and also evidence in the older children of a more difficult processing task producing a bigger decrease in recall, hence suggesting use of a common resource for processing and storage. Notably, however, the effect of processing difficulty was around 20%, which is not entirely consistent with the view that all of the available resource is devoted either to processing or to storage. Nevertheless, Barrouillet and Camos proposed a model that incorporates both decay and shared use of a common, limited-capacity attention system to account for their data.

Barrouillet, Bernardin, and Camos (2004) proposed a time-based resource-sharing (TBRS) model in which attention is proposed to underlie both processing and storage; when attention is engaged in a processing task, it is unable to sustain memory representations, which will otherwise decay over time. Equally, when attention is given to refreshing memory items, processing cannot be supported. Rather than the effect of the complexity of a processing task per se, they argue that a complex task reduces the opportunities rapidly to switch attention between the processing task and refreshing the memory representations. They reported a series of experiments in which they varied the number of processing operations to be carried out in fixed time periods. The faster the processing rate, the poorer was recall performance. The pace of processing was referred to as cognitive load, and the authors argue that even a simple task, completed at a fast pace, will result in a high cognitive load and poor recall.

Lewandowsky, Oberauer, and Brown (2009a) argued that a single processing item following memory items can produce interference-based forgetting that is not affected by increasing the number of items and reducing the time for processing (Oberauer & Lewandowsky, 2008). Lewandowsky, Oberauer, and Brown (2009a) also reanalyzed data that had previously been interpreted as reflecting decay (Portrat, Barrouillet, & Camos, 2008) and showed that poor recall could be attributed to post-error monitoring of difficult processing; thus disruption to recall could arise from interference during rehearsal or retrieval rather than decay during processing. Lewandowsky, Oberauer, and Brown (2009b) point out further that the TBRS is unable to account for the poorer recall of phonologically similar compared with phonologically distinct items, nor can it account for some basic findings in serial recall tasks such as serial position curves.

A recent version of the TBRS hypothesis (Camos, Lagner, & Barrouillet, 2009) proposes both a domain-specific rehearsal mechanism and a central attention mechanism that is domain-general. The latter serves to refresh the representations of the information to be maintained; these rehearsal and refreshing mechanisms work together to support maintenance of to-be-recalled information. Camos, Lagner, and Barrouillet (2009) note that when articulatory suppression has been employed in previous studies, there remains a residual number of items that can be recalled; they propose that it is the attentional refreshing mechanism that allows this continued maintenance, by reactivating representations through allocation of attention. As in previous versions of the TBRS, this attention – when engaged in a processing task – is not available to preserve activation of items for maintenance. This version of the model is illustrated with a series of experiments that sought to establish the independence of attentional refreshing and rehearsal mechanisms. They devised a complex span procedure in which processing required either completion or reading aloud of simple arithmetic equations, coupled with recall of letters presented following each equation. Attentional demand was considered to be lower for reading than for completion, and the number of words to be articulated was equal in both versions. Completion of sums was found to produce worse complex span recall performance than did reading, and this was interpreted as suggesting that the requirement to direct attention to the processing task had the effect of preventing the refreshing process.

A further experiment (Camos, Lagner, & Barrouillet, 2009, Expt. 4) varied both attentional demand and articulatory suppression. Low attention demand in the processing task required identification of a target number in sequentially presented number sequences. High attention demand required verification of two sequentially presented sums. Articulatory suppression was manipulated by requiring participants, while responding to the processing task by key press, to either voice aloud the task they were performing (high-suppression condition) or read the task silently (low-suppression condition). Additionally, pace was manipulated by slow or fast presentation of items. Results showed that both attention demand and overt articulation had a detrimental effect on recall performance and, additionally, that faster pace resulted in poorer recall. This last result reinforces the idea that when attention is restricted by the time available, then this results in poorer recall. The authors further note that the lack of an interaction between the effect of demands on attention and the effect of articulatory suppression establishes the independence of the suggested attention-based refreshing mechanism and the domain-specific rehearsal mechanism. It appears, however, that an effect of attention demand was found in a slow pace condition while no effect of attention demand was found at a fast pace. This result is not consistent with the TBRS hypothesis and is not specifically addressed by the authors.

Camos, Lagner, and Barrouillet (2009) concluded that since attention-based refreshing and rehearsal have additive effects on performance, then they comprise independent mechanisms that both operate on the same memory traces. It was therefore asserted that format of information representation is multimodal (including phonological features) and, consequently, that the TBRS is not compatible with a multiple-component model (Baddeley & Logie, 1999) in which a storage system is code-specific (the phonological loop) and does not involve domain-general attention (the central executive) in maintenance. It is proposed that the addition of the episodic buffer (Baddeley, 2000), which allows for a multimodal store and executive involvement in maintenance, is more congruent with the modified TBRS model.

A possible alternative account can be drawn from a paper by Saito, Logie, Morita, and Law (2008; see also Logie, Della Sala, Wynn, & Baddeley, 2000) in which they demonstrated visual similarity effects and phonological similarity effects in recall of visually presented verbal material. Articulatory suppression affected phonological similarity but not visual similarity, and the similarity effects were additive. This suggested the concurrent use of both visual codes and phonological codes for retaining the same visually presented verbal material. Given these findings, the Camos, Lagner, and Barrouillet (2009) data could be interpreted as reflecting the use of both visual and phonological codes for the visually presented material for recall. Their attention and pace manipulations could have simply placed greater demands on visual processing, making it difficult to encode and retain the visual codes, while the overt articulation might have disrupted phonological codes used for the same material. So, the refreshing mechanism proposed by Camos, Lagner, and Barrouillet (2009) could be interpreted as a domain-specific visual rehearsal process (Logie, 1995, 2003, 2011a; Logie & van der Meulen, 2009), which complements the phonological rehearsal process viewed as an aspect of the phonological loop component of the multi-component model of WM (Baddeley & Logie, 1999).

The Camos, Lagner, and Barrouillet (2009) version of the TBRS attempts to address some criticisms of the previous version of the model raised by Oberauer and Lewandowsky (2008; Lewandowsky, Oberauer, & Brown, 2009a, 2009b). However, some predictions resulting from the TBRS model in which attention is allocated both to processing and to maintenance appear irreconcilable with data such as that of Duff and Logie (1999, 2001; Logie & Duff, 2007) in which participants perform processing and recall tasks at their individual maximum ability and at a fast pace. Participants were found to achieve complex span recall at, or only slightly below, that of simple span recall while performing processing tasks presented at speed equal to that of their maximum performance in a single processing task condition (Duff & Logie, 1999, 2001; Logie & Duff, 2007). Moreover, participants' reaction times were shown to decrease (Duff & Logie, 1999, 2001) or stay stable (Logie & Duff, 2007) across list lengths in complex conditions. In other words, Duff and Logie found that, if anything, complex span performance was poorer in the low-demand conditions than in the high-demand conditions, when level of demand was set according to the capacity of each individual participant. It is notable that in the Camos, Lagner, and Barrouillet (2009) experiments, demand was operationally defined for the experiment and was the same for all participants. This might be a crucial difference in the procedures used. It is also notable that in a paper by Vergauwe, Barrouillet, and Camos (2009), the Duff and Logie (1999, 2001) results are misrepresented in that Vergauwe, Barrouillet, and Camos point to the slowing of response time in the low-demand processing plus storage condition used by Duff and Logie but fail to mention that there was no slowing of responses in the high-demand condition.

Complex span and visuo-spatial resources

Domain specificity for both storage and processing components of complex span tasks was indicated by Shah and Miyake (1996) in an investigation of complex visuo-spatial span. A letter rotation task was developed as a visuo-spatial analogue to the reading span task; a series of letters was presented with each letter shown in a different orientation and either as normally printed or mirror-reversed. For each letter, participants were to respond whether the letter was presented in a normal format or as a mirror image. After the series, participants recalled the orientation of each letter in the order shown. Performance was measured by recall span performance. In the first of two experiments, participants completed two WM tasks (reading span, letter rotation), three tests to index spatial ability, and a task measuring perceptual speed; verbal SAT scores (scores from academic testing) were reported by participants and included in the analysis. A simple visuo-spatial span was also employed in which a sequence of centrally presented arrows, each of a different orientation, was shown to participants, and at the end of a trial of a given list length they were required to indicate, on a response grid, the orientation of each arrow in the order in which these had occurred. Spatial WM span was found to correlate significantly with this spatial ability measure ($r = .66$), as did the simple visuo-spatial span ($r = .62$). However, neither of these memory tasks correlated with the verbal ability measure (SAT scores). Conversely, reading span correlated significantly with verbal ability ($r = .45$), but not with spatial ability. Furthermore, spatial span and reading span produced only a low, nonsignificant correlation. Complex visuo-spatial span and simple visuo-spatial span were significantly correlated ($r = .52$), and both of these tasks correlated independently with the spatial ability measure when their shared variance was controlled. This last result, together with reports from participants, led Shah and Miyake (1996) to propose that strategy use was employed in simple span in order to deal with the memory load. This option was not available in WM task performance due to processing demands, thus different processes were brought into play for completion of simple or complex tasks. Subsequent factor analysis revealed two factors, loading on only spatial or verbal measures respectively, indicating domain specificity in cognitive resources.

Concentrating solely on the visuo-spatial domain, Miyake, Friedman, Rettinger, Shah, and Hegarty (2001) examined the relationship of simple span to WM complex span and the relationship of each to executive functions. Confirmatory factor analysis found a good fit to the data from a two-factor model in which the simple and complex tasks loaded on the same factor and the second factor represented executive functions. A three-factor model (STM, WMC, and executive functions) also provided a good fit of the data. Miyake et al. (2001) selected a two-factor representation in the name of parsimony (however, this choice has subsequently been questioned – see, e.g., Kane et al., 2004). In both the two-factor and the three-factor models, variance shared between the factors representing recall performance and that representing executive functions was high ($r = .56$ to $.59$), suggesting an important role for executive resources in STM and WM recall.

Kane et al. (2004) assessed simple and complex span performance in both the verbal and spatial domains for unique and common variance – that is, common variance across domains and across tasks. Confirmatory factor analysis suggested that a four-factor model was the best representation of the data, with tasks labeled verbal STM, spatial STM, verbal WMC, and spatial WMC. The authors emphasized the greater relationship between WMC factors compared to that found between STM factors, noting that domain-general resources make a greater contribution to WMC performance whereas domain-specific resources appear to account for a larger proportion of STM performance.

In a recent study using complex span and individual differences methodology, Vergauwe, Barrouillet, and Camos (2009) contrasted their version of the TBRS hypothesis with the multiple-component model of WM (e.g., Baddeley, 1986; Baddeley & Logie, 1999; Klauer & Zhao, 2004). From the perspective of the TBRS model, information maintained in the storage system requires attentional refreshing, otherwise it is subject to decay. This refreshing is challenged by any other attention-demanding task – the frequency of which in a given time period determines the cognitive load (CL) of the distracting task and the subsequent extent of performance impairment in the storage task. Information in the storage systems is also considered subject to representation-based interference; Vergauwe et al. propose that previous fractionations in the visuo-spatial system, as demonstrated through interference, have been at the level they term "peripheral" – that is, limited to a storage system and due to representation-based interference. It was claimed that possible centrally based interference has not been established or duly considered. If information pertaining to two different domains (proposed subdomains within the visuo-spatial domain) recruits the same attentional resources, competition for these resources should produce a detriment in performance of any task requiring them, regardless of domain. Vergauwe, Barrouillet, and Camos (2009) varied processing and storage combinations in order to assess whether same-domain (visual or spatial) processing tasks produce a greater decrement in (visual or spatial) storage performance, or whether storage performance was consistent across processing tasks, which would indicate a domain-general central attentional resource. Vergauwe, Barrouillet, and Camos also manipulated the cognitive load of processing tasks utilized in order to test the premise of the TBRS that cognitive load determines extent of impairment from interference.

Four combinations of processing and storage complex span were created from tasks that they classified as visual storage, spatial storage, visual processing, and spatial processing. The task thought to assess visual storage required viewing and recalling a series of 2×3 matrix patterns. Their spatial processing task required responding with a judgment as to whether a presented line would fit within two presented points. Spatial storage required memory for a series of ball locations and resulting movements as used by Kane et al. (2004), with one location and associated movement per storage "item". Spatial processing combined with spatial storage consisted of participants providing responses as to the presence or absence of symmetry along the vertical axis of half-filled (6 cell $\times$ 6 cell) matrices. Visual processing required judgment as to whether a color presented was more blue or red in its composition. Cognitive load was manipulated by altering the number of processing segments presented, and to be completed, within a given processing period; participants were required to respond to either three, five, or seven processing requirements per processing episode, and all processing episodes were of a fixed time limit (8.5 s).

Only one of each combination of processing, storage, and cognitive load was performed by a participant, so all manipulations were between-subjects manipulations, and only the memory storage performance was analyzed. Participants performed the assigned complex span task at their own individually assessed span, and scoring was based on proportion correct (Friedman & Miyake, 2005; Conway et al., 2005). Analysis of storage performance revealed no difference between visual recall when performed with a visual processing task or with a spatial processing task, and spatial recall performance was not significantly different between concurrent visual or concurrent spatial processing tasks. Single task recall performance was not recorded as a control against which to ascertain effect of presence of a processing task. However, higher cognitive load resulted in poorer recall performance, interpreted as an effect of processing on recall. An analysis of the time taken up by "active" processing during a processing episode was carried out for participants in each cognitive load condition; time taken to respond to processing items was summed to create a total "time occupied" score for each processing episode. The mean total times were then divided by the time allocated to a processing episode (8.5 s), in order to create a specific measure of cognitive load. Recall performance was predicted by this time-based representation of cognitive load in each of the four combinations of complex span, with variance in recall performance explained by the time-based measure of cognitive load ranging from 89% to 99%. It was thus argued that processing affects storage performance and that the cognitive load of a concurrent processing task determines the degree of interference observed in recall performance in a complex span task. Furthermore, visual and spatial memory were shown to share resources at a "central" level, so the effect of processing and cognitive load was concluded to be domain-general.

Vergauwe, Barrouillet, and Camos (2009) argue that an effect of processing on storage, and the domain generality of central resources, means the findings are in contrast to the multiple-component model views of visual and spatial performance. However, domain generality of "central" resources is patently not incompatible with conceptualizations of central executive resources in this latter framework (e.g., Baddeley, 1986; Baddeley & Logie, 1999; Logie, 1995, 2003; Logie & van der Meulen, 2009). Moreover, while Vergauwe, Barrouillet, and Camos (2009) aimed to ascertain the generality or specificity of resources beyond a peripheral level (see also a discussion on fractionation within the visuospatial WM in chapter 5, this volume), there were several limitations in their experimental design that undermine their conclusions. Specifically, Vergauwe, Barrouillet, and Camos (2009) describe the visual storage task used as an adapted version of the visual pattern test (e.g., Della Sala, Gray, Baddeley, Allamano, & Wilson, 1999; Logie & Pearson, 1997). However, in the typical use of the visual pattern task, a single matrix pattern is presented for subsequent recall or recognition, and pattern span is assessed as the most complex single pattern that can be retained. It is not at all clear what kind of cognitive resources would be required to retain a sequence of 2×3 matrix patterns for subsequent recall. Indeed, Phillips and Christie (1977) demonstrated that this kind of task results in a one-item recency effect, with participants recalling the final item correctly but performing only just above chance on earlier items in the sequence. Broadbent and Broadbent (1981) suggested that those earlier items that were recalled might have relied on verbal labeling of patterns that happen to resemble familiar shapes. So, we do not know if the Vergauwe, Barrouillet, and Camos (2009) task actually relied on temporary visual codes. The apparent demonstration of an increase in cognitive load as producing greater interference could equally be the result of allowing less time to verbally code items in this task. The requirement to remember a series of locations within matrices could also be more spatial than visual, or even involve some executive resources for encoding a spatial sequence (see, e.g., Della Sala et al., 1999; Logie, 1995; Logie & Pearson, 1997; Mammarella et al., 2006; Pickering, Gathercole, Hall, & Lloyd, 2001; Rudkin, Pearson, & Logie, 2007).

There are several other problems with this study. For example, the authors utilized a processing task (matrix symmetry judgment) and storage task (ball span) from Kane et al., 2004. However, the appropriateness of these tasks is arguable – for example, the ball span task could have relied on visual codes to label the starting point for each of the movements presented, given that movement direction and starting point were confounded. Kane et al. (2004) made use of a number of different tasks to index spatial resources in a latent variable analysis, and the validity of each component of the tasks Kane et al. employed was not verified as specific to either visual or spatial resources. Finally, it is rather difficult to interpret the results of a between-subject design used to investigate effects of differential cognitive loads, given that there is no way to determine the relationship between the loads imposed on the capacities of the individuals in each participant group. Therefore, the Vergauwe, Barrouillet, and Camos (2009) study does not unequivocally establish the requirement of domain-general resources to support verbal or spatial storage, and evidence for the use of domain-specific resources that we have described in detail appears to be more consistent with the idea of an ensemble of domain-specific cognitive functions, which act in concert with domain-general executive functions (Baddeley, 2007; Baddeley & Logie, 1999; Logie, 2003, 2011b).

Summary

There is evidence for independence of resources supporting processing and storage (Duff & Logie, 1999, 2001; Logie & Duff, 2007), and for the case that multiple resources underlie completion of complex span tasks (Bayliss et al., 2003, 2005; Unsworth et al., 2009; Waters & Caplan, 1996). There is also an indication of executive resource involvement in recall performance (Bayliss et al., 2005; Kane et al., 2004; Miyake et al., 2001; Shah & Miyake, 1996) that suggests executive resources could supplement those resources reserved for storage (see also Ang & Lee, 2008). Initially, complex span tasks were thought to prevent maintenance strategies (e.g., La Pointe & Engle, 1990; Turner & Engle, 1989) seen in simple span performance. However, it has subsequently been demonstrated that strategies (e.g., subvocal rehearsal) can be, and frequently are, applied in complex span tasks (Friedman & Miyake, 2004; McNamara & Scott, 2001; Turley-Ames & Whitfield, 2003), though likely (Unsworth & Engle, 2007a) operating in a reduced form. In addition to strategy use, evidence of the presence of executive resources in complex span performance has previously been variously suggested as due to support of active maintenance in the presence of proactive interference, prevention of intrusion of irrelevant information, suppression of habitual responses (Engle, Kane, & Tuholski, 1999; Heitz, Unsworth, & Engle, 2005; Kane et al., 2008), and retrieval of information displaced into LTM from STM by processing of information (Healey & Miyake, 2009; Unsworth & Engle, 2007b). All of these proposed accounts would predict that executive resource involvement would be evident even at short list lengths in complex span tasks. Executive resources use is also proposed to underlie the coordination required for dual tasking of processing and storage (Duff & Logie, 1999, 2001; Logie & Duff, 2007), the effects of which can result in slightly reduced recall performance compared with simple span or processing without a memory load.

Executive variance in simple span performance, previously thought minimal (e.g., Duff & Logie, 1999, 2001; Engle, Kane, & Tuholski, 1999; Logie & Duff, 2007), appears to be evident in measures representing long list-length performance. Executive resource involvement in verbal and spatial simple span storage performance at longer list lengths has been argued to be equivalent (Kane et al., 2004). However, studies of the visuo-spatial domain have provided evidence for executive resource use in spatial recall in particular (Ang & Lee, 2008; Bayliss et al., 2005; Miyake et al., 2001). The precise nature of executive resource involvement remains unclear; encoding strategies (Ang & Lee, 2008; Kane et al., 2004; Miyake et al., 2001), retrieval from LTM, and efficiency of encoding information for LTM retrieval (Healey & Miyake, 2009; Mogel, Lovett, Stawski, & Sliwinski, 2008; Unsworth, Brewer, & Spillers, 2009; Unsworth & Engle, 2007b) are primary potential candidates. Previous indications of asymmetric executive employment between the verbal (e.g., Engle et al., 1999) and spatial (e.g., Miyake et al., 2001) domains could be reconciled with current indications by suggesting a requirement for executive resources in strategies to deal with memory demands that exceed storage capacity (e.g., Logie et al., 1996). Commonly practiced verbal strategies (e.g., rehearsal and chunking) would require little executive involvement until information exceeds these simple strategies. For example, novel strategies might be deployed unsuccessfully for supra-span items, and/or executive resources might be utilized to retrieve these supra-span items. The use of uncommon strategies for spatial information would be more common for shorter list lengths.

The endeavor to connect the experimental and individual differences literature in the visuo-spatial domain is a necessary step; the disconnection between the two literatures on WM – with a few notable exceptions – constitutes a lacuna in the literature. However, as is evident in our critical review of several studies above, the way in which complex span methodology has been employed previously, and fruitfully, in the verbal domain is largely unsuitable for investigating visuo-spatial fractionation. Due to the inherently serial nature of complex span presentation (a single storage item presented after each processing episode), investigation into the possibility of fractionation on the basis of serial presentation, for example, is likely unworkable in the traditional complex span approaches. These traditional methods involve pitting two storage mechanisms against each other in complex span form, manipulating processing and storage combinations and properties, or assessing predictive value of complex span performance for higher order cognition. Information regarding performance on simultaneous tasks is currently limited to presence or absence of simple correlations, such as the satisfactory fit of a task included within latent variables representing STM or joint STM functions within a broader WM system (Miyake et al., 2001). As detailed above, however, acknowledgment of findings from the complex span literature leads to further consideration of clearly pertinent issues including, but not limited to, resource allocation, performance strategies, whole system performance, and executive resource contributions to storage and recall performance. Information gained through this literature on the resources underlying complex span performance can, furthermore, be used to further illuminate the processes underlying simple span performance.

In sum, the jury is still out on the ensemble of WM functions compared with limited-capacity attentional control. Clearly, different forms of processing and storage must rely on different, but possibly overlapping, networks in the brain (for reviews, see Osaka, Logie, & D'Esposito, 2007). One major aspect of the debate considered in this chapter is about what is different and what overlaps. A further debate is whether the different methodologies are asking the same research questions. Individual difference approaches primarily focus on what are the cognitive drivers of those differences, and why a straightforward task such as reading a series of sentences and recalling the last words of each sentence correlates so highly with such a wide variety of mental ability measures. One answer could be that this apparently straightforward task actually uses a wide range of different cognitive resources for successful completion, and the more demanding it becomes, the larger is the range of different cognitive resources required. So high-demand complex span and low-demand complex span are actually measuring different mental abilities and are not simply taxing the same ability at different levels of demand. This alone could account for the overlapping variance with other cognitive ability measures that also require the use of a wide range of different cognitive resources.

Administering a WM span test is certainly much easier than using a full-scale intelligence test to measure mental ability, in children and in adults. However, it is not clear whether the theoretical interpretations that have been derived from individual difference studies actually yield as much insight into the underlying cognition as might have been assumed. One reason for this is that people vary in the strategies that they use for performing complex tasks; also, people vary in the strengths and weaknesses of the different cognitive abilities that might contribute to task performance and in how those strengths and weaknesses change differentially with age in different individuals (for an extended discussion, see Johnson, Logie, & Brockmole, 2010). If different people perform the same task in different ways, and rise to the challenge of increased cognitive demand in different ways, this rather complicates the job of identifying any common patterns across individuals in the nature of the cognitive resources on which those individuals can and do draw in performing that task.

A further complication of the individual differences approach is that any task will require the use of cognitive abilities at well below the capacity of those abilities, as well as cognitive abilities that are being stretched to their limits by increasing task demand. For example, if we were to measure how loudly each of a large number of people could speak, and also to measure the ability of those same people to recall orally a sequence of digits, the correlation between these two measures would be negligible. However, if an individual were to catch a cold and lose his or her voice, his or her ability to orally recall digits would be impaired. A measure of the maximum capacity for speech volume is not required to perform a digit span task, but some minimum level of speech volume *is* required. Measures of individual differences are measures of the maximum capacity of the ability being measured, but this approach would be completely insensitive to the contributions from other abilities that are required but only at some minimum level of competence. So, again, an individual differences approach is not an ideal way to identify the architecture of cognition. Results from such studies could complement, but cannot effectively challenge, results from other methodologies that are designed specifically to ask questions about that architecture.

We started this chapter by referring to concepts about the nature of on-line cognition that have their roots in the thinking of seventeenth- and eighteenth-century philosophers. The seminal ideas of Locke and Hume continue to pervade contemporary theorizing, with reference to primary and secondary memory, or to WM and LTM. However, philosophers during "The Period of Enlightenment" as it is known, tended to rely heavily on their own introspections about the workings of the mind, and the idea of a limited-capacity, domain-general attentional system offers a compelling match with our subjective experience of mental operations. However, there is a substantial body of evidence, some of which is reviewed in this chapter, to indicate that there are multiple different cognitive functions on which we can draw, and some of those functions can operate in parallel, even if we are not aware of them doing so. Temporary storage interspersed with on-line processing, such as is required of complex span tasks, offers an example where our subjective experience is of focusing on either the processing or the storage, possibly with the mental experience of rapid switching between them. But that subjective experience does not necessarily reflect the cognitive operations that are engaged. Pylyshyn (1973) noted some time ago that not all that is available to conscious inspection is necessarily functional, and that not all that is functional is necessarily available to conscious inspection (for recent discussions see Della Sala, van der Meulen, Bestelmeyer, & Logie, 2010; Zeman et al., 2010). Working memory is not consciousness (for a discussion, see Logie, 2009). It is a collection of cognitive functions on which the brain can draw to perform tasks. Identifying those cognitive functions and how they act together to achieve task goals will require converging objective evidence from a range of methodologies. As should also be clear from our review, large elements of contemporary research have tended to neglect converging evidence from different approaches and methodologies, and tend not to recognize the weaknesses as well as the strengths of each. There has also been a tendency to neglect accumulated findings that are incompatible with some contemporary theorizing. For research to advance our knowledge rather than recycle previously rehearsed debates (e.g., McGeoch, 1932), it is essential that the research builds on the several decades of experimental research, neuropsychology, brain imaging, and individual differences studies on the ensemble of WM, so as to clarify the nature of the cognitive instruments that contribute.

References

Alloway, T. P., & Gathercole, S. E. (2006). *Working memory and neurodevelopmental disorders*. Hove, UK: Psychology Press.

Anderson, J. R., Bothell, D., Byrne, M. D., Douglass, S., Lebiere, C., & Qin, Y. (2004). An integrated theory of mind. *Psychological Review, 111*, 1036–1060.

Anderson, J. R., Fincham, J. M., Qin, Y., & Stoccoet, A. (2008). A central circuit of the mind. *Trends in Cognitive Sciences, 12*, 136–143.

Ang, S. Y., & Lee, K. (2008). Central executive involvement in children's spatial memory. *Memory, 16*, 918–933.

Atkinson, R. C., & Shiffrin, R. M. (1968). Human memory: A proposed system and its control processes. In K. W. Spence & J. T. Spence (Eds.), *The psychology of learning and motivation: Advances in research and theory* (Vol. 2, pp. 89–105). New York: Academic Press.

Baars, B. J. (1997). *In the theater of consciousness: The workspace of the mind*. New York: Oxford University Press.

Baddeley, A. D. (1986). *Working memory*. Oxford, UK: Oxford University Press.

Baddeley, A. D. (2000). The episodic buffer: A new component of working memory? *Trends in Cognitive Sciences, 4*, 417–423.

Baddeley, A. D. (2007). *Working memory in thought and action*. Oxford, UK: Oxford University Press.

Baddeley, A. D., & Hitch, G. I. (1974). Working memory. In G. A. Bower (Ed.), *The psychology of learning and motivation* (Vol. 8, pp. 47–90). New York: Academic Press.

Baddeley, A. D., Lewis, V. J., & Vallar, G. (1984). Exploring the articulatory loop. *Quarterly Journal of Experimental Psychology, 36*, 233–252.

Baddeley, A. D., & Logie, R. H. (1999). Working memory: The multiple-component model. In A. Miyake & P. Shah (Eds.), *Models of working memory* (pp. 28–61). New York: Cambridge University Press.

Baddeley, A. D., Logie, R. H., Nimmo-Smith, I., & Brereton, N. (1985). Components of fluent reading. *Journal of Memory and Language, 24*, 119–131.

Barrouillet, P., Bernardin, S., & Camos, V. (2004). Time constraints and resource sharing in adult's working memory spans. *Journal of Experimental Psychology: General, 133*, 83–100.

Barrouillet, P., & Camos, V. (2001). Developmental increase in working memory span: Resource sharing or temporal decay. *Journal of Memory and Language, 45*, 1–20.

Bartlett, F. (1958). *Thinking: An experimental and social study*. London: George Allen & Unwin.

Bayliss, D. M., Jarrold, C., Baddeley, A. D., & Gunn, D. M. (2005). The relationship between short-term memory and working memory: Complex span made simple? *Memory, 13*, 414–421.

Bayliss, D. M., Jarrold, C., Gunn, D. M., & Baddeley, A. D. (2003). The complexities of complex span: Explaining individual differences in working memory in children and adults. *Journal of Experimental Psychology: General, 132*, 71–92.

Broadbent, D. E. (1958). *Perception and communication*. London & New York: Pergamon.

Broadbent, D. E., & Broadbent, M. H. P. (1981). Recency effects in visual memory. *Quarterly Journal of Experimental Psychology, 33A*, 1–15.

Camos, V., Lagner, P., & Barrouillet, P. (2009). Two maintenance mechanisms of verbal information in working memory. *Journal of Memory and Language, 61*, 457–469.

Caplan, D., & Waters, G. S. (1999). Verbal working memory and sentence comprehension, *Behavioural and Brain Sciences, 22,* 77–94.

Case, R., Kurland, D. M., & Goldberg, J. (1982). Operational efficiency and the growth of short-term memory span. *Journal of Experimental Child Psychology, 33,* 386–404.

Conway, A. R. A., Cowan, N., & Bunting, M. F. (2001). The cocktail party phenomenon revisited: The importance of working memory capacity. *Psychonomic Bulletin and Review, 8,* 331–335.

Conway, A. R. A., Kane, M. J., Bunting, M. F., Hambrick, D. Z., Wilhelm, O., & Engle, R. W. (2005). Working memory span tasks: A methodological review and user's guide. *Psychonomic Bulletin and Review, 12,* 769–786.

Cowan, N. (1995). *Attention and memory: An integrated framework.* New York: Oxford University Press.

Cowan, N. (2005). *Working memory capacity.* Hove, UK: Psychology Press.

Daneman, M., & Carpenter, P. A. (1980). Individual differences in working memory and reading. *Journal of Verbal Learning and Verbal Behavior, 19,* 450–466.

Daneman, M., & Hannon, B. (2007). What do working memory span tasks like reading span really measure? In N. Osaka, R. H. Logie, & M. D'Esposito (Eds.), *The cognitive neuroscience of working memory* (pp. 21–42). New York: Oxford University Press.

Della Sala, S. (Ed.) (2010). *Forgetting.* Hove, UK: Psychology Press.

Della Sala, S., Gray, C., Baddeley, A., Allamano, N., & Wilson, L. (1999). Pattern span: A tool for unwelding visuo-spatial memory. *Neuropsychologica, 37,* 1189–1119.

Della Sala, S., van der Meulen, M., Bestelmeyer, P., & Logie, R. H. (2010). Evidence for a workspace model of working memory from semantic implicit processing in neglect. *Journal of Neuropsychology, 4,* 147–166.

Denis, M. (1996). Imagery and the description of spatial configurations. In M. de Vega, M. J. Intons-Peterson, P. N. Johnson-Laird, M. Denis, & M. Marschark (Eds.), *Models of visuospatial cognition* (pp. 128–197). New York: Oxford University Press.

Deyzac, E., Logie, R. H., & Denis, M. (2006). Visuospatial working memory and the processing of spatial descriptions. *British Journal of Psychology, 97,* 217–243.

Duff, S. C., & Logie, R. H. (1999). Storage and processing in visuo-spatial working memory. *Scandinavian Journal of Psychology, 40,* 251–259.

Duff, S. C., & Logie, R. H. (2001). Processing and storage in working memory span. *Quarterly Journal of Experimental Psychology, 54A,* 31–48.

Emerson, M. J., & Miyake, A. (2003). The role of inner speech in task switching: A dual-task investigation. *Journal of Memory and Language, 48,* 148–168.

Engle, R. W., Kane., M. J., & Tuholski, S. W. (1999). Individual differences in working memory capacity and what they tell us about controlled attention, general fluid intelligence, and functions of the prefrontal cortex. In A. Miyake & P. Shah (Eds.), *Models of working memory: Mechanisms of active maintenance and executive control* (pp. 102–134). New York: Cambridge University Press.

Engle, R. W., Tuholski, S. W., Laughlin, J. E., & Conway, A. R. A. (1999). Working memory, short-term memory, and general fluid intelligence: A latent-variable approach. *Journal of Experimental Psychology: General, 128,* 309–331.

Friedman, N. P., & Miyake, A. (2004). The reading span test and its predictive power for reading comprehension ability. *Journal of Memory and Language, 51,* 136–158.

Friedman, N. P., & Miyake, A. (2005). Comparison of four scoring methods for the reading span test. *Behavior Research Methods, 37,* 581–590.

Gathercole, S., & Baddeley, A. D. (1989). Evaluation of the role of phonological STM in the development of vocabulary in children: A longitudinal study. *Journal of Memory and Language, 28*, 200–213.

Gathercole, S., & Baddeley, A. D. (1993). *Working memory and language*. Hove, UK: Lawrence Erlbaum Associates.

Hasher, L., & Zacks, R. T. (1988). Working memory, comprehension and aging: A review and a new view. *Psychology of Learning & Motivation, 22*, 193–225.

Healey, M. K., & Miyake, A. (2009). The role of attention during retrieval in working-memory span: A dual-task study. *Quarterly Journal of Experimental Psychology, 62*, 733–745.

Heitz, R. P., Unsworth, N., & Engle, R. W. (2005). Working memory capacity, attention, and fluid intelligence. In O. Wilhelm & R. W. Engle (Eds.), *Understanding and measuring intelligence* (pp. 61–77). New York: Sage.

Hume, D. (1748). *An enquiry concerning human understanding*. New York: Liberal Arts Press, 1955.

James, W. (1890). *Principles of psychology* (Vol. 2). London: MacMillan & Co., 1902.

Johnson, W., Logie, R. H., & Brockmole, J. R. (2010). Working memory tasks differ in factor structure across age cohorts: Implications for differentiation. *Intelligence, 38*, 513–528.

Just, M. A., Carpenter, P. A., & Keller, T. A. (1996). The capacity theory of comprehension: New frontiers of evidence and arguments. *Psychological Review, 103*, 773–780.

Kane, M. J., Bleckley, M. K., Conway, A. R. A., & Engle, R. W. (2001). A controlled-attention view of working-memory capacity. *Journal of Experimental Psychology: General, 130*, 169–183.

Kane, M. J., Conway, A. R. A, Hambrick, D. Z., & Engle, R. W. (2008). Variation in working memory capacity as variation in executive attention and control. In A. R. A. Conway, C. Jarrold, M. J. Kane, A. Miyake, & J. N. Towse (Eds.), *Variation in working memory* (pp. 21–48). New York: Oxford University Press.

Kane, M. J., & Engle, R. W. (2002). The role of prefrontal cortex in working memory capacity, executive attention, and general fluid intelligence: An individual differences perspective. *Psychonomic Bulletin and Review, 9*, 637–671.

Kane, M. J., & Engle, R. W. (2003). Working memory capacity and the control of attention: The contributions of goal neglect, response competition, and task set to stroop interference. *Journal of Experimental Psychology: General, 132*, 47–70.

Kane, M. J., Hambrick, D. Z., Tuholski, S. W., Wilhelm, O., Payne, T. W., & Engle, R. W. (2004). The generality of working memory capacity: A latent-variable approach to verbal and visuospatial memory span and reasoning. *Journal of Experimental Psychology: General, 133*, 189–217.

Kane, M. J., Poole, B. J., Tuholski, S. W., & Engle, R. W. (2006). Working memory capacity and the top-down control of visual search: Exploring the boundaries of "executive attention". *Journal of Experimental Psychology: Learning, Memory and Cognition, 32*, 749–777.

Klauer, K. C., & Zhao, Z. (2004). Double dissociations in visual and spatial short-term memory. *Journal of Experimental Psychology: General, 133*, 355–381.

La Pointe, L. B., & Engle, R. W. (1990). Simple and complex word spans as measures of working memory capacity. *Journal of Experimental Psychology: Learning, Memory and Cognition, 16*, 1118–1133.

Larsen, J., & Baddeley, A. D. (2003). Disruption of verbal STM by irrelevant speech, articulatory suppression and manual tapping: Do they have a common source? *Quarterly Journal of Experimental Psychology, 56A*, 1249–1268.

Lewandowsky, S., Oberauer, K., & Brown, G. D. A. (2009a). No temporal decay in verbal short-term memory, *Trends in Cognitive Sciences, 13*, 120–126.

Lewandowsky, S., Oberauer, K., & Brown, G. D. A. (2009b). Response to Barrouillet and Camos: Interference or decay in working memory? *Trends in Cognitive Sciences, 13*, 146–147.

Lobley, K. J., Baddeley, A. D., & Gathercole, S. E. (2005). Phonological similarity effects in verbal complex span. *Quarterly Journal of Experimental Psychology, 58A*, 1462–1478.

Locke, J. (1690). *An essay concerning human understanding* (1st edition, Book II, Chapter X, 1–20). University of Aberdeen Archive Library, Aberdeen, UK.

Logie, R. H. (1995). *Visuo-spatial working memory*. Hove, UK: Lawrence Erlbaum Associates.

Logie, R. H. (1996). The seven ages of working memory. In J. T. E. Richardson, R. W. Engle, L. Hasher, R. H. Logie, E. R. Stoltzfus, & R. T. Zacks, *Working memory and human cognition*. New York: Oxford University Press.

Logie, R. H. (2003). Spatial and visual working memory: A mental workspace. In D. Irwin & B. Ross (Eds.), *Cognitive vision: The psychology of learning and motivation* (Vol. 42, pp. 37–78). New York: Elsevier Science.

Logie, R. H. (2009). Working memory and consciousness. In T. Bayne, A. Cleeremans, & P. Wilkin (Eds.), *The Oxford companion to consciousness* (pp. 667–670). Oxford, UK: Oxford University Press.

Logie, R. H. (2011a). The visual and the spatial of a multicomponent working memory. In A. Vandierendonck (Ed.), *Spatial working memory*. Hove, UK: Psychology Press.

Logie, R. H. (2011b). The functional organisation and the capacity limits of working memory. *Current Directions in Psychological Science, 20*(4), 240–245.

Logie, R. H., & Baddeley, A. D. (1987). Cognitive processes in counting. *Journal of Experimental Psychology: Learning, Memory and Cognition, 13*, 310–326.

Logie, R. H., Baddeley, A. D., Mane, A., Donchin, E., & Sheptak, R. (1989). Working memory and the analysis of a complex skill by secondary task methodology. *Acta Psychologica, 71*, 53–87.

Logie, R. H., Cocchini, G., Della Sala, S., & Baddeley, A. D. (2004). Is there a specific executive capacity for dual task co-ordination? Evidence from Alzheimer's disease. *Neuropsychology, 18*, 504–513.

Logie, R. H., & Della Sala, S. (2005). Disorders of visuo-spatial working memory. In A. Miyake & P. Shah (Eds.), *Handbook of visuospatial thinking* (pp. 81–120). New York: Cambridge University Press.

Logie, R. H., Della Sala, S., Laiacona, M., Chalmers, P., & Wynn, V. (1996). Group aggregates and individual reliability: The case of verbal short-term memory. *Memory & Cognition, 24*, 305–321.

Logie, R. H., Della Sala, S., MacPherson, S., & Cooper, J. (2007). Dual task demands on encoding and retrieval processes: Evidence from healthy adult ageing. *Cortex, 43*, 159–169.

Logie, R. H., Della Sala, S., Wynn, V., & Baddeley, A. D. (2000). Visual similarity effects in immediate verbal serial recall. *Quarterly Journal of Experimental Psychology, 53A*, 626–646.

Logie, R. H., & Duff, S. C. (2007). Separating processing from storage in working memory operation span. In N. Osaka, R. H. Logie, & M. D'Esposito (Eds.), *The cognitive neuroscience of working memory* (pp. 119–135). Oxford, UK: Oxford University Press.

Logie, R. H., Gilhooly, K. J., & Wynn, V. (1994). Counting on working memory in arithmetic problem solving. *Memory & Cognition, 22*, 395–410.

Logie, R. H., Trawley, S., & Law, A.S. (2011). Multitasking: Multiple, domain-specific cognitive functions in a virtual environment. *Memory and Cognition.* doi: 10.3758/s13421-011-0120-1

Logie, R. H., & Pearson, D. G. (1997). The inner eye and the inner scribe of visuo-spatial working memory: Evidence from developmental fractionation. *European Journal of Cognitive Psychology, 9*, 241–257.

Logie, R. H., & van der Meulen, M. (2009). Fragmenting and integrating visuo-spatial working memory. In J. R. Brockmole (Ed.), *Representing the visual world in memory* (pp. 1–32). Hove, UK: Psychology Press.

Mammarella, I. C., Cornoldi, C., Pazzaglia, F., Toso, C., Grimoldi, M., & Vio, C. (2006). Evidence for a double dissociation between spatial-simultaneous and spatial-sequential working memory in visuospatial (nonverbal) learning disabled children. *Brain and Cognition, 62*, 58–67.

McGeoch, J. A. (1932). Forgetting and the law of disuse. *Psychological Review, 39*, 352–370.

McNamara, D. S., & Scott, J. L. (2001). Working memory capacity and strategy use. *Memory & Cognition, 29*, 10–17.

Miyake, A. (2001). Individual differences in working memory: Introduction to the special section. *Journal of Experimental Psychology: General, 130*, 163–198.

Miyake, A., Friedman, N. P., Emerson, M. J., Witzki, A. H., Howerter, A., & Wager, T. D. (2000). The unity and diversity of executive functions and their contributions to complex "frontal Lobe" tasks: A latent variable analysis. *Cognitive Psychology, 41*, 49–100.

Miyake, A., Friedman, N. P., Rettinger, D. A., Shah, P., & Hegarty, M. (2001). How are visuospatial working memory, executive functioning, and spatial abilities related? A latent-variable analysis. *Journal of Experimental Psychology: General, 130*, 621–640.

Mogel, J. A., Lovett, B. J., Stawski, R. S., & Sliwinski, M. J. (2008). What's so special about working memory? An examination of the relationships among working memory, secondary memory, and fluid intelligence. *Psychological Science, 19*, 1071–1077.

Oberauer, K., & Lewandowsky, S. (2008). Forgetting in immediate serial recall: Decay, temporal distinctiveness, or interference? *Psychological Review, 115*, 544–576.

Osaka, N., Logie, R. H., & D'Esposito, M. (Eds.) (2007). *The cognitive neuroscience of working memory.* Oxford, UK: Oxford University Press.

Phillips, L. H., Gilhooly, K. J., Logie, R. H., Della Sala, S., & Wynn, V. (2003). Age, working memory, and the Tower of London task. *European Journal of Cognitive Psychology, 15*, 291–312.

Phillips, W. A., & Christie, D. F. M. (1977). Components of visual memory. *Quarterly Journal of Experimental Psychology, 29*, 117–133.

Pickering, S. J., Gathercole, S. E., Hall, M., & Lloyd, S. A. (2001). Development of memory for pattern and path: Further evidence for the fractionation of visuo-spatial memory. *Quarterly Journal of Experimental Psychology, 54A*, 397–420.

Portrat, S., Barrouillet, P., & Camos, V. (2008). Time-related decay or interference-based forgetting in working memory. *Journal of Experimental Psychology: Learning, Memory, and Cognition, 34*, 1561–1564.

Pylyshyn, Z. W. (1973). What the mind's eye tells the mind's brain: A critique of mental imagery. *Psychological Bulletin, 80*, 1–24.

Rudkin, S. J., Pearson, D. G., & Logie, R. H. (2007). Executive processes in visual and spatial working memory tasks. *Quarterly Journal of Experimental Psychology, 60*, 79–100.

Saito, S., Logie, R. H., Morita, A., & Law, A. (2008). Visual and phonological similarity effects in verbal immediate serial recall: A test with kanji materials. *Journal of Memory and Language, 59*, 1–17.

Saito, S., & Miyake, A. (2004). On the nature of forgetting and the processing–storage relationship in reading span performance. *Journal of Memory and Language, 50*, 425–443.

Shah, P., & Miyake, A. (1996). The separability of working memory resources for spatial thinking in language processing: An individual differences approach. *Journal of Experimental Psychology: General, 125*, 4–27.

Stoltzfus, E. R., Hasher, L., & Zacks, R. T. (1996). Working memory and aging: Current status and the inhibitory view. In J. T. E. Richardson, R. W. Engle, L. Hasher, R. H. Logie, E. R. Stoltzfus, & R. Zacks (Eds.), *Working memory and human cognition*. Oxford, UK: Oxford University Press.

Stout, G. F. (1898). *Manual of psychology*. London: University Tutorial Press.

Towse, J. N., Hitch, G. J., & Hutton, U. (1998). A re-evaluation of working memory capacity in children. *Journal of Memory and Language, 39*, 195–217.

Towse, J. N., Hitch, G. J., & Hutton, U. (2000). On the interpretation of working memory span in adults. *Memory & Cognition, 28*, 341–348.

Towse, J. N., Hitch, G. J., & Hutton, U. (2002). On the nature of the relationship between processing activity and item retention in children. *Journal of Experimental Child Psychology, 82*, 156–184.

Turley-Ames, K. J., & Whitfield, M. M. (2003). Strategy training and working memory task performance. *Journal of Memory and Language, 49*, 446–468.

Turner, M. L., & Engle, R. W. (1989). Is working memory capacity task dependent? *Journal of Memory and Language, 28*, 127–154.

Unsworth, N., Brewer, G. A., & Spillers, G. J. (2009). There's more to the working memory capacity–fluid intelligence relationship than just secondary memory. *Psychonomic Bulletin and Review, 16*, 931–937.

Unsworth, N., & Engle, R. W. (2006). Simple and complex memory spans and their relation to fluid abilities: Evidence from list-length effects. *Journal of Memory and Language, 54*, 68–80.

Unsworth, N., & Engle, R. W. (2007a). On the division of short-term and working memory: An examination of simple and complex span and their relation to higher order abilities. *Psychological Bulletin, 133*, 1038–1066.

Unsworth, N., & Engle, R. W. (2007b). The nature of individual differences in working memory capacity: Active maintenance in primary memory and controlled search from secondary memory. *Psychological Review, 114*, 104–132.

Unsworth, N., Redick, T. S., Heitz, R. P., Broadway, J. M., & Engle, R. W. (2009). Complex working memory span tasks and higher-order cognition: A latent-variable analysis of the relationship between processing and storage. *Memory, 17*, 635–654.

Vallar, G., & Shallice, T. (1990). *Neuropsychological impairments of short-term memory*. Cambridge, UK: Cambridge University Press.

van der Meulen, M., Logie, R. H., & Della Sala, S. (2009). Selective interference with image retention and generation: Evidence for the workspace model. *Quarterly Journal of Experimental Psychology, 62*, 1568–1580.

Vergauwe, E., Barrouillet, P., & Camos, V. (2009). Visual and spatial working memory are not that dissociated after all: A time-based resource-sharing account. *Journal of Experimental Psychology: Learning, Memory, and Cognition, 35*, 1012–1028.

Waters, G. S., & Caplan, D. (1996). The measurement of verbal working memory capacity and its relation to reading comprehension. *Quarterly Journal of Experimental Psychology, 49A*, 51–79.

Zeman, A., Della Sala, S., Torrens, L., Gountouna, E., McGonigle, D., & Logie, R. H. (2010). Loss of imagery phenomenology with intact visual imagery performance. *Neuropsychologia, 48*, 145–155.

5   Theories and debate in visuo-spatial working memory

The questions of access and rehearsal

J. Gerry Quinn

This chapter explores the architecture of visuo-spatial working memory, taking as its starting point the popular and influential model of Logie (1995). Two issues are emphasised that have sparked productive controversy over recent times: the means of access into the visual working memory system and the nature of rehearsal within the system. The implications for these issues brought out by dynamic visual noise are explored and evidence is brought to bear that argues for a change in the architecture. In particular, it is argued that many of the controversies can be solved with the addition of a visual buffer as an *independent* component within visual working memory. This addition will, in turn, have implications for the understanding of the visual cache. Second, it is argued that movement as the means of rehearsal of the content of visual memory has little unambiguous empirical support and that the mechanisms of attention should provide the required retention mechanism. Again, the implications for the inner scribe and its relation to the cache are noted. These arguments require reference to a number of alternative models of visual processing that are able to shed light on the cognitive processes involved in visual memory.

Introduction

For a long time it was held that visuo-spatial working memory (VSWM) was the poor relation of working memory research, with investigations of verbal processes more to the fore (for a more detailed account, see Chapter 4 this volume). However, there is now a robust maturity to the topic, which has come about for several reasons; one is the sheer amount of work that has been published on the topic over recent years. From a slow start in the 1980s, there are now several well-established and interrelated topics that have become the focus of VSWM researchers. However, these foci enjoy impact because of the increasingly sophisticated theoretical perspectives, which have provided solid interpretative frameworks. These perspectives have ensured that the constraints that point the way towards relevant questions and debates are in place and continue to provide the means of empirical and theoretical development. Over the years, the perspectives contributing to the success of VSWM research have included those of Kosslyn and colleagues (Kosslyn, 1994; Kosslyn, Thompson, & Ganis, 2006),

Logie (1995), and Cornoldi and Vecchi (2003). These three examples have adopted notably different theoretical positions, with the model of Logie having a strong relationship to the original working memory (WM) model of Baddeley and Hitch (1974), Cornoldi and Vecchi being less clearly related to the original model though often seen as an alternative model within the tradition of the WM model. Kosslyn's model is a more general model of visual information processing that enjoys an independent derivation. These models have had notable success in determining the nature of the research done in the field of visuo-spatial memory and in providing an interpretative basis for the results garnered. They have enabled VSWM research to develop the robustness noted above.

While the models are different and so have emphasized different empirical questions, and somewhat different theoretical advances, research on similar cognitive phenomena might be expected to coincide. Distinct theoretical positions based on similar behavioral phenomena should themselves mutually inform and shape. This chapter will look at some of the interplay among these models, with emphasis on the first two, to determine the extent to which the models may be brought closer together. Comment will be made on some of the components of the models, with a view to investigating the insight that each may provide.

It is clear that the Logie (1995) model has been particularly influential in bringing together into a coherent whole much of the disparate work carried out in visual and in spatial WM throughout the last 30 years. It has two major components: a visual cache, which stores visual information, including shape and color; and an inner scribe, which stores spatial information and is related to movement. Crucially, the scribe is considered to perform a rehearsal function for the cache.

While the success of the interpretative function of the model is beyond question, there have been areas of significant uncertainty from the outset. Two aspects can be mentioned here: first, unlike the verbal working model (Baddeley, 1986, 2007) with which it is often compared, and which permits direct access by verbal material from the outside world, visual information from the outside world has no direct access into the cache. Second, there is the question of the function of the inner scribe as a rehearsal mechanism for the cache.

Taking the first aspect of direct access, information that gains access to the visual cache can only do so via a knowledge base. Only after interpretation within the knowledge base can it be entered into the cache; information in the cache, therefore, represents an output from a semantic system. In contrast, a clear example of direct access in the case of verbal WM is unattended speech. Claims about direct access of unattended speech into verbal WM have served to provide a rich means of further developing our understanding of verbal WM. Debates initiated by the work of Salamé and Baddeley (1982) and continued principally by Jones and his associates (e.g., Jones, Hughes, & Macken, 2006, 2007; see also Saito, 1994) continue to benefit theoretical development and provide further impetus to re-appraisal.

While the claim of indirect access to visual WM itself has led to debate and has been strengthened by the inclusion of neurophysiological data (Beschin, Cocchini, Della Sala, & Logie, 1997; Logie, 2003), the claim may be difficult to sustain

(Baddeley, 2007). There are several broad lines of evidence that indicate this difficulty: first, the model, which in its depiction covers both visual and verbal phenomena, suggests that access to verbal *and* visuo-spatial WM – not simply the visuo-spatial component – is via semantic interpretation within a knowledge base. However, this runs contrary to the research on unattended speech where the uninterpreted phonological property of presented information is considered to have direct access. Second, there is work within the area of VSWM which would, taken at face value, seem to suggest direct access (Dean, Dewhurst, & Whittaker, 2008; Dent, 2010; McConnell & Quinn, 2000, 2004; Quinn & McConnell, 1996, 2006). These authors used the technique of dynamic visual noise (DVN) as an interference technique focused on visual WM and consider that it is indicative of direct access. The claim, contrary to the claim of Logie (1995, 2003), that there is direct access to the VSWM system is worth investigating further. As noted above, research that has indicated direct access to verbal WM has provided a rich seam of information and a means of theoretical development.

Direct access to VSWM: debate and resolutions

DVN involves the presentation of a flickering black-and-white dot pattern (Figure 5.1) concurrent with the presentation of the to-be-remembered informa-tion. The pattern flickers continually throughout its extent and was designed to minimize any possibility of semantic analysis and any likelihood of focusing attention at any time or to any place within the display. When this pattern is used with the presentation of material that is to be processed visually, it leads to the disruption of the recall of that information. The pattern causes interference *specifi-cally* with the presentation of material that is to be visually processed. It does not cause general interference; there is no effect of DVN on, for example, verbal material (Quinn & McConnell, 1996).

While initial use of DVN was promising, further use of the display pointed, intriguingly, to empirical limits to its effectiveness as an interfering technique. Typically, DVN has been used to interfere with a visual *image*, here defined as a visual stimulus generated internally in response to a nonvisual input. In their series of experiments, Quinn and McConnell have most often used the pegword mnemonic to encourage visual processing. With this mnemonic, participants learn to create a visual image of each word in a sequence of standard cue words. The cue words (bun, shoe, . . .) are presented in a given numerical order, such as:

One is a bun

Two is a shoe

and so on, usually up to ten. Once the participants have learned to create images to each of the cues, they are then presented with the sequence of words to be recalled and are instructed to link each of these words with each of the cues in a composite image. On presentation during the retrieval period of the first cue word of the pair, participants re-create the image in order to retrieve the associated word. Over a series of experiments, the authors report that DVN interferes with the visual image while DVN does not interfere with processes involved in verbal

Figure 5.1 A static illustration of DVN. The display comprises black and white squares, each square measuring 4 × 4 pixels. In its dynamic presentation, the squares switch from black to white, and vice versa. A standard switching rate of around 300 random squares per second has been used.

recall where participants verbally link and rehearse two paired words. In an important expansion of this work, Parker and Dagnall (2009) have demonstrated the effectiveness of DVN where explicit instruction to form a visual image is *not* given. They presented concrete and abstract words without accompanying imagery instructions and found that the recall advantage of concrete words – a robust phenomenon in experimental psychology – was significantly reduced. However, initial emphasis on visual image creation through a restricted number of mnemonics has been shown to result in a narrow empirical basis for any broad interpretation of visual cognitive processes. For example, the extent to which the technique interferes with a visual *memory* is less clear. A visual *memory* is here defined as a visual image initially presented as a visual percept. While results showing clear and specific interference with visual *imagery* have been reported many times and by several authors, including Andrade, Kemps, Werniers, and Szmalec (2002), results involving memory for visually presented percepts is much less certain. In addition to demonstrating the effectiveness of DVN with mnemonic images, Andrade et al. also demonstrated no effect on visual memory performance when the memory items were visually presented matrices and Chinese symbols. Control experiments made it clear that although there was no effect of DVN, visual processes were being used by the participants when encoding and retaining the items. Avons and Sestieri (2005) have also carried out an impressive series of experiments using visual memory under a number of conditions. These conditions included mental synthesis, where the memory items, mainly block diagrams, had to be kept in consciousness and manipulated. Avons and Sestieri (2005) again show no effects of DVN under the various conditions of their experimental series. These findings served to give credence to the view that visual imagery and visual memory use different cognitive processes. In some contrast, however, both Dean, Dewhurst, and Whittaker (2008) and Dent (2010) report that DVN does cause interference with visual memory, yet both these papers make it clear that the interference is greatly lessened with a visual memory; interference occurs only when precision and detail have to be retained. Notwithstanding these most recent findings, there does seem to be a difference between visual images and visual memories as defined above. The images that are constructed following the pegword mnemonic can be broad-brush and do not require detailed recall.

Several suggestions have been put forward to account for these differences, which have implications for access to VSWM. Most frequently it has been suggested, in the case of visual images, that DVN causes interference with the generation of the image rather than with any visual component (Andrade et al., 2002; Logie, 2003) – that is, that the interference is with the executive processes responsible for image generation. An advantage of this interpretation is that it maintains the integrity of the two component model of VSWM. There is no direct access required to either of the two visuo-spatial components. The cache, responsible for retention of an interpreted percept, remains intact and is impervious to direct DVN interference. The inner scribe, associated with targeted movement, would not be expected to show any sensitivity to DVN. Only the central executive (CE) and its processes of generation of an *image* are affected.

However, such an interpretation highlights some debatable aspects of executive processes. In both the Logie model and the original model of WM of Baddeley and Hitch (1974), executive processes are not considered to be modality-specific, hence any interference caused to the CE would act through domain-general processes. However, on the basis of the information available currently, DVN interferes exclusively with a visual image. At the time of writing, it has not been used to interfere with the generation of nonvisual stimuli. It is known that it does not interfere with the recall of verbally rehearsed, verbally presented information. It may interfere with yet another modality of presentation, but there is currently no evidence on the matter. If it is the case that DVN interferes only in the visual domain, it will follow that it is specifically visual generation that is disrupted. Such a view will require a development of the concept of the CE into a number of processes, which will include domain-specific processes; at the very least, this interpretation forces a closer examination of the status of the executive processes and their relationship to visual imagery.

The central executive – master or slave?

In an intriguing way, the Logie model makes reference to visual images that appears to separate them structurally from the visual cache. Consistent with the argument suggesting that DVN interferes with executive processes, Logie (1995, p. 129) considers that the executive may host the visual image. However, in an interesting twist, the executive in this regard is not independent but is reliant on the cache. The twist here – using the language often applied to the relationship between the CE and the subsidiary modality-specific systems within the Baddeley (1986, 2007) model – is that the master has become the slave. The image in the executive needs the processes of the slave. While the executive may be the host of the image, the image has no independent, executive-based existence. It is not a memory in and of itself. Instead, it is reliant on the cache. The cache is the only visual store within the Logie model. Hence, the image is reliant on the cache even though generated within the executive. This, in turn, would seem to suggest that that disruption of the image should cause no problems, as a "master copy" would reside in the cache. However, DVN causes forgetting of words processed as an image, with no acceptance that the cache is similarly affected, so it seems that the precise demarcation of the visual processes involved in the cache from the processes of the executive is required.

Relevance of the Kosslyn (1994) model

An alternative argument here is to consider that there is an independent short-term memory system in addition to a cache. Such a system would bear comparison with Kosslyn's (1994) visual buffer and, as is the case with the Kosslyn buffer, be . accessed directly from external sources or from internal structures (see chapters 2 and 3, this volume). In this regard, the cache could be considered an internal structure that can access the buffer – and be accessed from the buffer – and where material in the cache can be made more explicit. However, external, explicit information may also access the buffer. Within Kosslyn's model, the buffer is considered to be a memory structure, with the clear view that its content can be lost. In this case, the buffer is a short-term memory while the cache is pushed further back in the system where it is better described as an episodic memory, holding implicit, semantically coded information in keeping with the "compressed image" description used by Kosslyn (1994, p. 325) of his pattern activation system (PAS). Pearson (2001) has also presented a theoretical discussion of this sort.

Within this view, the buffer would again be the structure that contained the visually generated image held in visual consciousness. Exclusively, it would represent visual detail. Being directly susceptible to outside interference, it would be susceptible to interference from DVN. Following this argument, the cache would be, as Logie argues, a knowledge-based system holding interpreted information. It will communicate with the buffer but would not be directly accessible from external sources. The material it held would not be in conscious awareness. As such, it would be impervious to DVN.

How might this explain the inability of DVN to interfere with the block diagrams of Avons and Sestieri (2005), the matrices and Chinese characters of Andrade et al. (2002), and, more recently, the geometrical patterns of Burin, Irrazabal, and Quinn (2007)? It could be argued that such information does not need to be held in consciousness. Block diagrams, Chinese characters, and geometrical patterns can be rapidly interpreted and coded. Moreover, such forms are not new and are likely to have been encountered and coded before. The parsing mechanism is yet to be firmly established, but it could be speculated that a visual semantics associated with the meaning of form would be involved, resulting in Kosslyn's compressed image, or, using Logie's more prosaic language, it would follow that "the visual cache contains more visual information than does the conscious image" (Logie, 1995, p. 129). Information in this system, the PAS, or the cache, could be regenerated as needed to fulfill the functions required of the participants. The details of color or of pattern shown by Dean, Dewhurst, and Whittaker (2008) and Dent (2010), or the more idiosyncratic image associated with mnemonics, are less likely to be encoded in any semantic memory and may be more susceptible to the short-term processes associated with the visual buffer, and so be more vulnerable to external interference.

There is some empirical evidence for this position. Quinn and McConnell (2006) replicated the effect of DVN on the pegword mnemonic, showing interference during the encoding phase and the retrieval phase of their experiment. However, during the maintenance phase of several seconds, they found no indications of DVN interference. Nevertheless, during that period, reminiscence effects that are associated with visual processes (Erdelyi & Becker, 1974; Roediger & Payne, 1982) were strongly in evidence: whereas the expected fall in verbally processed memory of the items was seen during the maintenance period, words processed under the imagery condition improved during that period. It is clear form these results that there can be visual encoding that is not open to interference by DVN. This aspect of the research fits in with Andrade et al. (2002) and with Avons and Sestieri (2005), whose careful experiments also ensured that their materials showed evidence of visual processing yet remained impervious to interference. An interpretation in terms of two visual stores, each with independent memorial consequences, would begin to answer this problem. One of these stores would reflect the visual buffer and retain depictive information, in keeping with Kosslyn's (1994) approach, while the other would be a semantically based store, perhaps overlapping with the current understanding of Logie's (1995) cache.

Of some relevance here, Parker and Dagnall (2009) also talk of a two-step model based on event related potential (ERP) distribution when interpreting the effect of DVN on concrete words. Following the work of Schie, Wijers, Mars, Benjamins, and Stowe (2005), they differentiate cognitively between the initial frontal N400, perhaps associated with a previsual stage, and a slow negative wave that can emerge between 1,400 and 3,300 ms and may be associated with the visual buffer.

Function of inner scribe

The properties of both the PAS and the cache remain a matter of debate. The cache, in particular, has been difficult to pin down, mainly because, as the only visual memory component within the Logie visual memory model, it has been given rather a lot to do (Quinn, 2008). Moreover, separating out the cache from the executive and spatial processes is proving difficult. On the basis of the Logie model, an image that is generated and re-generated as a result of executive processes yet is reliant on the cache is likely to present particular problems of dissociation and definition. Zimmer and his colleagues (Zimmer, 2008; Zimmer, Speiser, & Seidler, 2003) have pointed out the contradictions and difficulties associated with the coding processes attributed to the visual cache and the inner scribe. Distinctions between apparently visual items such as color and form, and more spatial items such as location, extent, and movement, are difficult to sustain, in particular when the human operator is taken into account. In addition, complications in the memorability of spatial displays – for example, caused by path crossing – suggest that a purely spatial or movement type of coding may not provide a sufficient account of the processes involved (Parmentier & Andres, 2006; Parmentier, Elford, & Maybery, 2005). Indeed, problems of dissociation may not exist only among the visual cache, inner scribe, and executive processes; the Visual Patterns Test, a popular test of specifically visual memory (Della Sala, Gray, Baddeley, & Wilson, 1997) may involve a greater degree of reliance on verbal processes than has been previously considered (Brown, Forbes, & McConnell, 2006).

While the properties of the component parts of the cache and scribe may be difficult to pin down, the major function of the inner scribe is more clear. It is twofold: first, it is the means of representing space/movement; second, it is a rehearsal mechanism for the cache. This second role is particularly problematic. In addition to the close coupling issue alluded to by Annett (1995), where he notes the logical problem of having a spatial/movement mechanism as a rehearsal mechanism for a visual store compared to the less problematic verbal WM rehearsal mechanism where phonology is rehearsed by phonology, the evidence of movement as a means of rehearsal is now being reconsidered. Much of the information in favor of the inner scribe as a mechanism for rehearsing of the cache comes from a period in the development of the concept of WM where there was uncertainty about what counted as visuo-spatial processing. One reason for the uncertainty was the then heavy reliance on a very few empirical approaches borrowed from adjunct areas of research. Prominent among the empirical techniques were the Corsi block test and the series of experimental approaches introduced by Brooks (1967, 1968). These tests put the emphasis on spatial processing as reflecting VSWM. However, with subsequent evidence detailing the part given to visual processing (Logie, 1986), both visual and spatial components found their way into a composite model. The rehearsal function that is considered to define the relationship between the two components makes them awkward bedfellows. Initially the two parts were seen as a mirror of the two-component model of verbal WM, where an active phonological rehearsal component rehearsed a passive phonological store. While it is the case that a disruption of spatial retention, such as of the Brooks (1967) test, is caused by conflicting movements and that the Corsi block test is also disrupted by simultaneous tapping (e.g., Smyth, Pearson, & Pendleton, 1988), the failure to isolate the attention component of these interfering acts weakens any interpretation in terms of a movement mechanism disrupting a spatial retention.

Attention as a rehearsal mechanism for visual WM

Evidence apparently supporting the disruption of spatial retention by incompatible and simultaneous movement has been widely reported over several decades (e.g., Baddeley & Lieberman, 1980; Logie, Zucco, & Baddeley, 1990; Quinn & Ralston, 1986; Smyth, Pearson, & Pendleton, 1988). However, scrutiny of experiments showing the effect of incompatible movement with spatial processing shows that a confounding of movement with attention is apparently omnipresent. For example, Quinn and Ralston (1986) reported a clear affect of incompatible movement on recall of the Brooks (1967) test, and further reported disruption when the incompatible movement was claimed to be passive – that is, participants relaxed their hand and allowed it to be moved for them by the experimenter. This apparently passive movement strengthened the conclusion that it was the incompatible movement itself that caused interference. However, a further condition, introduced by Quinn (1994), served to undermine this conclusion. Quinn (1994) made the movement not only passive but also unpredictable by changing the incompatible movement from trial to trial. When the incompatible movement was not changed from trial to trial, as in the Quinn and Ralston (1986) report, there was clear disruption of the retention of the Brooks test. However, when the condition involving unpredictability was introduced, no disruption was to be found. Quinn (1994) concluded that the predictability of the incompatible movement was sufficient to engage attention processes and that it is these processes rather than any movement processes which caused the interference. In a more recent experiment that also used a dual-task technique to show disruption of spatial retention, Postle, Idzikowski, Della Sala, Logie, and Baddeley (2006) demonstrated that eye movement control was important in the maintenance of visuo-spatial information. Referencing a number of researchers, such as those mentioned above who have shown disruption to spatial WM using a number of different effectors, the authors further speculate that the common mechanism may be an effector-independent motor plan. However, as disruption was significant under instruction to the participants to move their eyes any way they liked (Postle et al., 2006, Expt. 4), any motor plan at least in this condition would have been of a rudimentary nature. The authors concede that the experimental series did not address the possibility that control of visual attention may be the relevant underpinning mechanism.

Nevertheless, they imply that the control of, in particular, eye movements is likely to play a part in VSWM on the grounds that when eye movements have been contrasted with only shifts of spatial attention, the latter leads to notably smaller disruption. Yet this suggestion is far from convincing, since a contrast between attention shifts and eye movements in the experimental evidence cited (Lawrence, Myerson, & Abrams, 2004; Pearson & Sahraie, 2003) involved the eyes having to be moved to and focused and refocused on particular targets. Focusing and re-focusing on the targets themselves, an activity that is likely to draw on attention, irrespective of the movement, may have contributed independently to the disruption caused. On the basis of these results, it seems more plausible to suggest that attention rather than movement or movement plan may underpin retention in VSWM.

In addition to any critique of an especially close and functional relationship between movement and short-term visual maintenance, a number of sources have pointed to the close involvement of attention and visuo-spatial memory. Awh, Jonides, and Reuter-Lorenz (1998) provided evidence for selective spatial attention being the mediator for spatial WM. Where information was to be displayed at a particular location, attention at that location improved stimulus processing. In an experiment that controlled overt eye movements, an explanation in terms of covert eye movements seems unlikely since, in addition to evidence that the processes of attention and oculomotor programming can be dissociated (e.g., Reuter-Lorenz & Fendrich, 1992), when attention was directed to nonmemorized locations, discrimination performance was poor. The relationship of spatial WM to attention has been noted for sometime. Quinn (1988) drew attention to this, and the greater dependence of spatial than, for example, verbal memory on executive resources has also been indicated by Salway and Logie (1995) and by Vandierendonck, Kemps, Fastame, and Szmalec (2004). In a similar vein, using a psychometric approach, Thompson et al. (2006) indicated that the Corsi block task was heavily loaded on executive processes yet showed no loading on a visual factor. Of some interest is their finding that although the visual patterns test (VPT) did show loading on a visual factor, it also had significant loading on executive processes, perhaps indicating a similarity of processes used in recalling the Corsi block task and the VPT or that visual memory also requires significant executive processes.

Recently, Narimoto (2011) and Narimoto and Quinn (2011) have looked closely at the relationship between imagery and visual memory along with the processes on which they depend. They directly compared performance on two tasks – one where participants had to follow instructions and generate an image of a figure from piecemeal input, and one involving the visual presentation of a complete visual figure. Both tasks were designed to be of equal difficulty. In the image task, participants had to build up a pattern by following instructions to put together a sequence of lines and then retain the pattern for 11 s before recalling it. In the visual condition, a pattern already constructed was presented for later recall. During the retention period, four interfering tasks were presented: first, and as a control, articulatory suppression that was not expected to have any effect; second, a tapping task where participants had to press a button on the four corners of a square shape; third, an irrelevant-pictures task where abstract drawing were presented to the participants, who had to watch the pictures but do nothing in addition to this; finally, participants had to complete a random number generation (RNG) task. The results showed that the image task where the image had to be built up line by line was affected by the RNG task, whereas the visual task was affected only by tapping. Figure 5.2 illustrates the performance of the participants under the interference conditions of the experiment.

The irrelevant-pictures task, using the abstract drawings, had no interfering effect. However, when the irrelevant pictures were changed to pictures of line drawings more similar to the primary task material, an interfering effect was found with the visual presentation but not with the constructed image. This last finding is similar to that reported by Burin, Irrazabal, and Quinn (2007), who reported that although DVN had no effect on the retention of geometric patterns, interference more similar to the patterns themselves did cause disruption. These results suggest a very strong affinity between visuo-spatial and executive processes. The distinction between spatial and executive processes is often difficult to sustain at the purely behavioral level, though the behavioral evidence for separable visual and executive processes is more clear.

The affinity between visuo-spatial processes and executive processes, particularly those involved with attention, suggests that the inner scribe as a rehearsal mechanism may not be the most convincing way of characterizing the relationship between it and the cache. Moreover, without its major function of rehearsing the contents of a cache, the concept of an inner scribe may require reconsideration.

Cornoldi and Vecchi (2003) have also provided a different characterization where spatial and visual are separate components without any specified functional relationship. Their perspective is less suited to a traditional "box" model; rather, theirs is a model where the elements within it are continuous in one, perhaps two,

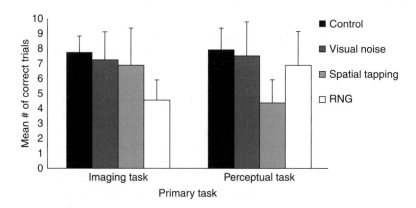

Figure 5.2 Mean numbers of correct trials and standard deviations in the imaging task and the perceptual task as a function of interference tasks: the control condition, the visual noise (VN) task, the spatial tapping task, and the random number generation (RNG) task. (Taken from Narimoto & Quinn, 2011.)

major dimensions, vertical and horizontal. Of interest here and referring to the horizontal dimension where modal specificity is retained, they consider that spatial WM should be considered to be a quite separate component from visual WM, with no particularly strong relationship between the two. Moreover, Cornoldi and Vecchi consider that the spatial element should be subdivided into sequentially and simultaneously presented spatial material. This distinction may well provide a theoretical context that serves to differentiate the elements within spatial encoding that are more associated or are less associated with executive processes and so place the distinction between the executive and spatial processes in a more revealing light. Evidence in favor of differentiating simultaneous and sequential processing comes principally from the field of individual differences, where they have shown that deficits can occur independently in spatial sequential and spatial simultaneous tasks (Mammarella et al., 2006). Developmental studies have also suggested that a distinction between active and passive visuo-spatial memory is required. Using a static and a dynamic presentation of matrix and maze forms, Pickering, Gathercole, Hall, and Lloyd (2001) were able to demonstrate fractionation between the two forms of presentation. Presentations of static matrix forms not only led to superior performance when compared to dynamic and sequential presentation of the matrices but the superior static performance increased more steeply with age. The same pattern of results was found when maze routes were used instead of matrices, illustrating that the effect was not associated with a particular stimulus type but reflected more general visuo-spatial processes.

The vertical dimension of the Cornoldi and Vecchi model represents some measure of cognitive activity such that an active task – for example, one involving manipulation of material – would be placed towards the apex of the model. Again, evidence has been provided suggesting that this perspective provides insight into behavior. Downs syndrome individuals were shown to perform normally where their VSWM tasks required little active control, but they performed poorly where there was a need for active control. Interestingly, performance in the verbal domain did not show this distinction, again indicating the independence of verbal and visuo-spatial phenomena (Lanfranchi, Cornoldi, & Vianello, 2004). While it is clear that the lower levels of the Cornoldi and Vecchi model incorporate modality specificity, the modal status of the higher levels remains unclear, a complication of a continuous model where modality specificity funnels up to a level of operation that is equally relevant to all modalities. At the very highest level, representing the most active level of cognitive undertaking, there appears to be amodality or multi-modality, as in the Baddeley and Hitch model (1974).

The results of Narimoto and Quinn (2011) contribute to the debate on the relationship among the retention of a constructed visual image, retention of a visual memory, and executive processes. RNG is generally regarded as a task that taxes executive processes (Baddeley, 2007), and while it has a verbal element, the lack of an effect of articulatory suppression suggests that its disruptive effect was mediated by the executive processes involved in the retention of the constructed image. This is consistent with the work of Andrade et al. (2002) and of Logie (2003), who have argued that there may be a significant executive element in the constructed image. However, this seems more plausible where the image is a line diagram generated line by line and less plausible where the image construction is appropriate to training on the pegword mnemonic where the visual processes are intuitively more prominent. Moreover, as the irrelevant-pictures task is a notably passive task, as might be defined by Cornoldi and Vecchi (2003), it would be expected to have its effect at a lower, more modality-specific, level. As there was no effect of the practiced tapping on the image, it appears that the constructed image of the line diagram is particularly dependent on executive coding, perhaps relating sequential or active spatial process more closely to executive processes. However, the visual memory was affected by tapping, suggesting that it was retained in a spatial rather than a visual mechanism. Yet, the subsequent interference caused by irrelevant similar pictures may reflect a visual coding or may imply that the similar primary and secondary tasks both had sufficiently similar spatial elements that constituted the main locus of the interference. At this stage, and following Burin, Irrazabal, and Quinn (2007), we cannot, with any confidence, rule out that the visual input could also be semantically coded into a cache-type system with the visual semantics coding properties sensitive to the form or shape of the items. The disruptive effects of the similar irrelevant pictures, in contrast to the abstract irrelevant pictures, would also be consistent with this interpretation. Similarly, the practiced tapping, forming the square shape, may have been sufficiently similar to the memory material to have caused some interference.

Conclusion

The main thrust of this chapter was to look at the contribution of theory to the continuing development of the concept of VSWM. In the process of doing so, certain interpretations – such as the means of access to the system and the interpretation of movement as a rehearsal mechanism for visual material – were re-examined. Initial evidence for this latter interpretation within the WM framework of Baddeley and Hitch (1974; Baddeley, 1986) was strong. However, alternative frameworks, including that of Kosslyn (1994) and more recently of Cornoldi and Vecchi (2003), suggested a different interpretation. It was argued that, for the most part, movement has been confounded with attention to that movement and that attention might underpin any disruption. Whenever movement has been distinguished from attention to the movement, no effect of movement can be seen. It was further argued that this holds for movements of the eyes; while there has been some suggestion that eye movements do contribute over and above the effects of attention, it was argued that the results apparently showing eye movement effects are also confounded, usually with the extra processes required to focus on discrete targets that play a crucial part in the relevant eye movement experiments. These results suggest, in keeping with the clear trend in VSWM, that the rehearsal mechanism for visual WM lies in the action of attention or executive processes. This is turn suggests that the models themselves should be reconfigured where necessary to bring attention more into focus and that the relationship between attention on the one hand and a spatial store and, perhaps to a lesser extent, a visual store on the other should be reconsidered. Kosslyn's (1994) model of visual processing has several component parts that seem to talk to this understanding of VSWM. Material in visual conscious awareness is contained in the visual buffer – more accurately, it is contained within the attention window of the visual buffer – and so the model makes explicit the intimate relationship held between attention and conscious visual memory. Within this model, the buffer is a separate memory store with properties distinct from the properties ascribed to the visual cache. Being a separate and independent store, disruption can cause material to be forgotten. Moreover, access can be direct from the environment or can be indirect from the PAS. Logie (1995) also discusses an image created through the action of executive processes. However, in spite of the executive processes of generation and regeneration and of zooming and manipulation associated with the image, Logie (1995) argues that the image is, in fact, reliant on the cache and is not independent of it. This would seem to give the image a structurally complicated and confusing status within WM. Cornoldi and Vecchi (2003) accept not only a distinction between visual and spatial processes but, additionally, break down the spatial into spatial simultaneous and spatial sequential. Such a distinction between the simultaneous and the sequential may be, in their terminology, in the vertical rather than the horizontal dimension, with the more active spatial sequential coding being more closely allied to executive involvement.

In arguing in favor of the role of attention in visual memory, no attempt is being made to argue against a spatial component of WM. Indeed, there is a wealth of evidence over the last thirty years testifying to the separate existence of visual and spatial mechanisms. The clear and convincing evidence comes from both cognitive and neuropsychology research (for reviews, see, among others, Baddeley, 1986, 2007; Logie, 2003). How best to conceptualize the relationship between visual and spatial material remains an issue. Several other models blur the identity between visual and spatial, or indeed between visual and verbal, with respect to rehearsal processes (Barrouillet, Bernardin, & Camos, 2004; Cowan, 2005). Indeed, Cornoldi and Vecchi's continuous model, where all modality-specific processes funnel up to what appears to be an amodel or multimodel apex related to high cognitive activation, leaves it unclear when modality specificity becomes apparent. The more discrete model of WM initiated by Baddeley and Hitch (1974) has separate modality-specific stores, with an executive component that was originally amodal and uniform. However, at least since Lehto's (1996) demonstration that there are likely to be a number of uncorrelated processes involved within the executive component, this is being reconsidered (Baddeley, 2007). The popularity of a perspective where visual attention has played a major part, including work on binding (Allen, Baddeley, & Hitch, 2006; Wheeler & Treisman, 2002), may suggest that executive processes should include a modality-specific visual and/or spatial attention component. Indeed, as is the case with the model of Kosslyn, there may be a notably strong relationship between visuo-spatial memory and visual attention which is not mirrored in the case of verbal material, an idea that has some support within the Baddeley and Hitch (1974) WM tradition (Quinn, 1991; Salway & Logie, 1995).

References

Allen, R., Baddeley, A. D., & Hitch, G. J. (2006). Is the binding of visual features in working memory resource-demanding? *Journal of Experimental Psychology: General*, *135*, 298–313.

Andrade, J., Kemps, E., Werniers, Y., & Szmalec, A. (2002). Insensitivity of visual short-term memory to irrelevant visual information. *Quarterly Journal of Experimental Psychology*, *55A*, 753–774.

Annett, J. (1995). Motor imagery: Perception or action? *Neuropsychologia*, *33*, 1395–1417.

Avons, S. E., & Sestieri, C. (2005). Dynamic visual noise: No interference with visual short-term memory or the construction of visual images. *European Journal of Cognitive Psychology*, *17*, 405–424.

Awh, E., Jonides, J., & Reuter-Lorenz, P. A. (1998). Rehearsal in spatial working memory. *Journal of Experimental Psychology: Human Perception and Performance*, *24*, 780–790.

Baddeley, A. (1986). *Working memory*. Oxford, UK: Oxford University Press.

Baddeley, A. (2007). *Working memory, thought and action*. Oxford, UK: Oxford University Press.

Baddeley, A. D., & Hitch, G. J. (1974). Working memory. In G. Bower (Ed.), *Recent advances in learning and motivation*, (Vol. 8, pp 47–90). New York: Academic Press.

Baddeley, A. D., & Lieberman, K. (1980). Spatial working memory. In R. Nickerson (Ed.), *Attention and performance VIII* (pp. 521–539). Hillsdale, NJ: Lawrence Erlbaum Associates.

Barrouillet, P., Bernardin, S., & Camos, C. (2004). Time constraints and resource sharing in adults' working memory spans. *Journal of Experimental Psychology: General*, *133*, 83–100.

Beschin, N., Cocchini, G., Della Sala, S., & Logie, R. H. (1997). What the eyes perceive the brain ignores: A case of pure unilateral representational neglect. *Cortex*, *33*, 3–26.

Brooks, L. R. (1967). The suppression of visualisation by reading. *Quarterly Journal of Experimental Psychology*, *19*, 289–299.

Brooks, L. R. (1968). Spatial and verbal components in the act of recall. *Canadian Journal of Psychology*, *22*, 349–368.

Brown, L. A., Forbes, D., & McConnell, J. (2006). Limiting the use of verbal coding in the Visual Patterns Test. *Quarterly Journal of Experimental Psychology*, *59*, 1169–1176.

Burin, D. I., Irrazabal, N., & Quinn, J. G. (2007). Maintenance in visuo-spatial working memory. *Psychologia*, *50*, 90–101.

Cornoldi, C., & Vecchi, T. (2003). *Visuo-spatial working memory and individual differences*. Hove, UK: Psychology Press

Cowan, N. (2005). *Working memory capacity*. Hove, UK: Psychology Press.

Dean, G. M., Dewhurst, S. A., & Whittaker, A. (2008). Dynamic visual noise interferes with storage in visual working memory. *Experimental Psychology*, *55*, 283–289.

Della Sala, S., Gray, C., Baddeley, A., & Wilson, L. (1997). *The Visual Patterns Test (VPT): A quick measure of short-term visual memory*. Bury St Edmunds, UK: Thames Valley Test Company.

Dent, K. (2010). Dynamic visual noise affects visual short-term memory for surface color but not spatial location. *Experimental Psychology, 57*, 17–26.

Erdelyi, M. H., & Becker, J. (1974). Hypermnesia for pictures: Incremental memory for pictures but not for words in multiple recall trials. *Cognitive Psychology, 6*, 159–171.

Jones, D., Hughes, R. W., & Macken, W. J. (2006). Perceptual organisation masquerading as phonological storage: Further support for the perceptual-gestural view of short-term memory. *Journal of Memory and Language, 54*, 265–281.

Jones, D., Hughes, R. W., & Macken, W. J. (2007). The phonological store abandoned. *Quarterly Journal of Experimental Psychology, 60*, 505–511.

Kosslyn, S. M. (1994). *Image and brain: The resolution of the imagery debate*. Cambridge, MA: MIT Press.

Kosslyn, S. M., Thompson, W. L., & Ganis, G. (2006). *The case for mental imagery*. Oxford, UK: Oxford University Press.

Lanfranchi, S., Cornoldi, C., & Vianello, R. (2004). Verbal and visuo-spatial working memory deficits in children with Down syndrome. *American Journal on Mental Retardation, 6*, 456–466.

Lawrence, B. M., Myerson, J., & Abrams, R. A. (2004). Interference with spatial working memory: An eye movement is more than a shift of attention. *Psychonomic Bulletin and Review, 11*, 488–494.

Lehto, J. (1996). Are executive function tests dependent on working memory capacity? *Quarterly Journal of Experimental Psychology, 49A*, 21–50.

Logie, R. H. (1986). Visuo-spatial processing in working memory. *Quarterly Journal of Experimental Psychology, 38A*, 229–247.

Logie, R. H. (1995). *Visuo-spatial working memory*. Hove, UK: Lawrence Erlbaum Associates.

Logie, R. H. (2003). Spatial and visual working memory: A mental workspace. In D. E. Irwin & B. H. Ross (Eds.), *The psychology of learning and motivation. Advances in research and theory: Cognitive vision* (Vol. 42, pp. 37–78). San Diego, CA: Academic Press.

Logie, R. H., Zucco, G., & Baddeley, A. (1990). Interference with visual short-term memory. *Acta Psychologica, 75*, 55–74.

Mammarella, I. C., Cornoldi, C., Pazzaglia, F., Toso, C., Grimoldi, M., & Vio, C. (2006). Evidence for a double dissociation between spatial-simultaneous and spatial-sequential working memory in visuo-spatial (nonverbal) learning. *Brain and Cognition, 62*, 58–67.

McConnell, J., & Quinn, J. G. (2000). Interference in visual working memory. *Quarterly Journal of Experimental Psychology, 53A*, 53–67.

McConnell, J., & Quinn, J. G. (2004). Complexity factors in visuo-spatial working *Memory, 12*, 338–350.

Narimoto, T. (2011). The role of the central executive in the storage of visually constructed images. *Japanese Journal of Cognitive Psychology, 8*, 99–108.

Narimoto, T., & Quinn, G. (2011). *The involvement of executive processes in visuo-spatial working memory: Differences between a visually generated image and a visually presented percept*. Manuscript submitted for publication.

Parker, A., & Dagnall, N. (2009). Concreteness effects revisited: The influence of dynamic visual noise on memory for concrete and abstract words. *Memory, 17*, 397–410.

Parmentier, F. B. R, & Andres, P. (2006). The impact of path crossing on visuo-spatial serial memory: Encoding or rehearsal effect? *Quarterly Journal of Experimental Psychology, 59*, 1867–1874.

Parmentier, F. B. R, Elford, G., & Maybery, M. T. (2005). Transitional information in spatial serial recall: Path characteristics affect recall performance. *Journal of Experimental Psychology: Learning, Memory and Cognition, 31*, 412–427.

Pearson, D. G. (2001). Imagery and the visuo-spatial sketchpad. In J. Andrade (Ed.), *Working memory in perspective*. Hove, UK: Psychology Press.

Pearson, D. G., & Sahraie, A. (2003). Oculomotor control and the maintenance of spatially and temporally distributed events in visuo-spatial working memory. *Quarterly Journal of Experimental Psychology, 56A*, 1089–1111.

Pickering, S. J., Gathercole, S. E., Hall, M., & Lloyd, S. A. (2001). Development of memory for pattern and path: Further evidence for the fractionation of visuo-spatial memory. *Quarterly Journal of Experimental Psychology, 54A*, 397–420.

Postle, B. R., Idzikowski, C., Della Sala, S., Logie, R. H., & Baddeley, A. D. (2006). The selective disruption of spatial working memory by eye movements. *Quarterly Journal of Experimental Psychology, 59*, 100–120.

Quinn, G. (1988). Interference effects in the visuo-spatial sketchpad. In M. Denis, J. Englekamp, & J. T. E. Richardson (Eds.), *Cognitive and neuropsychological approaches to mental imagery* (pp. 181–189). Amsterdam: Martinus Nijhoff.

Quinn, J. G. (1991). Encoding and maintenance of information in visual working memory. In R. H. Logie & M. Denis (Eds.), *Mental images in human cognition*. Amsterdam: Elsevier.

Quinn, J. G. (1994). Towards a clarification of spatial processing. *Quarterly Journal of Experimental Psychology, 47A*, 465–480.

Quinn, J. G. (2008). Movement and visual coding: The structure of visuo-spatial working memory. *Cognitive Processing, 9*, 35–43.

Quinn, J. G., & McConnell, J. (1996). Irrelevant pictures in visual working memory. *Quarterly Journal of Experimental Psychology, 49A*, 200–215.

Quinn, J. G., & McConnell, J. (2006). The interval for interference in conscious visual imagery. *Memory, 14*, 241–252.

Quinn, J. G., & Ralston, G. E. (1986). Movement and attention in visual working memory. *Quarterly Journal of Experimental Psychology, 38A*, 689–703.

Reuter-Lorenz, P. A., & Fendrich, R. (1992). Oculomotor readiness and covert orienting: Differences between central and peripheral precues. *Perception and Psychophysics, 52*, 336–344.

Roediger, H. L., & Payne, D. G. (1982). Hypermnesia: The role of repeated testing. *Journal of Experimental Psychology: Learning, Memory and Cognition, 8*, 66–72.

Saito, S. (1994). What effect can rhythmic finger tapping have on the phonological similarity effect? *Memory and Cognition, 22*, 181–187.

Salamé, P., & Baddeley, A. (1982). Disruption of short-term memory by unattended speech: Implications for the structure of working memory. *Journal of Verbal Learning and Verbal Behavior, 21*, 150–164.

Salway, A. F. S., & Logie, R. H. (1995). Visuospatial working memory, movement control and executive demands. *British Journal of Psychology, 86*, 253–269.

Schie, H. T., Wijers, A. A., Mars, R. B., Benjamins, J. S., & Stowe, L. A. (2005). Processing of visual semantic information to concrete words: Temporal dynamics and neural mechanisms indicated by event-related potentials. *Cognitive Neuropsychology, 22*, 364–386.

Smyth, M. M., Pearson, N. A., & Pendleton, R. A. (1988). Movement and working memory: Patterns and positions in space. *Quarterly Journal of Experimental Psychology, 41A*, 497–514.

Thompson, J. M., Hamilton, C., Gray, J. M., Quinn, J. G. Mackin, P., Young, A. H., et al. (2006). Executive and visuo-spatial sketchpad resources in euthymic bipolar disorder: Implications for visuospatial working memory architecture. *Memory, 14*, 437–451.

Vandierendonck, A., Kemps, E., Fastame M. C., & Szmalec, A. (2004). Working memory components of the Corsi blocks task. *British Journal of Psychology, 95*, 57–79.

Wheeler, M. E., & Treisman, A. M. (2002). Binding in short-term visual memory. *Journal of Experimental Psychology: General, 131*, 48–64.

Zimmer, H. D. (2008). Visual and spatial working memory: From boxes to networks. *Neuroscience & Biobehavioral Reviews, 32*, 1372–1395.

Zimmer, H. D., Speiser, H. R., & Seidler, B. (2003). Spatio-temporal working memory and short-term object location tasks use different memory mechanisms. *Acta Psychologica, 114*, 41–65.

Part IV

Language, space, and action

6 Individual differences in spatial text processing

Francesca Pazzaglia, Valérie Gyselinck, Cesare Cornoldi, and Rossana De Beni

Spatial cognition is the most basic of the cognitive abilities and is fundamental for the survival of any organism. In all species, the capacity to represent spatial information is involved in many crucial activities, such as fleeing from predators, finding food, or finding the way home. The processes involved in constructing mental representations of space have been studied intensively since the concept of "cognitive maps" was introduced in the first half of the twentieth century by Tolman (1948). A growing number of studies have now emerged in this field of research across various disciplines of the cognitive sciences (cognitive psychology, linguistics, and engineering). The findings from these studies cast light on the nature of our spatial representations and the processes by which they are constructed, taking into account the various cognitive constraints present. Finding the way around a large-scale environment is one of the multiple ways of learning and using information about space. Animals can build spatial representations of physical surroundings by viewing, hearing, touching, or moving around objects in the environment. But many other ways of acquiring spatial information are available, and the question then arises of what specific effects these various modalities of acquiring spatial information have on the characteristics of the spatial representations generated. In particular, humans have the capacity to construct abstract spatial representations through the use of symbolic supports such as language and maps. A number of recent studies have attempted to gain an understanding of spatial descriptions, in particular verbal itineraries (e.g., Denis, Daniel, Fontaine, & Pazzaglia, 2001); this constitutes a field in its own right, at the intersection between the study of text comprehension and that of spatial cognition.

But whatever the mode of presentation of spatial information, constructing a successful spatial representation involves a combination of capacities. Intact general cognitive capacities – including inferences and planning – are obvious necessities, as is verbal comprehension in the case of spatial descriptions. A number of more specific spatial skills also come into play, which typically show wide individual differences, such as mental rotation abilities, capacity to reason about spatial perspectives, memory for location, sense of direction, and map retention (Fields & Shelton, 2006). In addition, the ability to construct spatial representations varies between individuals and is presumed to change with age.

This chapter reviews a wide range of studies on the comprehension of spatial descriptions, in particular considering the role of individual differences. Evidence is shown that spatial abilities and visuospatial working memory (VSWM) are specifically involved in spatial text processing. These two related areas are receiving much attention today, very largely as a result of seminal work by Michel Denis.

To start, we give an overview of current text comprehension theories, with specific focus on Johnson-Laird's mental model theory (1980, 1983), widely used in the field of spatial text processing. The most widely recognized findings on spatial models are then reviewed, followed by an examination of individual differences with reference to spatial abilities, working memory (WM), imagery strategies, and aging. Evidence is given of the various levels of involvement of all these abilities and capacities in the processing of spatial descriptions.

Text comprehension

Three levels of representation

Theories of language comprehension commonly assume that texts or discourses are represented at three levels (Johnson-Laird, 1980, 1983; Kintsch, 1988; van Dijk & Kintsch, 1983). Van Dijk and Kintsch (1983) considered that, at the first level, a word-for-word representation is derived, which is called the surface level. At the second level, a propositional text-base is derived. This is a representation reflecting the microstructure and macrostructure of the text. Finally, at the third level, a more general representation (sometimes termed as a "situation model") is built. This contains the information that is implicit in the text. The situation model reflects the domain structure – that is, it is "a fragment of the world" (van Dijk, 1987) – and is the product of the interaction between information provided by the text and knowledge of the world, including knowledge of the reader's objectives and attitudes. Thus, to understand a text it is necessary to represent its meaning incorporating relevant world knowledge in the literal meaning of the text.

The three representation levels considered by Johnson-Laird (1983) are: a graphemic (or phonemic) representation, a propositional representation, and a mental model. The second stage of text comprehension is regarded as the automatic construction of a propositional or linguistic representation of the text that is close to the surface form of the text. In the third stage of comprehension, a procedural semantics acts on the propositional representation to construct a mental model. It is a representation of a state of affairs (objects, events, and processes) described in the text, not a description of the text itself. A mental model is defined as an internal model of the world that is analogous to the structure of the corresponding state of affairs in the world – as we perceive or conceive it.

Considering that surface and propositional representations alone were not sufficient to account for comprehension, various experiments were designed to validate the relevance of a representation of the situation portrayed by a text (e.g.,

Garnham, 1981; Mani & Johnson-Laird, 1982), while others were carried out to validate the three levels postulated by van Dijk and Kintsch (1983) (Fletcher & Chrysler, 1990; Perrig & Kintsch, 1985; Schmalhofer & Glavanov, 1986).

On one level of interpretation, situation models (as described by some authors – e.g., van Dijk & Kintsch, 1983) and mental models (as described by Johnson-Laird, 1983) are very similar, and several authors have used them synonymously. Both refer to the episodic representation of the situation presented in the text and, more generally, to the representation of what the text conveys beyond the linguistic representation of the text itself. According to the views of Johnson-Laird and of Kintsch, both explicit information in the text and the reader's inferences based on world knowledge contribute to text representation. Hence, inference processes play a central role in the construction of a mental model (or situation model), which is both the by-product of and the source for inferences. The acceptance of such a proposal leads to assessment of a subject's comprehension of a text via his or her ability to generate elaborative inferences (e.g., Kintsch, Welsch, Schmalhofer, & Zimny, 1990; Perrig & Kintsch, 1985; Tardieu, Ehrlich, & Gyselinck, 1992; Taylor & Tversky, 1992a). In contrast, using tasks that involve literal sentences or paraphrases should address the linguistic representation. Thus, the quality and/or speed of responses to such tests should reflect the quality and level of the representation built and, as such, are commonly used in studies on text processing.

Mental models and images

But despite the similarities between the views of Johnson-Laird and Kintsch, the propositional representation suggested by Johnson-Laird (1983) is not identical to the propositional text-base in the model described by van Dijk and Kintsch (1983). More importantly, a mental model is necessarily nonpropositional, whereas a situation model is mostly propositional (see Kintsch, 1988; Kintsch et al., 1990). A specific element of Johnson-Laird's theory is the notion of isomorphism to the world: a mental model has a structure analogous to that of the situation it represents, and its content corresponds to the objects and events of the world.

According to Johnson-Laird (1980), a propositional representation can thus be summarized as:

> A propositional representation is a description of a state of affairs, which may be true or false. It is evaluated with respect to a model representing that state of affairs.
>
> The initial, and sometimes perhaps only, stage in comprehension consists in creating a propositional representation: a linear string of symbols in a mental language that has an arbitrary (and as yet unknown) syntactic structure and a lexicon that closely corresponds to that of natural language. This representation can be used to construct a mental model, which represents information analogically: its structure is a crucial part of the representation. Models can also be set up directly from perception.

A propositional representation encodes determinate and indeterminate information in a uniform way, and makes no use of arbitrary assumptions. A mental model of the state of affairs described in a proposition may embody a number of arbitrary assumptions since language is inherently vague. Indeterminate information is encoded either by utilizing a set of alternative models, or else by incorporating a propositional representation in a "hybrid" way. The two sorts of representation do not necessarily yield the same equivalence classes, and hence there is no guarantee that a theory embodying one can be made to mimic the other.

A model represented in a dimensional space can be directly constructed, manipulated, or scanned, in any way that can be controlled by dimensional variables. A propositional representation lacks this flexibility and can be directly scanned only in those directions that have been laid down between the elements of the representation.

(Johnson-Laird, 1980, p. 108)

Thus, because of its analogical structure, a mental model is close to a mental image (see chapter 9, this volume). A mental model can be seen as a network of relations between representational elements, the tokens. Tokens represent characters, objects, or events of the world. The properties of these entities are represented in the model by the properties of the corresponding tokens, and the spatial, temporal, or causal relations between entities are represented in the model by the relations between tokens. If a reader constructs a mental model of the sentence "the circle is to the right of the triangle", then the model embodies a token corresponding to the circle whose properties correspond to those of the entity represented – a token triangle corresponds to the triangle, and the relationship between the two is represented by the spatial arrangement of the two tokens. The mental model can then be experienced as a mental image. Mental models, as mental images, are analogical internal representations that give the individual creating them a nonlinguistic equivalent to the world. But this similarity between a mental image and a mental model must not tempt us to consider them identical. In the view of Denis and de Vega (1993), both mental images and mental models provide readers with nonlinguistic equivalents of the world and allow for a kind of computation close to the computation one may apply to the world itself. A mental image is, however, a representation of a situation from a certain point of view, whereas a mental model should allow several points of view on a situation. A mental image would thus be one of the procedures contributing to the construction of mental models during the processing of descriptions. Once the model has been constructed, the mental image becomes a device for the instantiation of the model from a particular point of view. This would be true for models that include imaginable data, spatial or even quasi-spatial.

In sum, the assumptions that a mental model is not propositional and has an analogue structure give specificity to Johnson-Laird's view and certainly explain its success in the spatial domain. Many studies carried out on validation of the notion of mental model were conducted with spatial descriptions, and in the field of spatial cognition the notion of a spatial mental model has been largely accepted and is widely used, even though alternatives exist.

The dual-coding theory: an alternative view for spatial text processing?

Kulhavy and collaborators (Dean & Kulhavy, 1981; Kulhavy, Stock, Peterson, Pridemore, & Klein, 1992; Kulhavy, Stock, Verdi, Rittschof, & Savenye, 1993; Kulhavy, Stock, Woodard, & Haygood, 1993) explored the memory of spatial descriptions when these are presented along with a map of the environment, and they explained the facilitative effect of the map using the dual-coding theory (DCT) (Paivio, 1971, 1986). This theory has also been considered by researchers examining the role of imagery in texts. According to this theory, at least two coding systems are available: a verbal system and a nonverbal system. The two systems are independent but interconnected. Pictures (or mental images) are automatically stored in both the verbal system and the nonverbal system (whereas no such systematic claim is made for the processing of verbal material). As a result, pictures are thought to be memorized as such by the reader, who benefits from two memory traces, one in verbal form and one in nonverbal form. This theory has proved very fruitful for explaining a large number of memory effects, such as the image-superiority effect and the concreteness effect. On an initial interpretation, Paivio's theory might also be thought to explain some effects with spatial descriptions. It is sufficient to account for most effects of images and illustrations on the memory of simple material such as words and sentences. However, when the by-products of comprehension and not just memorization are considered, it is not clear how the DCT can account for text comprehension *per se* (for a discussion of some limits of the DCT with texts, see Marschark, 1985; Denis, 1991). Indeed, the DCT makes no assumptions about the construction of mental representations during the reading process, nor about the representational levels at which the interaction between the text and the images or illustrations occurs, and it also fails to explain how people can draw inferences from the information they are given. Nevertheless, Paivio (1986; see also Clark & Paivio, 1991; Sadoski, Paivio, & Goetz, 1991) has claimed that the DCT can account both for text comprehension and for other cognitive activities. He considers it unnecessary to postulate an integrated representation, the verbal and nonverbal systems being able to account for the generally observed results.

However, a study by Franklin and Tversky (1990) helps rule out the dual-coding hypothesis for the comprehension of spatial descriptions. Subjects read a narrative describing a character in a three-dimensional (3D) natural environment whose elements are described with reference to the character whose position is fixed. Subjects then read a second text where the perspective is modified relative to the first: the character is expected to rotate about the vertical (or even horizontal) axis. Reading is interrupted by the announcement of a direction (up/down, left/right, front/back), and subjects have to identify the one element (from five presented) that is actually located in the announced direction. Response times vary as a function of direction, indicating that the representation constructed cannot be similar to a graphical representation of space, since in this case the accessibility of every direction should be the same, the distance of the objects from the character being equal. If subjects imagine themselves in the place of the character, they have to perform a mental rotation to identify objects in the cued direction. Objects located in front of them would then be more accessible, those at the back less, and those resulting in a 90° rotation intermediate. The study's results show that the objects on the vertical axis are the most accessible, followed by objects on the sagittal axis, and finally those on the frontal axis. The authors' view is that a person's *experience* of space is the main determinant of the mental model constructed from complex descriptions such as these, rather than their *perception*. The model therefore lacks the analogical, quasi-perceptual nature of the representations studied during the scanning and transformation of mental images. The comprehension of spatial terms should be biased by the knowledge and the perceptive/motor experience the subjects have of the world (for more details, see chapter 8, this volume). The spatial model should be sufficiently general, abstract, and flexible to allow for different perspectives, in contrast with the mental image or a propositional representation, which represents only a certain point of view. These conclusions have been lent further support by Bryant, Tversky, and Franklin (1992), Franklin, Tversky, and Coon (1992), and Taylor and Tversky (1992a).

Spatial mental models: the early studies

In the 1980s and early 1990s, many experiments addressed the comprehension of texts that led to the construction of spatial models (e.g., Bower & Morrow, 1990; Denis & Cocude, 1989; Denis & Denhière, 1990; Ferguson & Hegarty, 1994; Franklin & Tversky, 1990; Glenberg, Meyer, & Lindem, 1987; Morrow, Bower, & Greenspan, 1989; Morrow, Greenspan, & Bower, 1987; Morrow, Leirer, Altieri, & Fitzimmons, 1994; Taylor & Tversky, 1992a, 1992b; Zwaan & van Oostendorp, 1993) and demonstrated the validity of the mental model construct. Some experiments also contributed to a description of the nature of the model and how it is updated during reading.

Morrow and collaborators (Bower & Morrow, 1990; Gray-Wilson, Rinck, McNamara, Bower, & Morrow, 1993; Morrow, Bower, & Greenspan, 1989; Morrow, Greenspan, & Bower, 1987; Morrow et al., 1994) designed a series of experiments to explore how a spatial mental model is updated during reading. In a typical procedure adopted in these experiments, subjects learn a map of a building containing rooms in which various objects are located. They then read a long text (19 lines) describing the actions and movements of a protagonist who is walking around inside the building from one place to another in pursuit of his goal (such as checking for something in the laboratory). After the presentation of a critical sentence describing the character moving from a source-room (the one he starts in) towards a goal-room (the one where he is headed), reading is interrupted by the presentation of a pair of test words (objects). Subjects are instructed to decide whether the two objects are in the same room or in different rooms. The hypothesis is that the mental model is organized around the main character and his actions. Activation of the elements of the model, evaluated through the speed of access to information about the objects, is assumed to depend on the importance – from the main character's point of view – of the elements and the spatial relations they have. Bower and Morrow (1990) describe the movements of the character as a spot of light moving over corresponding parts of the reader's mental model, thus lighting up the objects in the rooms as he progresses.

The results of Morrow, Greenspan, and Bower (1987) indicate that decision times are faster when objects are located in the goal-room than in the source-room or one of the other rooms, irrespective of the recency of the room mention in the text. Morrow, Bower, and Greenspan (1989) then showed that the accessibility of information does not depend on the mention of a physical movement of the character: decision times are shorter even when the objects are in a room the character is thinking about. Results also suggest that subjects are able to generate spatial inferences. Decision times are indeed shorter for objects in a room the character has to go through to get to the goal, but which is not explicitly mentioned in the text, than for objects of the source-room or of any other room (other than the goal-room). Overall, these results suggest that individuals build a model of the situation described in the text, and its elements are activated and deactivated as a function of the spatial relations they share with the main character around whom the model is organized. The accessibility of information during reading reflects the importance of this information, explicit or implicit, from the character's perspective. Recently, it has also been shown that reader expectations for character movement influence the accessibility of spatial information (Rapp, Klug, & Taylor, 2006).

Other information and the nature of spatial models

These spatial model results have been replicated and extended. Using the same material as Morrow, Bower, and Greenspan (1989), Gray-Wilson et al. (1993) found that subjects build a very detailed spatial mental model only when the task is to decide if an object is located in the same room as the main character of the story – that is, when they are motivated to follow the moves of the character very closely. The degree to which spatial models are precise was also discussed by Zwaan and van Oostendorp (1993). They cast doubts on readers' construction of such detailed mental models under naturalistic conditions of reading, for texts written not solely for experimental purposes. Zwaan and van Oostendorp (1993) gave a number of conditions that should be met in order for a given text to give rise to or facilitate the construction of a spatial model. The description must be determinate – that is, refer to a situation that is unique (Mani & Johnson-Laird, 1982) – continuous (Ehrlich & Johnson-Laird, 1982), and condensed. Indeed, the description might be continuous at the spatial model level, but not at the text surface level, since spatial information is usually mixed with other information. Zwaan and van Oostendorp (1993) took a text from a police novel which contained spatial and nonspatial information. Subjects had to read the text with either instruction to focus on spatial information or no specific instruction. Reading times were longer under the spatial instruction condition than for the no-instruction condition. Accuracy to a nonspatial inferences verification task was the same whatever the instruction, whereas spatial inferences were better verified when focus was on spatial information. This suggests that individuals construct a precise spatial model only when instructed to do so. In the same vein, results obtained by Denis and Denhière (1990) suggest that the construction of a spatial representation from a spatial description – which arouses spontaneous imagery strategies – is influenced by the structure of the text and also by the task put to the subject (see also, for a discussion of the availability of spatial information as a function of the task in hand, Hakala, 1999).

However, it is rare for a mental model to be uniquely spatial, and the question arises of the integration of nonspatial information into a spatial model. McNamara, Halpin, and Hardy (1992), for example, explored how readers associate facts to localizations. The subjects, who are familiar with a spatial environment, learn a series of facts associated with the landmarks (cities or buildings). In the test phase, a priming technique is used, and subjects have to decide if the localizations that are probed by their name or a fact associated to it are located in a specific part of the environment. Results of five experiments varying the conditions of presentation and tests indicate that judgments are faster, more accurate, or both when the target localization is primed by a fact associated to a place close by, rather than to one that is remote. The results suggest that readers integrate nonspatial information into their model, preserving distances between elements. These elements keep trace of their spatial characteristics but also of nonspatial information.

The studies presented so far show how subjects can use and update a model that has been constructed from a map as a function of a text. Several studies performed with young adults have also shown that a spatial representation built only from a verbal description reflects the spatial properties of the text, maintaining relations between objects (e.g., Avraamides, Loomis, Klatzky, & Golledge, 2004; Perrig & Kintsch, 1985) and preserving information about distance (e.g., Rinck, Hahnel, Bower, & Glowalla, 1997). Models derived from language have been shown to preserve many of the properties of real environments (for a review see Zwaan & Radvansky, 1998). This is true for representations derived from route descriptions, written from the perspective of a person traveling through an environment, in which landmarks are described from an egocentric perspective. It is also true if the representation derives from a survey description in which the frame of reference is extrinsic and fixed, providing a representation of the environment from a bird's-eye perspective (e.g., Noordzij & Postma, 2005). Some studies also suggest that, in a novel environment, people reading or listening to verbal descriptions create spatial representations that preserve the spatial perspective of the original source. However, ability to maintain a perspective and to switch from one perspective to another depends on familiarity with the environment (e.g., Brunyé & Taylor, 2008a) and can be modulated by the time spent acquiring spatial information (e.g., Sardone, Bosco, Scalisi, & Longoni, 1995).

As a first conclusion here, this series of studies shows the ability of the reader to construct or update spatial models from verbal descriptions, which can include information on physical properties as well as the relative positions of the elements described and the spatial distances separating them, and also the temporal distances (see, e.g., Rinck & Bower, 2000). These models are organized around a three-dimensional frame of reference centered on an observer whose body provides the up/down, front/back, and left/right dimensions (Morrow, 1994). Animated or non animated objects are located with reference to this frame, and the observer focuses on certain entities rather than on others, depending on the goal. Concerning the nature of spatial models, Langston, Kramer, and Glenberg (1998) considered the proposal that mental models, like real situations, are displayed in a medium analogous to Euclidean space, such that distance has functional consequences. For example, when mentally manipulating an element of the representation, an observer will notice other elements that are spatially close to it, and this will enhance their short-term accessibility. On the basis of empirical evidence, Langston, Kramer, and Glenberg (1998) claimed that the spatial models do not support automatic awareness of implicit spatial relations, and that spatial representation is likely to be more topological or functional than Euclidean.

In order to create a spatial model, readers use their knowledge of the meaning of words, the objects and the actions described, and the linguistic rules governing the interpretation of words as a function of the developing model and of the available cognitive resources – in particular, their WM capacity. This capacity is an element that probably contributes to the difficulty in building an accurate and detailed spatial model. Finally, even when readers have the ability (competency) and knowledge, and even if the text characteristics allow them to create a model, the probability of them constructing it will depend on the usefulness of this model for achieving the goals of the task in hand.

Cognitive mechanisms in spatial text processing

This section explores the cognitive functions that are involved in the construction of a mental model from spatial text comprehension. Above, support was given to the notion that the mental representation constructed from spatial texts maintains spatial properties of the environment described, such as landmarks location, distances, their visual features, and so on. Hence, it is plausible to expect that construction of a mental model from a spatial description requires not only verbal but also spatial functions. This was studied using both experimental and correlational methods, this latter very much focused on individual differences. The purpose here is not to give an exhaustive overview of these studies, but to select a number of them, largely derived from collaborations of the authors of the present chapter and partly inspired by their contacts with Michel Denis. In particular, these studies were devoted to examining the crucial role played by VSWM and by spatial and imagery ability in spatial mental model construction, using experimental studies (described below in this section) and in terms of individual differences studies (described in the final section).

Working memory and spatial text processing

Over the last two decades, a number of studies have investigated the cognitive abilities involved in the comprehension of spatial texts. Much investigation focused on which subcomponents of WM are required. In addition, the relationship between spatial abilities and spatial text comprehension has been examined closely.

The WM model most frequently adopted is that of Baddeley and Hitch (1974), and its subsequent updates (Baddeley, 1986, 2000). According to this model, WM is considered as a multicomponent system, composed of two distinct subcomponents: the visuospatial sketchpad and the phonological loop, devoted to the storing and processing of visuospatial and verbal information, respectively. They are coordinated by an executive control system that has mainly attentive functions. In the most recent updating of the model (Baddeley, 2000, 2003), a fourth component – the episodic buffer – was added: this has the role of integrating information from the two slave systems and making information from long-term memory available to WM. It can be thought of as an interface between a set of systems, each involving a different code, which uses a shared multidimensional code.

The paradigm most generally used to understand the extent of the involvement of the WM systems in spatial text processing is the selective interference paradigm. This paradigm consists of the request to perform a primary task (e.g., listening to or reading a text) concurrently with a secondary task involving specifically verbal working memory (VWM) and VSWM functions; the articulatory suppression (AS – continuous repetition of series of digits or syllables) competes for maintenance of phonological information in VWM; spatial tapping (ST – continuous tapping of series of keys or buttons) competes for maintenance of spatial information in VSWM (see, e.g., Farmer, Berman, & Fletcher, 1986). If the secondary task competes for the same limited resources of WM, performance in the primary task is reduced relative not only to a single task condition, but also to a condition requiring a nonspecific secondary task.

Investigation of the relation between WM and spatial text comprehension is based on a series of studies led by Brooks (1967, 1968). In particular, Brooks (1967) presented lists of sentences (abstract and spatial), where the abstract sentences consisted of numbers associated with adjectives and the spatial sentences were instructions that required some cells of an imagined 4 × 4 matrix to be filled in. The author found that recall of spatial sentences was more disrupted by reading than by listening, but that the opposite was true for abstract sentences, thus supporting the assumption that the processing of spatial sentences competes with the same visual resources as those involved in reading.

The findings of Brooks (1967) provided the first support to the notion that spatial functions are selectively involved in text processing. In the subsequent years, a number of studies demonstrated the involvement of VSWM in the processing of text accompanied by pictures. Using the dual-task paradigm, Kruley, Sciama, and Glenberg (1994) found that the comprehension of illustrated texts interfered with the performance of a VSWM task. Participants listened to 24 scientific texts, presented one sentence at a time. Text listening was/was not accompanied by a figure (text with/without illustration) and presented in either pre-load or control condition. In the pre-load condition, a 4×4 matrix, some of whose cells were filled with a black dot, was shown immediately before the sentence listening. Immediately afterwards, a second matrix was presented, and participants had to decide if it was the same as or different from the one just seen. Performance in the pre-load task was lower in the text-plus-illustration condition than in text only. The interpretation of the authors was that illustrations accompanying a text encourage the formation of a spatial mental model through the use of the WM sketchpad, and that this process interferes in the memory with the maintenance of the matrix configuration. In two subsequent studies (Gyselinck, Cornoldi, Dubois, De Beni, & Ehrlich, 2002; Gyselinck, Ehrlich, Cornoldi, De Beni, & Dubois, 2000), the dual-task paradigm was used to show how VSWM and the phonological loop were involved in processing scientific texts accompanied or not by illustrations. In Gyselinck et al. (2002, Expt. 1), the effects on text comprehension of two presentation formats (text-only and text-with-illustrations) were compared. Table 6.1 gives an example of text, while the related text-with-illustrations is shown in Figure 6.1.

Table 6.1 Examples of texts used by Gyselinck et al. (2002)

Title: Static Electricity

1 When two bodies are rubbed against each other, electricity is found on the parts rubbed. This is called static electricity.

2 Rubbing an ebonite rod with fur charges the rod with negative electricity, whereas the electricity produced on a Plexiglas ruler rubbed with silk is positive.

3 It is found that two bodies charged with the same kind of electricity repel each other.

4 On the other hand, two bodies charged with different electricity attract each other.

5 Other modes of electrification are possible: for instance, electric charges can flow from an electrified body to a neutral one by mere contact.

6 After contact, the charged body carries charges of the same kind as the item that electrified it.

7 Clouds may become charged with electricity by friction with the surrounding atmosphere.

8 When two bodies hold a large enough amount of opposite charge, an electric discharge can occur in certain circumstances.

9 A discharge between clouds produces lightning and discharge to the ground produces a thunderbolt.

Examples of questions

Paraphrase:

It can be verified that two bodies rubbed with cloth repel each other if the charges they bear are (a) identical, (b) different, (c) neutral (Answer: (a))

Inference:

After bringing a neutral body into contact with an electrified ebonite rod, as the two bodies are brought together, one observes (a) an attraction, (b) nothing, (c) a repulsion (Answer: (c))

Adapted from V. Gyselinck, C. Cornoldi, V. Dubois, R. De Beni, & M. F. Ehrlich, 2002. Visuospatial memory and phonological loop in learning from multimedia. *Applied Cognitive Psychology, 16*, 665–685.

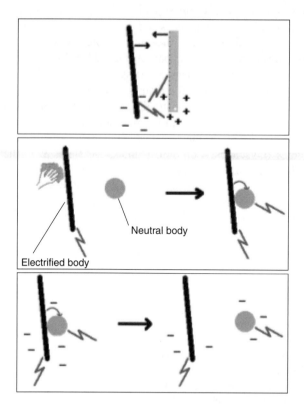

Figure 6.1 Illustrations associated with Sentences 4, 5, and 6 from the text shown in
Table 6.1. (Examples taken from V. Gyselinck, C. Cornoldi, V. Dubois,
R. De Beni, & M. F. Ehrlich, 2002. Visuospatial memory and phonological loop in learning from multimedia. *Applied Cognitive Psychology, 16*,
665–685. © Wiley Interscience, reprinted with permission.)

The results, which the authors discussed in term of a selective involvement of
VSWM in the comprehension of illustrated scientific texts, indicated that comprehension performance was better in the text-with-illustration condition (for a
consideration of the importance of depictions in human cognition, see chapter 1,
this volume). However, with a concurrent tapping task, the beneficial effect of
illustrations disappeared, while a concurrent articulatory task impaired performance similarly in both presentation formats.

The findings of these studies on illustrated texts can be interpreted as proof of
an implication of VSWM in the construction of mental models derived from illustrated texts. However, the objection could be raised that WM is involved in
processing illustrations only, not in the construction of a mental model from text.
The involvement of VSWM in the construction of mental models derived from
text is more evident when spatial texts without illustrations are examined. One of
the first studies to systematically test the assumption that different components of

WM were implied in spatial text processing was carried out by Pazzaglia and Cornoldi (1999). Differently from some studies described above, the authors employed not only short texts similar to those used by Brooks (1967), but also extended spatial and nonspatial texts not accompanied by pictures. The study outcomes support the idea that spatial text processing requires spatial functions as well as verbal functions. In Experiments 2 and 3 of the study by Pazzaglia and Cornoldi (1999), participants listened to various texts – one visual, one nonspatial, two spatial – and concurrently performed visual, verbal, or spatial concurrent tasks, assumed to load visual, verbal, or spatial WM subcomponents, respectively. As expected, the spatial concurrent tasks were found to selectively impair the memory performance of the spatial texts more than did the verbal tasks, whereas the opposite occurred with the nonspatial texts. An interesting result of this study was that it showed not only the involvement of the visuospatial sketchpad in the processing of spatial texts, but also that visuospatial processing could be further differentiated into visual, spatial-simultaneous, and spatial-sequential components. In accordance with the continuity model of WM (see Cornoldi & Vecchi, 2003), these three components partly shared the same resources, and differentiation from the verbal component was more clear-cut, but even so they also involved specific distinguishable resources. However, given the absence of a control group with no concurrent tasks in the Pazzaglia and Cornoldi study, it was impossible to establish how far, if at all, the verbal and the spatial concurrent tasks had any detrimental effect on the spatial and nonspatial texts, respectively.

To address this question, De Beni, Pazzaglia, Gyselinck, and Meneghetti (2005) carried out two experiments where three groups of participants listened to spatial and nonspatial texts in three different memory-load conditions. Table 6.2 presents the spatial and nonspatial texts used.

One group was given a concurrent spatial task (spatial tapping, ST) during text listening, the other had a verbal concurrent task (articulatory suppression, AS), while the third group (a control group) listened to the texts in no-concurrent-task condition. Results supported the hypothesis that verbal and spatial components of WM were differentially involved in the comprehension and memory of the spatial and nonspatial texts, with a selective interference effect of the spatial concurrent task on the spatial text, and an interference effect of the verbal concurrent task on both the spatial and the nonspatial texts. These effects emerged for recall, sentence verification of spatial relations that need to be inferred, and response times.

In the experiments by De Beni et al. (2005), the concurrent tasks were performed during text listening on the basis of the assumption that they would have blocked the construction of spatial mental models from texts. To also examine whether the retrieval of spatial mental models constructed from spatial text processing involved VSWM, Pazzaglia, De Beni, and Meneghetti (2007) ran two experiments where young adults listened to spatial and nonspatial texts while performing a spatial (Experiment 1) or verbal (Experiment 2) concurrent task during either encoding or retrieval. Text memorization and comprehension were tested by free-recall and sentence-verification tasks. The results (presented in Figure 6.2) showed that the concurrent spatial task was detrimental to memory performance for spatial

Table 6.2 Examples of texts and relative inferential questions used in De Beni et al. (2005)

Nonspatial text

. . . To produce red wines, the grapes are crushed and left in casks for 5 days. The grapes are then subject to fermentation at a constant temperature of 15°–18° C. to maximize the bouquet. . . . Before bottling, crystallization takes place by bringing the wine to subzero temperatures, . . . This procedure . . . allows the excess tartar to deposit so it can be eliminated later. . . .

Sentences

During fermentation the new wine stands at subzero temperatures. (False)

To eliminate tartar from wine it is left to stand at subzero temperatures. (True)

Spatial text

Immediately on your left you will see a well, . . . Go straight on until the end and you'll find a nice restaurant in front of you, situated in the other corner of the property. At the restaurant turn left . . . and continue to walk. . . . At the end of this side you will find several barns.

Sentences

After the well, if you turn right, you immediately find a bridge. (False)

Compared with the well, the barn is in the farthest corner. (True)

Adapted from R. De Beni, F. Pazzaglia, V. Gyselinck, & C. Meneghetti, 2005. Visuospatial working memory and mental representation of spatial description. *European Journal of Cognitive Psychology*, *17*, 75–95.

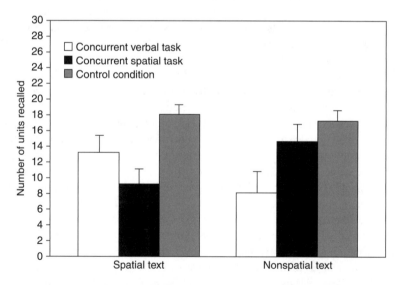

Figure 6.2 Mean overall number of information units correctly recalled for spatial and nonspatial texts as a function of concurrent tasks. (From R. De Beni, F. Pazzaglia, V. Gyselinck, & C. Meneghetti, 2005. Visuospatial working memory and mental representation of spatial description. *European Journal of Cognitive Psychology*, *17*, 75–95. © Psychology Press, reprinted with permission.)

text more than for nonspatial text. In contrast, the concurrent verbal task impaired memory performance equally for both spatial and nonspatial texts. Moreover, the spatial task interfered with both encoding and retrieval, in contrast with the verbal task, for which the interference effect was active only during encoding. Similar results were obtained by Brunyé and Taylor (2008b; Expts. 1, 3): Experiment 1 involved the reading of spatial texts in two perspectives (one route, one survey). Participants were split into three groups according to three concurrent task conditions. One group had no concurrent task (control condition); the other two had either a verbal (AS) task or a spatial (ST) task that had to be performed concurrently with reading. Text memory was tested using a sentence verification task, with verbatim, inferential, and paraphrased sentences, plus a map-drawing task. Whereas the AS impaired the memory performance of both texts, the ST task had a more detrimental effect on the route text than on the survey text. Experiment 3 used the same texts and concurrent tasks as those in Experiment 1, but this time the secondary task was carried out as part of the testing (i.e., statement verification and map drawing). The results showed that VSWM was called upon in statement verification involving inferencing about spatial environments, even though the detrimental effect of ST was more marked in response time than in accuracy.

Overall, these findings showed the involvement of VSWM in the construction and reactivation of mental models derived from spatial descriptions. However, they can be interpreted in two ways, either considered as support for the spatial nature of mental models constructed from spatial texts (given that VSWM is necessary for their reactivation) or else simply attributed to the fact that the retrieval phase required participants to (a) produce spatial language in order to freely recall information contained in the text and (b) process spatial language in order to perform the sentence verification task. It is possible that the spatial concurrent task interfered directly with the performance of testing tasks, rather than with the reactivation of the mental model previously formed. A third explanation – suggested by Brunyé and Taylor (2008b) – is that readers or listeners do not elicit all the possible spatial inferences during text processing, but produce them only when required for testing, and, in doing so, they need VSWM.

Working memory and the processing of spatial texts from different perspectives

Another question to be addressed is whether the processing of spatial texts from different perspectives needs distinct WM subcomponents. Literature on spatial descriptions shows that the description of an environment can assume two different main perspectives: route and survey (Tversky, 1991). Route descriptions assume the point of view of a person who is moving through the environment. They are characterized by the use of an intrinsic frame of reference and egocentric terms, such as right/left or front/back, and have a linear organization, given by the order in which landmarks appear along the route itself. Instead, survey descriptions provide an overview of the spatial layout, sometimes with a strong hierarchical organization (Taylor & Tversky, 1992a). An extrinsic frame of reference and canonical terms such as north, south, east, and west are used. Table 6.3 gives examples of route and survey descriptions from Pazzaglia and Cornoldi (1999).

The question of whether or not the mental model derived from spatial descriptions is dependent on text perspective has been investigated in various studies, but results are conflictual: in some cases spatial mental representation was found to be dependent on the perspective learnt (Bosco, Filomena, Sardone, Scalisi, & Longoni, 1996; Pazzaglia, Cornoldi, & Longoni, 1994; Perrig & Kintsch, 1985), but in others it was found to be independent of it (Brunyé, Rapp, & Taylor, 2008; Taylor & Tversky, 1992a). It seems that a number of factors influence the dependency (if there is any) between text perspective and mental representation: text learning time (Bosco et al., 1996; Brunyé & Taylor, 2008a), perspective switching within descriptions (Lee & Tversky, 2005), goals (Taylor, Naylor, & Chechile, 1999), instructions

Table 6.3 Examples of survey and route texts used in Pazzaglia and Cornoldi (1999)

Survey description

The zoo is situated in a large rectangular area.

There is only one entrance, at the center of the south side.

In front of the entrance there is a bar, which is exactly at the center of the zoo.

The other attractions of the zoo are situated in the four corners. In the south-west corner there is the park.

In the north-west corner there are the chimpanzees.

Close to the chimpanzees, to the south, there are the baboons.

In the north-east corner there are the polar bears.

South of the bears there are the penguins.

The penguins are at the center of the east side.

Route description

You are in front of the only entrance to the zoo.

Go into the zoo through the entrance, which is situated at the middle of one of its four sides.

After going through the entrance you can see a bar in front of you.

Turn left and go straight ahead until you arrive at a park.

Turn right and go straight ahead, leaving the park to your left.

Continue walking and you will be able to see the bar on your right.

Almost at the end you can see the baboons on your left.

Just after the baboons you will see the chimpanzees on your left.

Now, directly in front of you is one side of the zoo; turn right and go straight ahead until you find the polar bears in front of you.

Turn right and after a long walk you will be able to see the penguins on your left.

Adapted from F. Pazzaglia & C. Cornoldi, 1999. The role of distinct components of visuo-spatial working memory in the processing of texts. *Memory, 7,* 19–41.

(Noordzij, van der Lubbe, & Postma, 2005, 2006), and test type (Chabanne, Péruch, Denis, & Thinus-Blanc, 2003–2004; Noordzij & Postma, 2005; Shelton & McNamara, 2004). In any case, it is reasonable to assume that, apart from the final product of text processing, on-line processing can differentially involve VSWM as a function of the spatial text perspective. For survey descriptions, participants are initially provided with the general configuration of the environment and, successively, single items are mentioned and allocated within it. The comprehension process thus starts from a more global, visual structure, which is bit by bit filled in by local substructures. In contrast, route descriptions are characterized by a linear organization, the order of items being given in the order in which they are encountered along the route. Thus, in the latter case, comprehension requires implementation of sequential processes, characterized by continuous changes of perspective as a function of progress along the route. The hypothesis that the processing of route and spatial texts relies on different WM subcomponents has been tested by Brunyé and Taylor (2008b), Deyzac, Logie, and Denis (2006), Pazzaglia and Cornoldi (1999), and Pazzaglia, Meneghetti, De Beni, and Gyselinck (2010).

In fact, Pazzaglia and Cornoldi (1999) showed for the first time that processing of route and survey texts involves different components of VSWM. Some years later the issue was taken up again. As reported above, Brunyé and Taylor (2008b) found that ST interfered more with the memory performance of a route text than of a survey text. In the study of Deyzac, Logie, and Denis (2006), participants listened to short descriptions in either route or survey perspective in different concurrent task conditions: spatial (ST, Expt. 1), visual (brightness judgments and dynamic visual noise; Expts. 2 and 3, respectively), and verbal (AS, Expt. 4). Their results showed that the presentation of a spatial text concurrently with the ST task resulted in a larger interference effect on the recall of landmarks for the route descriptions than for the survey descriptions. The passive visual task (dynamic visual noise; Quinn & McConnell, 1996) produced interference effects for route texts but not survey texts. In contrast, a more active concurrent visual task (brightness judgment task, adapted from Logie, 1986) and an AS task produced the same interference for both types of spatial text.

In Pazzaglia et al. (2010, Expt. 1), participants listened to either a survey or a route text and concurrently performed either ST or AS. In line with previous studies (De Beni et al., 2005; Deyzac, Logie, & Denis, 2006), both concurrent tasks produced an interference effect on route-text processing, whereas a smaller disruptive effect from the ST was found for survey texts than for route texts. In Experiment 2, participants randomly assigned to three groups listened to a survey, route, or nonspatial text. Each group concurrently performed a sequential-spatial task, a simultaneous-spatial task, or no secondary task. Again, a different pattern of results emerged for the two texts: the survey text suffered from interference from the simultaneous concurrent task, whereas the route text was impaired by both the concurrent tasks, with a stronger effect from the sequential task; the detrimental effect of both spatial secondary tasks on nonspatial text was limited. Overall, the results described above support the notion that the online processing of route and survey texts taps specific WM components.

Further support that different mechanisms are implied in processing route and survey texts was given by a study by Noordzij and Postma (2005). Three groups of participants (early blind, late blind, and sighted) listened to route and survey texts and then performed a series of spatial tasks testing text spatial representation. The results showed that construction of a mental model from survey texts was poorer in blind people than in their sighted counterparts, whereas the opposite was found for the route text. In fact, in a distance-comparison task, blind people made more errors than did sighted people after studying a survey text, but the opposite pattern emerged for the route text, where it was the group of sighted people who made more errors (this study is discussed in more detail in chapter 7, this volume).

In summary, the overview presented so far in this section can be set out as three basic points: (1) Spatial texts differ from nonspatial in that the former require spatial WM components that are not involved in nonspatial text processing. (2) Within spatial texts there is a distinction that merits attention, namely the different perspective these texts can assume relative to the cognitive functions implied in their processing; the use of the dual-task paradigm revealed that sequential and simultaneous WM components are active in route-text processing. (3) In contrast, survey-text processing seems primarily to require the intervention of simultaneous components. The distinction between the two texts is supported also by the fact that blind people are facilitated by route- more than survey-text processing.

Imagery strategies in the memorization of spatial texts

The beneficial role of imagery in the comprehension and memorization of verbal material was intensively studied in the 1970s (for a review, see Denis, 1991). The theoretical background was provided by Paivio's (1971) dual-coding theory, which assumes that the use of imagery prompts visual, as well as verbal, encoding in language processing, facilitating memorization (see discussion of dual-coding theory in the first section of this chapter). In fact, a number of studies found that instructions to imagine the situation described by a text enhance the memory of concrete and spatial concepts, both explicitly stated and inferred (e.g., Fraisse & Léveillé, 1975; Giesen & Peeck, 1984). More recently, De Beni and Moè (2003) verified the efficacy of an imagery-based strategy in improving memory of spatial texts. Their participants were trained in the use of the loci-method, a traditional mnemonic that requires mental representation of a familiar route with a number of significant landmarks (loci) and, by the use of images, association of each landmark with a specific concept to remember. The efficacy of this strategy was compared to that of verbal rehearsal in improving memory of abstract, visual, and spatial texts, either read or listened to. As expected, imagery instructions proved more beneficial than repetition to the recall of the visual and spatial (but not abstract) texts for oral but not visual presentation. These findings show that the use of mental imagery can help the memorization of spatial texts and, at the same time, suggest that the construction of a spatial mental model is facilitated by the use of images. Indeed, when we process spatial descriptions we have the subjective experience of representing the situation described by the use of mental images. Although spatial mental models are something more complex and abstract than mental images, as explained in the opening sections of this chapter, it is well known that images help readers or listeners to construct a representation of the situation described that maintains the spatial relationships between landmarks (e.g., de Vega, Cocude, Denis, Rodrigo, & Zimmer, 2001); their use may involve the VSWM, and even explain why the VSWM is involved in spatial text processing.

The fact that spatial text mental representation is enhanced by the use of visual mental images also has relevance as regards applications: instructing people to construct good mental images can facilitate spatial text comprehension and memorization. This expectation was tested by Gyselinck, De Beni, Pazzaglia, Meneghetti, and Mondoloni (2007). In this study, participants were instructed to listen to a route description and to use two different memory strategies, one imagery-based and the other verbal-based. In the first case, they were asked to imagine themselves moving along the route described in the text, in the second to rehearse verbal information. Concurrently, they were invited to perform ST, AS, or no secondary task. Comprehension performance was measured using a sentence verification task. It emerged that the imagery-based strategy was more efficient in enhancing the spatial text processing than was verbal repetition. Moreover, the interference of ST and AS on text comprehension was modulated by the instructions participants received: ST impaired performance of the group instructed to use imagery, and it caused the beneficial effect of imagery instructions to vanish. By contrast, no interference effect of ST was found for the repetition group. Instead, AS interfered with text processing of both groups. These findings indicated that imagery instructions prompt subjects to form mental images (which help them form a spatial model) and that these processes involve both the VWM and the VSWM. In the case of the repetition instructions, however, participants appeared to rely only slightly on their VSWM for performing the comprehension task.

Overall, research findings to date with the dual-task paradigm all point to the conclusion that verbal and spatial resources are relevant in processing and in maintaining spatial mental representations in memory. These findings also question the interest of adding a new component such as the episodic buffer to account for the results obtained. The episodic buffer (Baddeley, 2000, 2003) was incorporated into the model to allow for temporary storage of information held in a multimodal code, capable of binding information from the subsidiary systems and from long-term memory into a unitary episodic representation. To date, however, there has been little mention of how this might take place, and how it might be tested experimentally without any confounding between the peripheral systems and the episodic buffer.

Individual differences in spatial text processing

Studying the cognitive functions implied in spatial text processing can be approached from another point of view, namely using the individual differences paradigm (for a discussion on the use of individual differences in the study of spatial cognition, see Cornoldi & Vecchi, 2003). Studies using this paradigm are mainly based on correlational or group-comparison methods. The latter assume that when two groups with different ability levels in a specific cognitive area (e.g., spatial ability) but matched in all other relevant aspects also differ in performance on a cognitive task (e.g., text comprehension), then the specific cognitive ability can be considered to be implied in the performance of the cognitive task.

In the context of spatial text processing, individual differences in many cognitive variables have been taken into account, not only in isolation but also in their mutual relationships. We will examine individual differences in spatial ability, VSWM, cognitive style in spatial representation, and their relation with spatial text comprehension. In addition, developmental studies and studies on one particular learning disability syndrome (nonverbal learning disability, NLD) will also be considered.

Spatial ability as a source of individual differences in spatial text processing

The literature distinguishes many different spatial sub-abilities within the general spatial domain (Cornoldi & Vecchi, 2003), including spatial perception, spatial visualization, and mental rotation (Linn & Petersen, 1985; Voyer, Voyer, & Bryden, 1995). Spatial visualization and mental rotation have been found to be associated with environmental learning (e.g., Allen, Kirasic, Dobson, Long, & Beck, 1996; Fields & Shelton, 2006; Hegarty, Montello, Richardson, Ishikawa, & Lovelace, 2006) also in cases where learning was based on spatial descriptions (de Vega, 1994; Bosco et al., 1996; Haenggi, Kintsch, & Gernsbacher, 1995).

For Linn and Petersen (1985), spatial perception can be defined as the ability to perceive and encode different features of spatial arrays and maintain them in memory. Spatial visualization is the ability to perform multistep manipulation of complex spatial information, and it is measured by, for example, the paper folding test (PFT; Ekstrom, French, & Harman, 1976) or the Minnesota paper form board (MPFB; Likert & Quasha, 1948). Mental rotation refers to the ability to mentally rotate two-dimensional (2D) or 3D stimuli rapidly and accurately. Stimuli for mental rotation tasks can be 2D, such as in the card rotation and cube comparison tests (CRT, CCT; Ekstrom, French, & Harman, 1976), or else 3D; in this latter case, the task most frequently used is the mental rotations test (MRT; Vandenberg & Kuse, 1978), which involves identifying objects in a rotated position in 3D space.

An overview of the literature reveals numerous studies identifying differences in text processing performance in individuals with different levels of spatial ability. Haenggi, Kintsch, and Gernsbacher (1995) showed that ability to rotate spatial information is important for constructing a mental model of a narrative text describing the actions of a person moving in a building. De Vega (1994) investigated spatial mental models derived from short texts describing a protagonist moving from one place to another, in an environment containing various objects.

The results in general demonstrated that the objects described in the text were more easily accessible as a function of the actual location of the protagonist. Beyond this general effect, it was found that the performance of participants varied as a function of their spatial ability, measured by the MPFB: participants with high MPFB performance proved to be more accurate than those with low MPFB performance. Similar results – although more specifically referred to the WM domain – were found by Pazzaglia and Cornoldi (1999, Expt. 1). Participants were high and low performers on the Corsi block test (Milner, 1971) but had identical performance on the digit span test (Wechsler, 1981). Again, the high-performance group outperformed the lower counterpart in a free-recall task of information derived from a spatial text. Overall, these results demonstrate that quantitative differences in spatial text processing can be attributed to spatial and VSWM abilities, even when verbal ability is controlled. More recently, Pazzaglia (2008) found similar effects in the comprehension of survey texts accompanied (or not) by pictures. The aim of this study was to investigate the role of different pictures in the comprehension of spatial text. In two experiments, survey texts were presented to three groups of participants with the instruction to memorize them. In Experiment 1, texts were presented under three different conditions: no-picture, single-picture, and map-picture. In the no-picture condition, only the text was presented. In the other two conditions, each individual sentence was accompanied by a picture representing the content of that sentence (single-picture), or a picture integrating the content of the sentence with that of the other sentences (map-picture). In Experiment 2, participants were also asked to perform the MRT. In general, the map-pictures were most effective in improving text processing. As regards individual differences, poor MRT participants had lower text comprehension than did participants with high MRT performance. Interestingly, all participants, whether high or low in MRT performance, benefited from the map-picture condition: it seems that the visual representation of items' relative positions facilitates the construction of a spatial mental model from text.

Meneghetti, Gyselinck, Pazzaglia, and De Beni (2009) examined how WM and spatial ability (as measured by the MRT) work together in spatial text comprehension. In this study, both dual-task and individual differences paradigms were adopted with the aim of clarifying the separate roles of WM and spatial ability in spatial text processing. The assumption was that both VSWM and spatial ability are implicated in spatial text processing, albeit with different functions: VSWM is mainly engaged in the maintenance of spatial information for the construction of a spatial mental model, whereas spatial ability is more actively implied in the mental manipulation of spatial information. As a consequence, participants with high and low performance on the MRT were expected to show different patterns of resistance to VSWM interference, the high-performance group being less impaired by the VSWM interference than their poorer performing counterparts. In two experimental sessions, two groups different in MRT were asked to listen to and memorize spatial and nonspatial descriptions similar to those used by De Beni et al. (2005) and concurrently perform AS and ST tasks. In line with the authors' expectations, low-MRT individuals proved less efficient than higher performing counterparts in their ability to build spatial mental representations derived from spatial descriptions when they had to concurrently perform a spatial task assumed to load VSWM. In fact, as shown in Figure 6.3, spatial text memory recall of the low MRT group was poorer in the ST condition than in the control condition (with no concurrent task), whereas the high MRT group had the same performance in the two conditions. Moreover, both groups were impaired by AS in both spatial and nonspatial text processing, supporting the notion that the resistance of the high MRT group to ST in spatial text processing was not attributable to a generally better ability to resist WM interference, but was specific for spatial interference during spatial text processing.

Overall, these results, obtained under dual-task and individual differences paradigms, prove that the higher spatial resources of high spatial ability individuals can compensate an overload in VSWM; the results also suggest a concurrent implication of spatial ability and VSWM in spatial text processing. They not only reveal the importance of taking account of VSWM and spatial abilities in explaining text processing performance, but also indicate that spatial and WM functions interact.

Individual differences in imagery and WM in relation to spatial text processing

While the beneficial role of image-based strategy in spatial text memorization is well acknowledged, it is not known whether all individuals or only those with

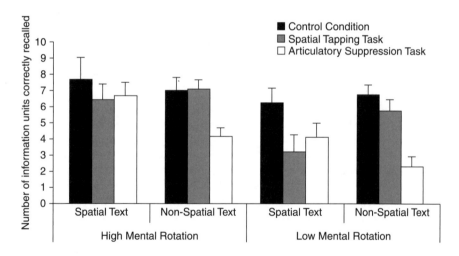

Figure 6.3 Means and standard errors of number of information units correctly recalled in free recall of high and low mental rotation groups in spatial and nonspatial text as a function of concurrent task conditions (control condition vs. spatial tapping task vs. articulatory suppression task). (From C. Meneghetti, V. Gyselinck, F. Pazzaglia, & R. De Beni, 2009. Individual differences in spatial text processing: High spatial ability can compensate for spatial working memory interference. *Learning and Individual Differences, 19,* 577–589. © Elsevier, reprinted with permission.)

good imagery ability can benefit from the use of image-based strategies. Gyselinck, Meneghetti, De Beni, and Pazzaglia (2009) ran a study where individual differences on imagery and spatial ability were considered in the context of possible benefit from imagery in spatial text memorization. As in Meneghetti et al. (2009), participants were trained to use either imagery or verbal strategies to process route spatial texts and had to concurrently perform either ST or AS. The overall results mirror those found in the previous study: participants demonstrated higher comprehension and memorization when instructed to imagine text contents than when they were asked to rehearse. Moreover, in the imagery condition, performance was impaired by both ST and AS, whereas only AS impaired performance in the repetition condition. However, the introduction of individual differences measures of imagery and spatial abilities changed the general pattern of results, underlining the importance of taking into account differences among participants. Ability to form vivid visual mental images was measured using the Vividness of Visual Images Questionnaire (VVIQ; Marks, 1973), a self-rating scale that provides a measure of ability to easily form vivid visual images. Ability to mentally manipulate spatial configurations was measured using the MRT (Vandenberg & Kuse, 1978). The two scores were combined to give a single measure of imagery and spatial ability. On the basis of this measure, participants were split into high and low and their text recall scores were examined as a function of strategies and concurrent task conditions. An interesting finding was that both groups were facilitated by the imagery strategy, performing better when asked to imagine than when having to rehearse verbally. This result indicates that imagery strategies are efficient irrespective of level of spatial and imagery abilities. However, the role of individual differences emerged when performance was analyzed as a function of ability, strategy, and concurrent task. A completely different pattern of resistance to ST was shown by the two groups using imagery instructions. While the low-ability group was impaired by the ST, just as for the total sample, the high-level group was not sensitive to spatial interference. These results provide evidence that individuals with high spatial ability can use imagery strategies in spatial text processing even when their WM components are loaded by performance of secondary tasks.

Do cognitive styles in spatial representation influence spatial text comprehension and memorization?

The spatial cognition literature proposed a distinction between intrinsic (or egocentric) and extrinsic (or allocentric) frames of reference in spatial representations (e.g., Carlson-Radvansky & Irwin, 1993; Friedman & Hall, 1996; Pani & Dupree, 1994). In intrinsic frames of reference, location is specified with respect to the observer, whereas in extrinsic frames it is specified with respect to objects in or features of the environment. In performing orientation tasks (e.g., wayfinding and production of route directions), intrinsic and extrinsic frames of reference are usually associated to the use of route and survey spatial strategies, respectively (e.g., Darken & Peterson, 2002; Evans, 1980; Lawton, 1994; Siegel & White, 1975).

Individual differences in spatial representation have been found to be particularly related to gender (Lawton, 1994; Lawton & Kallai, 2002) (males preferring survey representation, females preferring route) and with familiarity with the environment (Nori & Piccardi, 2009) (unfamiliar individuals adopting a route representation shifting to a survey representation only when familiarity increases). More recently, a number of studies revealed the existence of an individual cognitive style in spatial representation. Individuals, independently of gender or familiarity, prefer a spatial representation focused on landmarks (landmark representation), on route interconnecting landmarks (route representation), or a map-like representation (survey) (Pazzaglia, Cornoldi, & De Beni, 2000). Using a questionnaire on sense of direction and spatial representation (Pazzaglia et al., 2000), Nori and Giusberti (2003) selected three groups of participants who differed in their cognitive style in spatial representation. One group was characterized by a landmark-focused cognitive style, claiming to rely mainly on the visual features of salient landmarks in navigation. The second was classified as route, being characterized by use of navigation strategies based on the encoding and memorization of a number of salient landmarks and of their location. Finally, the third group, labeled as survey, stated preference for a map-like spatial representation. The authors assumed a hierarchical model, where survey individuals can flexibly adopt all three kinds of spatial representation, route individuals can use both route- and landmark-focused representations, and the third group only their own kind of preferred representation. Interestingly, the differences in performance of the three groups on spatial tasks were coherent with their cognitive styles: the three groups had the same performance on a visual task, but for a route task landmark-focused participants had worst performance, while for a survey task the survey group performed best.

But although "survey" individuals tend to perform best on spatial tasks, there are cases where a survey representation cannot be optimal. For example, in the city of Venice, Italy, where the organization of streets and channels is spatially unpredictable, people who rely on a survey representation can be disadvantaged (in fact, in view of its specific orientation difficulties, Venice has been the setting for various orienteering competitions; De Beni, Cornoldi, Larsson, Magnussen, & Ronnberg, 2007). In a study performed in Venice itself, Denis, Pazzaglia, Cornoldi, and Bertolo (1997) asked participants to read three different route directions and then follow the memorized instructions around the corresponding routes. They were split into participants with high or low preference for survey representation. Results showed that participants with high survey preference made more navigation errors when route directions were poor, whereas with good directions their performance was equal to that of the other group. This suggests that preferences for one particular spatial representation can influence spatial language processing. This assumption was addressed in a study by Meneghetti, Pazzaglia, and De Beni (2011) where two groups of participants were selected from a wider sample on the basis of their use of an allocentric frame of reference in spatial representation. This allowed selection of a group of participants who claimed to rely extensively on compass directions for orientation, and another group who made only rare use of compass directions. Both groups were presented with spatial texts in survey and route perspectives. An effect of dependency was found between preference for spatial representation and text perspective: individuals with high preference for use of compass directions memorized the survey texts better than did the other group. In another study (Pazzaglia & Meneghetti, 2011), participants were selected on the basis of their high or low preference for adopting a survey perspective in spatial representation. Again, memory performance in spatial text processing was found to relate to spatial representation preference: the high survey group was more accurate in a sentence verification task on text contents than were the low survey counterpart.

Individual differences in spatial text processing due to aging

A number of studies to date have supported the notion that older adults typically show a preserved ability to construct and use spatial mental models, even when they present other cognitive declines (e.g., Radvansky, Zwaan, Curiel, & Copeland, 2001); the effects of mental model use are the same as or sometimes stronger than those observed for young adults (Dijkstra, Yaxley, Madden, & Zwaan, 2004). However, although a number of potentially limiting factors need to be taken into account, older adults are impaired by the request to integrate ongoing information around multiple locations, or when multiple mental models have to be constructed. One study, by Copeland and Radvansky (2007), tested the assumption that limitations in WM functioning can impair mental model activation by older adults relative to younger adults.

In a set of three experiments they studied the construction of spatial mental models from the integration of list of sentences (Expt. 1), diagrams of words (Expt. 2), and display of simple objects (Expt. 3), which were presented continuously or discontinuously. Overall, older adults exhibited lower scores than did younger adults in accuracy, response times, and viewing times, demonstrating difficulty in integrating spatial information particularly when this was verbally presented (sentences or patterns of words). In Experiments 1 and 2, in fact, performance was very low, but improved in Experiment 3 where pictures were used. The authors concluded that older adults had difficulty in integrating spatial information into a mental model particularly when it is presented verbally, probably as a result of limitations in maintaining and processing resources in VWM. An analogous difficulty in translating verbal information into a spatial mental model was found by Meneghetti, Borella, Grasso, and De Beni (in press), who asked two groups of adults (one younger, one older) to learn a route in three different learning conditions: description (D), map (M), or map plus description (M+D). The older group was found to be particularly disadvantaged in the D condition, where performances on map-drawing and pointing tasks were lower than for their younger counterparts. However, age-related differences in map-drawing and aligned pointing tasks were no longer significant in learning conditions M and M+D. These findings suggest that the difficulty older adults have in route learning can be attenuated by type of input and recall task and can be interpreted as a difficulty in managing verbal information in the construction of a spatial mental model when a visuospatial support (e.g., a map) is not provided. Verbal WM limitations can explain these results.

Spatial text processing and special subjects: the case of children with NLD disabilities

Described for the first time by Rourke (1995), a Canadian clinical psychologist, nonverbal learning disabilities represent a developmental syndrome characterized by specific impairments in visuospatial-organizational, psychomotor, tactile-perceptual, and nonverbal problem-solving skills, which are associated with a right-hemisphere dysfunction (Nichelli & Venneri, 1995; Tranel, Hall, Olson, & Tranel, 1987). Children with NLD show deficits in all school disciplines that require the use of spatial skills. In everyday life they manifest topographical disorientation and poor motor coordination but perform normally in linguistic tasks such as rote verbal learning, verbal classification, and regular phoneme–grapheme matching. The observed discrepancy between verbal and visuospatial domains – NLD individuals are in fact characterized by average verbal skills and very poor spatial competencies – gives the examination of this syndrome parti-cular relevance in studies aimed at clarifying the roles of spatial and verbal abilities in spatial text processing.

The case of NLD children is interesting because they are characterized by good verbal abilities and any problems they have in text processing relate only to their visuospatial difficulties. Text comprehension in children with NLD is adequate, with minor difficulties in inferential processes that seem more marked when spatial inferences are required (Worling, Humphries, & Tannock, 1999). However, to date, very few studies have considered whether the pattern of impairments in spatial abilities is associated with specific problems in spatial text processing. A first study was run by Rigoni, Cornoldi, and Alcetti (1997), who presented NLD children and controls with short spatial descriptions, asking them to represent the spatial organization of the landmarks using a drawing. NLD children were dramat-ically poorer than controls. However, their poor performance could be due to their well-acknowledged poor drawing ability. For this reason, NLD children were given the possibility of using available reproductions of the landmarks, with the simple request of arranging them in a given space. Also in this case, NLD children performed worse than controls. Later studies, examining the processing of longer texts (distinguished between route and survey) further confirmed the difficulties of NLD children. In particular, Mammarella et al. (2009) carried out a study to distinguish the contributions of spatial abilities and verbal abilities to spatial text processing by comparing two groups of children, one with NLD and one with reading disabilities (RD). Their performance in spatial and nonspatial text processing was compared to that of a control (nondisabled) group. The goals were twofold: first to test the expectation that NLD children behave poorly in spatial text processing relative to both the control and RD groups; second, to verify whether spatial text perspective (route vs. survey) could influence their perfor-mance. Three types of text (nonspatial, spatial-survey, spatial-route) were orally presented, each immediately followed by a sentence verification task and a location task. Results showed that survey-text comprehension was particularly impaired in NLD children, who performed worse than RD and control groups in both the sentence verification and location tasks related to the survey text. Moreover, NLD children performed more poorly than the control group in the location task for route text.

These findings show that impairments in the spatial domain are related to an inability to process spatial information, even when the medium is verbal, and the findings confirm the results of the experimental and correlational studies reported earlier in this chapter in the context of clinical samples. Again, we see data supporting the conclusion that survey- and route-text processing rely on different cognitive mechanisms, given that the disadvantage of NLD children appears to be more critical with survey texts than with route texts. This result could reflect their incapacity to integrate the descriptions into a survey-like cognition map, this being due, for example, to specific deficits in processing simultaneous (rather than sequential) spatial information. Alternatively, the result could be associated with a delay in spatial ability development. Developmental models of spatial representation (e.g., Siegel & White, 1975), in fact, identify a more mature stage of spatial cognition in survey representation than in landmark-focused or route representation. It is possible that spatial deficits characterizing children with NLD bring about a delay, or even a definitive inability to obtain survey representation.

Conclusions

An overview of the notion of a mental model and the classical studies on spatial mental models was presented in the first part of the chapter. The validity of the mental model construct was confirmed and was used in the subsequent studies reported in the second and third sections, which deal with spatial text processing and individual differences. Our argument is that the consideration of the processes involved in the construction of the spatial model (WM, imagery strategies), together with the individual differences (in spatial ability, WM capacity, cognitive style, and also some developmental aspects) helps characterize the nature of the representation built. The studies overviewed in this chapter are demonstration of the specificity of spatial language relative to language in general. A number of conclusions about spatial language and some new routes of research can be drawn.

First of all, spatial text comprehension requires both VWM and VSWM abilities. This is seen very clearly both in experimental studies using the dual-task paradigm and in analysis of individual differences: concurrent spatial tasks impair comprehension of spatial texts much more than that of nonspatial texts; furthermore, individuals with poor VSWM capacity or very low spatial ability (in particular, spatial visualization and mental rotation) fail in spatial text processing much more than do people with average spatial skills. Analogous results have been obtained with special groups such as children affected by NLD and healthy elderly people. These data support the importance of VSWM and spatial ability in constructing spatial mental models, and show clearly that the capacities of maintaining and manipulating spatial information have a relevant role in spatial representation, even when visual and spatial perception are not involved. Extending spatial text comprehension studies to other pathological groups – such as brain-damaged patients who suffer from topographical disorientation, or cases with Alzheimer's disease or other dementias due to degenerative causes – could allow the specific role of perception and mental manipulation in spatial cognition to be determined.

Another area that deserves more investigation is the dependency (if there is any) of the spatial mental model on text perspective. A number of studies described here strongly suggest that on-line processing of survey texts and of route texts is supported by different cognitive mechanisms. However, it is not completely clear which particular mechanisms are involved. For example, it is well known that ST interferes with the processing of route texts (e.g., De Beni et al., 2005), but it is still not known which components of ST (motor involvement, sequentiality, intervention of executive processes) produce – alone or in interaction – this interference effect. At the same time, presentation of a configuration of dots is found to have an interference effect on survey-text processing, but whether this concurrent task relies on visual (Logie, 1995) or spatial-simultaneous WM subcomponents (Cornoldi & Vecchi, 2003; Pazzaglia & Cornoldi, 1999) is yet to be discovered.

It remains to define the nature of the spatial mental models constructed from survey and route descriptions. From the current state of our knowledge, it is in fact impossible to establish if the mental models stored in long-term memory are spatial and whether they present particular and distinct characteristics as a function of text perspective. Support for their having a spatial nature is found in the studies by Brunyé and Taylor (2008b) and Pazzaglia, De Beni, and Meneghetti (2007), where an interference effect of ST in the retrieval of information from a spatial text emerged. However, this effect has numerous alternative explanations – for example, being attributed to the fact that the stored model is spatial in nature, such that its reactivation requires spatial processes. Alternatively, it is possible that ST does not interfere with the reactivation of the mental model but, instead, with the processes required for testing tasks (free recall and sentence verification). Further research is necessary in this context.

Finally, a number of issues are raised by investigations on individual differences in spatial ability and spatial text processing. One example is the question of why individual differences in mental rotation are related to different levels of performance in the comprehension of spatial texts. It is possible that MRT and spatial text processing share a common ability to maintain and mentally manipulate visuospatial information. However, it remains to be established whether the underlying crucial factor is a general ability to process spatial information or, instead, the specific ability to mentally rotate spatial stimuli or assume different perspectives in space.

References

Allen, G. L., Kirasic, K. C., Dobson, S. H., Long, R. G., & Beck, S. (1996). Predicting environmental learning from spatial abilities: An indirect route. *Intelligence*, *22*, 327–355.
Avraamides, M. N., Loomis, J. M., Klatzky, R. L., & Golledge, R. G. (2004). Functional

equivalence of spatial representations derived from vision and language: Evidence from allocentric judgments. *Journal of Experimental Psychology: Learning, Memory, & Cognition, 30,* 801–814.

Baddeley, A. D. (1986). *Working Memory.* Oxford, UK: Oxford University Press.

Baddeley, A. D. (2000). The episodic buffer: A new component of working memory? *Trends in Cognitive Sciences, 4,* 417–423.

Baddeley, A. D. (2003). Working memory and language: An overview. *Journal of Communication Disorders, 36,* 198–208.

Baddeley, A. D., & Hitch, G. (1974). Working memory. In G. H. Bower (Ed.), *Recent advances in learning and motivation* (Vol. 8, pp. 47–89). New York: Academic Press.

Bosco, A., Filomena, S., Sardone, L., Scalisi, T. G., & Longoni, A. M. (1996). Spatial models derived from verbal descriptions of fictitious environments: The influence of study time and the individual differences in visuospatial ability. *Psychologische Beitrage, 38,* 451–464.

Bower, G. H., & Morrow, D. G. (1990). Mental models in narrative comprehension. *Science, 247,* 44–48.

Brooks, L. R. (1967). The suppression of visualization by reading. *Quarterly Journal of Experimental Psychology, 19,* 289–199.

Brooks, L. R. (1968). Spatial and verbal components of the act of recall. *Canadian Journal of Psychology, 22,* 349–368.

Brunyé, T. T., Rapp, D. N., & Taylor, H. A. (2008). Representational flexibility and specificity following spatial descriptions of real-world environments. *Cognition, 108,* 418–443.

Brunyé, T. T., & Taylor, H. A. (2008a). Extended experience benefits spatial mental model development with route but not survey descriptions. *Acta Psychologica, 127,* 340–354.

Brunyé, T. T., & Taylor, H. A. (2008b). Working memory in developing and applying mental models from spatial descriptions. *Journal of Memory and Language, 58,* 701–729.

Bryant, D. J., Tversky, B., & Franklin, N. (1992). Internal and external spatial frameworks for representing described scenes. *Journal of Memory and Language, 31,* 74–98.

Carlson-Radvansky, L. A., & Irwin, D. E. (1993). Frames of reference in vision and language: Where is above? *Cognition, 46,* 223–244.

Chabanne, V., Péruch, P., Denis, M., & Thinus-Blanc, C. (2003–2004). Mental scanning of images constructed from visual experience or verbal descriptions: The impact of survey versus route perspective. *Imagination, Cognition and Personality, 23,* 163–171.

Clark, J. M., & Paivio, A. (1991). Dual coding theory and education. *Educational Psychology Review, 3,* 149–210.

Copeland, D. E., & Radvansky, G. A. (2007). Aging and integrating spatial mental models. *Psychology and Aging, 22,* 569–579.

Cornoldi, C., & Vecchi, T. (2003). *Visuo-spatial working memory and individual differences.* Hove, UK: Psychology Press.

Darken, R., & Peterson, B. (2002). Spatial orientation, wayfinding and representation. In K. Stanney (Ed.), *Handbook of virtual environments: Design, implementation and applications.* Mahwah, NJ: Lawrence Erlbaum Associates.

Dean, R. S., & Kulhavy, R. W. (1981). The influence of spatial organization in prose learning. *Journal of Educational Psychology, 73,* 57–64.

De Beni, R., Cornoldi, C., Larsson, M., Magnussen, S., & Ronnberg, J. (2007). Memory experts: Visual learning, wine tasting, orienteering and speech-reading. In S. Magnussen & T. Helstrup (Eds.), *Everyday memory* (pp. 201–227). Hove, UK: Psychology Press.

De Beni, R., & Moè, A. (2003). Presentation modality effects in studying passages: Are mental images always effective? *Applied Cognitive Psychology*, *17*, 309–324.

De Beni, R., Pazzaglia, F., Gyselinck, V., & Meneghetti, C. (2005). Visuospatial working memory and mental representation of spatial description. *European Journal of Cognitive Psychology*, *17*, 75–95.

Denis, M. (1991). *Image and cognition*. New York: Harvester Wheatsheaf.

Denis, M., & Cocude, M. (1989). Scanning visual images generated from verbal description. *European Journal of Cognitive Psychology*, *1*, 293–307.

Denis, M., Daniel, M. P., Fontaine, S., & Pazzaglia, F. (2001). Language, spatial cognition and navigation. In M. Denis, R. H. Logie, C. Cornoldi, M. de Vega, & J. Engelkamp (Eds.), *Imagery, language and spatial representation* (pp. 137–160). Philadelphia, PA: Psychology Press.

Denis, M., & Denhière, G. (1990). Comprehension and recall of spatial descriptions. *European Bulletin of Cognitive Psychology*, *10*, 115–143.

Denis, M., & de Vega, M. (1993). Modèles mentaux et imagerie mentale. In M. F. Ehrlich, H. Tardieu, & M. Cavazza (Eds.), *Les modèles mentaux. Approche cognitive des représentations* (pp. 79–100). Paris : Masson.

Denis, M., Pazzaglia, F., Cornoldi, C., & Bertolo, L. (1997). Spatial discourse and navigation: An analysis of route directions in the city of Venice. *Applied Cognitive Psychology*, *13*, 145–174.

de Vega, M. (1994). Characters and their perspectives in narratives describing spatial environments. *Psychological Research*, *56*, 116–126.

de Vega, M., Cocude, M., Denis, M., Rodrigo M. J., & Zimmer, H. D. (2001). The interface between language and visuo-spatial representations. In M. Denis, R. H. Logie, C. Cornoldi, M. de Vega, & J. Engelkamp (Eds.), *Imagery, language and visuo-spatial thinking* (pp. 109–136). New York: Psychology Press.

Deyzac, E., Logie, R., & Denis, M. (2006). Visuospatial working memory and the processing of spatial descriptions. *British Journal of Psychology*, *97*, 271–243.

Dijkstra, K., Yaxley, R. H., Madden, C. J., & Zwaan, R. A. (2004). The role of age and perceptual symbols in language comprehension. *Psychology and Aging*, *19*, 352–356.

Ehrlich, K., & Johnson-Laird, P. N. (1982). Spatial descriptions and referential continuity. *Journal of Verbal Learning and Verbal Behavior*, *21*, 296–326.

Ekstrom, R. B., French, J. W., & Harman, H. H. (1976). *Manual for kit of Factor Referenced Cognitive Tests*. Princeton, NJ: Educational Testing Service.

Evans, G. W. (1980). Environmental cognition. *Psychological Bulletin*, *88*, 259–287.

Farmer, E. W., Berman, J. V. F., & Fletcher, Y. L. (1986). Evidence for a visuo-spatial scratch-pad in working memory. *Quarterly Journal of Experimental Psychology*, *38*, 375–688.

Ferguson, E. L., & Hegarty, M. (1994). Properties of cognitive maps constructed from texts. *Memory and Cognition*, *22*, 455–473.

Fields, A. W., & Shelton A. L. (2006). Individual skill differences and large-scale environmental learning. *Journal of Experimental Psychology: Learning, Memory, and Cognition*, *32*, 506–515.

Fletcher, C. R., & Chrysler, S. T. (1990). Surface forms, textbases, and situation models: Recognition memory for three types of textual information. *Discourse Processes*, *13*, 175–190.

Fraisse, P., & Léveillé, M. (1975). Influence du codage visuel de phrases sur leur mémorisation à court terme. *L'Année Psychologique*, *75*, 409–416.

Franklin, N., & Tversky, B. (1990). Searching imagined environments. *Journal of Experimental Psychology: General, 119*, 63–76.

Franklin, N., Tversky, B., & Coon, V. (1992). Switching points of view in spatial mental models. *Memory & Cognition, 20*, 507–518.

Friedman, A., & Hall, D. L. (1996). The importance of being upright: Use of environmental and viewer-centered reference frames in shape discriminations of novel three-dimensional objects. *Memory & Cognition, 24*, 285–295.

Garnham, A. (1981). Mental models as representations of text. *Memory & Cognition, 9*, 560–565.

Giesen, C., & Peeck, J. (1984). Effects of imagery instruction on reading and retaining a literary text. *Journal of Mental Imagery, 8*, 79–90.

Glenberg, A. M., Meyer, M., & Lindem, K. (1987). Mental models contribute to fore-grounding during text comprehension. *Journal of Memory and Language, 26*, 69–83.

Gray-Wilson, S., Rinck, M., McNamara, T. P., Bower, G. H., & Morrow, D. G. (1993). Mental models and narrative comprehension: Some qualifications. *Journal of Memory and Language, 32*, 141–154.

Gyselinck, V., Cornoldi, C., Dubois, V., De Beni, R., & Ehrlich, M. F. (2002). Visuospatial memory and phonological loop in learning from multimedia. *Applied Cognitive Psychology, 16*, 665–685.

Gyselinck, V., De Beni, R., Pazzaglia, F., Meneghetti, C., & Mondoloni, A. (2007). Working memory components and imagery instructions in the elaboration of a spatial mental model. *Psychological Research, 71*(3), 373–382.

Gyselinck, V., Ehrlich, M. F., Cornoldi, C., De Beni, R., & Dubois, V. (2000). Visuospatial working memory in learning from multimedia systems. *Journal of Computer Assisted Learning, 16*, 166–175.

Gyselinck, V., Meneghetti, C., De Beni, R., & Pazzaglia, F. (2009). The role of working memory in spatial text processing: What benefit of imagery strategy and visuospatial abilities? *Learning and Individual Differences, 19*, 12–20.

Haenggi, D., Kintsch, W., & Gernsbacher, M. A. (1995). Spatial situation models and text comprehension. *Discourse Processes, 19*, 173–199.

Hakala, M. (1999). Accessibility of spatial information in a situation model. *Discourse Processes, 27*, 261–279.

Hegarty, M., Montello, D. R., Richardson, A. E., Ishikawa, T., & Lovelace, K. (2006). Spatial abilities at different scales: Individual differences in aptitude-test performance and spatial-layout learning. *Intelligence, 34*, 151–176.

Johnson-Laird, P. N. (1980). Mental models in cognitive science. *Cognitive Science, 4*, 71–115.

Johnson-Laird, P. N. (1983). *Mental models: Towards a cognitive science of language, inference, and consciousness*. Cambridge, UK: Cambridge University Press.

Kintsch, W. (1988). The use of knowledge in discourse processing: A construction-integration model. *Psychological Review, 95*, 163–182.

Kintsch, W., Welsch, D., Schmalhofer, F., & Zimny, S. (1990). Sentence memory: A theoretical analysis. *Journal of Memory and Language, 29*, 133–159.

Kruley, P., Sciama S. C., & Glenberg, A. M. (1994). On-line processing of textual illustrations in the visuospatial sketchpad: Evidence from dual-task studies. *Memory & Cognition, 22*, 261–272.

Kulhavy, R. W., Stock, W. A., Peterson, S. E., Pridemore, D. R., & Klein, J. D. (1992). Using maps to retrieve text: A test of conjoint retention. *Contemporary Educational Psychology, 17*, 56–70.

Kulhavy, R. W., Stock, W. A., Verdi, M. P., Rittschof, K. A., & Savenye, W. (1993). Why maps improve memory for text: The influence of structural information on working memory operations. *European Journal of Cognitive Psychology, 5*, 375–392.

Kulhavy, R. W., & Stock, W. A., Woodard, K. A., & Haygood, R. C. (1993). Comparing elaboration and dual coding theories: The case of maps and text. *American Journal of Psychology, 106*, 483–498.

Langston, W., Kramer, D. C., & Glenberg, A. M. (1998). The representation of space in mental models derived from text. *Memory and Cognition, 26*, 247–262.

Lawton, C. A. (1994). Gender differences in way-finding strategies: Relationship to spatial ability and spatial anxiety. *Sex Roles, 30*, 765–779.

Lawton, C. A., & Kallai, J. (2002). Gender differences in wayfinding strategies and anxiety about wayfinding: A cross-cultural comparison. *Sex Roles, 47*, 389–401.

Lee, P., & Tversky, B. (2005). Interplay between visual and spatial: The effect of landmark descriptions on comprehension of route/survey spatial descriptions. *Spatial Cognition and Computation, 5*, 163–185.

Likert, R., & Quasha, W. H. (1948). *Revised Minnesota Paper Form Board Test*. San Antonio, TX: Psychological Corporation.

Linn, M. C., & Petersen, A. C. (1985). Emergence and characterization of sex differences in spatial ability: A meta-analysis. *Child Development, 56*, 1479–1498.

Logie, R. H. (1986). Visuo-spatial processing in working memory. *Quarterly Journal of Experimental Psychology, 38*, 229–247.

Logie, R. H. (1995). *Visuo-spatial working memory*. Hove, UK: Lawrence Erlbaum Associates.

Mammarella, I. C., Meneghetti, C., Pazzaglia, F., Gitti, F., Gomez, C., & Cornoldi, C. (2009). Representation of survey and route spatial descriptions in children with nonverbal (visuospatial) learning disabilities. *Brain and Cognition, 71*, 173–179.

Mani, K., & Johnson-Laird, P. N. (1982). The mental representation of spatial descriptions. *Memory and Cognition, 10*, 181–187.

Marks, D. F. (1973). Visual imagery differences in the recall of pictures. *British Journal of Psychology, 64*, 17–24.

Marschark, M. (1985). Imagery and organization in the recall of prose. *Journal of Memory and Language, 24*, 734–745.

McNamara, T. P., Halpin, J. A., & Hardy J. K. (1992). The representation and integration in memory of spatial and nonspatial information. *Memory & Cognition, 20*, 519–532.

Meneghetti, C., Borella, E., Grasso, I., & De Beni, R. (2011). Environment learning with map and/or description: Age-related differences in young and older adults. *Environmental Psychology*. Manuscript submitted for publication.

Meneghetti, C., Gyselinck, V., Pazzaglia, F., & De Beni, R. (2009). Individual differences in spatial text processing: High spatial ability can compensate for spatial working memory interference. *Learning and Individual Differences, 19*, 577–589.

Meneghetti, C., Pazzaglia, F., & De Beni R. (2011). Spatial mental representations derived from survey and route descriptions: When individuals prefer extrinsic frame of reference. *Learning and Individual Differences, 21*, 150–157.

Milner, B. (1971). Interhemispheric differences in the localization of psychological processes in man. *British Medical Bulletin, 27*, 272–277.

Morrow, D. G. (1994). Spatial models created from text. In H. van Oostendorp & R. A. Zwaan (Eds.) (pp. 57–78). *Naturalistic text comprehension*, Norwood, NJ: Ablex.

Morrow, D. G., Bower, G. H., & Greenspan, S. L. (1989). Updating situation models during narrative comprehension. *Journal of Memory and Language, 28*, 292–312.

Morrow, D. G., Greenspan, S. L., & Bower, G. H. (1987). Accessibility and situation models in narrative comprehension. *Journal of Memory and Language, 26*, 165–187.

Morrow, D. G., Leirer, V., Altieri, P., & Fitzimmons, C. (1994). Age differences in creating spatial models from narratives. *Language and Cognitive Processes, 9*, 203–220.

Nichelli, P., & Venneri, A. (1995). Right hemisphere developmental learning disability: A case study. *Neurocase, 1*, 173–177.

Noordzij, M. L., & Postma, A. (2005). Categorical and metric distance information in mental representations derived from route and survey descriptions. *Psychological Research, 69*, 221–232.

Noordzij, M. L., van der Lubbe, R. H. J., & Postma, A. (2005). Strategic and automatic components in the processing of linguistic spatial relations. *Acta Psychologica, 119*, 1–20.

Noordzij, M. L., van der Lubbe, R. H. J., & Postma, A. (2006). Electrophysiological support for strategic processing of spatial sentences. *Psychophysiology, 43*, 277–286.

Nori, R., & Giusberti, F. (2003). Cognitive styles: Errors in directional judgments. *Perception, 32*, 307–320.

Nori, R., & Piccardi, L. (2009). Familiarity and spatial cognitive style: How important are they for spatial representation? In J. B. Thomas (Ed.), *Spatial memory: Visuospatial processes, cognitive performance and developmental effects* (pp. 123–144). New York: Nova Science.

Paivio, A. (1971). *Imagery and verbal processes.* New York: Holt, Rinehart and Winston.

Paivio, A. (1986). *Mental representations: A dual coding approach.* New York: Oxford University Press.

Pani, J. R., & Dupree, D. (1994). Spatial reference systems in the comprehension of rotational motion. *Perception, 23*, 929–946.

Pazzaglia, F. (2008). The specific involvement of verbal and visuospatial working memory in hypermedia learning. *British Journal of Educational Technology, 39*, 110–124.

Pazzaglia, F., & Cornoldi, C. (1999). The role of distinct components of visuo-spatial working memory in the processing of texts. *Memory, 7*, 19–41.

Pazzaglia, F., Cornoldi, C., & De Beni, R. (2000). Differenze individuali nella rappresentazione dello spazio e nell'abilità di orientamento. Presentazione di un questionario auto valutativo [Individual differences in representation of space: Presentation of questionnaire]. *Giornale Italiano di Psicologia, 3*, 627–650.

Pazzaglia, F., Cornoldi, C., & Longoni, A. M. (1994). Limiti di memoria e specificità di rappresentazione nel ricordo di descrizioni spaziali "dall'alto" ed "entro il percorso" [Limits of memory and the specificity of representations in the memory of survey and route descriptions]. *Giornale Italiano di Psicologia, 21*, 267–286.

Pazzaglia, F., De Beni, R., & Meneghetti, C. (2007). The effects of verbal and spatial interference in the encoding and retrieval of spatial and nonspatial texts. *Psychological Research, 71*, 484–494.

Pazzaglia, F., & Meneghetti, C. (2011). Spatial text processing in relation to preferential style in spatial representation. *European Journal of Cognitive Psychology.* Manuscript submitted for publication.

Pazzaglia, F., Meneghetti, C., De Beni, R., Gyselinck, V. (2010). Working memory components in survey and route spatial text processing, *Cognitive Processing, 11*, 359–369.

Perrig, W., & Kintsch, W. (1985). Propositional and situational representations of text. *Journal of Memory and Language, 24*, 503–518.

Quinn, J. G., & McConnell, J. (1996). Irrelevant pictures in visual working memory. *Quarterly Journal of Experimental Pshychology, 49*, 200–215.

160   *Language, space, and action*

Radvansky, G. A., Zwaan, R. A., Curiel, J. M., & Copeland, D. E. (2001). Situation models and aging. *Psychology and Aging, 16*, 145–160.

Rapp, D. N., Klug, J. L., & Taylor, H. A. (2006). Character movement and the representation of space during narrative comprehension. *Memory & Cognition, 34*, 1193–1205.

Rigoni, F., Cornoldi, C., & Alcetti, A. (1997). Difficolta' nella comprensione e rappresentazione di descrizioni visuospaziali in bambini con disturbi non-verbali dell'apprendimento [Reading comprehension difficulties and mental representation of spatial descriptions in children with nonverbal disabilities]. *Psicologia Clinica dello Sviluppo, 1*, 187–215.

Rinck, M., & Bower, G. H. (2000). Temporal and spatial distance in situation models. *Memory & Cognition, 8*, 1310–1320.

Rinck, M., Hahnel, A., Bower, G. H., & Glowalla, U. (1997). The metrics of spatial situation models. *Journal of Experimental Psychology: Learning, Memory, Cognition, 23*, 622–637.

Rourke, B. P. (Ed.). (1995). *Syndrome of nonverbal learning disabilities: Neurodevelopmental manifestations*. New York: Guilford Press.

Sadoski, M., Paivio, A., & Goetz, E. T. (1991). A critique of schema theory in reading and a dual coding alternative. *Reading Research Quarterly, 26*, 463–484.

Sardone, L., Bosco, A., Scalisi T. G., & Longoni A. M. (1995). The effects of study time on mental representations of spatial information acquired from texts. *Ricerche di Psicologia, 19*, 131–163.

Schmalhofer, F., & Glavanov, D. (1986). Three components of understanding a programmer's manual: Verbatim, propositional and situational representations. *Journal of Memory and Language, 25*, 279–294.

Shelton, A. L., & McNamara T. P. (2004). Orientation and perspective dependence in route and survey learning. *Journal of Experimental Psychology, 30*, 158–170.

Siegel, A. W., & White, S. H. (1975). The development of spatial representations of large-scale environments. In H. W. Reese (Ed.), *Advances in child development and behavior* (Vol. 10, pp. 9–55). New York: Academic Press.

Tardieu, H., Ehrlich, M. F., & Gyselinck, V. (1992). Levels of representation and domain-specific knowledge in comprehension of scientific texts. *Language and Cognitive Processes, 7*, 335–352.

Taylor, H. A., Naylor, S. J., & Chechile, N. A. (1999). Goal-specific influences on the representation of spatial perspective. *Memory & Cognition, 27*, 309–319.

Taylor, H. A., & Tversky, B. (1992a). Spatial mental models derived from survey and route descriptions. *Journal of Memory and Language, 31*, 261–292.

Taylor, H. A., & Tversky, B. (1992b). Descriptions and depictions of environments. *Memory & Cognition, 20*, 483–496.

Tolman, E. C. (1948). Cognitive maps in rats and men. *Psychological Review, 55*, 189–208.

Tranel, D., Hall, L. E., Olson, S., & Tranel, N. N. (1987). Evidence for a right-hemisphere developmental learning disability. *Developmental Neuropsychology, 3*, 113–127.

Tversky, B. (1991). Spatial mental models. In G. H. Bower (Ed.), *The psychology of learning and motivation: Advances in research and theory* (Vol. 27, pp. 109–145). New York: Academic Press.

Vandenberg, S. G., & Kuse, A. R. (1978). Mental rotations, a group test of three-dimensional spatial visualization. *Perceptual and Motor Skills, 47*, 599–604.

van Dijk, T. A. (1987). Episodic models in discourse processing. In R. Horowitz & S. J. Samuels (Eds.). *Comprehending Oral and Written Language*, New York: Academic Press, 161–196.

van Dijk, T. A., & Kintsch, W. (1983). *Strategies of discourse comprehension.* New York: Academic Press.

Voyer, D., Voyer, S., & Bryden, M. P. (1995). Magnitude of sex difference in spatial abilities: A meta-analysis and consideration of critical variables. *Psychological Bulletin, 117,* 250–270.

Wechsler, D. (1981). *Wechsler Adult Intelligence Scale – Revised.* New York: Psychological Corporation.

Worling, D. E., Humphries, T., & Tannock, R. (1999). Spatial and emotional aspects of language inferencing in nonverbal learning disabilities. *Brain and Language, 70,* 220–239.

Zwaan, R. A., & Radvansky, G. A. (1998). Situation models in language comprehension and memory. *Psychological Bulletin, 123,* 162–185.

Zwaan, R. A., & van Oostendorp, H. (1993). Do readers construct spatial representations in naturalistic story comprehension? *Discourse Processes, 16,* 125–144.

7 Language of space

A comparison between blind and sighted individuals

Matthijs L. Noordzij and Albert Postma

Introduction

People talk about many things, and most of the time conversations are about other people, objects, or events that are not directly perceivable. This is not true for spatial language use. An important characteristic of spatial communication is that it often relies on a tight coupling between linguistic and visual information. An utterance such as *"Your car keys are on the coffee table"* could be seen as a linguistic starting point or an imperative from one person, which will result in a visual search by another person. This coupling has been captured in a detailed and rigorous fashion by Carlson and Logan in a theoretical framework, experimental work, and a computational model (e.g., Carlson, 1999; Carlson-Radvansky & Irwin, 1994; Logan & Compton, 1996; Logan & Sadler, 1996; Regier & Carlson, 2001). To describe this work in detail is beyond the scope of this chapter, but it is important to note that it predicts how visual attention is directed over a visual scene to establish a link between a conceptual representation (of the spatial sentence) and a perceptual representation (of the visual scene). However, these ideas become hard to apply in a situation where a spatial sentence is encountered without accompanying visual information. This could happen when a person hears a route description of a town that he or she is about to visit in the near future, or when someone is incapable of receiving visual information (i.e., when this person is blind). The question of how sighted and blind people represent and memorize these "isolated" spatial descriptions is the theme of this chapter.

One could argue that the study of spatial language use by the blind should actually be one of the main research directions in scientific investigations into the production and comprehension of spatial language. There are at least two (sets of) reasons for this. First, because blind people cannot use their visual modality, they cannot establish a coupling between linguistic and visual information. However, we established above that this coupling is a defining feature of spatial language use. Studying how blind people represent spatial language thus provides a unique opportunity to study spatial language use separate from visual processing. We could mention several other reasons along these lines (e.g., what the effect is of replacing a primary linguistic–visual coupling with a primary linguistic–haptic coupling), and these would all fall within the realm of fundamental cognitive (neuro)science. Second, because blind people face all kinds of orientation and mobility challenges in their daily lives, one could argue that well-designed spatial descriptions might be an important tool to enhance their wayfinding skills. Of course, blind people can use tactile maps and other wayfinding aids, but the flexibility and accessibility (everyone can give them on the spot) of spatial descriptions make them a primary means to convey spatial information to the blind. This second reason falls more within the realm of applied (cognitive) psychology. In this chapter, we focus on fundamental scientific studies on spatial language processing in the blind and sighted, but we also aim to provide some guidelines for more applied work. Specifically, by the end of this chapter, we can give a scientifically motivated answer to the questions: Is spatial language really a helpful tool for enhancing and supporting the orientation and mobility capacities of blind people? And, should spatial communication directed at the blind have particular characteristics in order to be efficient?

In order to answer these questions, this chapter sets out to describe work on spatial representations in the blind and sighted in general. Much work has been done on this topic, and many of these findings are relevant for the special case of representations based on spatial language. In addition, we introduce a framework for spatial representations that encompasses both sensory and linguistic inputs and that will serve as a basis for describing the results from studies on spatial language. After this general introduction on spatial representations, we discuss very basic spatial sentences and how they are represented, both functionally and neurally, in the blind and in the sighted. Subsequently, we move on to more complex spatial descriptions and outline to what extent representations based on these are similar to what people memorize when they study visual maps or through actual navigation. Finally, we focus on the influence of text perspective in spatial descriptions and whether blind and sighted people have different preferences related to this variable. We conclude by summarizing the presented information and answering the questions of whether spatial language is a helpful tool to the blind and whether it should have certain characteristics in order to be helpful.

Spatial representations and the blind

For sighted people, many of their spatial abilities are inextricably bound up with their visual capacities. Grasping your cup of coffee, finding your way in a new town, avoiding approaching cars when crossing the road, all might intuitively seem very difficult without sight. There are also scientific studies that show that blind people have severe problems with spatial tasks (e.g., Kitchin & Jacobsen, 1997). In line with this, Warren (1984) reviewed developmental differences between blind and sighted children using a "blindness as deficit" approach. This type of approach assumes that visual inputs form the basis of the ability to build a spatial representation of the world (or a spatial image – see below) that is not directly dependent on the original sensory input. Furthermore, the visual modality is the "right" modality, and a lack of this modality will have serious negative consequences for the ability to form spatial images.

It is clear that congenitally blind people cannot have, and have never had, the opportunity to receive visual input, but they can and have relied on tactile and auditory input. It could be that they could form spatial representations on the basis of these alternative inputs. For the sake of clarity, we introduce two diagrams at this point (see Figure 7.1; adapted from Struiksma, Noordzij, & Postma, 2009) that will serve as basic building blocks for our discussions of representations that the blind and sighted can form on the basis of sensory and verbal (or linguistic) inputs. What becomes clear from these diagrams is that both the sighted (Figure 7.1A) and the blind (Figure 7.1B) can form spatial images, which are mental representations of the physical world, that can contain information about the relative position of objects, metric distances between objects, and the orientation of objects (de Vega, Intons-Peterson, Johnson-Laird, Denis, & Marschark, 1996). These spatial images are assumed to have supramodal qualities in the sense that they rely both on modality-specific brain areas (e.g., in the case of visual input, the primary visual cortex) and also on supramodal areas, which are activated independently from the original input channel (for a review, see Cattaneo et al., 2008). Furthermore, the different modalities contribute to the spatial images with different weights. For the sighted, the visual modality has the highest weight, while the other modalities have relatively modest contributions. In contrast, for the blind, the visual modality has no weight, while the other modalities have relatively substantial contributions. Finally, Figure 7.1 indicates that amodal input (namely linguistic information) can contribute to spatial images. This amodal view on linguistic information can be debated, because words themselves are always encountered through a particular modality. However, to view the encoding of linguistic information into an amodal conceptual representation ("a set of propositions") is an influential theoretical position and one that is encountered quite often in the processing of spatial language. Therefore, this option is included in Figure 7.1, and we return to it below when discussing studies directly related to spatial language.

Given that the blind can rely on, among other things, tactile and auditory information to form a spatial image, while the sighted have a strong dependence on the visual modality, a "blindness as deficit" model does not seem very appropriate. Instead, the different pathways leading up to a supramodal spatial image leave the option open that spatial images of the blind and sighted are actually very similar. On the one hand, this is in accordance with many studies on spatial (imagery) tasks where performance and functional behavior of the blind and sighted were the same (for a review, see Kaski, 2002). On the other hand, this does not do justice to the fact that, as mentioned above, there are also many studies that do find differences. Therefore, more intermediate theoretical positions have been suggested on the consequence of blindness for the quality of the resulting spatial images. For example, the so-called difference theory (see Fletcher, 1980) argues that blind individuals can understand spatial concepts and process them in ways functionally equivalent to that of the sighted, although taking longer and requiring a greater cognitive effort. This difference in time and effort could be the result of the difference in input channels. Tactile input is laborious, slow, and serial, while

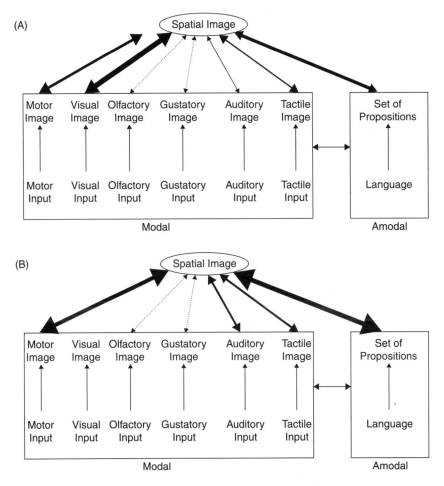

Figure 7.1 Diagram to elucidate a supramodal view on the formation of spatial images for both the sighted and the blind (adapted from Struiksma, Noordzij, & Postma, 2009). (A) A variety of modal inputs are available to sighted people to create a supramodal spatial representation. The width of the arrows indicates the relative importance of a certain modality for the spatial representation. For the sighted, the visual modality is most important. Next to the modal inputs, amodal input to the spatial image results from linguistic information. (B) A similar diagram but now aimed at describing the processes for the blind. The other modalities gain in importance for the creation of a spatial image. This holds in particular for the motor, auditory, tactile, and linguistic inputs.

visual input (in comparison) is easy, fast, and parallel (but for a criticism of this point and a critical discussion of the "fastness" of the visual channel, see Thinus-Blanc & Gaunet, 1997). A related theory – the "continuity" model (see Cornoldi & Vecchi, 2003) – has the assumption that blind representations are subjected to limitations due to the specific type of information and to the complexity of required operations, namely that the necessity to combine multiple spatial images (in working memory) in a short time frame and the manipulation of three-dimensional information are indicated as specifically problematic.

The "compensatory view" assumes that the blind can compensate or look for more familiar strategies: the blind seem to have superior tactile acuity (Goldreich & Kanics, 2006), to be better at auditory localization (Lessard, Pare, Lepore, & Lassonde, 1998; Röder, Teder-Salejarvi, Sterr, Rösler, Hillyard, & Neville, 1999), and to be more accurate than sighted individuals in self-positioning in the environment on the basis of auditory cues. In line with this notion, research on the coding of space by blind people in haptic and locomotor tasks has shown that certain strategies might differ from those employed by the sighted with respect to the preferred reference frame (Millar, 1994; Postma, Zuidhoek, Noordzij, & Kappers, 2008). Millar argues that blind people tend to code spatial information (especially of large spaces) in the form of a local, sequential representation (i.e., egocentric representation/ bias), whereas sighted people mostly code spatial information in the form of a more global, externally based representation (allocentric representation/ bias).

Simple spatial sentences and imagery

Now that we have given an introduction on spatial images in the blind, we will move on to the main topic of this chapter: spatial language processing in the blind. A starting point for discussing the representation of spatial language could very well be to look at a (relatively) simple sentence such as "*the plus is above the star*", in which a single spatial relation is identified. Classic studies on the representation of spatial sentences employed the sentence–picture verification task (using, in fact, the above-mentioned sentence as one of the stimuli; Carpenter & Just, 1975; Chase & Clark, 1972; Clark & Chase, 1972). In this task participants are first asked to read a spatial sentence, after which they are confronted with a picture for which they have to indicate whether the information is the same as in the sentence. The two options for the representational format of a spatial sentence that have been proposed for the sentence–picture verification task echo those from the "imagery debate": a set of propositions (amodal) or a visual mental image (modal) (see Figure 7.1A) (MacLeod, Hunt, & Mathews, 1978).

In the decades that followed, several theoretical models were formed that can, to some extent, be traced back to this distinction. First, the model of Carlson and Logan mentioned in the introduction assumes that the spatial sentence is always represented propositionally. Second, theories that get their inspiration from embodied cognition (see chapter 8, this volume) assume that language use always entails some kind of mental simulation that is grounded in the relevant modality (Barsalou, 1999; Barsalou, Simmons, Barbey, & Wilson, 2003; Zwaan, 2004). Third, the concept of a dual code (Paivio, 1983), which suggests that both forms of representation are available at the same time, has been put forward in mental model theory (Johnson-Laird, 1983; van Dijk & Kintsch, 1983). Fourth, it might be that, as a default, a propositional, amodal code (Struiksma, Noordzij, & Postma,

2009) is formed of a spatial sentence and that a visual mental image is created strategically. Evidence for this last idea comes from some of our own studies (Noordzij, van der Lubbe, Neggers, & Postma, 2004; Noordzij, van der Lubbe, & Postma, 2005, 2006). For example, by employing electroencephalogram (EEG) measures during sentence–picture and sentence–sentence verification tasks, we were able to establish whether spatial sentences elicited different event-related potentials (ERPs) depending on the context – visual or verbal – in which the sentence was read (Noordzij, van der Lubbe, & Postma, 2006). We found a transient slow wave between ± 600 and 1,200 ms after spatial sentence presentation in parieto-occipital regions associated with imagery processes (Bosch, Mecklinger, & Friederici, 2001). This slow wave was much stronger in a visual context than in a verbal context, suggesting that people only or more strongly employed visual imagery during spatial sentence processing when they know they will use the information in the sentence to evaluate, at a later point in time, a particular visual scene. What becomes clear from the above-mentioned models (see Figure 7.1) is that in almost all cases a basic, amodal representation is assumed for the processing of simple spatial sentences. In the next section, we further examine the possibility that this amodal code is "the bridge" that allows the blind and sighted to communicate about space.

A shared code for the blind and the sighted?

It is clear that it is possible for blind and sighted people to exchange ideas about their surroundings using spatial language. If we now follow the simple dichotomy that was proposed between mental images and propositions, a good candidate for a shared representation, which would allow for communication between those with and without vision, would be the propositional, amodal code. Can we provide any evidence for such a shared code? We try to argue for this by looking at possible similarities in how categories of spatial words are represented in the brain of blind and sighted individuals.

At the heart of spatial language use lies the word category of spatial prepositions such as "*above*", "*in front of*", and "*beside*". This is actually a small class of words (about 70) in most languages, and Landau and Jackendoff (1993) had already suggested that semantic aspects of processing this class of words might be subserved by parts of the parietal lobe (in contrast to more inferior, temporal areas usually associated with other word categories). Neuropsychological and neuroimaging studies further corroborated and refined this hypothesis. Tranel and Kemmerer (2004) tested 78 patients with various brain lesions and found that matching and naming spatial prepositions was impaired in a small subset of six patients. Lesion overlap techniques revealed that these patients all had lesions in a particular part of their parietal lobe (the left supramarginal gyrus, SMG). Neuroimaging research with healthy adults also revealed that the SMG was more activated for naming spatial prepositions compared to naming tools and other utensils (Damasio et al., 2001). We showed that in sentence–picture and sentence–sentence verification tasks, the SMG was more activated for sentences containing spatial prepositions (compared to sentences with nonspatial conjunction terms, Noordzij, Neggers, Ramsey, & Postma, 2008; for a further review of neural correlates of spatial terms, see Kemmerer, 2006). This last finding is especially relevant given the fact that the context (visual or verbal) in which the spatial sentence was read did not influence the activity in the SMG. This suggests that this region is involved with amodal encoding and thus might support the above-mentioned propositional code.

Evidence for this idea of a shared code comes from a recent fMRI study (Struiksma, Noordzij, Neggers, Bosker, & Postma, 2011) in which both congenitally blind and sighted participants were asked to listen to two sentences and verify whether they contained the same information. Comparing spatial sentences with nonspatial sentences revealed that for both the blind and the sighted, activity in the left SMG was higher for the spatial stimuli. On the one hand, this provides – neurally, at least – evidence for a possible shared code between blind and sighted people, which could serve as a basis for common ground related to the understanding of spatial language. On the other hand, it becomes necessary to stress the fact that purely looking for a shared code on a propositional level is too limited. As we have indicated in our introduction on spatial images, congenitally blind people do not engage in spatial imagery on the basis of visual input, but they can rely on their other senses for this (for a recent review, see Struiksma, Noordzij, & Postma, 2009). It has been shown that in many cases blind people do show different functional behavior from that of the sighted in spatial imagery tasks (without a verbal component). On the level of simple spatial sentences, these differences are not readily apparent. For example, Fleming, Ball, Ormerod, and Collins (2006) found evidence that both blind and sighted individuals remembered linguistically described spatial relations equally well (although verbatim memory was surprisingly inferior in the blind). They argue that both the blind and the sighted spontaneously created analogues representations (i.e., spatial images) of these spatial sentences. It might be that more pronounced differences between the blind and the sighted can be found when the spatial descriptions (and the described layout) become more complex (Vecchi, 1998).

Complex spatial descriptions and imagery

Up to this point we have discussed scientific work that has measured responses from people to single spatial sentences (e.g., *"the plus is above the star"*). Typically, participants read or listen to only one of those sentences in any given trial. We will now move on to other studies where sighted participants listen to and memorize a set of spatial sentences.[1] Typically, these extended descriptions give information on a complex configuration of landmarks, which implicitly implies metric information. These descriptions can also be dynamic, because they guide the attention of the listener from one landmark to the next. This dynamic process can be either egocentric or only with reference to the landmarks; the consequences of this distinction for memorization are worked out further below. A good example stems from the work of Denis and Zimmer (1992). In this study, a series of experiments were done in which participants memorized a variety of spatial layouts by reading spatial texts with elements such as *"In the extreme northwestern part of the island, there is a bridge. East of the bridge, there are skyscrapers. . .".* After participants memorized this extensive spatial description, their memory was tested and probed by means of mental scanning, distance comparison, and priming tasks. These three tasks had been previously used (e.g., Kosslyn, Ball, & Reiser, 1978; McNamara, 1986) to establish whether certain characteristics such as spatial proximity and distance were present in representations based on perceptual experience (i.e., maps). Denis and Zimmer (1992) found similar results (e.g., a symbolic distance effect – see Moyer & Bayer, 1976) for participants who studied a map or a verbal description. From this they argued for the structural isomorphism of representations based on spatial descriptions. This idea of similar structural properties for perceptually and verbally based representations has since received strong experimental corroboration and theoretical follow-ups (e.g., Avraamides, Loomis, Klatzky, & Golledge, 2004; Cocude, Mellet, & Denis, 1999; Denis, 2008; Loomis, Klatzky, Avraamides, Lippa, & Golledge, 2007).

It is important to note that spatial information that is communicated by means of a verbal description is usually restricted to categorical spatial relations, such as *"the cat lies on the ground under the table".* Although it is possible to say *"the cat lies on the ground, 60.7 cm. under the table",* people almost always leave out this detailed, metric spatial information from their verbal descriptions. In contrast, a photograph of your living room, with the aforementioned cat on her favorite spot under the table, would contain this detailed information. The differences between, on the one hand, the lack of detail in spatial descriptions and, on the other, the precise metric detail in direct perceptual experience might also be reflected in the mental representations people build up from descriptions or perception. Hence, it could be that representations from descriptions are rather crude and contain only categorical spatial information, whereas representations based on direct perception contain metric spatial information (Jager & Postma, 2003). The above-mentioned work of Denis and others contradicts this line of reasoning. There is a structural isomorphism (i.e., including metric detail) for representations based on both verbal and perceptual experiences.

Some of our own work has further strengthened this claim. A problem with many of the studies on extensive spatial descriptions is that the spatial information is described with direct reference to an iconic visual form or is supported by visual aids that explicitly show a particular form. For example, the position of objects is described in terms of their place on a circle (*"the lighthouse is at 2 o'clock, the tree is at 6 o'clock, and the mountain is at 11 o'clock"*), or participants see a visual matrix of possible object locations after which the spatial description "fills in" this matrix at certain spots. One could argue that metric detail that might exist in the visual mental image originates from the reactivation from memory of the iconic form or the presented visual form. To counter this claim, we conducted a study in which people listened to a fairly complex spatial description of an unknown spatial configuration (Noordzij & Postma, 2005). Despite the lack of a reference to an existing geometrical form or explicit visual aids, we found that people exhibited spatial priming and symbolic distance effects in their responses to recognition/priming and distance comparison tasks. This strengthens the original claims by Denis and others by showing that response patterns indicative of isomorphism do not disappear when people cannot rely on information other than that which was presented in a complex spatial description.

Complex spatial descriptions, blindness, and perspective

Although there is an abundance of evidence that sighted people can build detailed mental representations (spatial mental models) of complex spatial descriptions (see chapter 6, this volume), this does not necessarily mean that blind people can do the same. A person listening to a spatial description that contains several sentences needs to continually integrate and transform different pieces of spatial information in order to build a coherent spatial mental model (Zwaan & Radvansky, 1998). It has been suggested that these kinds of active, on-line spatial processes might be more difficult for the (congenitally) blind (Cornoldi & Vecchi, 2000). This would mean that blind people would build up a propositional representation of a complex spatial description, which would allow them to "playback" the description at a later point in time, but it would limit their ability to make spatial inferences. This latter line of reasoning has been further qualified by some of our research. We asked blind participants to memorize complex spatial descriptions and subsequently tested and probed their memory of these descriptions (Noordzij, Zuidhoek, & Postma, 2006). Identical to the behavior of sighted participants in the original studies of Denis described above, the blind participants showed spatial priming effects and symbolic distance effects. This indicates that the representations on which they were relying to answer our (spatial) questions contained spatial information that allowed for metric spatial inferences.

Besides the question of whether people build up a spatial representation at all, many researchers have looked into the issue of what the influence of several characteristics of complex spatial descriptions is on spatial representations (Brunyé, Rapp, & Taylor, 2008; Rinck & Denis, 2004; Rinck, Hähnel, Bower, & Glowalla, 1997; Shelton & McNamara, 2004; Taylor & Tversky, 1992). Communicating information involves making choices about *how* to tell something. These choices involve the level of detail in a story, the amount of emotion included, and the perspective from which everything is described. Consequently, the choices people make pertaining to *how* to describe something might have a great impact on *what* the listener or reader thinks the information actually is or means. Especially relevant for spatial descriptions is the perspective with which spatial information is communicated. Speakers mostly seem to choose between two types of spatial perspectives in realistic everyday descriptions, or a mix between the two (e.g., Hund, Haney, & Seanor, 2008). The first consists of taking listeners or readers on a mental tour, using terms such as "to the left" and "to the right", and maintaining a linear structure. This is termed a route perspective; the second consists of taking a viewpoint that is above the environment, using terms such as "North of" and "to the West", and maintaining a hierarchical structure. This is termed a survey perspective.

The perspective of a spatial text is especially relevant for blind people. As mentioned in our introduction on spatial images in the blind, we know from research on their spatial learning skills in haptic and locomotor tasks that they prefer to code spatial information in relation to their own body, resulting in quite local, sequential representations. This can be contrasted with the more global, externally based representations of the sighted (Millar, 1994; Postma et al., 2008; Thinus-Blanc & Gaunet, 1997). This local/global contrast can also be found in the two text perspectives described above. Route descriptions describe landmarks relative to a moving person/body, never foreshadowing anything that is not directly in the vicinity. Survey descriptions start out with giving global information about the environment, clearly giving the listener an overview in which landmarks are described relative to one another (eliminating any egocentric references). It turns out that, similar to what happens in the haptic and locomotor domain, blind people prefer (i.e., have better memories of) route descriptions to survey descriptions (Noordzij, Zuidhoek, & Postma, 2006). In contrast, sighted people prefer survey descriptions, because their spatial mental models based on survey descriptions contain more metric detail (Noordzij & Postma, 2005) and are learned with greater ease than those based on route descriptions (Brunyé & Taylor, 2008).

Now that we have discussed how blind and sighted people represent both simple and complex spatial descriptions, we can relate this to the general model we provided in Figure 7.1 and tailor it specifically for the case of spatial language. Sighted and blind people can represent spatial language in the following way, where option 1(a) is relevant for the sighted and option 1(b) is (most) relevant for the blind:

1 (a) Through a mental spatial representation (bound to visual/global information).
  (b) Through a mental spatial representation (bound to haptic/local information).

2 Through a propositional (amodal) code.

Conclusions

In this chapter we have provided a description of the representational options that are available to blind and sighted people when they are confronted with "isolated" spatial sentences. These two groups have a lot in common. Denis and Zimmer (1992) showed that sighted people show remarkably similar responses when they have to answer spatial questions based on either a visual map or a verbal description. In turn, Noordzij, Zuidhoek, and Postma (2006) observed that blind people show remarkably similar responses to sighted people when answering spatial questions about complex spatial texts they have studied. These similarities allow us to answer in the affirmative the first question we asked in the introduction "*Is spatial language really a helpful tool for enhancing and supporting the orientation and mobility capacities of blind people?"* People can create these complex spatial descriptions on the fly, and, as the research presented in this chapter demonstrates, both blind and sighted people can subsequently create detailed spatial images from them. This is a remarkable feat and something that should not be overlooked when trying to strengthen the orientation and mobility skills of the blind. There are also differences between the blind and the sighted. The blind prefer spatial descriptions that are presented as a route. The sequential nature of these route descriptions fits better with how they experience the world and probably plays to their strengths in terms of their superior serial memory skills (Raz, Striem, Pundak, Orlov, & Zohary, 2007). From this we can formulate an answer to the second question we posed at the beginning of this chapter: *"Should spatial communication directed at the blind have particular characteristics in order to be efficient?"* We think the answer is: Yes, it should! Namely, people addressing the blind with the aim of providing spatial information efficiently should take care that their descriptions always take into account the position of the listener and consequently relate any landmark or turn to the relative position of the virtually) moving body of the listener. By doing this, a spatial description can be as informative to the blind as a good visual map is to the sighted.

The recommendations above are useful because they are based on general biases found in rigorous scientific work. However, they are based on differences on a group level. On an individual level, a certain group bias might be reversed. In our work on text perspective (Noordzij, Zuidhoek, & Postma, 2006) we found that, in general, the blind preferred route descriptions. However, on an individual level there was one congenitally blind individual who greatly preferred a survey description (and memorized the spatial layout very accurately on the basis of this global, map-like description). In real life, people also typically mix perspectives (Taylor & Tversky, 1996) and do not strictly adhere to one perspective. In a recent applied study, the most effective way to describe census data to the blind was examined (Thomas, Sripida, & Noordzij, in press). Census data can contain information about the frequency distribution of a certain demographic variable (i.e., incidence of crime in different regions in a country). This type of data is typically illustrated to the sighted by means of a map with different colored regions. For the blind, these maps are inaccessible, and therefore spatial descriptions are an obvious alternative. It seemed that the blind preferred egocentric terms (to the right) over allocentric terms (to the east). However, the most preferred way of receiving spatial descriptions on these data and locations was actually by providing composite descriptions (i.e., crime was highest to the east and to the right). Although these composite descriptions in essence provided no more information than a single description, they were without exception indicated as the preferred ones. This is an example where strictly applying the biases found from fundamental science might have seemed very successful (i.e., the blind gave higher ratings to egocentric than to allocentric sentences). Yet, by introducing a more realistic set of stimuli (mixing perspectives and providing redundant information), an even better alternative was found for solving a real-world problem. Therefore, much work still needs to be done on the application of findings from fundamental cognitive work to the reality of providing effective spatial descriptions to the blind.

Note

1 We will continue the comparison with the blind in the following section, but most of the earlier studies on complex spatial descriptions only recruited sighted participants.

References

Avraamides, M. N., Loomis, J. M., Klatzky, R. L., & Golledge, R. G. (2004). Functional equivalence of spatial representations derived from vision and language: Evidence from allocentric judgments. *Journal of Experimental Psychology: Learning, Memory, & Cognition, 30*, 801–814.

Barsalou, L. W. (1999). Perceptual symbol systems. *Behavioral & Brain Sciences, 22*, 577–660.

Barsalou, L. W., Simmons, W. K., Barbey, A. K., & Wilson, C. D. (2003). Grounding conceptual knowledge in modality-specific systems. *TRENDS in Cognitive Sciences, 7*, 84–91.

Bosch, V., Mecklinger, A., & Friederici, A. D. (2001). Slow cortical potentials during retention of object, spatial and verbal information. *Cognitive Brain Research, 10*, 219–237.

Brunyé, T. T., Rapp, D. N., & Taylor, H. A. (2008). Representational flexibility and specificity following spatial descriptions of real-world environments. *Cognition, 108*, 418–443.

Brunyé, T. T., & Taylor, H. A. (2008). Extended experience benefits spatial mental model development with route but not survey descriptions. *Acta Psychologica, 127*, 340–354.

Carlson, L. A. (1999). Selecting a reference frame. *Spatial Cognition and Computation, 1*, 365–379.

Carlson-Radvansky, L. A., & Irwin, D. E. (1994). Reference frame activation during spatial term assignment. *Journal of Memory & Language, 33*, 646–671.

Carpenter, P. A., & Just, M. A. (1975). Sentence comprehension: A psycholinguistic processing model of verification. *Psychological Review, 82*, 45–73.

Cattaneo, Z., Vecchi, T., Cornoldi, C., Mammarella, I., Bonino, D., Ricciardi, E., et al. (2008). Imagery and spatial processes in blindness and visual impairment. *Neuroscience & Biobehavioral Reviews, 32*, 1346–1360.

Chase, W. G., & Clark, H. H. (1972). Mental operations in the comparison of sentences and pictures. In L. W. Gregg (Ed.), *Cognition in learning and memory*. New York: Wiley.

Clark, H. H., & Chase, W. G. (1972). On the process of comparing sentences against pictures. *Cognitive Psychology, 3*, 472–517.

Cocude, M., Mellet, E., & Denis, M. (1999). Visual and mental exploration of visuo-spatial configurations: Behavioral and neuroimaging approaches. *Psychological Research, 62*, 93–106.

Cornoldi, C., & Vecchi, T. (2000). Mental imagery in blind people: The role of passive and active visuospatial processes. In M. A. Heller (Ed.), *Touch, representation, and blindness* (pp. 143–181). Oxford, UK: Oxford University Press.

Cornoldi, C., & Vecchi, T. (2003). *Visuo-spatial working memory and individual differences*. Hove, UK: Psychology Press.

Damasio, H., Grabowski, T. J., Tranel, D., Ponto, L. L. B., Hichwa, R. D., & Damasio, A. R. (2001). neural correlates of naming actions and of naming spatial relations. *NeuroImage, 13*, 1053–1064.

Denis, M. (2008). Assessing the symbolic distance effect in mental images constructed from verbal descriptions: A study of individual differences in the mental comparison of distances. *Acta Psychologica, 127*, 197–210.

Denis, M., & Zimmer, H. D. (1992). Analog properties of cognitive maps constructed from verbal descriptions. *Psychological Research, 54*, 286–298.

de Vega, M., Intons-Peterson, M. J., Johnson-Laird, P. N., Denis, M., & Marschark, M. (Eds.). (1996). *Models of visuospatial cognition.* New York: Oxford University Press.

Fleming, P., Ball, L. J., Ormerod, T. C., & Collins, A. F. (2006). Analogue versus propositional representation in congenitally blind individuals. *Psychonomic Bulletin & Review, 13*, 1049–1055.

Fletcher, J. (1980). Spatial representation in blind children. 1: Development compared to sighted children. *Journal of Visual Impairment & Blindness, 74*(10), 381–385.

Goldreich, D., & Kanics, I. M. (2006). Performance of blind and sighted humans on a tactile grating detection task. *Perception & Psychophysics, 68*, 1363–1371.

Hund, A. M., Haney, K. H., & Seanor, B. D. (2008). The role of recipient perspective in giving and following wayfinding directions. *Applied Cognitive Psychology, 22*, 896–916.

Jager, G., & Postma, A. (2003). On the hemispheric specialization for categorical and coordinate spatial relations: A review of the current evidence. *Neuropsychologia, 41*, 504–515.

Johnson-Laird, P. N. (1983). *Mental models.* Cambridge, MA: Harvard University Press.

Kaski, D. (2002). Revision: Is visual perception a requisite for visual imagery? *Perception, 31*, 717–731.

Kemmerer, D. (2006). The semantics of space: Integrating linguistic typology and cognitive neuroscience. *Neuropsychologia, 44*, 1607–1621.

Kitchin, R., & Jacobsen, R. (1997). Techniques to collect and analyze the cognitive map knowledge of people with visual impairments or blindness. *Journal of Visual Impairment & Blindness, 9*, 360–376.

Kosslyn, S. M., Ball, T. M., & Reiser, B. J. (1978). Visual images preserve metric spatial information: Evidence from studies of image scanning. *Journal of Experimental Psychology: Human Perception & Performance, 4*, 47–60.

Landau, B., & Jackendoff, R. (1993). "What" and "where" in spatial language and spatial cognition. *Behavioral & Brain Sciences, 16*, 217–265.

Lessard, N., Pare, M., Lepore, F., & Lassonde, M. (1998). Early-blind human subjects localize sound sources better than sighted subjects. *Nature, 395*(6699), 278–280.

Logan, G. D., & Compton, B. J. (1996). Distance and distraction effects in the apprehension of spatial relations. *Journal of Experimental Psychology: Human Perception & Performance, 22*, 159–172.

Logan, G. D., & Sadler, D. D. (1996). A computational analysis of the apprehension of spatial relations. In P. Bloom, M. A. Peterson, L. Nadel, & M. F. Garret (Eds.), *Language and space* (pp. 493–529). Cambridge, MA: MIT Press.

Loomis, J. M., Klatzky, R. L., Avraamides, M. N., Lippa, Y., & Golledge, R. G. (2007). Functional equivalence of spatial images produced by perception and spatial language. In F. Mast & L. Jäncke (Eds.), *Spatial processing in navigation, imagery, and perception* (pp. 29–48). New York: Springer.

MacLeod, C. M., Hunt, E. B., & Mathews, N. N. (1978). Individual differences in the verification of sentence–picture relationships. *Journal of Verbal Learning & Verbal Behavior, 17*, 493–507.

McNamara, T. P. (1986). Mental representations of spatial relations. *Cognitive Psychology, 18*, 87–121.

Millar, S. (1994). *Understanding and representing space: Theory and evidence from studies with blind and sighted children*. Oxford, UK: Oxford University Press.

Moyer, R. S., & Bayer, R. H. (1976). Mental comparison and the symbolic distance effect. *Cognitive Psychology*, *8*, 228–246.

Noordzij, M. L., Neggers, S. F. W., Ramsey, N. F., & Postma, A. (2008). Neural correlates of locative prepositions. *Neuropsychologia*, *46*, 1576–1580.

Noordzij, M. L., & Postma, A. (2005). Categorical and metric distance information in mental representations derived from route and survey descriptions. *Psychological Research*, *69*, 221–232.

Noordzij, M. L., van der Lubbe, R. H., Neggers, S. F. W., & Postma, A. (2004). Spatial tapping interferes with the processing of linguistic spatial relations. *Canadian Journal of Experimental Psychology*, *58*, 259–271.

Noordzij, M. L., van der Lubbe, R. H., & Postma, A. (2005). Strategic and automatic components in the processing of linguistic spatial relations. *Acta Psychologica*, *119*, 1–20.

Noordzij, M. L., van der Lubbe, R. H. J., & Postma, A. (2006). Electrophysiological support for strategic processing of spatial sentences. *Psychophysiology*, *43*, 277–286.

Noordzij, M. L., Zuidhoek, S., & Postma, A. (2006). The influence of visual experience on the ability to form spatial mental models based on route and survey descriptions. *Cognition*, *100*, 321–342.

Paivio, A. (1983). The empirical case for dual coding. In J. C. Yuille (Ed.), *Imagery, memory and cognition*. Hillsdale, NJ: Lawrence Erlbaum Associates.

Postma, A., Zuidhoek, S., Noordzij, M. L., & Kappers, A. M. (2008). Haptic orientation perception benefits from visual experience: Evidence from early blind, late blind and sighted people. *Perception and Psychophysics*, *70*, 1197–1206.

Raz, N., Striem, E., Pundak, G., Orlov, T., & Zohary, E. (2007). Superior serial memory in the blind: A case of cognitive compensatory adjustment. *Current Biology*, *17*, 1129–1133.

Regier, T., & Carlson, L. A. (2001). Grounding spatial language in perception: An empirical and computational investigation. *Journal of Experimental Psychology: General*, *130*, 273–298.

Rinck, M., & Denis, M. (2004). The metrics of spatial distance traversed during mental imagery. *Journal of Experimental Psychology: Learning, Memory, & Cognition*, *30*, 1211–1218.

Rinck, M., Hähnel, A., Bower, G. H., & Glowalla, U. (1997). The metrics of spatial situation models. *Journal of Experimental Psychology: Learning, Memory, & Cognition*, *23*, 622–637.

Röder, B., Teder-Salejarvi, W., Sterr, A., Rösler, F., Hillyard, S. A., & Neville, H. J. (1999). Improved auditory spatial tuning in blind humans. *Nature*, *400*(6740), 162–166.

Shelton, A. L., & McNamara, T. P. (2004). Orientation and perspective dependence in route and survey learning. *Journal of Experimental Psychology: Learning, Memory, & Cognition*, *30*, 158–170.

Struiksma, M. E., Noordzij, M. L., Neggers, S. F. W., Bosker, W. M., & Postma, A. (2011). Spatial language processing in the blind: Evidence for a supramodal representation and cortical reorganization. *PLoS ONE*, *6*(9), e24253. doi: 10.1371/journal.pone.0024253

Struiksma, M. E., Noordzij, M. L., & Postma, A. (2009). What is the link between language and spatial images? Behavioral and neural findings in blind and sighted individuals. *Acta Psychologica*, *132*, 145–156.

Taylor, H. A., & Tversky, B. (1992). Spatial mental models derived from survey and route descriptions. *Journal of Memory & Language*, *31*, 261–292.

Taylor, H. A., & Tversky, B. (1996). Perspective in spatial descriptions. *Journal of Memory & Language, 35*, 371–391.

Thinus-Blanc, C., & Gaunet, F. (1997). Representation of space in blind persons: Vision as a spatial sense? *Psychological Bulletin, 121*, 20–42.

Thomas, K., Sripada, S., & Noordzij, M. L. (in press). Atlas.txt: Exploring linguistic grounding techniques for communicating spatial information to blind users. *Universal Access in the Information Society.*

Tranel, D., & Kemmerer, D. (2004). Neuroanatomical correlates of locative prepositions. *Cognitive Neuropsychology, 21*(7), 719–749.

van Dijk, T. A., & Kintsch, W. (1983). *Strategies of discourse comprehension.* New York: Academic Press.

Vecchi, T. (1998). Visuo-spatial imagery in congenitally totally blind people. *Memory, 6*, 91–102.

Warren, D. H. (1984). *Blindness and early childhood development.* New York: American Foundation for the Blind.

Zwaan, R. A. (2004). The immersed experiencer: Toward an embodied theory of language comprehension. In B. H. Ross (Ed.), *The psychology of learning and motivation* (Vol. 44). New York: Academic Press.

Zwaan, R. A., & Radvansky, G. A. (1998). Situation models in language comprehension and memory. *Psychological Bulletin, 123*, 162–185.

8 Language and action

An approach to embodied cognition

Manuel de Vega

Introduction

There are two general approaches to linguistic meaning: symbolist theories and embodiment theories. The symbolist approach assumes that words and sentences activate mental symbols in our mind, which are abstract, arbitrary, and amodal. For symbolists, comprehension basically consists of a translation process from an external symbolic language (words) into an internal symbolic language (mental symbols). Thus, if you read or listen to the word "cat", you would activate an abstract symbol in your mind, which is connected to other equally abstract symbols, none of which have any similarity to your visual, auditory, tactile, or motor experience with cats. The symbolist doctrine has been quite successful in cognitive sciences, because it allowed computational analyses of language meaning in terms of symbolic codes such as propositions, lists of features, semantic networks, semantic dimensions, statistical covariations, etc. One problem with symbolism, however, is that language meaning lacks grounding in the world (Harnad, 1990; Searle, 1980; Shapiro, 2008). Namely, words only refer to abstract symbols, associated with other symbols, which in turn are associated with other symbols, and so on; thus, language meaning remains in a sort of "Chinese room", never interfacing with the world experience (Searle, 1980).

The need of grounding in the world is evident in conversational settings, where speakers continuously refer to entities and events in the current environment and, thus, words have to be mapped into perception and action to be fully understood. But even when we refer to absent events, we must be able to establish a correspondence between the linguistic utterances and the real world. For instance, in a route description task, it is useful for the addressee to build an embodied representation that guides her or him to identify the described landmarks and to produce the appropriate navigation (straight walks and turns) in the real environment (e.g., Denis, Daniel, Fontaine, & Pazzaglia, 2001) (for an account of representations of spatial descriptions, see chapters 6 and 7, this volume). However, for traditional symbolic theories, the grounding problem remains unsolved.

By contrast, the embodiment approach to meaning considers that language is grounded on the world. This means that the same perceptual, motor, and emotional brain mechanisms used in real-world experience are involved to some extend in the processing of linguistic meaning. According to this view, meaning consists of the mental simulation of the objects, events, and situations to which words refer. For instance, if you read or listened to the sentence "*John hammered a nail into the wall*", this would briefly activate in your mind visual, auditory, motor, and even emotional images of the scene. And if your brain activity were recorded, we could expect small activations in the visual, auditory, and motor cortex, overlapping the regions involved in the performance of hammering a nail. But is this true?

Fortunately, the embodiment approach relies on experimental methods, using both behavioral and brain measures, and the literature provides many empirical demonstrations of embodiment phenomena. This chapter is related to the embodiment approach to language meaning, focusing on action-related language. The main purpose is to provide and discuss evidence on how action-related language activates motor simulations in the brain. The chapter will be organized as follows. The first section below describes behavioral experiments supporting the idea that understanding action-related sentences activates motor representations; the second section provides neuroscience data demonstrating that the understanding of action-related sentences activates premotor and motor areas in the brain; the third section discusses some theoretical interpretations of embodied meaning, based on behavioral and neuroscience experiments; the fourth section describes some advantages of the embodiment approach in comparison with disembodied theories; the fifth section discusses one challenge to embodied theories, namely abstract language; and the final section offers some conclusions.

Behavioral studies on action-related language

One way to test whether action language involves a motor simulation is to use double-task paradigms, in which the comprehension of action-related sentences overlaps or immediately precedes the performance of a related action. In the basic procedure, participants are asked to understand sentences describing motor events and to perform a motor task designed to match or mismatch the meaning of the sentences. The rationale is that when the action described by the sentence and the motor action match, a meaning–action interaction might be observed, indicating that both share motor processes. With this paradigm, a meaning–action facilitatory effect was reported in some cases. That is, the meaning–action matching conditions produce faster responses than the mismatching conditions (Borreggine & Kaschak, 2006; Glenberg & Kaschak, 2002; Zwaan & Taylor, 2006). Thus, Glenberg and Kaschak (2002) asked people to judge how sensible were sentences describing a motion toward or away from you (e.g., "Andy delivered the pizza to you" or "You delivered the pizza to Andy") or nonsense sentences. For some participants, the "yes" response involved a hand motion towards their body, and the "no" response a hand motion away from their body; for other participants, it was the other way around. The judgments for sensible sentences were faster for the matching conditions (e.g., sentences describing a transfer towards you, responding "yes" towards you) than for the mismatching conditions. Zwaan and Taylor (2006) obtained a similar meaning–action facilitatory effect, using sentences describing actions that usually involve a clockwise (e.g., "Louis sharpened the pencil") or counterclockwise hand rotation (e.g., "Eric turned down the volume"). In their Experiment 2, participants were given each sentence auditorily and made a speedy sensibility judgment, by turning a knob clockwise or counterclockwise. As in the previous meaning–action effect experiments, Zwaan and Taylor found faster sensibility judgments for the matching condition.

Other studies have found interference rather than facilitation for the meaning–action matching conditions (Buccino et al., 2005; de Vega, Moreno, & Castillo, 2011). For instance, Buccino et al. (2005) gave participants hand-action sentences (e.g., "He took the cup"), foot-action sentences (e.g., "He kicked the ball"), or abstract sentences, and they had to respond if the sentence described an action, and refrain from responding otherwise. Hand responses were faster for foot-action than for hand-action sentences, and foot responses were faster for hand-action than for foot-action sentences. In other words, using the same effectors as those implicit in the sentence meaning interferes rather than facilitates motor responses. In another experiment, Buccino et al. (2005) sent single-pulse transcranial magnetic stimulation (TMS) to participants' hand-motion brain areas or foot-motion brain areas synchronized with the motion verb of each sentence. They recorded the motor evoked potentials (MEP) at muscles related to hand motion and foot motion and again found interference in the matching conditions – namely, decreasing MEP at hand sites for hand-motion sentences, and decreasing MEP at foot sites for foot-motion sentences.

Several factors could contribute to the discrepancy in the meaning–action effect results, either of facilitation or interference in the matching conditions. The experiments differ in the complexity of the linguistic materials (single words, single-clause sentences, or double-clause sentences), the semantic task (sensibility judgments, categorical judgments, lexical decision), the response paradigm (choice, go/no-go, self-paced reading), and the temporal overlap between the linguistic stimulus and the motor response.

To explore the role of meaning–action temporal overlap, de Vega, Moreno, and Castillo (2011) manipulated the temporal delay between the comprehension process and the production of the motor response. The motor action accompanying the sentences was a simple directional response to an apparent motion cue. This psychophysical response did not require the burden of a semantic judgment, and the apparent motion cue could be placed at specific times in the sentence without need to process the whole sentence. De Vega, Moreno, and Castillo (2011) used transfer sentences describing motions towards (e.g., "my friend *passed* me the sharpener") or away from oneself (e.g., "I *passed* my friend the sharpener") and collected the motor responses at several delays following the transfer verb. For short verb-action delays (100–200 ms), they found interference – namely, slower responses in the matching conditions (e.g., transfer away/motion away) than in the mismatching condition (e.g., transfer towards/motion away). By contrast, when the motion cue was given with a delay of 350 ms after the transfer verb, there was facilitation in the matching conditions, indicating priming between meaning and action.

The most interesting effect was the interference observed in the matching conditions, when the action verb and the motor response were temporally close. A possible explanation is that in this case neural competition for the same motor resources takes place. For instance, it might be the case that constructing a simulation of an away transfer motion during language comprehension requires the activation of some specific neurons in the motor cortex that are tuned to respond to planning or execution actions in that direction, and this causes a momentary competition for the same neuronal resources when the participant performs an away motion. However, it seems that the neural overload fades quite soon, because when the motion was delayed more than 200 ms the standard facilitation for meaning–action matching conditions was found. The early onset and short life of the motor effect fits well with neuroscience data that also demonstrate a fast and brief activation of action-related meaning, as we will see in the next section (Pulvermüller, Shtyrov, & Ilmoniemi, 2003).

The meaning–action effect not only occurs for concrete sentences describing physical actions, but also for abstract sentences such as counterfactuals and metaphors. People use counterfactuals to make conjectures about how past events might have been if just a relatively small change in the situation had occurred. For instance, "If I had studied last week, I would have passed the exam". Counterfactuals involve two meanings: a realistic meaning, or how things really happened (I did not study nor pass the exam); and an alternative meaning, or how things would have happened (I did study and passed the exam). The two meanings are necessary to fully produce or understand counterfactuals. In some experiments performed by de Vega and Urrutia (2011), participants listened to sentences including a transfer action either in counterfactual (e.g., "If my brother had been generous he would have lent me the Harry Potter novel"), or factual format (e.g., "Since my brother is generous he has lent me the Harry Potter novel"). At the moment of the transfer verb (*lent*) presentation, participants received a visual cue prompting them to move their finger away or towards themselves to press a given key. As in previous experiments (de Vega, Moreno, & Castillo, 2011), the motor response was slower in the matching conditions, in both the factual and the counterfactual sentences, suggesting that neural competition in the motor brain occurs also for the counterfactual meaning.

In the same vein, Santana and de Vega (2011) performed another study with orientational metaphors, like those originally described by Lakoff and Johnson (1980), to test whether metaphorical meaning activates motor representations on-line. Participants read for comprehension; among other conditions, orientational metaphors (e.g., "she climbed up in the company") and concrete literal sentences (e.g., "she climbed up the hill). While reading each sentence, participants performed an upward or downward hand motion that either matched or mismatched the direction conveyed by the sentence meaning. In Experiment 1, the hand motion was prompted by a dynamic visual cue (an upward or downward animation of the sentence verb), and the results showed faster responses in the matching conditions for concrete literals as well as for metaphors. For instance, understanding the metaphor "she climbed up in the company" speeded upward motions, whereas understanding the metaphor "she buried his hopes" speeded downward motions. In other words, meaning–action facilitation was obtained both for literal sentences describing physical vertical motions and for orientational metaphors describing abstract events, as Figure 8.1 illustrates. In this experiment, however, there was a possible confounding between the visual-motion effect and the hand-motion effect. Thus, in Experiment 2 the visual-motion cue substituted a static cue (a color switch of the verb) prompting a particular hand motion. In spite of this, the meaning–action facilitation was similar in literal sentences and metaphor, indicating that the motor component was sufficient to produce meaning–action effects. Finally, in Experiment 3 the motor motion was ruled out, whereas the visual motion was kept. In a go/no-go paradigm, participants pressed a single key when the verb moved upward or downward, and they did not respond otherwise. In this case, the facilitation effect faded – in other words, the visual component of motion did not interact with the meaning of orientational metaphors nor literal sentences describing vertical motions, suggesting that only the motor component (an implicit motor motion) is involved in the meaning of these sentences.

Although, strictly speaking, emotions are not actions (we do not execute fear or anger; we *feel* them), their expression involves motor components, such as motions of the face muscles, motions of the trunk and hands, or changes in the muscle tone. Some studies have shown that understanding emotional sentences is modulated by the participants' facial expression. For instance, in an experiment by Havas, Glenberg, and Rinck (2007), participants were given sentences describing pleasant ("You and your lover embrace after a long separation") and unpleasant situations ("The police car rapidly pulls up behind you, siren blaring"). While listening to the sentences, some participants were asked to keep a pen in the

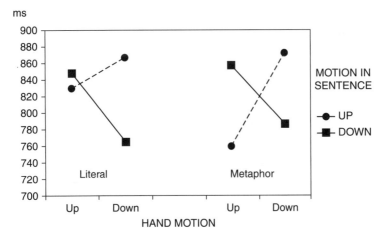

Figure 8.1 Meaning–action interaction. Upward and downward hand motions are primed by a concurrent sentence that refers to a matching motion. This effect occurs with both literal sentences and orientational metaphors (Santana & de Vega, 2011).

mouth using just the teeth (like smiling) or just the lips (like frowning). For each sentence, they were instructed to give judgments on whether it was "pleasant" or "unpleasant" by pressing the assigned keys on the keyboard. The results showed faster responses for pleasant sentences in the pen-with-teeth condition and faster responses for unpleasant sentences in the pen-with-lips condition. In other words, emotional sentences were better understood when their emotional valence was consistent with the expression forced by the mouth-keeping task.

In the same vein, Havas, Glenberg, Gutowski, Lucarelli, and Davidson (2010) used a self-paced reading task in which participants received sentences describing happy situations ("You spring up the stairs to your lover's apartment"), angry situations ("Reeling from the fight with that stubborn bigot, you slam the car door"), and sad situations ("You hold back your tears as you enter the funeral home"). The study was run in two sessions, and, before the second one, participants were injected with a drug (botox) that temporarily paralyzed the muscles used for frowning (corrugators). After the botox administration, the reading times for the angry and the sad situation sentences increased, whereas the reading times for the happy situation sentences did not change. That is, the comprehension of emotional sentences was interfered with when the muscles used to express the corresponding emotions were blocked. This fact is quite remarkable, because it reverses the expected causal order (emotions cause face expressions), showing that expressions modulate the comprehension of emotional-related language, a clear embodiment phenomenon.

In summary, the behavioral studies demonstrated that during the comprehension of action-related sentences, motor activation of the peripheral effectors occurs, demonstrating embodied simulation of the corresponding actions. The motor simulations take place not only when the sentences describe factual concrete events, but also when they describe counterfactual and metaphorical events. In addition, the face muscles involved in emotional expressions are also recruited to get proper understanding of emotional sentences. These results support an embodiment explanation of meaning, rather than a disembodied or symbolic explanation. However, the above studies do not provide direct evidence of sensorimotor activations in the brain associated with meaning. In contrast, in the next section I describe some neuroscience studies that provided relevant data on the activation of the motor and premotor cortex in the comprehension of action-related language.

Neuroscience studies on action language

Recently, some experiments on cognitive science have reinforced the notion that language comprehension could involve a mental simulation of embodied experience. Thus, Pulvermüller, Hauk, Nikulin, and Ilmoniemi (2005) have studied the neural activity underlying the comprehension of action verbs. In one experiment, participants listened to action verbs while their brain hemodynamic response was recorded by means of functional magnetic resonance imaging (fMRI). The verbs referred to motions either of the mouth (e.g., lick), the finger and hands (e.g., pick), or the legs (e.g., kick). In another experimental session, the same participants performed real motions of their mouth, hands, and legs. The results were clear: performing physical actions activated the expected somatotopic regions in the motor and premotor cortex. Thus, mouth motions produced specific activations in regions near the Sylvian fissure, hand and arm motions activated dorsolateral areas, and foot and leg motions showed activation in the vertex and interhemispheric sulcus. Most importantly, listening to action verbs caused partial activation of the same areas activated when executing the corresponding actions. Notice that participants just listened to the words passively – they were not asked to perform any particular task with them or even to pay them attention. In spite of this, the obtained somatotopic activation indicates that it was quite automatic, suggesting strongly established connections between the neurons responsible for word recognition and the specific motor areas in the brain.

Other experiments have shown that not only isolated action verbs, but also action-related sentences activate motor and premotor brain areas (Aziz-Zadeh, Wilson, Rizolatti, & Iacoboni, 2006; Tettamanti et al. 2008). For instance, in another fMRI study Tettamanti et al. (2008) recorded brain activity while participants listened to sentences that described motions of the mouth ("I bite the apple"), hands ("I grasp a knife"), or legs ("I kick the ball"). They also listened to abstract sentences as a control condition ("I appreciate the sincerity"). The results showed that all the action-related sentences, unlike the control sentences, share activation in a specific subregion of the Broca area (pars triangularis) in the left inferior frontal gyrus. The role of the Broca area in the comprehension of action-related language is not surprising, because this is a genuine motor area, involved not only in the production of language but also in the comprehension and execution of actions (e.g., Hamzei et al., 2003). Tettamanti and his collaborators also reported that the somatotopic regions, mentioned above, were selectively activated by mouth-, hand-, and leg-related sentences. Globally, these results suggest that action-related language triggers a relatively abstract representation of actions associated with activation in the Broca area, and also specific motor programs associated with the corresponding somatotopic regions.

The neuronal overlapping between performing actions and understanding action-sentences was also observed when action effort was manipulated. Moving a heavy object demands more physical effort and, in some cases, more planning than moving a light object. Not surprisingly, effort has a correlate in brain activity. Thus, motor and premotor areas of the brain are activated differentially according to the degree of physical effort necessary for the target action, as reported in some recent papers. For instance, producing different degrees of effort in a squeezing task correlated with the volume of activation in the contralateral sensorimotor cortex and the supplementary motor area (Cramer et al., 2002). In the same vein, manipulating the objects' weight in a lifting task, randomly alternating heavy and light weights in an unpredictable way, determined activation in the right inferior parietal cortex (supramarginal gyrus) for all trials and additional activity in the left primary motor and the somatosensory cortices when the object was heavier than expected (Jenmalm, Schmitz, Forssberg, & Ehrsson, 2006).

More importantly for the purpose of this chapter, sentences describing actions with different degrees of effort also differentially activate motor areas in the brain.

Thus, when people understand action-related sentences, the implicit weight of the objects involved in the action plays a role in the embodied simulations of meaning. In an event-related fMRI study, Moody and Gennari (2009) recorded brain activity while participants read sentences describing actions towards objects differing in weight and therefore demanding varying degrees of physical effort: high-effort (e.g., pushing the piano), low-effort (e.g., pushing the chair), and no-effort (e.g., remembering the piano). They also obtained functional regions of interest when the same participants performed a physical-effort task (squeezing a ball). The results of the reading task indicated that motor and premotor regions, overlapping with those activated by the squeezing task, were sensitive to the degree of effort implicit in the action-related sentences. Thus the Broca area, among others, was specifically engaged in sentences describing high-effort actions, whereas the left inferior parietal lobe was sensitive to sentences describing both high- and low-effort actions. The observed sensitivity of the motor brain to the implicit effort of sentences demonstrated that language comprehension elicits action representations that are object-specific. In addition, these object-specific representations were built on-line, namely during the combinatorial process that integrates the verb and the noun meanings.

In another study, Urrutia, de Vega, and Gennari (2009) tested whether sentences describing hypothetical scenarios were also sensitive to effort manipulation. They used counterfactual sentences describing low- and high-effort actions, such as "If Pedro had decided to paint the room, he would have moved the picture/sofa". Notice that counterfactual sentences do not describe "real" events, but just imaginary events that did not happen. Thus, it may be unnecessary to activate embodied representations of counterfactual events because they do not have a real-world referent. In spite of this, Urrutia, de Vega, and Gennari reported more activation in high- than in low-effort counterfactuals in the left inferior parietal lobe, extending to the supramarginal gyrus (see Figure 8.2), which is a motor region associated with action-planning processes, including assessment of size, weight, and muscles involved in the action (Glover, 2004).

The neuroimaging studies provide important insights into how the brain motor networks play a role in the comprehension of action-related language. However, the poor temporal resolution of this technique makes it convenient to use other complementary techniques that permit accurate tracing of the temporal course of motor activation in the brain. Thus, Pulvermüller et al. (2005) used magnetoencephalography (MEG) to explore the temporal pattern of activation of brain regions while participants listened to the same action verbs employed in the aforementioned neuroimaging experiment. They observed activations in the specific somatotopic brain areas as soon as 200 ms after the word onset, and only 30 ms after activation in the Broca area. These activations, however, were short-lived and faded very soon, confirming the automaticity of resonance established also by behavioral studies.

Another technique recently used to explore the time course of motor activation consists of analyzing brain-rhythm changes associated with action-related language. Specifically, EEG studies have found that the mu rhythms are a good

(A)   (B)

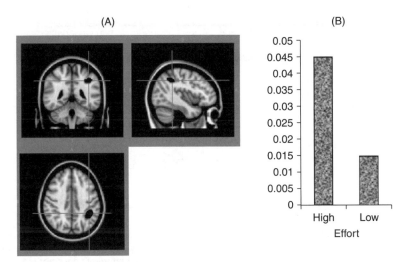

Figure 8.2 (A) Counterfactual sentences mentioning actions with light or heavy objects (e.g., "If Daniel had celebrated his wedding he would have raised his cup/bride") activate differentially the left inferior parietal lobe, shown in the left side of the brain sections. (B) The percent change in the hemodynamic response in this region is also shown for low- and high-effort sentences (Urrutia, de Vega, & Gennari, 2009).

marker of motor processes in the brain. The mu rhythms have a frequency of 8–14 Hz, similar to the alpha band rhythms although differing in their distribution (central in mu, and posterior in alpha) and their functionality. In particular, mu rhythms are synchronized in resting states, and they become desynchronized when individuals perform actions, when they see others' actions, or when they image performing actions themselves (see review by Pineda, 2005). In a recent experiment, Moreno, León, and de Vega (2011) collected EEG data while participants listened to action-related sentences ("I hammer a nail") or abstract sentences ("I trust in friendship") or observed action-related videos. Resting periods between blocks of trials were used as the baseline condition. The EEG-induced activity was analyzed by computing the power in the mu band, and a significant desynchronization was observed for action-related sentences, as well as action observations in the central electrodes (C3, Cz, C4). By contrast, the mu activity was kept at the baseline level in the abstract sentences. Figure 8.3 illustrates these results. The modulation of mu rhythms by action-related language can be considered a strong evidence of motor resonance and, when using time-frequency analysis of the EEG signal, provides an accurate timing of the phenomenon.

In a recent paper, van Elk, van Schie, Zwaan, and Bekkering (2010) also explored mu sensitivity to action-related sentences, using time-frequency analysis of the EEG signal. They employed sentences with action verbs involving an animal or a human agent ("The duck is *swimming* in the pond" vs. "The woman is

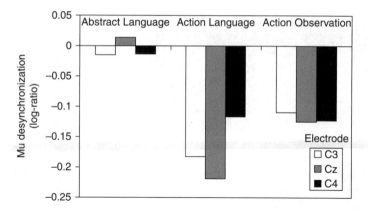

Figure 8.3 Desynchronization of mu rhythms in the central electrodes (C3, Cz, and C4) is a marker of motor processes in the brain. Action-related language and action observations desynchronize mu, whereas abstract language does not (Moreno, León & de Vega, 2011).

swimming in the water"), and they found larger mu and beta rhythm desynchronization starting 200 ms after the verb onset, which was stronger in the animal rather than the human agent condition. This could be counterintuitive, because the kinematics of swimming is very different in ducks and humans, and thus motor resonance should be larger for human actions, which are in our motor repertoire, than for animal actions, which are not. The authors' explanation for this paradoxical result is that motor resonance is associated with lexical–semantic processes of words, rather than motor images. Human agents are associated with a great number of predicates and, thus, a motor action like swimming is not very predictable, whereas the number of predicates applicable to animal agents is much more limited. Consequently, the motor resonance is more active in the former than in the later. In any case, mu suppression associated with action language was obtained similar to that in Moreno, León, and de Vega (2011).

The evidence provided by the neuroscience data is quite conclusive, clearly showing that understanding action verbs and sentences produces resonance in the somatotopic motor cortex. However, skeptical arguments are still possible. For instance, the neuroscience results are correlational rather than causal or explanatory. The fact that words and sentences trigger motor activations does not necessarily mean that these activations are relevant. In other words, the data do not demonstrate that resonance of the motor brain is a functional facet of linguistic meaning. It could be the case that sensorimotor resonance is just an associative phenomenon that fades without contributing to word and sentence meaning (Mahon & Caramazza, 2008). After all, according to the construction–integration theory many associative traces are activated during the stage of "construction", which are almost immediately suppressed at the stage of meaning "integration" (Kintsch, 1998).

The strength of the argument that meaning cannot be identified with motor resonance can be better appreciated if you consider that people who never bicycled or skied, and therefore do not have these skills in their motor repertoire, still could understand the verbs "bicycling" and "skiing". A tentative answer to this claim is that people who lack a given motor skill are still exposed to other embodied cues such as visual images of bicycling and skiing, and even they could roughly mimic the motor processes by means of their mirror-neuron system. A more empirical response could be demonstrating that, in fact, the lack of motor skills determines drawbacks in comprehension. For instance, some recent studies have shown that patients with Parkinson disease, who have damage in their motor brain, also show selective difficulties in understanding verbs (Boulenger et al., 2008; Castner et al., 2008; Crescentini, Mondolo, Biasutti, & Shallice, 2008). In the same vein, the behavioral studies described early in this chapter have shown that motor processes can be interfered with or facilitated by the comprehension of action-related sentences matching in a spatial parameter, such as direction of motion. A possible conclusion in this case is that action-related language mobilizes not only the motor brain but also peripheral responses in the muscles.

In summary, the neuroscience data are convergent with the behavioral data previously described in demonstrating underlying motor processes in the comprehension of action-related language. The neuroscience data are, however, more detailed, revealing activations in specific regions of the frontal and parietal cortex that partially overlap the motor and premotor cortex involved in the performance of real actions. In addition, both the behavioral and the neuroscience data coincide in showing that these activations occur on-line, starting as soon as 200 ms after the critical word onset, and that they are short-lived.

Theories of embodied meaning

The contributors to the embodiment approach have gone beyond the description of embodiment phenomena. They have provided theoretical interpretations of the empirical facts, proposing cognitive hypotheses to explain them (perceptual symbols, simulators, meshing of affordances), as well as possible neurological mechanisms for embodiment in the brain (motor resonance, Hebbian assemblies, mirror neurons). In this section, I focus briefly on the latter.

Motor resonance

A plausible neuronal mechanism for embodied meaning is resonance, or the reactivation of sensorimotor areas when words are processed (Fisher & Zwaan, 2008; Zwaan & Taylor, 2006). For instance, the meaning–action effects observed in behavioral studies or the motor activations for action-related language observed by means of neuroimaging could be explained by the interconnection between the brain areas responsible for processing word forms (e.g., Broca's and Wernicke's areas) and the motor areas in the brain. The connectivity among these areas determines that the activation of the language cortex *resonates* in the motor cortex.

Similar resonant circuitries can be established between concrete nouns and sensory areas in the brain that usually process color, shape, sound, smell, and the like, explaining how visual-related language is also embodied.

Hebbian assemblies

But why are language-related brain areas connected with the motor and premotor cortex? One possible mechanism for establishing these connections consists of cell assemblies that form a neuronal-learning mechanism (Hebb, 1949). According to Hebb, neurons that are connected to each other and fire together frequently strengthen their connections, whereas neurons that fire independently from each other tend to weaken their links. In other words, the coactivation of cortical neurons causes the strengthening of connections. Following the Hebbian hypothesis, Pulvermüller (1999, 2008) argues that the current neuroscience data confirm the existence of these neuronal assemblies' mechanisms, and these very mechanisms are responsible for embodied meaning. The functional consequence of these Hebbian assemblies is a resonance process. When a part of a Hebbian circuitry is activated by a sensory input, other associated circuitries also become activated; in the case of language, action-related words are processed first in the language cortex, which creates resonance in the corresponding motor cortex (Zwaan & Taylor, 2006; Fisher & Zwaan, 2008). The fast onset of resonance effects observed with meaning–action effect paradigms, as well as magnetoencephalographic methods, is consistent with the expected timing of a Hebbian neuronal mechanism.

Mirror neurons

The embodiment approach has also benefitted from the discovery of mirror neurons (Gallese, Keysers, & Rizzolatti, 2004). Mirror neurons are located in the motor cortex, but they are multimodal – that is, they fire when people execute an action, but also when people observe another individual performing an action, when they listen to the sound of an action, or even when they image themselves performing an action. These neurons were initially located in brain area F5 of the monkey's cortex, but other mirror neurons are located in the temporal and the parietal lobes as well as the insula. Recent studies both with animals and with humans have revealed important functions for the mirror-neuron system, including the comprehension of others' actions and intentions, or empathic emotions. Most importantly, language functions could also be associated with mirror neurons. We mentioned in the previous section that, according to fMRI studies, action-related language activates brain regions considered as part of the human mirror system. For instance, a subregion of the Broca area (pars triangularis), the human homologous of the monkey's F5, and the left parietal lobe were both differentially activated by action language (e.g., Aziz-Zadeh et al., 2006; Moody & Gennari, 2009; Tettamanti et al., 2008). These facts made Rizzolatti and Arbib (1998) speculate that language evolved in our species as a functional extension of the mirror-neuron system.

Not only seeing actions activates mirror motor neurons, but also seeing some objects can trigger activation in the motor cortex. Thus, graspable objects can activate some neurons in the monkey's F5 area (Fadiga & Craighero, 2003), even though the animal is neither performing nor observing any action. This fact could support the traditional notion of *affordance*. We not only perceive the visual features of objects, but we also perceive what they afford to us (they are graspable, edible, portable, seat-able, etc). In other words, they mobilize functional actions that could rely on a subset of the mirror neurons. The mirror-neuron system has also been associated with mu rhythms in the EEG because, as mentioned before, they are desynchronized both when the individuals perform actions and when they observe another's actions, and also – as we have seen above – when people under-stand action-related sentences.

Advantages of embodied meaning

The functional advantages of embodied meaning are clear. I mentioned above that symbolist theories (at least in their extreme version) are not able to solve the grounding problem, whereas embodied meaning is by definition grounded. I now discuss the functional advantages of embodied meaning in more detail, focusing on the functions of motor resonance in action-related language: (1) motor reso-nance facilitates the interface with the physical events, preparing the organism to get ready for action (or inaction); (2) motor resonance facilitates communication between speakers, providing a mechanism for common ground; and (3) motor resonance provides biological evaluation of the events.

Interface with the physical world

A functional advantage of embodied meaning is that it provides a better interface with the world than that of the symbolist approach. Embodied representations provide direct grounding of words into the world or, more accurately, into the perceptual and motor experience of the world, overcoming in this way the grounding problem of symbolism. Generally speaking, embodied representations are situational and prepare agents for situated action; in contrast, symbolic repre-sentations provide only categorical information (as in a dictionary or encyclo-pedia entry) and, thus, only prepare agents for retrieving associated symbols (e.g., Barsalou, Santos, Simmons, & Wilson, 2008).

The need for embodied/situated meaning is quite obvious in conversational settings, in which the speakers frequently refer to current events. Thus, the refer-ents of pronouns (I, you, she) or demonstratives (this, that) demand a direct connection between words and ongoing perceptual and motor experiences (de Vega, 2008). But even when conversations deal with events that are not in the current situation, the connection with world referents is necessary in many cases, as in route descriptions, working instructions, and the like. The idea that embodied meaning is an efficient "preparation for action" is also germane to the notion of meaning as mobilization of affordances postulated by Glenberg and Kaschak

(2002). Thus, nouns corresponding to objects would automatically activate motor affordances. For example, the word "paper" activates motor affordances such as "getting", "tearing", "throwing", or "writing", depending on the particular context.

Even speaking robots must use embodied representations to accomplish simple orders, such as "get the bottle to your left and give it to me". To accomplish the order, the robot must be able to connect words with entities and actions in the environment; for instance, the noun "bottle" must be mapped into the robot's visual world to identify the target, and the verbs "get" and "give" must trigger appropriate "motor" programs such as moving the mechanical arm and closing the mechanical hand, etc. (Roy, 2008). A purely symbolic robot wouldn't work.

Communication

A primary function of language is communication, and successful communication needs alignment of the interlocutors' representations (e.g., Garrod & Pickering, 2004). In other words, we understand each other to the extent that we are able to build similar referents for words and sentences. Embodied representations seem an efficient way to do so, because the interlocutors use the same perceptual-motor machinery (shared by all individuals) to build embodied simulations. For instance, motor resonance would be similar both in the speaker who says "give me the bottle" and in the addressee who understands the request. Rizzolatti and Arbib (1998) propose the mirror-neuron system as a possible neural mechanism for the building of shared representations between interlocutors. Mirror neurons have the property of parity: they are fired in both the agent and the observer, and this very property is necessary for shared meaning and successful communication.

Evaluation

Embodied meaning allows a fast emotional assessment of the biological value of events. According to Damasio (1994), the primary emotional brain (e.g., the amygdala in the limbic system) evolved to ensure the survival of the body, generating body responses to face biological risks and threats, such as the proximity of predators or competitors. When complex brains capable of thinking and talking evolved, connections between the frontal cortex and the limbic system emerged, allowing the assessment of cognitive and linguistic information with the same embodied markers (emotions) primarily used for survival. For this reason, language can trigger emotions that provide immediate information about the adaptive value of the message. Just think of the intensive emotions that good news, bad news, insults, or flattery provoke in us and how these kinds of linguistic information guide or modulate our behavior. Some of the experiments described in the section on action-related language clearly showed that understanding stories with emotional content even causes subliminal activation of expression-related muscles in the reader's face.

Abstract language

The previous arguments concerning the functional advantages of embodied meaning and the empirical data from cognitive psychology and neuroscience supporting this approach are not sufficient for some researchers. Some skeptical arguments on embodied cognition have been raised (e.g., Mahon & Caramazza, 2008; for a debate on this issue, see also de Vega, Glenberg, & Graesser, 2008). One of these arguments deserves special attention: the difficulty of the embodiment approach to explain abstract language. Most experiments that support the embodiment approach have used concrete words or sentences referring to objects, actions, or emotional reactions as experimental materials. These are important contents in human cognition and language, but people also use language to describe experiences beyond those provided by concrete words and sentences. Symbolists feel quite comfortable with abstractions, and radical symbolists consider that all symbols are ultimately abstract. In contrast, abstraction seems a challenge to the embodiment approach because abstract words and sentences often do not appear to be grounded in embodied experiences. The best hope for the embodiment approach is to demonstrate that abstract words and sentences are also grounded on perception and action, but this seems rather counterintuitive. Let us consider some facets of abstraction – metaphors, granularity grammatical markers, and abstract words – and how the embodiment account of meaning faces these challenges.

Metaphors

In some cases, embodiment theories provide appropriate explanations for abstract meaning. For instance, metaphorical meaning is abstract, although in some cases it could activate embodied representations, as mentioned before. Thus, positive and negative events can be expressed in terms of the spatial vertical dimension (Meier & Robinson, 2006; Santana & de Vega, 2011), causality can be expressed in terms of force dynamics (Talmy, 2001; Wolff, 2007), social exclusion can be expressed as physical pain (Eisenberger, Lieberman, & Williams, 2003), moral indignation can be expressed as disgust (Moll & de Oliveira-Souza, 2007), and so forth. In some of these cases, metaphorical meaning and the corresponding physical experience even share brain activity. But metaphors are a special case of hybrid meaning because, although they refer to abstract ideas, their linguistic support is still concrete (perceptual and motor words).

Granularity

Granularity is another aspect of abstraction. Granularity specifies the level of detail or scope of conceptual or linguistic descriptions. Speakers and listeners can focus on coarse- or fine-grained conceptualizations of events and situations. Compare, for instance, the difference in granularity between "There was somebody in the street" and "There was an old man with a hat at the left corner of the street". The question comes up: how detailed must linguistic meaning be to consider it embodied? For instance, when people understand action-related sentences, do they activate just a high-order (abstract) representation of the action or do they activate fine-grained motor programs of hand and arm motions? Let us consider some of the meaning–action interaction studies reported in this chapter (e.g., de Vega, Moreno, & Castillo, 2011; Glenberg & Kaschak, 2002). They employed transfer verbs referring to actions with quite different motor programs (e.g., throwing a ball vs. telling a story), and all them differed considerably from the motor response (e.g., pressing a key or moving a lever) used as the concurrent task. In spite of that, meaning–action interaction occurred, which suggests that actions are simulated at a relatively abstract level of motor processing (e.g., gross directional parameters) rather than in detail (e.g., at the level of motor programs) (de Vega, 2008; Sanford, 2008). A complementary argument is that specific motor programs must be suppressed to avoid enactment of the actions during language comprehension. It is quite obvious that enactment would be rather inconvenient for most ordinary comprehension tasks. When we listen to or read a sentence about someone performing an action – say, "hammering a nail" – resonance of the premotor areas in the brain should not extend to the motor areas responsible for triggering the action of hammering the nail.

Finally, language-based simulations may also differ from real actions in their temporality. Whereas performing or observing real actions provides analogue on-line temporal information about the ongoing action, this is not the case for action-related language (Fisher & Zwaan, 2008). For instance, the sentence "Mary played the piano for an hour" does not produce a longer mental simulation (or longer reading time) than the sentence "Mary played the piano for one minute". However, it is still possible that the gross temporal structure of the events (e.g., the order or simultaneity of actions, or their relative duration) is preserved in mental simulations (e.g., de Vega, Robertson, Glenberg, Kaschak, & Rinck, 2004).

Thus, we can face a paradoxical situation: action-related sentences activate embodied simulations, but these simulations are "abstract" rather than detailed representations of actions. However, the relative abstraction of action meaning considerably departs from the amodal and arbitrary symbols posited by traditional symbolic theories. In addition, the motor network in the brain is itself highly hierarchical, involving the premotor and parietal cortex responsible for high-order planning of actions and the primary motor cortex responsible for action execution (Glover, 2004). It might be possible that language relies mainly on the high-order planning and interpretation level of action processing.

Grammatical words

There are linguistic markers that appear much more abstract than metaphors and posit a real challenge to embodiment theories. For instance, the negation "not", the disjunctive "or", the adversative "but", or the conditional "if" are similar to "logical operators", and they do not seem to refer to perceptual entities or relations. Some researchers in the embodiment approach consider that these linguistic markers are indeed processed as embodied simulations. For instance, Zwaan and

Madden (2004) propose that negation in a sentence like "the eagle was not in the nest" prompts the reader to initially represent the negated situation (the eagle in the nest) and later on the actual situation (the nest without the eagle). In the same vein, counterfactual sentences such as "If I had been generous, I would have lent you the Harry Potter novel" determines a momentary simulation of the transfer action in spite of the fact that such action is not described as actual (de Vega & Urrutia, 2011). Negation and counterfactuals seem to demand the management in time of a dual meaning: the simulation of a "false" scenario immediately followed by (or simultaneous to) an alternative simulation of the "real" scenario.

Abstract words

Finally, how do we process abstract words such as "truth", "justice", or "idea" that apparently do not refer to any physical entity? This question seems to be a fundamental challenge for embodied theories. A traditional answer was given by Paivio's dual-code theory – concrete words are processed by both the symbolic (verbal) and the embodiment (imagery) systems, whereas abstract words are processed just by the symbolic system (Paivio, 1971) – and many experiments in recent decades supported this dual approach. Concrete words are better recalled, recognized faster, and produce a stronger electrophysiological N400 signature than do abstract words (Glaser, 1992, Kounios & Holcomb, 1994). Paivio's dual theory is a hybrid account of meaning, with the assumption that both embodied and symbolic representations are possible in language.

However, some researchers within the embodiment approach attempt a different hypothesis: abstract and concrete words, although differing in the content and complexity of their meanings, are both grounded in situated knowledge, and some of the situated knowledge is embodied (Barsalou & Wiemer-Hastings, 2005; Barsalou et al., 2008). The critical difference is that concrete words activate a specific set of sensorimotor traces, whereas abstract words activate a heterogeneous set of traces because they are compatible with a much broader range of situations. For this reason, when both kinds of words are presented without context (e.g., a list of words or pairs of words) for a memory task, abstract words fail to retrieve a particular context and are processed superficially, resulting in worse recall. The abstract-word disadvantage disappears, however, when they are incorporated into rich linguistic or nonlinguistic contexts. Thus the concept "truth" in a given context (e.g., someone says "it's true that it is raining") requires consideration of a number of situational parameters: (1) a speaker says something on a world state (it is raining), (2) a listener builds a representation of this world state, (3) the listener then performs some checking operation, such as a visual exploration of the street, (4) the speaker contrasts the original utterance with the outcome of her or his visual exploration; (5) if there is a matching, the concept "true" is applied, otherwise the concept "false" is applied. All these operations are situated, and the meaning of "true" or "truth" becomes much more concrete.

Even the neurological differences between concrete and abstract words fade when words are included in contexts, or when the participants actively engage in generating contexts. In those cases, abstract words produce as strong an N400 in the ERP signal as concrete words (Holcomb, Kounios, Anderson, & West, 1999), and neuroimaging shows an activation of content-related sensorimotor brain areas ("simulators") in addition to the most typically linguistic Broca area (Barsalou et al., 2008). Levels of processing modulate considerably how abstract words are processed. When the processing is shallow, such as in a word recognition task, concrete words provide a better grounding in situation knowledge and abstract words are processed almost exclusively by the linguistic system, as Paivio suggested. However, notice that the linguistic system cannot be assimilated to a symbolic processing system. All words, whether concrete or abstract, are physical signals that are immediately encoded by the linguistic system in terms of phonological or ortho-graphical categories (e.g., Barsalou et al., 2008). According to this conception, the linguistic system encodes word forms rather than amodal symbols. The main differ-ence between concrete and abstract words presented in isolation is that the former easily activate situated meaning or embodied simulations, whereas the former do not. But rather than proposing a special "abstract" meaning for abstract words, we could conceive that these words presented in isolation are almost devoid of meaning.

Concluding remarks

The action system is primarily responsible for planning and executing motor programs aimed at moving our body in the environment or interacting with objects. In this chapter, I have presented and discussed evidence that this action system also plays a functional role in language comprehension. When people understand action-related language, they activate motor brain areas that partially overlap with those activated by performing actions. Furthermore, peripheral activity of the effectors is also relevant to understanding action-related language, as some behavioral studies have demonstrated. The empirical evidence for these claims is overwhelming and clearly supports the theoretical approach of embodied meaning. However, some challenges to this approach still remain. Abstract language posits limits, in some cases, to the notion of embodied meaning, and although the experimental data supporting embodied meaning are accepted by most researchers, alternative (disembodied) interpretations have been raised. Further research is essential to clarify these points, but overall the embodiment approach is quite robust and extremely productive, guiding behavioral and neuro-logical research that provides exciting new data on human cognition.

The embodiment approach in this chapter is not a substitute for the study of visuospatial cognition developed in other chapters in this book. It only puts more emphasis on motor processes and representations and their role in language comprehension. However, it should be noted that visuospatial cognition is also "embodied" and may also underlie language comprehension. Many linguistic utterances describe visual entities, and therefore they could activate visual rather than, or in addition to, motor simulations. This is perfectly compatible with the notion of embodied meaning, which proposes not only motor resonance, but also other sensory modality resonances, including visual resonance. In fact, there are many experiments from the embodiment approach reporting visual activations occurring during language comprehension, but this is beyond the scope of this chapter.

On the other hand, action and vision share important features and are functionally complementary. Thus, performing actions can be considered a genuine case of visuospatial cognition, because when we move our body or parts of our body in space, we rely on the visual system to some extent. For instance, in grasping an object, your visual system provides you with information on the shape, size, or distance of the object, which is necessary to plan your motions, and you also receive visual information on your own body that enters a feedback loop to control your movements accurately. The most remarkable demonstration of the functional relationship between action and vision is the recent discovery of the mirror-neuron system, mentioned in this chapter. These neurons are located in the motor cortex and are activated when individuals (either monkeys or humans) perform an action, but also when they observe another's action. Moreover, mirror neurons also play an important role in the comprehension of action-related language according to the neuroscience data discussed above.

Another functional similarity between action and vision is that not only do they operate *on-line* to perceive and/or respond to current stimuli, but they also could operate *off-line* as mental imagery systems. In the field of visuospatial cognition, the notion of mental imagery has been firmly established and developed by many researchers including the contributors to this book (e.g., Cornoldi, Logie, Bradimonte, Kaufmann, & Reisberg, 1996; Denis, 1989; Kosslyn, 1980; Logie, 1995; Richardson, 1980). But the study of motor imagery has also provided important insights contributing to the consolidation of the field of motor cognition (e.g., Jeannerod, 2006; Sommerville & Decety, 2006).

A final remark concerns the relationship between mental imagery and simulations (or neural resonances) generated during language comprehension. Generally speaking, mental images – either visual or motoric – are slow and cognitively demanding processes generated in the context of problem-solving tasks. For instance, the typical mental scanning experiments require, first, learning a map (or a description of a map), followed by generating and continuously refreshing in memory a mental image of the map to perform the scanning process on it (e.g., Borst & Kosslyn, 2008; Denis & Cocude, 1997). In contrast, the simulations/resonances occurring during the comprehension of action-related or visual-related language are automatic, short-lived, and subliminal processes rather than controlled and optional processes. Further research will be necessary to disentangle the properties of mental images and mental simulations. They could be similar processes differing just in slow or fast timing and cognitive cost, or they could be different processes involving nonoverlapping neural networks.

Acknowledgments

The preparation of this paper was supported by the Grant SEJ2007–66916 from the Spanish Ministry of Science and Innovation, and by the Grant NEUROCOG from the Canary Agency for Research, Innovation, the Society of Information, and the European Regional Development Fund.

References

Aziz-Zadeh, L., Wilson, S. M., Rizzolatti, G., & Iacoboni, M. (2006). Congruent embodied representations for visually presented actions and linguistic phrases describing actions. *Current Biology, 16*, 1–6.

Barsalou, L., Santos, A., Simmons, W. K., & Wilson, C. D. (2008). Language and simulation in conceptual processing. In M. de Vega, A. Glenberg, & A. Graesser (Eds.), *Symbols and embodiment: Debates on meaning and cognition* (pp. 245–284). New York: Oxford University Press.

Barsalou, L., & Wiemer-Hastings, K. (2005). Situating abstract concepts. In D. Pecher & R. Zwaan (Eds.), *Grounding cognition: The role of perception and action in memory, language, and thought* (pp. 129–163). New York: Cambridge University Press.

Borreggine, K. L., & Kaschak, M. P. (2006). The action–sentence compatibility effect: It's all in the timing. *Cognitive Science, 30*, 1097–1112.

Borst, G., & Kosslyn, S. M. (2008). Visual mental imagery and visual perception: Structural equivalence revealed by scanning processes. *Memory & Cognition, 36*, 849–862.

Boulenger, V., Mechtouff, L., Thobois, S., Broussolle, E., Jeannerod, M., & Nazir, T. A. (2008). Word processing in Parkinson's disease is impaired for action verbs but not for concrete nouns. *Neuropsychologia, 46*, 743–756.

Buccino, G., Riggio, G., Melli, F., Binkofski, V., Gallese, G., & Rizzolatti, G. (2005). Listening to action-related sentences modulates the activity of the motor system: A combined TMS and behavioral study. *Cognitive Brain Research, 24*, 355–363.

Castner, J. E., Chenery, H. J., Silburn, P. A., Coyne, T. J., Sinclair, F., Smith, E. R., et al. (2008). Effects of subthalamic deep brain stimulation on noun/verb generation and selection from competing alternatives in Parkinson's disease. *Journal of Neurology, Neurosurgery, and Psychiatry, 79*, 700–705.

Cornoldi, C., Logie, R. H., Bradimonte, M. A., Kaufmann, G., & Reisberg, D. (1996). *Stretching the imagination: Representation and transformation in mental imagery.* New York: Oxford University Press.

Cramer, S. C., Weisskoff, R. M., Schaechter, J. D., Nelles, G., Foley, M., Finklestein, S. P., & Rosen, B. R. (2002). Motor cortex activation is related to force of squeezing. *Human Brain Mapping, 16*, 197–205.

Crescentini, C., Mondolo, F., Biasutti, E., & Shallice, T. (2008). Supervisory and routine processes in noun and verb generation in nondemented patients with Parkinson's disease. *Neuropsychologia, 46*, 434–447.

Damasio, A. R. (1994). *Descartes' error: Emotion, reason and the human brain.* New York: Putnam's Sons.

Denis, M. (1989). *Image et cognition.* Paris: Presses Universitaires de France.

Denis, M., & Cocude, M. (1997). On the metric properties of visual images generated from verbal descriptions: Evidence for the robustness of the mental scanning effect. *European Journal of Cognitive Psychology, 9*, 353–379.

Denis, M., Daniel, M. P., Fontaine, S., & Pazzaglia, F. (2001). Language, spatial cognition, and navigation. In M. Denis, R. H. Logie, C. Cornoldi, M. de Vega, & J. Engelkamp (Eds.), *Imagery, language, and visuo-spatial thinking* (pp. 137–160). Hove, UK: Psychology Press.

de Vega, M. (2008). Levels of embodiment: From pointing to counterfactuals. In M. de Vega, A. M. Glenberg, & A. C. Graesser (Eds.), *Symbols and embodiment: Debates on meaning and cognition* (pp. 285–308). New York: Oxford University Press.

de Vega, M., Glenberg, A. M., & Graesser, A. C. (2008). *Symbols and embodiment: Debates on meaning and cognition.* New York: Oxford University Press.

de Vega, M., Moreno, V., & Castillo, M. D. (2011). The comprehension of action-related sentences may cause interference rather than facilitation on matching actions. *Psychological Research.* doi: 10.1007/s00426–011–0356–1

de Vega, M., Robertson, D. A., Glenberg, A. M., Kaschak, M. P., & Rinck, M. (2004). On doing two things at once: Temporal constraints on action in language comprehension. *Memory & Cognition, 32,* 1033–1043.

de Vega, M., & Urrutia, M. (2011). Counterfactual sentences activate embodied meaning: An action–sentence compatibility effect study. *Journal of Cognitive Psychology.* doi: 10.1080/20445911.2011.590471

Eisenberger, N. I., Lieberman, M. D., & Williams, K. D. (2003). Does rejection hurt? An fMRI study of social exclusion. *Science, 302,* 290–292.

Fadiga, L., & Craighero, L. (2003). New insights on sensorimotor integration: From hand action to speech perception. *Brain and Cognition, 53,* 514–524.

Fisher, M. H., & Zwaan, R. A. (2008). Embodied language: A review of the role of the motor system in language comprehension. *Quarterly Journal of Experimental Psychology, 61,* 825–850.

Gallese, V., Keysers, C., & Rizzolatti, G. (2004). A unifying view of the basis of social cognition. *Trends in Cognitive Sciences, 8,* 396–403.

Garrod, S., & Pickering, M. J. (2004). Why is conversation so easy? *Trends in Cognitive Sciences, 8,* 8–11.

Glaser, W. R. (1992). Picture naming. *Cognition, 42,* 61–105.

Glenberg, A. M., & Kaschak, M. P. (2002). Grounding language in action. *Psychonomic Bulletin & Review, 9,* 558–565.

Glover, S. (2004). Separate visual representations in the planning and control of action. *Behavioral and Brain Sciences, 27,* 3–78.

Hamzei, F., Rijntjes, M., Dettmers, C., Glauche, V., Weiller, C., & Buëchel, C. (2003). The human action recognition system and its relationship to Broca's area: An fMRI study. *NeuroImage, 19,* 637–644.

Harnad, S. (1990). The symbol grounding problem. *Physica D, 42,* 335–346.

Havas, D. A., Glenberg, A. M., Gutowski, K. A., Lucarelli, M. J., & Davidson, R. J. (2010). Cosmetic use of botulinum toxin-A affects processing of emotional language. *Psychological Science, 20,* 1–6.

Havas, D. A., Glenberg, A. M., & Rinck, M. (2007). Emotion simulation during language comprehension. *Psychonomic Bulletin and Review, 14,* 436–441.

Hebb, D. O. (1949). *The organization of behaviour: A neuropsychological theory.* New York: John Wiley.

Holcomb, P., Kounios, J., Anderson, J., & West, W. (1999). Dual-coding, context-availability, and concreteness effects in sentence comprehension: An electrophysiological investigation. *Journal of Experimental Psychology: Learning, Memory, and Cognition, 25,* 721–742.

Jeannerod, M. (2006). *Motor cognition: What actions tell the self.* Oxford, UK: Oxford University Press.

Jenmalm, P., Schmitz, C., Forssberg, H., & Ehrsson, H. (2006). Lighter or heavier than predicted: Neural correlates of corrective mechanisms during erroneously programmed lifts. *Journal of Neuroscience, 26,* 9015–9021.

Kintsch, W. (1998). The role of knowledge in discourse comprehension: A construction-integration model. *Psychological Review, 95,* 163–182.

Kosslyn, S. M. (1980). *Image and mind.* Cambridge, MA: Harvard University Press.

Kounios, J., & Holcomb, P. (1994). Concreteness effects in semantic processing: ERP evidence supporting dual-coding theory. *Journal of Experimental Psychology: Learning, Memory, and Cognition, 20,* 804–823.

Lakoff, G., & Johnson, M. (1980). *Metaphors we live by.* Chicago, IL: University of Chicago Press.

Logie, R. H. (1995). *Visuo-spatial working memory.* Hillsdale, NJ: Lawrence Erlbaum Associates.

Mahon, B. Z., & Caramazza, A. (2008). A critical look at the embodied cognition hypothesis and a new proposal for grounding conceptual content. *Journal of Physiology – Paris, 102,* 59–70.

Meier, B. P., & Robinson, M. D. (2006). Does "feeling down" mean seeing down? Depressive symptoms and vertical selective attention. *Journal of Research in Personality, 40,* 451–461.

Moll, J., & de Oliveira-Souza, R. (2007). Moral judgments, emotions and the utilitarian brain. *Trends in Cognitive Sciences, 11,* 319–321.

Moody, C. L., & Gennari, S. P. (2009). Effects of implied physical effort in sensory-motor and pre-frontal cortex during language comprehension. *NeuroImage, 49,* 782–793.

Moreno, I., León, I., & de Vega, M. (2011). *Action-related language produces mu suppression.* Manuscript in preparation.

Paivio, A. (1971). *Imagery and verbal processes.* New York: Holt, Rinehart, & Winston.

Pineda, J. (2005). The functional significance of mu rhythms: Translating "seeing" and "hearing" into "doing". *Brain Research Reviews, 50,* 57–68.

Pulvermüller, F. (1999). Words in the brain's language. *Behavioural and Brain Sciences, 22,* 253–336.

Pulvermüller, F. (2008). Grounding language in the brain. In M. de Vega, A. M. Glenberg, & A. C. Graesser (Eds.), *Symbols and embodiment: Debates on meaning and cognition* (pp. 85–116). New York: Oxford University Press.

Pulvermüller, F., Hauk, O., Nikulin, V., & Ilmoniemi, R. J. (2005). Functional links between motor and language systems. *European Journal of Neuroscience, 21,* 793–797.

Pulvermüller, F., Shtyrov, Y., & Ilmoniemi, R. J. (2003). Spatiotemporal patterns of neural language processing: An MEG study using minimum-norm current estimates. *NeuroImage, 20,* 1020–1025.

Richardson, J. T. E. (1980). *Mental imagery and human memory.* London: Macmillan.

Rizzolatti, G., & Arbib, M. A. (1998). Language within our grasp. *Trends in Neuroscience, 21,* 188–194.

Roy, D. (2008). A mechanistic model of three facets of meaning. In M. de Vega, A. M. Glenberg, & A. C. Graesser (Eds.), *Symbols and embodiment: Debates on meaning and cognition* (pp. 195–220). New York: Oxford University Press.

Sanford, A. J. (2008). Defining embodiment in understanding. In M. de Vega, A. M. Glenberg, & A. C. Graesser (Eds.), *Symbols and embodiment: Debates on meaning and cognition* (pp. 181–194). New York: Oxford University Press.

Santana, E., & de Vega, M. (2011). Metaphors are embodied, and so are their literal counterparts. *Frontiers in Psychology.* doi: 10.3389/fpsyg.2011.00090

Searle, J. R. (1980). Minds, brains and programs. *Behavioral & Brain Sciences, 3,* 417–424.

Shapiro, L. (2008). Symbolism, embodied cognition, and the broader debate. In M. de Vega, A. M. Glenberg, & A. C. Graesser (Eds.), *Symbols and embodiment: Debates on meaning and cognition* (pp. 57–74). New York: Oxford University Press.

Sommerville, J. A., & Decety, J. (2006). Weaving the fabric of social interaction: Articulating developmental psychology and cognitive neuroscience in the domain of motor cognition. *Psychonomic Bulletin & Review, 13,* 179–200.

Talmy, L. (2001). *Toward a cognitive semantics. Vol. 1: Concept structuring systems.* Cambridge, MA: MIT Press.

Tettamanti, M., Manenti, R., Della Rosa, P., Falini, A., Perani, D., Cappa, S., et al. (2008). Negation in the brain: Modulating action representations. *NeuroImage, 43,* 358–367.

Urrutia, M., de Vega, M., & Gennari, S. (2009). *The force is with you . . . or would have been with you: An fMRI study of action language.* Workshop on Embodied and Situated Language Processing, Rotterdam, The Netherlands (July).

van Elk, M., van Schie, H. T., Zwaan, R. A., & Bekkering, H. (2010). The functional role of motor activation in language processing: Motor cortical oscillations support lexical-semantic retrieval. *NeuroImage, 50,* 665–677.

Wolff, P. (2007). Representing causation. *Journal of Experimental Psychology: General, 36,* 82–111.

Zwaan, R. A., & Madden, C. (2004). Commentary and reply: Updating situation models. *Journal of Experimental Psychology: Learning, Memory, and Cognition, 30,* 283–288.

Zwaan, R. A., & Taylor, L. J. (2006). Seeing, acting, understanding: Motor resonance in language comprehension. *Journal of Experimental Psychology: General, 135,* 1–11.

Part V
Interconnections

9 Decades of images

Reminiscences of a shared scientific journey

Michel Denis

Introduction: scanning forty years of imagery research

Most of the contributors to this volume share the privilege of having been involved in the process by which the concept of imagery reemerged in modern cognitive psychology. One of the critical landmarks in the revival of the concept four decades ago was the theoretical paper that Allan Paivio published in *Psychological Review* in 1969 (see Figure 9.1). This paper reviewed empirical findings demonstrating the effectiveness of using mental images in learning and memory, but, still more importantly, it argued for the explanatory and heuristic value of the imagery concept in psychology.

Since the publication of this strong claim, a number of psychologists have rallied to the view that attempting to account for the functions and architecture of the human mind implies adopting a comprehensive approach. In this context, "comprehensive" means taking into account all the facets of cognition – that is, both its verbal and nonverbal aspects. Many of us were taught in the 1960s and 1970s by people who gave a focal importance to language as the ultimate expression and paramount achievement of human cognition. This view has not completely disappeared from the communities dedicated to cognitive science. Despite all the respect due to language, which is the vehicle of both daily communication and scientific exchanges, we were committed to recognizing the significance of imagery in a variety of cognitive functions including memory, reasoning, and mental anticipation, and even in the acquisition of motor skills.

By the mid-1960s, Robert Holt, a distinguished scholar from New York University, aptly described the return of imagery into modern psychology as "the return of the ostracized" (Holt, 1964). Of course, the return of a concept that has been set aside for a long time in a discipline is a noteworthy event, but in this case, what was particularly important was the fact that psychologists imposed an obligation on themselves to free the imagery concept from naive Associationist views and to subject the process to a systematic analytical approach. That was precisely what Allan Paivio's scientific program at that time was designed to achieve (Paivio, 1971). Later, the broader concept of a "neomentalism" emerged as the behavioral approach to internal mental events (Paivio, 1975).

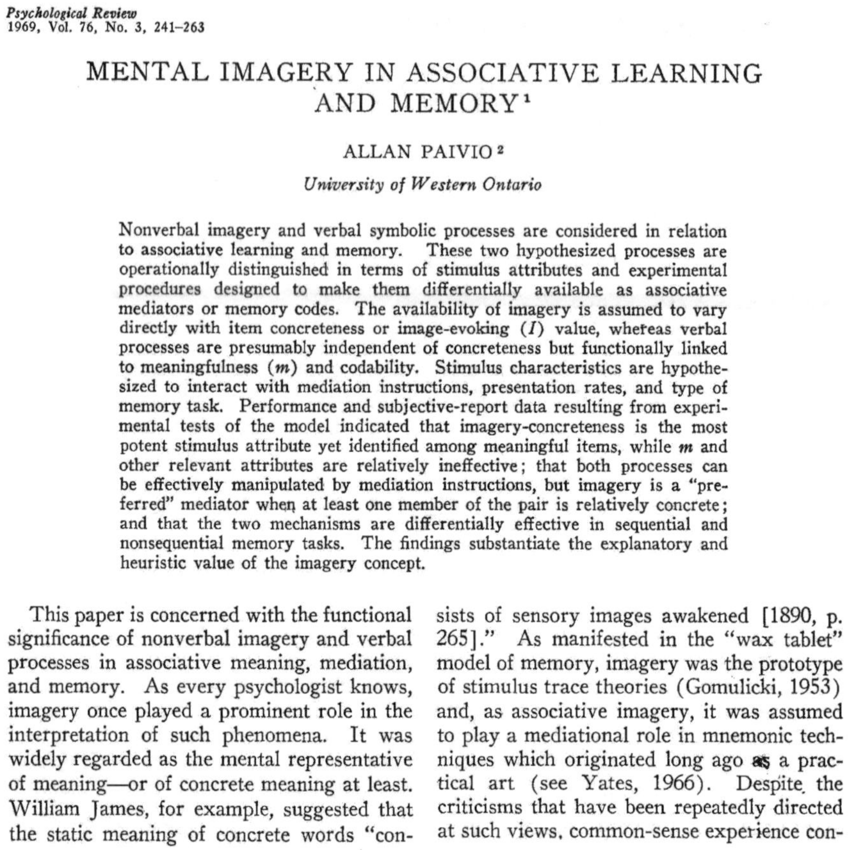

Psychological Review
1969, Vol. 76, No. 3, 241–263

MENTAL IMAGERY IN ASSOCIATIVE LEARNING AND MEMORY[1]

ALLAN PAIVIO[2]

University of Western Ontario

Nonverbal imagery and verbal symbolic processes are considered in relation to associative learning and memory. These two hypothesized processes are operationally distinguished in terms of stimulus attributes and experimental procedures designed to make them differentially available as associative mediators or memory codes. The availability of imagery is assumed to vary directly with item concreteness or image-evoking (*I*) value, whereas verbal processes are presumably independent of concreteness but functionally linked to meaningfulness (*m*) and codability. Stimulus characteristics are hypothesized to interact with mediation instructions, presentation rates, and type of memory task. Performance and subjective-report data resulting from experimental tests of the model indicated that imagery-concreteness is the most potent stimulus attribute yet identified among meaningful items, while *m* and other relevant attributes are relatively ineffective; that both processes can be effectively manipulated by mediation instructions, but imagery is a "preferred" mediator when at least one member of the pair is relatively concrete; and that the two mechanisms are differentially effective in sequential and nonsequential memory tasks. The findings substantiate the explanatory and heuristic value of the imagery concept.

This paper is concerned with the functional significance of nonverbal imagery and verbal processes in associative meaning, mediation, and memory. As every psychologist knows, imagery once played a prominent role in the interpretation of such phenomena. It was widely regarded as the mental representative of meaning—or of concrete meaning at least. William James, for example, suggested that the static meaning of concrete words "consists of sensory images awakened [1890, p. 265]." As manifested in the "wax tablet" model of memory, imagery was the prototype of stimulus trace theories (Gomulicki, 1953) and, as associative imagery, it was assumed to play a mediational role in mnemonic techniques which originated long ago as a practical art (see Yates, 1966). Despite the criticisms that have been repeatedly directed at such views, common-sense experience con-

Figure 9.1 This is the first page of Allan Paivio's seminal paper in *Psychological Review* (1969), which triggered the research programs of the scientists who discovered mental imagery in the early 1970s. (Copyright © 1969 by the American Psychological Association. Reprinted with permission.)

One of the most impressive contributions to this enterprise was the theoretical and empirical work of Steve Kosslyn, who split a complex process into a set of distinct functional components (Kosslyn, 1980, 1983). At the same time, imagery was also integrated into more comprehensive theories of human cognition and articulated with the other modules of the cognitive architecture. The challenge facing imagery researchers was to provide explicit information about the functional relationships between this process and other, nonimaginal forms of mental representation.

Various doubts and suspicions against imagery-based accounts of cognition eventually prevailed. Imagery researchers had to withstand the propositionalist conceptions of the human mind. To be more exact, what was targeted were the *purely* propositionalist conceptions, such as those defended by Pylyshyn (1973) or Anderson and Bower (1973). Remember that the model of mental imagery proposed by Kosslyn at about this time included both pictorial (imaginal) *and* propositional representations, each in its respective place and with its distinct functions (see Kosslyn, 1975; Kosslyn & Pomerantz, 1977).

This controversy reached its peak in the early 1980s. I made a modest contribution to the debate in a study conducted with Maryvonne Carfantan about what people know about images (Denis & Carfantan, 1985; see Figure 9.2). What we found was that ordinary people (i.e., not imagery researchers!) actually know quite a lot about mental images. This subjective experience makes sense to them, and they readily

Cognition, 20 (1985) 49–60

3

People's knowledge about images*

MICHEL DENIS
MARYVONNE CARFANTAN
Université de Paris-Sud

Abstract

Adult subjects were given a questionnaire containing short descriptions of classic imagery experiments and asked to predict what the typical outcomes of these experiments would be. A majority of subjects correctly predicted that imagery would have positive effects on learning of verbal material, and on spatial and deductive reasoning. Only a small number of subjects, however, predicted effects of mental practice on learning motor skills. Furthermore, very few subjects were capable of predicting results typically obtained in mental rotation experiments (viz., more time is required to accomplish greater amounts of rotation on images), mental scanning experiments (longer distances in images take longer to scan), and experiments demonstrating longer verification times for properties of objects in small-sized images. The extremely poor abilities of subjects to predict these results can hardly be accounted for by a 'tacit knowledge' hypothesis, since, assuming that knowledge of the relationships linking speed, time, and physical distance normally 'penetrates' image processing, in this case the consequence would be that such knowledge is likely to be used for making rather accurate predictions concerning these experimental situations.

Figure 9.2 A contribution to the debate on tacit knowledge about mental imagery, in *Cognition* (1985). (Copyright © 1985 by Elsevier. Reprinted with permission.)

claim that images are useful in memory or reasoning tasks, as has been demonstrated by hundreds of published experiments. When asked, these people are even able to predict the outcomes of the classic experiments that nearly all of us have conducted. In contrast, when people are asked to predict the results of experiments concerning the intimate mechanisms of imagery, such as image scanning or mental rotation, they appear to be unable to anticipate the well-established empirical facts – for instance, that it takes longer to scan longer distances in visual images. The opacity of such phenomena to introspection is noteworthy, and this is something that would not fit in with the theory that knowledge penetrates imagery and ultimately governs the chronometric results of mental scanning and mental rotation experiments. Some years later, Cesare Cornoldi and his collaborators nicely extended this issue, demonstrating that people's beliefs about images affect their behavior when they take part in imagery experiments (Cornoldi, De Beni, & Giusberti, 1996).

In 1994, Steve Kosslyn published his major book, *Image and Brain*. This book had a rather optimistic subtitle: *The Resolution of the Imagery Debate*. It included an impressive compilation of the theoretical and empirical arguments exchanged by the proponents of the two views over the previous twenty years. However, in spite of Kosslyn's optimistic (and mildly provocative) claim, I am afraid that the controversy left the two points of view at loggerheads, without either of them prevailing (see Kosslyn, Thompson, & Ganis, 2006; Paivio, 2007; Pylyshyn, 2003; see also Zimmer, chapter 3, this volume). In fact, what we learned was that any radical interpretation of human cognition is not viable. Imagery does not constitute the whole of thought. Language and propositions don't either. The multimodal approach to the mind developed on this basis.

Something else we have learned is the value of developing *analytic* approaches to cognitive phenomena such as mental imagery – that is, splitting a complex, multifactorial process into a set of articulated, but nonetheless distinct functional components. One of the most impressive contributions was Kosslyn's computational analysis of imagery processes, based on an extensive analysis of individual differences (Kosslyn, Brunn, Cave, & Wallach, 1984). This line of thinking inspired a (much more modest) experiment in which Marguerite Cocude and I collected evidence that the generation and maintenance of visual images are governed by different mechanisms. The time taken to generate an image does not predict the time for which it can be maintained in the visual buffer (Cocude & Denis, 1988). Another lesson learned from Kosslyn's approach was the need to be explicit about the functional relationships between mental imagery and the other nonimaginal forms of mental representation (Kosslyn, 1980, 1994).

Last, but not least, the constant efforts of psychologists to account for the underlying mechanisms of visual cognition, together with the tremendous development of brain imaging techniques, resulted in the establishment and full recognition of a cognitive neuroscience of mental imagery. Two of my most intellectually thrilling experiences were the fruits of my long-standing collaboration with Bernard Mazoyer, at the Orsay Hospital, and one of our co-tutored students at that time, Emmanuel Mellet. One of these experiences was what turned out to be the first positron emission tomography (PET) study of mental imagery conducted in a

French laboratory (Mellet, Tzourio, Denis, & Mazoyer, 1995). We were honored when the very first vivid color images of brain activation from this study were used as the cover illustrations for a textbook, *Imagery*, that John Richardson published a few years later (1999) (see Figure 9.3). Further studies, in which Alain Berthoz, from the Collège de France, was also involved, documented the role of the right hippocampus in the mental exploration of an environment previously learned either by actual navigation or from a map (see Mellet, Bricogne, et al., 2000).

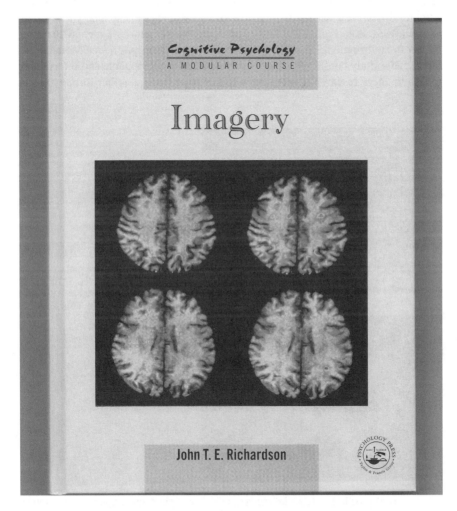

Figure 9.3 The cover of John Richardson's book, *Imagery* (published in 1999 by Psychology Press), showed the first color images of brain activation obtained in an image scanning task by a team of French researchers using positron emission tomography. This is a black-and-white reproduction of the original color figures, as published in the article by Mellet, Tzourio, Denis, & Mazoyer (1995). (Copyright © 1999 by Psychology Press, Ltd. Reprinted with permission.)

My second thrilling experience was related to another neuroimaging study in which, along with Emmanuel Mellet and Steve Kosslyn, we found that the same cerebral networks were activated by images generated from visual experience and those generated from language (see Mellet, Tzourio-Mazoyer, et al., 2000; see Figure 9.4). This finding confirmed the long-standing efforts of my lab to investigate the structural and functional similarities between images derived from perceptual experience and those derived from verbal descriptions (Denis, 1991; Denis & Cocude, 1989, 1992, 1997; Denis, Gonçalves, & Memmi, 1995; Denis & Zimmer, 1992). The last step in this series of PET studies was especially rewarding, as it allowed us to record the first neurocognitive signature of mental scanning across an environment learned from a purely verbal description (see Mellet et al., 2002). This study confirmed image scanning as a highly valuable and informative tool in imagery research. I am grateful to Grégoire Borst, another former student

Visual scene

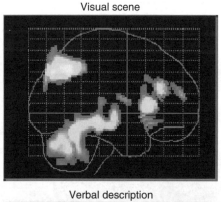

Verbal description

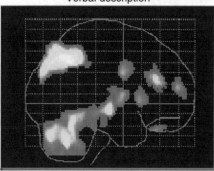

Figure 9.4 Although reproduced here in black and white, these figures clearly reflect the similarity of the brain activation patterns obtained when people form images after being exposed to a visual scene or listening to a verbal description of the scene. (From E. Mellet, N. Tzourio-Mazoyer, S. Bricogne, B. Mazoyer, S. M. Kosslyn, & M. Denis, 2000. Functional anatomy of high-resolution visual mental imagery. *Journal of Cognitive Neuroscience*, *12*, 101. Copyright © 2000 by the Massachusetts Institute of Technology. Adapted with permission.)

of mine, who brilliantly extended this line of research in several highly regarded publications (e.g., Borst & Kosslyn, 2008, 2010; Borst, Kosslyn, & Denis, 2006; see also Borst & Kosslyn, chapter 2, this volume).

The return of imagery in modern cognitive psychology also had an impact on the progress of knowledge in other domains. In some specific fields of psychology, each with its own history, research programs were launched that were intended to account for the mechanisms by which imagery contributes to other vision- or space-related processes. For instance, the concept of imagery was present in the discussions that led to differentiating the subsystems of the working memory, in particular the visuo-spatial sketchpad. A sustained discussion ensued about the possible overlap between this component of the working memory model and the visual buffer of Kosslyn's computational theory. Another area into which mental imagery penetrated in a rather useful way was the mental model theory. The confrontation between the two concepts offered us an opportunity to clarify the respective functional status of mental images and mental models as internal representations. In the field of spatial cognition and navigation, the role of imagery in the construction of mental representations of routes and environments should not be ignored either, even though nowadays the emphasis tends to be on more abstract, amodal forms of representation of spatial knowledge. Lastly, the investigation of the properties of images constructed from language has provided imagery researchers with an opportunity to contribute to investigating blind people's mental representations of their environment.

In these various domains, the pursuit of the imagery concept has led to productive interactions with cognate concepts (i.e., the working memory, mental models, the mental representation of space, and cognition in the blind). I will review these topics separately for the sake of clarity, while acknowledging the close connections existing between them. In this chapter, I want to emphasize the fact that imagery, as a cognitive construct, has broadened the perspectives of psychologists, and that imagery research has contributed substantially to other areas of psychology.

Imagery and working memory

Although the working memory (WM) theory developed quite separately from research on mental imagery, the parallels between the issues involved in these two approaches soon became evident. For Baddeley and Hitch (1974), the founding postulate was that WM makes it possible to execute tasks that require the transient availability of information and the ability to process it. WM involves a central executive that supervises two slave systems. One system, the phonological loop, is involved in processing all kinds of verbal material, whereas the other, the visuospatial sketchpad (VSSP), directs the functions related to the processing of visuospatial information (Baddeley, 1986).

The visuospatial sketchpad

The theoretical speculations and experimental investigations of the VSSP closely paralleled the development of theories of mental imagery during the 1970s and

1980s. One of the first encounters between these two lines of research occurred in studies demonstrating that a concurrent task involving visuospatial tracking hindered the efficiency of mnemonic techniques based on the generation of visual images (Baddeley & Lieberman, 1980). The negative effect of irrelevant visual inputs during the manipulation of visual images was another important landmark. It was interpreted as strongly suggesting an overlap between visual perception and visual memory (Logie, 1986). Subsequent experiments were devoted to analyzing subjective ratings of the vividness of imagery when participants were processing secondary tasks simultaneously. The results showed that the execution of tasks intended to disrupt the VSSP affected the vividness rating of imagery (Baddeley & Andrade, 2000).

The dominant and most influential theory of mental imagery was articulated in the early 1980s by Kosslyn (1980). This theory was intended to account for a set of processes operating on a short-term visual buffer. This structure was thought to hold images generated from the long-term memory as well as images coded from perceptual inputs or verbal descriptions. Like the proponents of the WM theory, Kosslyn and his collaborators amply documented the functional overlap between visual perception and visual imagery, and they further postulated that both functions relied on the same cerebral substratum (e.g., Farah, 1985; Finke, 1985). The visual buffer concept was found to be consistent with the concept of VSSP, and a large body of mutually relevant data was obtained by researchers working within these two frameworks. Interestingly, one feature shared by the visual buffer and VSSP is that both have a limited capacity. Furthermore, both have to undergo some kind of refreshment process in order to offset the effects of decay over time.

The characterization of images as cognitive tools that make it possible to execute tasks in a wide spectrum of activities, ranging from memory through language comprehension to reasoning and problem solving, is specific to research dedicated to visual imagery. This aspect of images was the focus of early imagery research conducted under the umbrella of the dual-coding theory (Paivio, 1971). Subsequently, the main objective of the researchers in the Kosslyn (1975) and Shepard (1978) traditions was to determine to what extent imagery and perception share common features. The same current of research also tackled the issue of whether imagery relies on analogical or propositional processes (a concern that was largely absent from the agenda of the WM theory). The debate on the analogue vs. propositional nature of the representations underlying imagery coincided with the launching of analytical approaches to account for the processes underpinning mental imagery, and how these processes are related to those underlying perception (see Kosslyn et al., 1984).

Everyone involved in human cognition research nowadays sees visual imagery as a component of a more complex cognitive architecture. The study of mental images has moved on from the analysis of the phenomenon of imagery itself to the exploration of its role in the interface between perception, memory, and language. From the outset, WM theory has also included definite assumptions about the architecture of cognition.

The visuospatial working memory

Following on from Baddeley's original insights, the proponents of WM with an interest in visual cognition realized that the concept that a single system was in charge of all the visuospatial processes was probably an oversimplification. An important step forward was taken by Bob Logie in his book, *Visuo-spatial Working Memory*, published in 1995. Logie preferred the concept of "visuo-spatial working memory" (VSWM) to that of the traditional "visuo-spatial sketchpad". The VSWM was presented as the function of the WM that deals with visual and spatial information. Underlying this concept was the postulate that the corresponding memory codes entertain a direct relationship with the characteristics of the materials processed by the system. The idea of structural similarity between perceived objects and their mental counterparts was consonant with the basic tenet of Kosslyn's theory at that time. More importantly, Logie's contribution was to offer a revised model of WM comprising two distinct stores, one visual and one spatial. In this model, a passive "visual cache" holds information transiently, while an active "inner scribe" is responsible for rehearsing these contents in order to prevent decay (see Logie, 1995; Logie & Pearson, 1997). An emergent property of this rehearsal function is that it can represent movement, a characteristic that is of special relevance in tasks involving the encoding of motor information, particularly when such information is activated in the form of mental images of actions (see Engelkamp, 1991; Engelkamp, Zimmer, & Denis, 1989).

In addition to these revisions, interesting encounters occurred between the two conceptual approaches. One of them is illustrated by a study of mental rotation (a task requiring the implementation of dynamic visuospatial imagery). Logie and Salway (1990) invited people to perform mental rotation while executing various concurrent tasks taken from the classic WM paradigms. Articulatory suppression did not affect performance on the mental rotation task, but spatial tapping caused a significant impairment of performance, indicating that the spatial component of VSWM is involved in mental rotation. Interestingly, a concurrent task of oral random generation of digits (a task expected to tap the resources of the central executive) proved to be even more detrimental to the main task than was spatial suppression. Not surprisingly, the findings of this experiment supported the involvement of VSWM in a mental imagery task and, in addition, the notion that a task placing a load on the central executive would also interfere with mental rotation.

Another imagery task that elicited interest in this context was mental synthesis, a task in which discrete parts in an image are mentally manipulated and transformed in order to form new patterns or lead to new insights (see Finke, Pinker, & Farah, 1989). In two studies, David Pearson investigated the role that WM plays during such a task (Pearson, Logie, & Gilhooly, 1999; Pearson, Logie, & Green, 1996). The results showed that mental synthesis was disrupted by concurrent spatial tapping, confirming that the inner-scribe component of the VSWM was involved during the dynamic processing of images. The random generation of digits, which is thought to demand executive resources, also substantially interfered with the primary task and, furthermore, significantly reduced the participants' conscious experience of imagery. A further finding was that the participants' exposure to concurrent dynamic visual noise (Quinn & McConnell, 1999) did not affect their performance in the synthesis task. This is worth noting, since efforts to assess the compatibility between the two lines of research gave rise to the view that the visual cache, as the structure in which visual images are maintained, shares the properties of the visual buffer in Kosslyn's model.

At the turn of the century, further conceptual developments of the WM system were introduced by Cornoldi and Vecchi (2003), who held that mental imagery belongs to the set of WM functions. Mental images can be used to execute various tasks, but whatever the context in which they are used, their generation, maintenance, and manipulation are functions that are jointly ascribed to VSWM and to the central executive of the WM model. As Pearson, De Beni, and Cornoldi (2001) pointed out, beyond the fact that both the WM theory and Kosslyn's computational theory of imagery refer to image maintenance and image transformation, the two models can hardly be seen as compatible, if only because they have evolved in order to address distinct empirical questions. Whereas the VSSP was originally characterized as being responsible for the generation and maintenance of visual images, the new approach posited that imagery processes should more probably be assigned to the active component of the VSWM and to the central executive. According to this scenario, the visual cache acts only as a temporary storage system for materials to which a conscious experience of image is attached.

Whereas the WM model attempts to separate the storage and processing functions, this separation within a cognitive task is not so clear in Kosslyn's model. We should note that in Paivio's dual-coding theory, both imagery and the verbal system have storage and processing functions, whereas Logie's VSWM appears to be mainly dedicated to storage. A further notable advantage of the WM theory is that it provides a comprehensive framework that accounts for the interactions between verbal encoding and imagery (as Paivio's dual coding does), whereas the relationships between imagery and language receive little attention in Kosslyn's computational model. This relative lack of concern with verbal coding is mitigated by a deep and detailed analysis of the processes and subprocesses that underlie the performance in tasks such as mental rotation, image scanning, size comparisons, and the like. Beyond Kosslyn's claim that mental imagery is "a good example of the kind of representation used in working memory" (Kosslyn, Thompson, & Ganis, 2006, p. 22), the issue of the relationships between the imagery system and the components of the WM architecture still needs further exploration. Logie and van der Meulen (2009) have provided a substantial documented update of these issues (see also Logie & Niven, chapter 4, and Quinn, chapter 5, this volume).

Neuropsychological evidence

Another interesting feature is that, beyond the individual peculiarities of the two research traditions, what they have had in common in the past two or three decades is a strategy of extending the range of experimental paradigms and an effort to extend behavioral research into neuropsychological, neurobiological, and neuro-imaging research (a trend evident throughout cognitive psychology). I would like to focus on one example, which again illustrates a valuable encounter between WM and imagery research in the neuropsychology of visual cognition. This can also be used as an example of the advantages of having the company of inspiring colleagues ready to join in scientific ventures concerning challenging issues. This is what I found with Bob Logie and Sergio Della Sala, who are both respected experts in the neuropsychology of visuospatial cognition.

As I pointed out above, Kosslyn's theory stresses the notion of an intimate overlap between perception and visual imagery, a concept supported by neuro-cognitive evidence. For neuropsychologists, unilateral spatial neglect is diagnosed when a patient is unable to report details from one hemispace (usually the left) of the immediate environment or from mental reconstructions (mental images) of familiar scenes. The former is referred to as "perceptual neglect", and the latter as "representational neglect". Several patients have been reported to display both forms, suggesting that there are close links between perception and mental repre-sentations. However, there are also reports of patients suffering from purely perceptual neglect, or purely representational neglect. This double dissociation indicates that the links between perception and representation may not be as direct as is sometimes postulated.

One plausible explanation of representational neglect is that it reflects an impairment of VSWM. The WM framework has no difficulty in coping with the view that impairment of the perceptual input might not affect the representations held in the VSWM and that, conversely, impairments of the VSWM would not necessarily result in deficits in the processing of perceptual inputs.

In our first study (Denis, Beschin, Logie, & Della Sala, 2002), we wanted to establish how representational neglect might affect both the immediate recall of recently perceived novel visual scenes and also the recall of novel scenes that had been presented in the form of auditory verbal descriptions (without any visual input) (see Figure 9.5). Under both these conditions, neglect patients had a poorer ability to report objects depicted or described on the left than on the right side of each scene. Overall, the results indicated that representational neglect does not depend on the presence of perceptual neglect, that visual perception and mental representations mediated by visual imagery are less closely linked than had been thought, and that visuospatial images have similar functional characteristics regardless of whether they are derived from perception or from linguistic descrip-tions. Subsequent studies confirmed this interpretation and provided data suggesting that at least some of the processes that operate on images (such as mental rotation) appear to be intact in patients with representational neglect (see Della Sala, Logie, Beschin, & Denis, 2004; Logie, Della Sala, Beschin, & Denis, 2005).

To summarize, the general pattern of results supports the view that representa-tional neglect is an impairment of VSWM. Representational neglect not only occurs when patients try to retrieve visual information stored in long-term memory. It also affects visual information that has been perceived recently or has

Visual scene

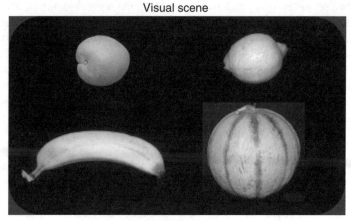

Verbal description

The banana is in front of the apricot.
The apricot is on the left of the lemon.
The lemon is behind the melon.
The melon is on the right of the banana.

Figure 9.5 Materials similar to those used in the experiment with neglect patients, as reported by Denis, Beschin, Logie, and Della Sala (2002).

been constructed from verbal descriptions. The argument here is that the mental representation constructed by using visual imagery is independent of visual perception, and that WM is separate from visual perception.

Images and mental models

The notion that the mind forms "models" of reality and uses them in reasoning was introduced into psychology by Kenneth Craik (1943), in a book published just two years before the author's untimely death. Four decades elapsed before the concept was revived and integrated into a fully fleshed-out theory. The modern concept of "mental model" emerged in the early 1980s. It was forged by Phil Johnson-Laird (1980) at a time where researchers were realizing that accounts of human reasoning based exclusively on the propositional coding of the premises had severe limitations. An internal representation that is a structural analogue of a situation or state of affairs is known as a mental model. This concept was described and integrated into a comprehensive account of human reasoning in Johnson-Laird's (1983) book, *Mental Models*. In the same year, van Dijk and Kintsch (1983) introduced the concept of a "situation model" into a theory whose basic components consisted essentially of propositions. This conceptualization was motivated by the same objective as the mental model theory – that is, a desire to go beyond a purely propositionalist approach – even though in fact the two theories underwent separate developments.

The concept of mental model became very popular and flourished in diverse areas of psychology, such as comprehension (Bower & Morrow, 1989; Glenberg, Meyer, & Lindem, 1987), reasoning (Byrne & Johnson-Laird, 1989; Rodrigo, de Vega, & Castaneda, 1992), and spatial cognition (Franklin & Tversky, 1990; Taylor & Tversky, 1992). Note also that a variant of the concept of mental model was introduced at about the same time to account for people's mental representations of physical processes and their qualitative reasoning about space and motion (see Gentner & Stevens, 1983).

Mental images in the mental model theory

In the history of psychological concepts, decades elapsed between the initial approaches to mental imagery and the proposal of a theory of mental models. Despite this long interval, the two concepts share several features, which explains why imagery researchers have been interested in mental model conceptualization.

Johnson-Laird's basic assumption about reasoning was that besides propositions, which are processed using formal logic, there are alternative modes of representation that can be used to create mental analogues of the domain to which reasoning is applied and thus can derive inferences without performing any proposition-based operations. This line of thinking was originally applied to reasoning, but it was rapidly extended to language processing, a domain where the role of imagery had long been investigated (see Garnham, 1987; Perrig & Kintsch, 1985). The idea was that the human mind is able to perform computations on cognitive entities constructed from linguistic inputs without relying on formal logic. This approach highlights the human mind's propensity to create cognitive representations of absent entities.

In addition, in their respective theoretical areas, mental images and mental models are both viewed in contrast to the same alternative mode of representation, namely propositional representations. For logicians (from whom the concept was borrowed by cognitive psychologists), propositions are chains of symbols structured in the same way as language, and they are composed of arbitrary symbols. In contrast, images and models are nonarbitrary symbols, and their structure analogically reflects the structure of the entities represented. Both are based on a *semantic of resemblance*, and both exhibit similar cognitive advantages and similar limitations with respect to propositions. For instance, in the processing of language, the advantage of propositional representations over images or models is the ease with which they are constructed, due to the direct correspondence between lexical items and the symbols composing the propositions. However, they have the disadvantage that the only inferential machinery that operates on them is a system based on meaning postulates and formal logic. In contrast, images and models provide a cognitive equivalent of the represented world, and they have a structure that undergoes the same types of processing as the world itself. This advantage, however, can also be a drawback. In indeterminate cases, several images or several models may be necessary to cope with that indeterminacy, whereas propositional representations make it useless to construct several alternative models.

Johnson-Laird's theory of mental models was grounded on an analysis of situations in which people process verbal information, mainly deductive reasoning and discourse comprehension. In contrast, most studies of mental imagery have been devoted to situations or processes with a perceptual source, eliciting questions about how images reflect the visual world and how people retrieve visual information from the activation of such representations. One question about mental models has long been ignored: Is the exploration of the perceptual world a source for the elaboration of models? The numerous demonstrations that graphic information helps readers to construct mental models while reading a text suggest that it is. Bower and Morrow's (1989) experiments demonstrated the possibility of intimate articulation between the processing of a text and of map information. Glenberg and Langston (1992) showed that the spatial structure of illustrations enhances the comprehension and memorizing of texts describing the steps of a process. Gyselinck and Tardieu (1994) also provided evidence that graphic illustrations really do make it easier to understand complex processes described in instructional texts.

In his 1983 book, Johnson-Laird devoted a full chapter to a discussion of imagery as a form of mental representation. He established a parallel between images and mental models, pointing out that both are representations in which information is not inscribed according to an arbitrary syntactical structure. He also introduced the idea that a mental model may display varying degrees of analogy. In fact, analogy is not an all-or-nothing property of a representational system. Various degrees of analogy may be achieved between a represented world and its representation. Undoubtedly, there has to be some degree of analogy in any mental model. However, when a model is intended to represent the spatial relations existing among a set of elements, analogy may go a significant step further if the model is organized by a dimensional structure within which distances are represented by distances and relationships between distances are preserved. If the model incorporates visual features, an image can act as an expression of the model, so that the model is apprehended from a particular point of view. Imagery gives the mental representation its figural features and also gives it spatial extension. In other words, the image provides the model with a transient figural appearance.

In this regard, Johnson-Laird's theory evolved substantially from its original formulation. In his 1983 book, Johnson-Laird proposed a distinction between "physical" mental models (which represent states of the physical world) and "conceptual" mental models (which represent more abstract entities). Johnson-Laird distinguished six types of physical models, which are listed here in order of increasing specification: simple relational models, spatial models, temporal models, kinematic models, dynamic models, and lastly *images*. The inclusion of images in the list of "models" is nevertheless questionable. For Johnson-Laird, an image is an observer-centered representation that displays the visible characteristics of a model. It corresponds to a certain "view" of the object or the situation represented in that model. In an effort to clarify the relationships between images and models, Manuel de Vega and I argued that rather than being a "sort of model", an image should, rather, be seen as a "tool" intended to make it easier to figure out a mental model. In other words, mental imagery should be viewed as a mode of specification (or instantiation) of mental models that include data likely to be figured out, such as spatial mental models (Denis & de Vega, 1993).

Reasoning with mental models

Interestingly, Johnson-Laird (1996) subsequently revisited his original conception of visual images as a "special case" of mental models and stressed the view that images and models are "distinct sorts of representations calling for distinct sorts of processes" (p. 92). Johnson-Laird introduced an explicit "triple-code" hypothesis, involving propositional representations, mental models, and images. Models are distinct from images inasmuch as they contain abstract elements that cannot be visualized. Furthermore, they do not correspond to a single situation (as images typically do), but to a class of situations. However, both models and images can be used to reason.

The issue, then, is to find out whether a specific reasoning episode will depend primarily on images or models. If the person reasoning relies on visual images, he or she can be expected to cope better with premises that are easy to visualize. However, the validity of the long-standing (and dominant) view of the role of visual imagery in reasoning (e.g., Shaver, Pierson, & Lang, 1975) needs to be reconsidered. In particular, the classical studies did not distinguish between the ease of visualization and the ease of constructing mental models. In a series of experiments in which the visual and the spatial characters of the relationships were dealt with separately, Knauff and Johnson-Laird (2002) provided evidence that visual images are not critical for deductive reasoning and that sometimes they can even impede the reasoning process. Further neurocognitive arguments have been provided in support of the view that only spatial mental models are effective in helping people to reason deductively (Knauff, 2009; Knauff, Fangmeier, Ruff, & Johnson-Laird, 2003).

Johnson-Laird's conception of the respective values of images and mental models in reasoning was aptly summarized in his most recent book, *How We Reason* (2006). Here, Johnson-Laird highlights the fact that both images and models of a spatial layout are *iconic* in nature (i.e., their parts and the relations among them correspond to the parts of the layout and the relations among them) and reminds us that the mind "eschews abstract representations in favor of representations rooted in perception" (p. 31). But visualization alone cannot solve a problem, which means that "images need to be backed up by an independent representation of the problem if they are to be used to solve it" (p. 35). Johnson-Laird then offers the best summary of the specificities of the two types of iconic representations:

An image of a scene makes manifest the visual characteristics of the objects in the scene from a particular point of view. Mental models are different. Their content is available to consciousness, but we cannot inspect them as we can inspect images. They are often abstract and represent a small amount of information. But their power lies in their abstraction. A mental model can represent what is common to all the different ways in which a possibility might occur. Each model therefore corresponds to a *set* of possibilities.

(Johnson-Laird, 2006, p. 36)

Spatial mental models

During the past 10–15 years, a number of research programs have been dedicated to the investigation of mental models and their ability to underpin reasoning and language comprehension. As de Vega and Marschark (1996) pointed out, the emphasis of these two areas of research is somewhat different. The focus in reasoning research has primarily been on the number of models activated during the processing of a problem (especially, in reasoning using indeterminate statements), whereas researchers investigating comprehension were more interested in the dynamic, incremental nature of models and, in particular, their enrichment and on-line updating during comprehension. For instance, de Vega (1994) showed that after constructing a spatial model from a narrative describing a spatial environment, people are able to switch their perspective and adopt various points of view. However, their responses in a sentence verification task reveal that adopting a new point of view has a cognitive cost. Furthermore, sentence verification is faster when the narrative introduces several characters all viewing the described layout from the same direction than when the characters have different points of view. It is also worth noting that the participants with the highest visuospatial abilities perform better and more rapidly in the verification task. In further studies, de Vega (1995) provided evidence that people are able to track the position and surroundings of a moving protagonist during the continuous reading of a narrative.

A related topic of interest is that of the representation of metric information in mental models. This issue is relevant if one recalls that visual imagery is a form of representation that preserves Euclidean distances and that the functional value of this representation is clearer in people with good visuospatial imagery capacities (Denis, 2008; Denis & Kosslyn, 1999). With spatial models, the situation is somewhat different. For instance, Langston, Kramer, and Glenberg (1998) provided empirical arguments favoring the view that spatial mental models derived from text are topological rather than Euclidean forms of representation. At about the same time, Mike Rinck conducted a number of experiments intended to document this issue, based on a paradigm initially developed by Morrow, Greenspan, and Bower (1987; Morrow, Bower, & Greenspan, 1989; Rinck, Williams, Bower, & Becker, 1996; see also Haenggi, Kintsch, & Gernsbacher, 1995). In one of these studies (Rinck, Hähnel, Bower, & Glowalla, 1997), the participants first studied the layout of a complex building in which various objects were located in the different rooms. They then read a narrative describing the movement of a protagonist in the building. Based on participants' responses to sentences referring to objects contained in the various rooms in the building, the accessibility of the objects was shown to decrease with increasing spatial distance between the objects and the reader's current focus of attention. However, this decrease depended not on the actual distance, but on the number of rooms located between the object and the current focus of attention. In other terms, the effect of spatial distance was only categorical, with no evidence that Euclidean distance had any effect on responses.

Mike Rinck and I were interested in pushing the investigation a bit further (Rinck & Denis, 2004). Our objective was to find out whether the previously established pattern of results would persist if the participants, after learning the spatial layout of the building, were invited to perform a mental imagery task – specifically, to imagine themselves walking through the building from one room to another. We manipulated both Euclidean distance (as measured on the layout) and categorical distance (with movements passing through one or two rooms) (see Figure 9.6). Measures of the reading times of room-to-room instructions revealed that both variables were effective. The participants took longer to imagine moving along longer paths and also (independently) to move along paths involving two rooms rather than just one, reflecting that both Euclidean distance and categorical distance were represented during the mental imagery task. Test probes showed also that both types of spatial distance yielded similar effects, without any dominance of categorical over Euclidean distance in probe response times.

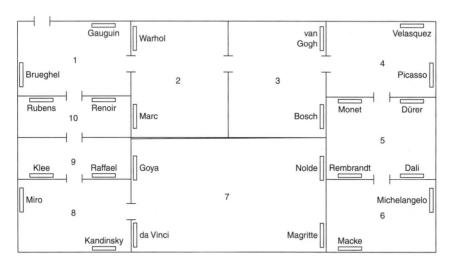

Figure 9.6 This shows the layout of the fictitious art museum in which participants in the Rinck and Denis experiments performed a mental imagery task. (Reprinted from M. Rinck & M. Denis, 2004. The metrics of spatial distance traversed during mental imagery. *Journal of Experimental Psychology: Learning, Memory, and Cognition, 30,* 1212. Copyright © 2004 by the American Psychological Association. Reprinted with permission.)

The fact that only categorical distance had affected the measures in the previous studies (Rinck et al., 1997) reflects the fact that in narrative comprehension, readers create only rough, categorical representations of spatial distance, whereas during the mental imagery task in the Rinck and Denis (2004) study, they represent spatial distance at the more detailed level of Euclidean distance. This does not mean that the demands of a particular task could not incite a reader to create more detailed spatial representations if this becomes necessary.

Mental models and working memory

What we have learned from research comparing images and models can be summarized as follows. Compared with models, images are representations that can reach a high degree of analogy with the real world that they depict. They can preserve quite detailed spatial relations, metric distances, and kinematic transformations. On the other hand, mental models are representations constructed by a system that, to a large extent, fulfills a data-reduction function. In many situations involving comprehension or reasoning, there is no need for the reader or listener to construct an accurate representation of metric distances or to perform continuous mental scanning across all available information. Models are in fact simplified representations, which selectively emphasize the features that are the most relevant to the task in hand. For instance, in order to execute a given task correctly, it may be sufficient to construct a model of the relative positions of two objects while ignoring the exact distance separating them, or to represent the starting point and the target of a moving object without implementing continuous image scanning between the two points. Mental models are thought to use resources available in WM. Given the capacity limitations of WM, it is advantageous for mental models to construct reduced or simplified representations rather than models with a high degree of resolution (see Denis, 1996; Denis & de Vega, 1993).

The relationships between WM and mental models, and the impact of individual imagery capacities, are precisely the focus of an important research program conducted jointly by Francesca Pazzaglia and Valérie Gyselinck. The starting point of their research was a set of experiments showing that the verbal and spatial components of WM are involved in different ways in the comprehension and memory of spatial and nonspatial texts, with a concurrent spatial task having a selective interference effect on the processing of a spatial text, and a concurrent verbal task having an interference effect on the processing of both spatial and nonspatial texts. Consistent with the basic tenet of the WM theory, the verbal component of WM appears to be involved in text comprehension in general, whereas VSWM is only involved for texts that convey visuospatial information (De Beni & Moè, 2003; De Beni, Pazzaglia, Gyselinck, & Meneghetti, 2005; Pazzaglia & Cornoldi, 1999).

Gyselinck and her collaborators then focused on the mental models elaborated from spatial texts (descriptions of outdoor environments, such as a tourist center, a nature reserve, or a holiday farm, involving route instructions). In one study (Gyselinck, De Beni, Pazzaglia, Meneghetti, & Mondoloni, 2007), one group of

participants received imagery instructions (they were invited to imagine themselves moving around in the described environment), while another group received
repetition instructions (they were instructed to repeat each individual sentence
mentally after reading it). While they were reading, each group undertook concurrent tasks expected to make use of either spatial or verbal WM resources (spatial
tapping and articulatory suppression, respectively). The finding relevant to the
present discussion was that the tapping task impaired sentence verification performance in the imagery instructions group, but not in the repetition instructions
group – that is, it eliminated the usual beneficial effect of imagery instructions
(which, in a control condition, was confirmed in the absence of any concurrent
task). There was no similar finding for the concurrent articulatory task, and interference effects were of similar magnitude in the two groups. Overall, these data
confirmed that VSWM is involved when people generate mental images. Further
studies (Gyselinck, Meneghetti, De Beni, & Pazzaglia, 2009; Meneghetti,
Gyselinck, Pazzaglia, & De Beni, 2009) showed that while all readers benefitted
from receiving imagery instructions, only the "low imagers" (i.e., those reporting
less vivid imagery and/or scoring low on a mental rotation test) were sensitive to
spatial interference. The greater spatial resources available to "high imagers"
helped them to compensate for spatial interference during the construction of
a spatial mental model, a finding that nicely corroborates the idea of intimate
relationships between mental modeling, working memory, and mental imagery
(see Pazzaglia, Gyselinck, Cornoldi, & De Beni, chapter 6, this volume).

On the whole, the literature of recent years supports the notion that mental
models of spatial environments cannot be equated to visual images in a narrow
sense. Spatial models of described environments are not simply figural representations of these environments. As Barbara Tversky (1991) aptly pointed out,
models should be conceived of as "spatial frameworks" that people use to perform
computations on relations not explicitly asserted in the texts from which they are
generated.

Imagery and spatial cognition

An integral aspect of the study of spatial behavior in humans and animals – from
simple homing behavior to the calculation of shortcuts in complex environments
– is the formulation of hypotheses about the nature and functions of the mental
representations underlying spatial performance (see Figure 9.7). The introduction
of the concept of "cognitive map" (Tolman, 1948) marked the emergence of
psychologists' concern about the mechanisms that underlie the construction of
spatial knowledge and the use of such knowledge in adaptive behavior within an
environment. However, the new concept pushed the issue towards new frontiers
and made it necessary to ask new questions. What are cognitive maps made of?
Which sensory modalities contribute to their construction? Are these modalities
involved in the mechanisms that determine how people adapt to novel spatial environments, such as spatial updating or path integration? Has visual imagery anything
to do with people's mental representations of their spatial environments?

Figure 9.7 As a passionate collector of road signs and direction arrows, I see this nice combination of an arrow and a question mark in a foggy North-American landscape as a visual metaphor of my continuous search for answers to the questions that arise from the investigation of spatial cognition. (Photograph by M. Denis.)

These questions have led to a vast amount of research and the formation of a scientific community (e.g., Allen, 2004, 2006; Golledge, 1999; O'Keefe & Nadel, 1978; Portugali, 1996; see Denis & Loomis, 2007). The issue of the sensory modalities that are responsible for the encoding of spatial information concerned imagery researchers. In particular, a lot of research was motivated by the contrast between vision and body-based senses (proprioception and kinesthesis), as sources of information for the spatial memory. The critical role of visual cues in creating internal representations of a spatial layout received abundant support from behavioral and neurocognitive studies (e.g., Janzen, Wagensveld, & van Turennout, 2007; Thinus-Blanc & Gaunet, 1997), and the contribution of the vestibular system to spatial learning and spatial updating has also been attested, in particular in the absence of vision (e.g., Klatzky, Loomis, Beall, Chance, & Golledge, 1998; Waller & Greenauer, 2007). The particular significance of visual cues has elicited questions about the role of mental imagery as a means of encoding the visual information used as landmarks in navigation. In 2006, a comprehensive volume was edited by Tomaso Vecchi and Gabriella Bottini under the title: *Imagery and Spatial Cognition: Methods, Models and Cognitive Assessment*. This volume includes a very useful summary of the methods used to assess imagery and VSWM functions in children and adults (see Mammarella, Pazzaglia, & Cornoldi, 2006).

Scales of psychological space

The increasing interest in the cognitive factors of space-related behavior led researchers to more accurately define distinct categories of phenomena that are likely to call various different mechanisms into play. It soon became evident that various types of space must be differentiated, first of all in terms of their size, from small spaces (visually apprehended from a single vantage point) to large ones (inviting navigation and being apprehended perceptually through successive views).

Dan Montello (1993) aptly argued that space is not scale-independent. He identified several qualitatively distinct classes of space on the basis of the projective size of the space relative to the human body, namely figural, vista, and environmental spaces. Figural space is smaller than the human body and is external to the individual. It can be apprehended from a single viewpoint, and its properties are perceived without locomotion. Vista space is at least as large as the body, but it can be visually apprehended from a single place without locomotion. Environmental space is larger than the body and "contains" the individual. It requires locomotion to be apprehended, and it typically calls for the integration of information apprehended from several points of view (see also Montello, 2009). In a similar effort to develop a conceptual distinction between different scales of psychological space, Barbara Tversky proposed distinguishing three types of functional space: the space of the body, the space around the body, and the space of navigation (see Tversky, Morrison, Franklin, & Bryant, 1999). "Each of these is conceptualized differently, depending on the functions it serves, the activities invoked, and the entities involved" (Tversky, 2003, p. 77). Not only do spatial entities at different scales involve distinct cognitive structures and mechanisms, but the processing of information about them involves different brain structures and mechanisms. Small-scale spatial tasks (such as mental rotation) are typically associated with parietal activity, whereas learning about large-scale spaces mainly involves the hippocampus and the medial temporal lobes.

Mary Hegarty and her colleagues investigated whether the mechanisms underlying the processing of different scales of space are common or separate (see Hegarty, Montello, Richardson, Ishikawa, & Lovelace, 2006). The authors' idea was to develop an approach based on individual behavioral measures in two families of spatial tasks. One group of tasks consisted of psychometric tests of spatial ability involving the inspection, imagination, or mental transformation of small shapes or manipulable objects, which correspond to the "figural" scale. The other group included tasks of wayfinding and navigation through large spaces surrounding the body and involving the integration of successive views at the "environmental" scale. One feature that made this study especially valuable to imagery researchers is that the measures of spatial abilities at the scale of figural space relied on tests from the repertoire of psychometric instruments typically used to assess individual abilities in visuospatial imagery (such as mental rotation tests or measures of VSWM). This approach offered the possibility of documenting an issue of interest to both communities – that is, establishing whether individual abilities in the processing of visuospatial information in paper-and-pencil psychometric tests are also mobilized to navigate in large-scale environments. The results of the study indicated that small-scale spatial ability is indeed predictive of performance in environmental learning tasks, which is compatible with the assumption of partial, but not total, overlap between spatial abilities at different scales.

The impact of basic visuospatial abilities on navigational performance has been clearly established by studies in which people were requested to execute distracting tasks involving VSWM resources while moving in an environment. In a very elegant study conducted by Garden, Cornoldi, and Logie (2002) in the streets of the city of Padua, Italy, people were invited to follow a previously learned trajectory. Their navigational performance (as assessed by the frequency of directional errors) was significantly impaired when they were asked to carry out a concurrent distracting task making use of their visuospatial resources. This effect was even more marked in the people with the highest visuospatial capacities, indicating that only these people effectively relied on the visuospatial components of WM during navigation in a real environment. A similar paradigm was used in a virtual-reality setting by Meilinger, Knauff, and Bülthoff (2008). The participants were invited to memorize two routes through the streets of the ancient city of Tübingen, Germany. During the learning phase, they had to perform a secondary task, which was either verbal or visuospatial in nature. In this latter case, the task was either mainly visual or mainly spatial. The participants' memorization of the routes was then tested (by measuring the navigation time, the distance covered, the number of stops, and the number of errors). Both verbal and visuospatial interference had an impact on performance, and the spatial task was more detrimental to performance than was the visual task. This finding reflected the primary involvement of spatial WM in the learning of routes, and it corroborated Hegarty et al.'s (2006) conclusion that basic visuospatial abilities play a functional role in people's navigational performance.

Verbal descriptions of spatial environments

Whereas vision and locomotion as sources of spatial knowledge have attracted the attention of researchers for several decades, it was only from the early 1990s that a genuine interest emerged for the situations in which *language* is used to convey information about spatial environments and to help in elaborating mental representations of space (see Denis, 1996). A variety of verbal statements may be generated with the aim of providing someone with spatial representations. They may consist of descriptions of static environments seen from a given viewpoint, or of verbal instructions intended to assist a person engaged in wayfinding. The concern for "spatial language" has elicited a large amount of research in both psychology and linguistics (see Bloom, Peterson, Nadel, & Garrett, 1996; Dasen

& Mishra, 2010; Denis, 1997a; Evans & Chilton, 2010; Hickmann & Robert, 2006; Levinson, 2003) and has also become a focus of interest for researchers in artificial intelligence, human–machine interactions, and cognitive ergonomics (e.g., Freksa, Newcombe, Gärdenfors, & Wölfl, 2008).

At the scale of figural space (as defined above; see Montello, 1993), the capacity of language to convey valid spatial information by eliciting visual mental imagery was at the heart of the research program that I launched when I joined LIMSI-CNRS on the Orsay campus of the Université de Paris-Sud in 1992. My objective was to assess whether purely verbal information might, under certain conditions, help people create internal representations with structural properties similar to those of images derived from visual experience. Image scanning and the mental comparison of distances were the paradigms mainly used in my lab to serve this objective.

When creating experimental situations that make use of descriptive materials, one is sooner or later confronted with the issue of the internal structure of descriptions and its impact on the ease and effectiveness with which they can be processed (see Denis & Cocude, 1992; Denis & Denhière, 1990). This means that before looking at the *processing* and *use* of spatial language, one must first investigate the processes involved in its *production*. In this respect, it is well established that a major cognitive problem for a speaker or a writer is the fact that language generates linear, unidirectional outputs. Translating a multidimensional spatial entity into the form of a linear linguistic output requires the construction of a sequential structure, which has to be selected from among numerous alternatives (see Figure 9.8).

Some studies have shown that dominant structures regulate the sequential description of certain spatial objects. The descriptions of apartments or rooms made from memory are often cited as an example of this (see Ehrich & Koster, 1983; Linde & Labov, 1975; Shanon, 1984). The speaker reviews an internal representation, presumably a visual image, and guides the listener along an imaginary "tour" of the environment being described in such a way that the listener constructs the representation according to a sequence that matches the order in which the speaker explores his or her own representation. Such regularities or descriptive schemata were reported and analyzed by Pim Levelt (1982, 1989). For instance, in the absence of any intrinsic sequential constraint imposed by the structure of the object or the scene to be described, most speakers solve the "linearization problem" by adopting strategies that minimize the number of items that they have to store simultaneously in their WM (or the duration of their storage). This corresponds to what Levelt called the "principle of minimal effort", based on economizing short-term memory.

Of course, it was more than tempting to try to find out whether the description of an imagined scene matches the description of a currently perceived layout. We adapted Levelt's paradigm in order to compare the strategies used to describe either visually presented scenes or mental images of the same scenes. When people described their mental images, their modes of linearization exhibited strong similarities to those used to describe physically present configurations

Figure 9.8 The research program in which several of my experiments have been undertaken can be summarized by the situation shown in this figure. The situation
involves two people. Person A is looking at a visual scene. Person B is at some
distance, in some other location (another room, or maybe even in another city),
and cannot see the scene. A's task is to describe the scene to B solely by speech,
in such a way as to allow B to construct a representation as similar as possible
to that which he would have constructed after looking at the scene himself.
"Similar", here, means "carrying the same information" and, more importantly,
"likely to support the same kinds of cognitive operations". For instance, if A
has described a territory, B may be required to draw a map of this territory, or
use his mental representation in order to compare distances between landmarks, or plan an appropriate route through the scene depicted. (From M.
Denis, 1996. Imagery and the description of spatial configurations (p. 129). In
M. de Vega, M. J. Intons-Peterson, P. N. Johnson-Laird, M. Denis, & M.
Marschark, *Models of Visuospatial Cognition* (pp. 128–197). New York:
Oxford University Press. Copyright © 1996 by Oxford University Press, Inc.
Reprinted with permission.)

(Robin & Denis, 1991). This finding is consistent with the hypothesis that similar
processes are implemented to access perceptual events and visual images of
spatial configurations. We did not find any reliable difference between high and
low imagers as regards their tendency to use the dominant descriptive strategies
for a given set of configurations. The only difference between the two groups was
that high imagers consistently had shorter description latencies than did low
imagers (and they consistently devoted more time to studying the visual scenes
during the memorization phase) (Denis, 1996).

Let us now turn to the verbal descriptions of larger spatial entities at the scale
of environmental space and to the processes by which someone reading or
listening to such descriptions constructs internal representations intended to assist
navigation or wayfinding. There is no doubt that the major distinction introduced
in this domain is that made by Taylor and Tversky (1992) between route and

survey perspectives in the description of environments, and the corresponding textual outputs reflecting these perspectives. A *route description* typically forces the reader or listener to adopt the perspective of a person moving along a route through an environment. The description adopts an egocentric, frontal view of the environment, involving continuous changes in orientation. The language used consists mainly of egocentric terms (e.g., "right"/"left"). In contrast, in a *survey description*, the environment is described from a bird's-eye perspective. It provides an overview of a scene, with an allocentric point of view that remains unchanged throughout the description. The language used is more likely to include canonical terms (e.g., "east"/"west"). Processing these two perspectives imposes different cognitive constraints. If imagery is associated with the processing of such descriptions, it may not display the same type of visual information in both cases, and this difference may have consequences for the operations by which a reader or listener first constructs an internal representation and later makes use of it. The route/survey distinction and, more generally, the related issues of spatial reference frames, multiple systems of spatial memory, and the processing of visual vs. described scenes have been widely documented and continue to inspire a good number of "rising stars" working in spatial cognition (see Avraamides & Kelly, 2010; Brunyé & Taylor, 2008; Janzen, 2006; Kozhevnikov, Motes, Rasch, & Blajenkova, 2006; Noordzij & Postma, 2005; Pazzaglia, Meneghetti, De Beni, & Gyselinck, 2010).

I would like to mention our contribution to the studies investigating the implication of WM in the processing of route and survey texts. In this study, which was conducted with Bob Logie and Emilie Deyzac, we tested people's ability to draw sketch-maps of environments learned from route or survey perspectives while executing various concurrent tasks (see Deyzac, Logie, & Denis, 2006; see also Figure 9.9). The resulting patterns of interference indicated that the processing of landmarks mobilized both the visual and the spatial components of WM when people were processing route descriptions, whereas the processing of moves (using a route perspective) and locations (using a survey perspective) essentially relied on the spatial component of VSWM. These findings, plus those of others—notably those of Brunyé and Taylor (2008), Gyselinck et al. (2007), and Pazzaglia et al. (2010)—provided evidence that the processing of route descriptions and the processing of corresponding survey descriptions rely on distinct components of WM.

Production and comprehension of route directions

A particular aspect of the relationships between language and spatial cognition which has greatly occupied me (and several of my colleagues and doctoral students) is the situation in which one person gives route directions to another person. This situation has aroused considerable interest for many years, not only because it is a very common situation encountered on a daily basis, but because it invites researchers to try to account for the functional connections between language, spatial cognition, and mental imagery, three major domains of the

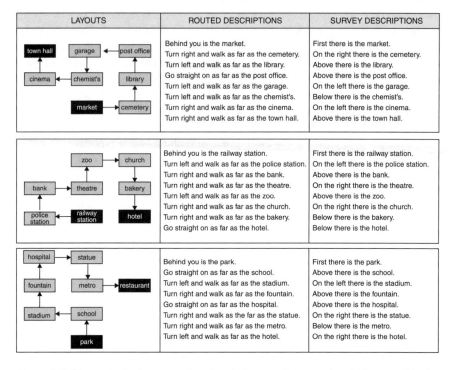

LAYOUTS	ROUTED DESCRIPTIONS	SURVEY DESCRIPTIONS
(layout diagram: town hall, garage, post office, cinema, chemist's, library, market, cemetery)	Behind you is the market. Turn right and walk as far as the cemetery. Turn left and walk as far as the library. Go straight on as far as the post office. Turn left and walk as far as the garage. Turn left and walk as far as the chemist's. Turn right and walk as far as the cinema. Turn right and walk as far as the town hall.	First there is the market. On the right there is the cemetery. Above there is the library. Above there is the post office. On the left there is the garage. Below there is the chemist's. On the left there is the cinema. Above there is the town hall.
(layout diagram: zoo, church, bank, theatre, bakery, police station, railway station, hotel)	Behind you is the railway station. Turn left and walk as far as the police station. Turn right and walk as far as the bank. Turn right and walk as far as the theatre. Turn left and walk as far as the zoo. Turn right and walk as far as the church. Turn right and walk as far as the bakery. Go straight on as far as the hotel.	First there is the railway station. On the left there is the police station. Above there is the bank. On the right there is the theatre. Above there is the zoo. On the right there is the church. Below there is the bakery. Below there is the hotel.
(layout diagram: hospital, statue, fountain, metro, restaurant, stadium, school, park)	Behind you is the park. Go straight on as far as the school. Turn left and walk as far as the stadium. Turn right and walk as far as the fountain. Go straight on as far as the hospital. Turn right and walk as the far as the statue. Turn right and walk as far as the metro. Turn left and walk as far as the hotel.	First there is the park. Above there is the school. On the left there is the stadium. Above there is the fountain. Above there is the hospital. On the right there is the statue. Below there is the metro. On the right there is the hotel.

Figure 9.9 These are the layouts, route descriptions, and survey descriptions used in the Deyzac, Logie, and Denis (2006) experiments. (Reprinted from E. Deyzac, R. H. Logie, & M. Denis, 2006. Visuospatial working memory and the processing of spatial descriptions. *British Journal of Psychology*, *97*, 224. Copyright © 2006 by the British Psychological Society. Reprinted with permission.)

cognitive architecture, each of which has its own representational system, organization, and mechanisms. In 1997, I proposed a model of the processes by which speakers or writers generate route directions (Denis, 1997b). This model was based on the analysis of a large number of descriptions collected in natural settings. At that time, a survey of the psychological literature revealed that no more than seven journal articles and five book chapters had specifically addressed this issue. One of them was a thoughtful analysis of route directions proposed by Wolfgang Klein (1982).

Our general framework considered three cognitive macro-operations: activating an internal representation of the territory in which a displacement is to take place; planning a route between the starting point and the destination in the relevant subspace of the activated representation; and formulating the procedure that the user will have to execute to move along the route and eventually reach the destination. The resulting verbal output involves a series of prescriptions of actions along a succession of segments, in which these actions are triggered when the person moving along the route comes across specific landmarks. Our approach included a classification of the statements contained in route directions and their elementary components (references to landmarks and prescriptions of actions). It introduced the concept of "skeletal description" as the abstract description reflecting the essentials of a navigational procedure. Based on a selection of statements from among a set of actual descriptions, a skeletal description is thought to be fully informative, while containing the smallest set of landmarks and instructions needed to navigate appropriately.

Several subsequent studies allowed us and others to refine and extend the model – in particular, the concept of the skeletal description. This was done in joint empirical studies undertaken with my colleague Marie-Paule Daniel (see Daniel & Denis, 2004; Daniel, Mores Dibo-Cohen, Carité, Boyer, & Denis, 2007). The approach was also extended with the objective of finding iconic equivalents to verbal route directions. In particular, Tversky and Lee (1998, 1999) analyzed a corpus of route directions and route maps and found that the same type of information constituted the content of both route descriptions and depictions, suggesting that the same underlying mental representations might generate both (see also Fontaine, Edwards, Tversky, & Denis, 2005; Tversky, chapter 1, this volume). Route instructions also inspired Gary Allen, who provided a thoughtful analysis of the conventions used for conveying wayfinding information and recommended a set of principle-based practices for communicating route knowledge (Allen, 1997, 2000).

Now, what about the role of mental imagery in the production and comprehension of route directions? Very little empirical data is available about this, but it seems reasonable to hypothesize that if the generation of a description relies on the activation of an internal representation with a visual content, mental images could be particularly helpful to someone reviewing the landmarks to be included in his or her description. On the comprehension side, a reader or listener with a strong inclination to generating images would be more likely to visualize the landmarks and scenes conveyed by the description. The limited information so far available supports both these hypotheses.

In tasks requiring the production of route directions, Vanetti and Allen (1988) showed that participants with high visuospatial abilities produced more effective spatial discourse than did low visuospatial imagers. The data from my investigation of the production of route instructions did not reveal any difference between the high and low visuospatial imagers as regards the rating of the quality of their descriptions, but the descriptions provided by high visuospatial imagers included more frequent references to landmarks. This finding is consistent with the expectation that people who are more likely to retrieve visuospatial information from their memories are also more likely to include such information in their verbal production (Denis, 1997b). If we now look at the cognitive processes implemented during the *processing* of route directions, a highly consistent pattern emerges. In the first doctoral thesis to be completed in my lab on the issue of route instructions, we found that high visuospatial imagers were faster at processing route instructions delivered in written form, a finding suggesting that they made efficient use of their ability to create visuospatial representations while reading. Furthermore, their recall of the actions prescribed by the instructions was higher than that of low imagers (Fernandez, 2000).

However, while it can be useful to test the abilities of readers or listeners to generate visuospatial representations and recall them verbally or by drawing, the ultimate test of the value of such representations is people's ability to *use* them effectively for actual navigation. This was the objective of what is undoubtedly my most cherished experimental study in my decades of research. This study has a special place in my affections not only because the experimental setting was one of the most fascinating real environments that an experimenter could ever have dreamt of – the city of Venice! – but also because this was an opportunity to collaborate with stimulating colleagues in designing, conducting, and subsequently sharing with the community some ambitious experimental work and an exciting experience (see Denis, Pazzaglia, Cornoldi, & Bertolo, 1999; see also Figures 9.10 and 9.11). The study consisted first of collecting various descriptions of routes from residents of Venice. The communicative value of these descriptions was rated by independent judges, and skeletal descriptions reflecting the essentials needed for navigation were designed. We then tested the navigational

Figure 9.10   Lost in Venezia! The intricate street and channel network in the city of Venice offers a challenging environment for spatial orientation. It has provided an exceptional setting for the navigation experiments conducted by Denis, Pazzaglia, Cornoldi, and Bertolo (1999). (Photograph by F. Pazzaglia.)

Figure 9.11 The city of Venice provides a variety of directional arrows to help visitors find their way through the city. (Photographs by M. Denis.)

performance of new participants who were unfamiliar with the city of Venice and had been provided either with descriptions rated as "good" or "poor" or with skeletal descriptions. The data showed that navigation with good descriptions resulted in significantly lower error scores than did navigation with poor descriptions, and that skeletal descriptions gave scores similar to those of good descriptions. Poor descriptions also resulted in more errors by participants who tended to use a survey perspective than by participants expressing a preference for visual memories of landmarks (which are likely to be encoded as visual images).

As we noted in our discussion of these results, the survey perspective is generally considered to be a rather sophisticated mode of representation, which involves recoding egocentric visual and/or locomotor experience as map-like mental representations. The construction of a survey representation from route directions (i.e., materials that impose a route perspective) probably involves a high cognitive cost. The intriguing finding here was that the participants who seemed most likely to construct survey representations experienced particular difficulty with the navigation task. This is easy to explain if we assume that these people abandoned their preferred (spontaneous) strategy as soon as they realized how difficult it was to construct a survey representation when they were forced to rely on a confusing route description. These difficulties were certainly increased by the specific features of the topography of Venice, a city with narrow streets that restrict distant views of important landmarks and thus make it especially difficult for a moving person to construct a map-like representation of the environment traversed by the routes. In contrast, people who spontaneously tended to rely on the encoding of visual scenes and landmarks were less perturbed when exposed to a poorly organized spatial discourse. As a consequence, a navigation episode anchored to salient visual landmarks (which had presumably been encoded as visual images) resulted in better performance than any attempt to construct a comprehensive survey representation.

The data from the Venice study clearly suggested that navigational performance based on the processing of spatial discourse depends on interactions between individual cognitive characteristics or preferences, properties of the environment, and intrinsic characteristics of the linguistic material. Note that the findings regarding the value of verbal descriptions for assisting navigational performance have been repeatedly confirmed in field studies conducted in other spatial contexts. Although far less splendid than the setting offered by the Serenissima, environments like the Orsay campus (Daniel, Tom, Manghi, & Denis, 2003) and the suburbs of Paris (Tom & Denis, 2003) allowed us to confirm the broad lines of our Venetian findings!

Spatial mental models, again!

To conclude this section, let us note that when researchers investigate the representations and mechanisms involved in spatial cognition, mental imagery is waiting in the wings, ready to come onto the stage at some point. And indeed, there are some hints of the fact that imagery may contribute to the construction of spatial mental representations. However, the main current theories of spatial cognition tend to invoke mechanisms that are autonomous with regard to imagery. Images are good companions of spatial representations, but a growing body of evidence suggests that the various inputs collected during encoding of spatial information (whether visual, kinesthetic, verbal, etc.) may lead to functionally equivalent amodal representations, such as the "spatial image" advocated by Jack Loomis – a kind of representation that supports behavior in an equivalent manner independent of the encoding modality (see Avraamides, Loomis, Klatzky, &

Golledge, 2004; Loomis, Lippa, Klatzky, & Golledge, 2002). A similar view was more recently expressed by Struiksma, Noordzij, and Postma (2009) in favor of spatial images as abstract ("supramodal") mental representations.

This view was to a large extent presaged by the insightful theoretical perspective promoted by Barbara Tversky in her writings of the 1990s. Based on substantial empirical work with Nancy Franklin – a highlight in the literature of spatial cognition (Franklin & Tversky, 1990) – her "spatial framework" approach ruled out the idea that all the dimensions of a spatial model are equally available, as a strong imagery hypothesis would claim. Rather, a spatial mental model is an abstract representation. It looks like "something analogous to an architect's 3-D model of a town that can be viewed or visualized from many different perspectives, but cannot be viewed or visualized as a whole" (Tversky, 1991, p. 128). It flows from this statement that the view that cognitive maps are like real maps available to inspection, in the same way as mental images displaying accurate Euclidean metrics, is no longer tenable. As a substitute for the classic "cognitive map" metaphor, the concept of "cognitive collage" (Tversky, 1993) conveys better the fact that mental representations of large spaces are constructed from pieces of information extracted from different sources and modalities and which reflect different perspectives.

Imagery without visual experience

It is hardly surprising that researchers in visuospatial cognition have been persistently interested in the cognitive impact of blindness on mental imagery processes. An early review of this issue was proposed by Ernest (1987), and more recent state-of-the-art syntheses have been provided by Kaski (2002) and Dulin, Hatwell, Pylyshyn, and Chokron (2008). The same question runs through these reviews and can be summarized as follows: In the absence of vision, and hence presumably in the absence of any visual imagery, would people with congenital blindness be disadvantaged when performing tasks that are known to depend on visual imagery in sighted people? This question led to a number of research programs, of which only a selected subset is reviewed here.

Do blind people use visual imagery?

Given the abundant evidence that visual imagery is based on visual experience, one would expect people without such experience to be unable to form visual images, while being able to construct images derived from other sensory modalities. An early test of this assumption was made by Allan Paivio in the framework of his dual-coding hypothesis. Paivio and Okovita (1971) tested memory performance of sighted and congenitally blind people in paired-associate learning involving words with high or low imagery values in either visual or auditory modalities. The results showed that blind people had a poorer recall of words evoking mainly visual images (such as "rainbow") than of words evoking auditory images (such as "thunder"), while the reverse was true for the sighted people, in whom the visual sense is predominant.

Other studies have reported findings suggesting that, on the contrary, the performance of blind people in tasks thought to involve visual imagery is not severely impaired and that in some cases the difference in performance from sighted people might be quantitative rather than qualitative. Marmor and Zaback (1976) compared congenitally blind, adventitiously blind, and blindfolded sighted people in a mental rotation task, of which a tactile version had been devised. In all three groups, the same linear increase in response times as a function of the angular disparity between the compared forms was found. The only difference was in the speed of mental rotation, with the congenitally blind participants being much slower than either of the other groups (which did not differ from each other). This finding was interpreted as indicating that strategies other than visual ones might be implemented by the congenitally blind, even though they are less efficient in terms of speed. The important point here is that *visual* imagery might not be the essential process involved when people rotate mental images. Mental rotation also includes kinesthetic components, which may also be used by sighted people in conjunction with visual imagery.

In a series of studies involving a variety of memory tasks, Zimler and Keenan (1983) showed that congenitally blind people recalled high-imagery words as well as other words and in similar proportions to sighted controls. This finding attested that a permanent deficit in visual imagery may be compensated for by representations of another nature that are as efficient in terms of memory performance. The same conclusion was drawn from independently collected data reported by Nancy Kerr (1983). Kerr's experiments revealed that congenitally blind people were capable of preserving and processing images of spatial configurations in a manner quite similar to that of sighted controls. Here again, blind people took longer than sighted people to process these images.

A high point in this area where imagery meets blindness studies was the research reported by De Beni and Cornoldi (1988). The authors tested the effect of imagery instructions on a memory task involving single nouns, pairs of nouns, or triplets of nouns. The results showed that total congenitally blind participants took advantage of instructions to create interactive images, just as sighted controls did, but that their recall was impaired when images of interacting objects involved noun pairs and triplets (i.e., with higher memory load). The blind participants appeared to experience special difficulty in manipulating multiple images as well as in linking images sequentially. In subsequent studies, similar capacity limitations were observed, resulting in a fall-off in performance when the blind participants had to process complex three-dimensional patterns (Cornoldi, Cortesi, & Preti, 1991). In line with these findings, in a task inviting people to memorize spatial positions of objects in matrices, the differences between sighted and congenitally blind people were more marked when the task was more demanding (involving three-dimensional rather than two-dimensional matrices) and when the task included an active component (focusing on pathways rather than on positions of objects) (Vecchi, 1998). All these findings converge on a notion that the absence of sight does not make it impossible to process visuospatial information, but that the representations constructed by blind people may well be based on information conveyed with support from other sensory modalities. Visuospatial imagery may then be conceived as relying on a variety of sources of information, including information originating from haptic experience or from language (see Hollins, 1985).

The supposed difficulty experienced by blind people in processing visuospatial information remains a controversial topic. Depending on which indicators are used to explore the issue, researchers come to conclusions that emphasize either the differences or the similarities between the cognitive performance of sighted and blind people. There is no doubt that some aspects of visual imagery are absent from the mental representations of congenitally blind people. For instance, when sighted people form images of objects and are asked to judge visual angles, they seem to construct images whose size varies as a function of the distance separating the participant and the imagined object. For the congenitally blind, there is no such decrease in the size of imagined objects with increased image distance, a finding that suggests that they do not have any concept of perspective (Arditi, Holtzman, & Kosslyn, 1988). However, in other domains of visuospatial cognition, no such differences appear. For instance, when asked to estimate the absolute distances between pairs of objects in a familiar room, both sighted and blind people provide estimates that have genuine metric properties and are related to actual distances (Haber, Haber, Levin, & Hollyfield, 1993). This absence of qualitative difference as a function of blindness is consistent with the previously mentioned facts that blind people sometimes take longer than their sighted counterparts to process visuospatial information, and that they experience difficulty when they have to process images overloaded with information.

Cognitive maps of large spaces

Spatial orientation is usually preserved in congenitally blind people, who construct internal representations of their surrounding space and make use of the information contained in them to find their way around in the environment. As mentioned in the previous section on imagery and spatial cognition, sighted people's cognitive maps cannot be reduced to mere visual mental images, and it is obvious that sensory modalities other than vision must be used to construct the representations that enable blind people to orient themselves in space.

There is a consensus about the functional role of vision (and presumably visual imagery) in the construction of spatial representations by sighted people (see Millar, 1994). Specific impairments typical of congenitally blind people have been reported, such as their weaker sensitivity to changes in perspective during locomotion (Rieser, Guth, & Hill, 1986), their relative lack of accuracy when assessing directions or distances (Veraart & Wanet-Defalque, 1987), or the fact that they tend to linearize curved paths (Golledge, Klatzky, & Loomis, 1996). Most of these findings are taken as reflecting the role of early visual experience and visual imagery in the mental representation of space. Visual experience is thought to facilitate the perception of relationships between objects and to be particularly helpful in the construction of survey views of environments. However, in spite of their permanent lack of sight, blind people often perform remarkably well in many spatial situations. If such performance is not underpinned by sight, we can only assume that other sensory modalities must underlie their construction of functional spatial representations.

Tests of spatial performance are usually divided into two broad categories. The first consists of tasks in which people provide responses based on a spatial relation that has been directly experienced in an environment. The second category consists of tasks that require people to *infer* a new relationship based on previous experience. While the former only implies some form of spatial coding, the latter requires the transformation of previously coded information (see Ungar, 2000). Both types of task are used in experimental investigations of the spatial abilities of blind people, but tasks involving some kind of inference or elaboration of spatial information are particularly useful, since they are expected to reveal the most sophisticated aspects of spatial mental representations.

Several research programs have generated findings that provide little indication, if any, that spatial competence essentially depends on prior visual experience. In an extensive study on navigation without vision (with blindfolded sighted, adventitiously blind, and congenitally blind people), Jack Loomis did not find any significant differences in error scores between the groups in several locomotion tasks, regardless of whether they were rather simple (reproduce and estimate walked distances and turns) or more complex (complete a triangle after walking two segments, retrace the route in reverse, return to the starting point with a shortcut, or point to targets). The only differences observed were in response latencies, which tended to be longer for the congenitally blind people than for those who were sighted, although not consistently so across all tasks (see Loomis et al., 1993). It is also important to note that considerable differences exist among blind people as regards their mobility skills and experience of independent travel, which probably accounts for the inconsistencies in the literature as regards the spatial capacities of blind people compared to those of sighted people.

More recently, Tinti, Adenzato, Tamietto, and Cornoldi (2006) reported a study in which blind and blindfolded sighted people learned novel pathways and were then tested in tasks that are generally considered to rely on survey representations (proceed from the departure point to the arrival point via the shortest way, estimate directions by pointing after locomotion and perspective change, judge straight-line distances, and draw the explored pathways). In this study, blind people performed *better* than the blindfolded sighted controls, attesting that in the permanent absence of sight, successful spatial encoding can occur and can result in the construction of reliable internal representations. Thus, while visual experience and visual imagery considerably facilitate the encoding of spatial environments as compared to other sensory modalities, they can hardly be claimed to be *necessary* conditions for the development of complex spatial representations.

In previous sections, I referred to the situations in which people construct mental representations of spatial environments from linguistic sources. Most sighted people spontaneously generate visual images during the construction of spatial mental models from language. Verbal descriptions are communication devices that blind people will inevitably use to create spatial knowledge (see

Noordzij & Postma, chapter 7, this volume). Are blind people able to benefit fully from such descriptions in spite of their lack of visual imagery? More specifically, will the distinction between survey and route perspective in spatial descriptions be relevant when blind people are exposed to spatial descriptions? Still more precisely, will the perspective imposed by a spatial description be likely to affect the representation of metric information in the cognitive maps of blind people?

Experiments with sighted people have shown that their assessment of the metric features of a described environment (by performing mental comparisons of distances) is affected by the type of descriptions previously processed. The frequency of correct responses is higher and the response times are shorter when the participants have learned about the environment from a survey rather than from a route perspective. The advantage of survey over route descriptions suggests that the former help people to construct more fine-grained representations than do the latter. In other words, although the representations from sources involving either perspective can contain veridical metric information, it is more difficult to access that information when it has been constructed from a route perspective (see Noordzij & Postma, 2005; Péruch, Chabanne, Nesa, Thinus-Blanc, & Denis, 2006).

An interesting extension of this approach to blind people was undertaken by Noordzij, Zuidhoek, and Postma (2006), from Utrecht University. In a similar task involving the mental comparison of distances, blind people were found to be able to form spatial mental models from both route and survey descriptions. They also exhibited the same patterns of chronometric responses as sighted people. However, unlike sighted people, these blind participants performed better after listening to the route description than to the survey description of the environment.

These findings are consistent with Millar's (1994) observation that blind people tend to encode spatial relations primarily from an egocentric perspective and, as a result, to form route-based sequential representations, in contrast to the stronger tendency of sighted people to build allocentric (map-like) survey representations. This overall pattern, however, does not preclude the possibility that blind people may form survey representations from descriptions conveying a route perspective, even though a greater cognitive effort is probably required to achieve this trans-formation. This kind of translation from route to survey perspective was probably the process at work in the experiments of Tinti et al. (2006), where blind people who had learned a route by locomotion proved to be successful in providing responses reflecting their capacity to manipulate survey information.

Scanning studies

Image scanning is recognized as one of the best ways to assess the ability of visual images to preserve the Euclidean properties of the objects or configurations they represent. When people mentally scan the image of an object or a scene, their scanning time increases linearly with the scanned distance, a finding that is taken to demonstrate that the image preserves the metrics of the object or scene repre-sented (see Denis & Kosslyn, 1999). However, do such properties of images essentially depend on their visuospatial nature? Several experiments were undertaken to find out whether the acquisition of spatial information mediated by nonvisual modalities, in particular by blind people, results in the construction of internal representations that have the same analogical properties.

The first attempt to involve participants in mental scanning tasks where a spatial configuration had been learned via the haptic modality was reported by Kerr (1983). The experiment involved congenitally blind participants who learned a configuration by tactile exploration of a board to which raised figures were affixed. In the subsequent mental scanning task, the participants' scanning times appeared to increase linearly with increasing distances, indicating that the representation they had constructed from haptic learning included accurate metric information. Kerr also found that blind people tended to have longer scanning times than the sighted controls who had learned the same configuration by visual inspection. In another study, Röder and Rösler (1998) replicated the finding that congenitally blind people's responses displayed the same time/distance linear relationship, but they found that their scanning times were not different from those of their blind-folded sighted counterparts. More recently, Amandine Afonso and several other colleagues from Orsay and Harvard conducted scanning experiments with blind participants who were tested after being assigned to various learning conditions (see Afonso et al., 2010). In one of these experiments involving haptic learning of a small-size configuration, we did obtain the expected time/distance correlation, but only for the sighted and late-blind participants. The congenitally blind partici-pants did not appear to construct a representation of a small-scale configuration in which distances were consistently represented (see Figure 9.12). Furthermore, in line with Kerr's findings, the scanning times of the congenitally blind participants were much longer than those of the sighted controls and the late-blind participants. Analysis of the data revealed that the discrepancy between our results and those of Röder and Rösler were attributable to differences in the learning procedure.

In the absence of sight, locomotor experience is an obvious alternative source of information for constructing the mental representation of a spatial environ-ment. We have pointed out above that blind people are able to construct cognitive maps by locomotor exploration of their surroundings. Iachini and Giusberti (2004) used mental scanning as a method for assessing the metric properties of represen-tations constructed by walking. They did so with sighted participants who first learned a configuration on the floor of a room, either by visual inspection of the paths connecting landmarks or by walking along these paths (while they were blindfolded and guided by the experimenter). The participants then mentally scanned distances of various lengths by imagining that they were moving from a designated landmark to another one. Both learning conditions produced the typical time/distance correlation, but overall the scanning times were shorter after visual learning than after locomotor learning.

To find out whether the mental representations of blind people preserve the metric properties of the learned environment, we obviously had to conduct a similar experiment with blind participants. The study by Afonso et al. (2010) included a condition in which blindfolded sighted, late-blind, and congenitally blind participants performed locomotor learning in an indoor environment.

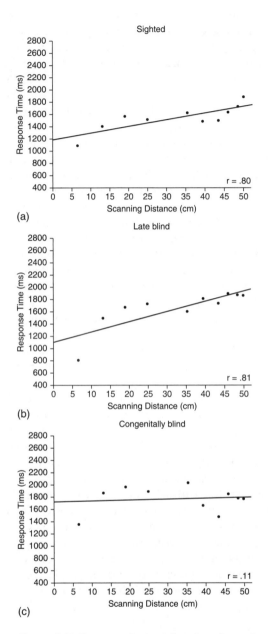

Figure 9.12 Response time as a function of scanning distance after haptic exploration for sighted, late-blind, and congenitally blind participants. (From A. Afonso, A. Blum, B. F. G. Katz, P. Tarroux, G. Borst, & M. Denis, 2010. Structural properties of spatial representations in blind people: Scanning images constructed from haptic exploration or from locomotion in a 3-D audio virtual environment. *Memory & Cognition, 38,* 596. Copyright © 2010 by the Psychonomic Society, Inc. Reprinted with permission.)

Whereas people with all three types of visual history were able to construct a metrically valid representation from listening to verbal descriptions (attesting to their capacity to handle analogue spatial representations), there was a striking contrast between the responses of the blind participants and those of their sighted counterparts when learning was based on locomotor experience. The former exhibited a robust pattern of time/distance relationship, while for the latter there was no trace of any correlation between times and distances (see Figure 9.13). The cognitive difficulty experienced by sighted people in constructing a representation of the environment from navigation while blindfolded was evident, at least, after the amount of learning permitted in the experiment. Within the same time frame, the blind participants displayed their ability to use the distances explored by navigation to construct an efficient, realistic representation of the environment.

Another variation on the scanning paradigm was recently reported by Iachini and Ruggiero (2010), who used an actual outdoor medium-scale environment as a location for locomotor learning with movement alone (for congenitally blind, adventitiously blind, and blindfolded sighted participants) or vision plus movement (for sighted participants). In this study, an increase in scanning time with increasing path length was found in all the groups (including the blindfolded sighted participants), but similar to the study of Afonso et al. (2010), the two groups of blind people had shorter scanning times than the two sighted groups. An interesting finding emerged from the analysis of the strategies used for mental scanning, based on the participants' reports in post-experimental interviews. Two scanning strategies were identified. One was termed "configurational", and the participants declared that they had focused on some representation of the configuration without any reference to themselves as moving along the paths; the other was termed "kinesthetic", and here the participants reported using images of their bodies moving along the paths or referred to feeling as if they were moving. Most of the participants, but especially the congenitally blind, preferred the kinesthetic strategy. Furthermore, the results showed that this strategy was consistently associated with longer scanning times than was the configurational strategy.

Together, the studies of Afonso et al. (2010) and of Iachini and Ruggiero (2010) indicate that the spatial images of blind people based on locomotor experience preserve metric information, as do the visual images of sighted people. Some inconsistencies in the published findings may result from the use of environments of different sizes. The scale of locomotor space is likely to affect the processing of various distances. It is therefore crucial for visually impaired people to encode spatial information on the basis of their most reliable currently functional sensorimotor system.

A closing note: imagery research in perspective

In writing this chapter, my intention was to carry out a kind of "subjective" exercise while reviewing four decades of imagery research. By "subjective", I certainly did not mean idiosyncratic, gratuitous, or unjustified. What I hope I have made clear is the scientific intent that has guided these reminiscences. My objective was

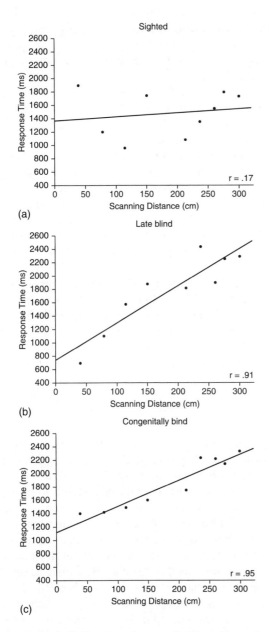

Figure 9.13 Response time as a function of scanning distance after locomotor experience for sighted, late-blind, and congenitally blind participants. (From A.
Afonso, A. Blum, B. F. G. Katz, P. Tarroux, G. Borst, & M. Denis, 2010.
Structural properties of spatial representations in blind people: Scanning
images constructed from haptic exploration or from locomotion in a 3-D
audio virtual environment. *Memory & Cognition, 38,* 601. Copyright ©
2010 by the Psychonomic Society, Inc. Reprinted with permission.)

to identify the areas of cognitive psychology to which imagery researchers have made a contribution, by adding new information to the literature or by contributing to theoretical debates concerning human cognition. This retrospective exercise was developed from the point of view of this particular researcher, with his own topics of interest and thematic preferences. Nevertheless, I have done my best to point out some of the highlights of imagery research, as well as the main lines along which this research has developed and its constructive interactions with other areas of cognitive research. In her chapter, Barbara Tversky (chapter 1, this volume) offers an interesting complementary perspective on these years of research.

When I started on my journey in mental imagery, my research interests led on directly from a period of my life dedicated to another facet of images, namely, film and motion pictures. In one of my "previous lives", I happened to write a couple of essays on cinema, including one on the life and work of Buster Keaton (see Figure 9.14), the famous comedian and silent film-maker (Denis, 1971). I am grateful to Allan Paivio (2007, p. 337; see Figure 9.15), who seems to be the only scientist who ever dared to refer to my monograph in one of his most serious scientific writings!

In 1968, the CNRS offered me the opportunity of launching a program of research into the perception and memory of film. In retrospect, I realize that this was a real challenge. The studies, which involved adults and children and compared memory of film and of verbal narratives, were the source of some very exciting experiences, but I was frustrated by the fact that in those ancient (pre-video) times, the editing of experimental films was a rather cumbersome technical matter. For this reason and others, I soon switched from animated images to still images (line drawings, in studies *à la* Paivio, comparing memory of pictures and of words), and eventually to mental images, which led me into the fascinating and rewarding world of mental imagery!

I soon became interested in language as one possible input into the process of image formation, in the extremely demanding situations in which people have to construct their visual knowledge of objects that are currently out of view, based solely on a sequence of verbal statements. Later on, I devoted myself to investigating the mental representations of more complex scenes or environments with a spatial extension, in which images and language entertain close relationships. The title chosen by the editors for the present book – *From Mental Imagery to Spatial Cognition and Language* – could not be a more explicit summary of the intellectual journey retraced in this chapter. I am sure that this title also expresses something of the itineraries of several of the authors of the preceding chapters.

This book is coming out just a decade after another one, *Imagery, Language, and Visuo-Spatial Thinking*, a volume stemming from the joint efforts of scholars of five European labs mostly active in imagery research (see Denis, Logie, Cornoldi, de Vega, & Engelkamp, 2001). Today, the chapters compiled by Valérie Gyselinck and Francesca Pazzaglia provide the readers with an opportunity to appreciate the progress and achievements of imagery research in the past ten years, acknowledging the role of other European colleagues who have become involved more recently, as well as researchers from the North American community.

Figure 9.14 Buster Keaton's elegant profile shown in wide-open space (from the 1924 film, *The Navigator*). (Copyright © The Picture Desk, Ltd. Reprinted with permission.) The art of film, and the films of Buster Keaton in particular, were a source of great interest to me before I embarked on a career in psychological science. Keaton was famous for creating a character who did not reveal anything of his emotions or inner feelings on his face, but expressed himself solely through his actions and performance. Undoubtedly, Keaton would have been of exceptional interest as an experimental subject for the defenders of a strongly behavior-oriented psychology. Ironically, one may note that *The Navigator* was released in 1924, the very same year that John B. Watson published his book, *Behaviorism*. After decades devoted to studying mental imagery, I am convinced that behind Keaton's legendary "frozen face", intense emotional mental images were certainly at work!

This chapter, like the entire volume, attests to the fact that imagery has opened researchers' minds to wider perspectives, which form the basis of a more integrated vision of human cognition. By saying this, I do not intend to display naive satisfaction. Of course, many questions remain to be solved. But it is remarkable that a cognitive construct like imagery broadened the perspectives of students of

Figure 9.15 Allan Paivio presents his book, *Mind and Its Evolution: A Dual Coding Theoretical Approach* (2007), at an international conference in Anaheim, California, in 2006. (Photograph by M. Denis.)

human cognition and was introduced profitably into other domains of psychology. None of the scholars who have dedicated themselves to imagery research appear to have entertained a "narrow" approach to their subject, but all have incorporated the topic into broader areas of interest.

The imagery community has long proven to be a creative and stimulating one. Despite the scientific controversies that it has traversed, the imagery family has always remained a friendly community, a feature that should not be overlooked if a "social history" of imagery research is written some day. This is attested by the success of regular scientific meetings, like the European Workshop on Imagery and Cognition (EWIC), which has been held since 1986, and the Conference on Spatial Information Theory (COSIT), which has continuously provided opportunities for psychologists, computer scientists, and geographers to interact since 1993.

Let me close this chapter by a brief look forward. Are there any areas in cognitive psychology – other than working memory, mental models, spatial cognition, and blindness, all of which have been reviewed above – in which imagery researchers are likely to be keen to get involved in the years to come? The answer is probably "yes". For instance, none of us can ignore the increasing popularity of models referring to the concept of embodiment (e.g., de Vega, Glenberg, & Graesser, 2008; Zwaan & Taylor, 2006). The basic tenet here is that the conceptual and linguistic structures that shape the human mind are rooted in the mechanisms that govern perception and action, which implies that in order to fully understand how the mind works, one has to study the intimate interactions between mind and body. This approach naturally leads to an increased interest in the contributions of sensory modalities and their mental simulation to higher order cognition, as opposed to the traditional view of cognition as pure computation based on abstract symbols (see Barsalou, 2008; Postma & Barsalou, 2009; Tversky, 2009; see also de Vega, chapter 8, this volume).

Interactions between imagery research and other emerging areas can probably also be anticipated. There is no doubt that new lines of research will develop in the areas concerned, as will more comprehensive accounts of the human mind.

Acknowledgments

There are dozens of eminent scholars, colleagues, graduate students, as well as hundreds of anonymous participants in experiments, who deserve my thanks for their contribution to my research. A number of them (although not all) have been mentioned in this chapter. I would like to express my very special gratitude to Allan Paivio and Steve Kosslyn, both of whom have been inspiring colleagues, gentlemen, and genuine friends, who helped me to find my way in the wonderful world of mental images. I also want to say how indebted I am to Maryvonne Carfantan, colleague and spouse, without whom both my work and my personal life would have been much less rewarding.

References

Afonso, A., Blum, A., Katz, B. F. G., Tarroux, P., Borst, G., & Denis, M. (2010). Structural properties of spatial representations in blind people: Scanning images constructed from haptic exploration or from locomotion in a 3-D audio virtual environment. *Memory & Cognition, 38*, 591–604.

Allen, G. L. (1997). From knowledge to words to wayfinding: Issues in the production and comprehension of route directions. In S. C. Hirtle & A. U. Frank (Eds.), *Spatial information theory: A theoretical basis for GIS* (pp. 363–372). Berlin: Springer.

Allen, G. L. (2000). Principles and practices for communicating route knowledge. *Applied Cognitive Psychology, 14*, 333–359.

Allen, G. L. (Ed.) (2004). *Human spatial memory: Remembering where*. Mahwah, NJ: Lawrence Erlbaum Associates.

Allen, G. L. (Ed.) (2006). *Applied spatial cognition: From research to cognitive technology*. Mahwah, NJ: Lawrence Erlbaum Associates.

Anderson, J. R., & Bower, G. H. (1973). *Human associative memory*. Washington, DC: Winston.

Arditi, A., Holtzman, J. D., & Kosslyn, S. M. (1988). Mental imagery and sensory experience in congenital blindness. *Neuropsychologia, 26*, 1–12.

Avraamides, M. N., & Kelly, J. W. (2010). Multiple systems of spatial memory: Evidence from described scenes. *Journal of Experimental Psychology: Learning, Memory, and Cognition, 36*, 635–645.

Avraamides, M. N., Loomis, J. M., Klatzky, R. L., & Golledge, R. G. (2004). Functional equivalence of spatial representations derived from vision and language: Evidence from allocentric judgments. *Journal of Experimental Psychology: Learning, Memory, and Cognition, 30*, 801–814.

Baddeley, A. D. (1986). *Working memory*. Oxford, UK: Clarendon Press.

Baddeley, A. D., & Andrade, J. (2000). Working memory and vividness of imagery. *Journal of Experimental Psychology: General, 129*, 126–145.

Baddeley, A. D., & Hitch, G. J. (1974). Working memory. In G. H. Bower (Ed.), *The psychology of learning and motivation: Advances in research and theory* (Vol. 8, pp. 47–89). New York: Academic Press.

Baddeley, A. D., & Lieberman, K. (1980). Spatial working memory. In R. S. Nickerson (Ed.), *Attention and Performance VIII* (pp. 521–539). Hillsdale, NJ: Lawrence Erlbaum Associates.

Barsalou, L. W. (2008). Grounded cognition. *Annual Review of Psychology, 59*, 617–645.

Bloom, P., Peterson, M. A., Nadel, L., & Garrett, M. F. (Eds.) (1996). *Language and space*. Cambridge, MA: MIT Press.

Borst, G., & Kosslyn, S. M. (2008). Visual mental imagery and visual perception: Structural equivalence revealed by scanning processes. *Memory & Cognition, 36*, 849–862.

Borst, G., & Kosslyn, S. M. (2010). Individual differences in spatial mental imagery. *Quarterly Journal of Experimental Psychology, 63*, 2031–2050.

Borst, G., Kosslyn, S. M., & Denis, M. (2006). Different cognitive processes in two image-scanning paradigms. *Memory & Cognition, 34*, 475–490.

Bower, G. H., & Morrow, D. G. (1989). Mental models in narrative comprehension. *Science, 247*, 44–48.

Brunyé, T. T., & Taylor, H. A. (2008). Working memory in developing and applying mental models from spatial descriptions. *Journal of Memory and Language, 58*, 701–729.

Byrne, R. M. J., & Johnson-Laird, P. N. (1989). Spatial reasoning. *Journal of Memory and Language, 28*, 564–575.

Cocude, M., & Denis, M. (1988). Measuring the temporal characteristics of visual images. *Journal of Mental Imagery, 12*, 89–101.

Cornoldi, C., Cortesi, A., & Preti, D. (1991). Individual differences in the capacity limitations of visuospatial short-term memory: Research on sighted and totally congenitally blind people. *Memory & Cognition, 19*, 459–468.

Cornoldi, C., De Beni, R., & Giusberti, F. (1996). Meta-imagery: Conceptualization of mental imagery and its relationship with cognitive behavior. *Psychologische Beiträge, 38*, 484–499.

Cornoldi, C., & Vecchi, T. (2003). *Visuo-spatial working memory and individual differences*. Hove, UK: Psychology Press.

Craik, K. (1943). *The nature of explanation*. Cambridge, UK: Cambridge University Press.

Daniel, M.-P., & Denis, M. (2004). The production of route directions: Investigating conditions that favour conciseness in spatial discourse. *Applied Cognitive Psychology, 18*, 57–75.

Daniel, M.-P., Mores Dibo-Cohen, C., Carité, L., Boyer, P., & Denis, M. (2007). Dysfunctions of spatial cognition in schizophrenic patients. *Spatial Cognition and Computation, 7*, 287–309.

Daniel, M.-P., Tom, A., Manghi, E., & Denis, M. (2003). Testing the value of route directions through navigational performance. *Spatial Cognition and Computation, 3,* 269–289.

Dasen, P. R., & Mishra, R. C. (2010). *Development of geocentric spatial language and cognition: An eco-cultural perspective.* Cambridge, UK: Cambridge University Press.

De Beni, R., & Cornoldi, C. (1988). Imagery limitations in totally congenitally blind subjects. *Journal of Experimental Psychology: Learning, Memory, and Cognition, 14,* 650–655.

De Beni, R., & Moè, A. (2003). Presentation modality effects in studying passages: Are mental images always effective? *Applied Cognitive Psychology, 17,* 309–324.

De Beni, R., Pazzaglia, F., Gyselinck, V., & Meneghetti, C. (2005). Visuospatial working memory and mental representation of spatial descriptions. *European Journal of Cognitive Psychology, 17,* 77–95.

Della Sala, S., Logie, R. H., Beschin, N., & Denis, M. (2004). Preserved visuo-spatial transformations in representational neglect. *Neuropsychologia, 42,* 1358–1364.

Denis, M. (1971). *Buster Keaton.* Paris: Editions de l'Avant-Scène.

Denis, M. (1991). *Image and cognition.* New York: Harvester Wheatsheaf.

Denis, M. (1996). Imagery and the description of spatial configurations. In M. de Vega, M. J. Intons-Peterson, P. N. Johnson-Laird, M. Denis, & M. Marschark, *Models of visuospatial cognition* (pp. 128–197). New York: Oxford University Press.

Denis, M. (Ed.) (1997a). *Langage et cognition spatiale* [Language and spatial cognition]. Paris: Masson.

Denis, M. (1997b). The description of routes: A cognitive approach to the production of spatial discourse. *Current Psychology of Cognition, 16,* 409–458.

Denis, M. (2008). Assessing the symbolic distance effect in mental images constructed from verbal descriptions: A study of individual differences in the mental comparison of distances. *Acta Psychologica, 127,* 197–210.

Denis, M., Beschin, N., Logie, R. H., & Della Sala, S. (2002). Visual perception and verbal descriptions as sources for generating mental representations: Evidence from representational neglect. *Cognitive Neuropsychology, 19,* 97–112.

Denis, M., & Carfantan, M. (1985). People's knowledge about images. *Cognition, 20,* 49–60.

Denis, M., & Cocude, M. (1989). Scanning visual images generated from verbal descriptions. *European Journal of Cognitive Psychology, 1,* 293–307.

Denis, M., & Cocude, M. (1992). Structural properties of visual images constructed from poorly or well-structured verbal descriptions. *Memory & Cognition, 20,* 497–506.

Denis, M., & Cocude, M. (1997). On the metric properties of visual images generated from verbal descriptions: Evidence for the robustness of the mental scanning effect. *European Journal of Cognitive Psychology, 9,* 353–379.

Denis, M., & Denhière, G. (1990). Comprehension and recall of spatial descriptions. *Cahiers de Psychologie Cognitive/European Bulletin of Cognitive Psychology, 10,* 115–143.

Denis, M., & de Vega, M. (1993). Modèles mentaux et imagerie mentale [Mental models and mental imagery]. In M.-F. Ehrlich, H. Tardieu, & M. Cavazza (Eds.), *Les modèles mentaux: Approche cognitive des représentations* (pp. 79–100). Paris: Masson.

Denis, M., Gonçalves, M.-R., & Memmi, D. (1995). Mental scanning of visual images generated from verbal descriptions: Towards a model of image accuracy. *Neuropsychologia, 33,* 1511–1530.

Denis, M., & Kosslyn, S. M. (1999). Scanning visual mental images: A window on the mind. *Current Psychology of Cognition, 18,* 409–465.

Denis, M., Logie, R. H., Cornoldi, C., de Vega, M., & Engelkamp, J. (Eds.) (2001). *Imagery, language, and visuo-spatial thinking*. Hove, UK: Psychology Press.

Denis, M., & Loomis, J. M. (2007). Perspectives on human spatial cognition: Memory, navigation, and environmental learning. *Psychological Research, 71*, 235–239.

Denis, M., Pazzaglia, F., Cornoldi, C., & Bertolo, L. (1999). Spatial discourse and navigation: An analysis of route directions in the city of Venice. *Applied Cognitive Psychology, 13*, 145–174.

Denis, M., & Zimmer, H. D. (1992). Analog properties of cognitive maps constructed from verbal descriptions. *Psychological Research, 54*, 286–298.

de Vega, M. (1994). Characters and their perspective in narratives describing spatial environments. *Psychological Research, 56*, 116–126.

de Vega, M. (1995). Backward updating of mental models during continuous reading of narratives. *Journal of Experimental Psychology: Learning, Memory, and Cognition, 21*, 373–385.

de Vega, M., Glenberg, A. M., & Graesser, A. C. (Eds.) (2008). *Symbols and embodiment: Debates on meaning and cognition*. Oxford, UK: Oxford University Press.

de Vega, M., & Marschark, M. (1996). Visuospatial cognition: An historical and theoretical introduction. In M. de Vega, M. J. Intons-Peterson, P. N. Johnson-Laird, M. Denis, & M. Marschark, *Models of visuospatial cognition* (pp. 3–19). New York: Oxford University Press.

Deyzac, E., Logie, R. H., & Denis, M. (2006). Visuospatial working memory and the processing of spatial descriptions. *British Journal of Psychology, 97*, 217–243.

Dulin, D., Hatwell, Y., Pylyshyn, Z., & Chokron, S. (2008). Effects of peripheral and central visual impairment on mental imagery capacity. *Neuroscience and Biobehavioral Reviews, 32*, 1396–1408.

Ehrich, V., & Koster, C. (1983). Discourse organization and sentence form: The structure of room descriptions in Dutch. *Discourse Processes, 6*, 169–195.

Engelkamp, J. (1991). Imagery and enactment in paired-associate learning. In R. H. Logie & M. Denis (Eds.), *Mental images in human cognition* (pp. 119–128). Amsterdam: North-Holland.

Engelkamp, J., Zimmer, H. D., & Denis, M. (1989). Paired associate learning of action verbs with visual- or motor-imaginal encoding instructions. *Psychological Research, 50*, 257–263.

Ernest, C. H. (1987). Imagery and memory in the blind: A review. In M. A. McDaniel & M. Pressley (Eds.), *Imagery and related mnemonic processes: Theories, individual differences, and applications* (pp. 218–238). New York: Springer-Verlag.

Evans, V., & Chilton, P. (Eds.) (2010). *Language, cognition and space: The state of the art and new directions*. London: Equinox.

Farah, M. J. (1985). Psychophysical evidence for a shared representational medium for mental images and percepts. *Journal of Experimental Psychology: General, 114*, 91–103.

Fernandez, G. (2000). *Processus cognitifs mis en oeuvre dans la compréhension et la mémorisation de descriptions d'itinéraires: Une approche différentielle* [Cognitive processes in the comprehension and memory of route directions: A differential approach]. Unpublished doctoral thesis, Université René-Descartes, Boulogne-Billancourt/LIMSI-CNRS, Orsay.

Finke, R. A. (1985). Theories relating mental imagery to perception. *Psychological Bulletin, 98*, 236–259.

Finke, R. A., Pinker, S., & Farah, M. J. (1989). Reinterpreting visual patterns in mental imagery. *Cognitive Science, 13*, 51–78.

Fontaine, S., Edwards, G., Tversky, B., & Denis, M. (2005). Expert and non-expert knowledge of loosely structured environments. In A. G. Cohn & D. M. Mark (Eds.), *Spatial information theory* (pp. 363–378). Berlin: Springer.

Franklin, N., & Tversky, B. (1990). Searching imagined environments. *Journal of Experimental Psychology: General, 119*, 63–76.

Freksa, C., Newcombe, N., Gärdenfors, P., & Wölfl, S. (Eds.) (2008). *Spatial cognition VI: Learning, reasoning, and talking about space.* Berlin: Springer.

Garden, S., Cornoldi, & Logie, R. H. (2002). Visuo-spatial working memory in navigation. *Applied Cognitive Psychology, 16*, 35–50.

Garnham, A. (1987). *Mental models as representations of discourse and text.* Chichester, UK: Ellis Horwood.

Gentner, D., & Stevens, A. L. (1983). *Mental models.* Hillsdale, NJ: Lawrence Erlbaum Associates.

Glenberg, A. M., & Langston, W. E. (1992). Comprehension of illustrated text: Pictures help to build mental models. *Journal of Memory and Language, 31*, 129–151.

Glenberg, A. M., Meyer, M., & Lindem, K. (1987). Mental models contribute to foregrounding during text comprehension. *Journal of Memory and Language, 26*, 69–83.

Golledge, R. G. (Ed.) (1999). *Wayfinding behavior: Cognitive mapping and other spatial processes.* Baltimore, MD: Johns Hopkins University Press.

Golledge, R. G., Klatzky, R. L., & Loomis, J. M. (1996). Cognitive mapping by adults without vision. In J. Portugali (Ed.), *The construction of cognitive maps* (pp. 215–246). Dordrecht, The Netherlands: Kluwer.

Gyselinck, V., De Beni, R., Pazzaglia, F., Meneghetti, C., & Mondoloni, A. (2007). Working memory components and imagery instructions in the elaboration of a spatial mental model. *Psychological Research, 71*, 373–382.

Gyselinck, V., Meneghetti, C., De Beni, R., & Pazzaglia, F. (2009). The role of working memory in spatial text processing: What benefit of imagery strategy and visuospatial abilities? *Learning and Individual Differences, 19*, 12–20.

Gyselinck, V., & Tardieu, H. (1994). Illustrations, mental models, and comprehension of instructional text. In W. Schnotz & R. W. Kulhavy (Eds.), *Comprehension of graphics* (pp. 139–151). Amsterdam: North-Holland.

Haber, R. N., Haber, L. R., Levin, C. A., & Hollyfield, R. (1993). Properties of spatial representations: Data from sighted and blind subjects. *Perception and Psychophysics, 54*, 1–13.

Haenggi, D., Kintsch, W., & Gernsbacher, M. A. (1995). Spatial situation models and text comprehension. *Discourse Processes, 19*, 173–199.

Hegarty, M., Montello, D. R., Richardson, A. E., Ishikawa, T., & Lovelace, K. (2006). Spatial abilities at different scales: Individual differences in aptitude-test performance and spatial-layout learning. *Intelligence, 34*, 151–176.

Hickmann, M., & Robert, S. (Eds.) (2006). *Space in languages: Linguistic systems and cognitive categories.* Amsterdam: John Benjamins.

Hollins, M. (1985). Styles of mental imagery in blind adults. *Neuropsychologia, 23*, 561–566.

Holt, R. R. (1964). Imagery: The return of the ostracized. *American Psychologist, 19*, 254–264.

Iachini, T., & Giusberti, F. (2004). Metric properties of spatial images generated from locomotion: The effect of absolute size on mental scanning. *European Journal of Cognitive Psychology, 16*, 573–596.

Iachini, T., & Ruggiero, G. (2010). The role of visual experience in mental scanning of actual pathways: Evidence from blind and sighted people. *Perception, 39*, 953–969.

Janzen, G. (2006). Memory for object location and route direction in virtual large-scale space. *Quarterly Journal of Experimental Psychology*, *59*, 493–508.

Janzen, G., Wagensveld, B., & van Turennout, M. (2007). Neural representation of navigational relevance is rapidly induced and long lasting. *Cerebral Cortex*, *17*, 975–981.

Johnson-Laird, P. N. (1980). Mental models in cognitive science. *Cognitive Science*, *4*, 71–115.

Johnson-Laird, P. N. (1983). *Mental models: Towards a cognitive science of language, inference, and consciousness.* Cambridge, UK: Cambridge University Press.

Johnson-Laird, P. N. (1996). Images, models, and propositional representations. In M. de Vega, M. J. Intons-Peterson, P. N. Johnson-Laird, M. Denis, & M. Marschark, *Models of visuospatial cognition* (pp. 90–127). New York: Oxford University Press.

Johnson-Laird, P. N. (2006). *How we reason.* New York: Oxford University Press.

Kaski, D. (2002). Revision: Is visual perception a requisite for visual imagery? *Perception*, *31*, 717–731.

Kerr, N. H. (1983). The role of vision in "visual imagery" experiments: Evidence from the congenitally blind. *Journal of Experimental Psychology: General*, *112*, 265–277.

Klatzky, R. L., Loomis, J. M., Beall, A. C., Chance, S. S., & Golledge, R. G. (1998). Spatial updating of self-position and orientation during real, imagined, and virtual locomotion. *Psychological Science*, *9*, 293–298.

Klein, W. (1982). Local deixis in route directions. In R. J. Jarvella & W. Klein (Eds.), *Speech, place, and action* (pp. 161–182). Chichester, UK: Wiley.

Knauff, M. (2009). A neuro-cognitive theory of deductive relational reasoning with mental models and visual images. *Spatial Cognition and Computation*, *9*, 109–137.

Knauff, M., Fangmeier, T., Ruff, C. C., & Johnson-Laird, P. N. (2003). Reasoning, models, and images: Behavioral measures and cortical activity. *Journal of Cognitive Neuroscience*, *15*, 559–573.

Knauff, M., & Johnson-Laird, P. N. (2002). Visual imagery can impede reasoning. *Memory & Cognition*, *30*, 363–371.

Kosslyn, S. M. (1975). Information representation in visual images. *Cognitive Psychology*, *7*, 341–370.

Kosslyn, S. M. (1980). *Image and mind.* Cambridge, MA: Harvard University Press.

Kosslyn, S. M. (1983). *Ghosts in the mind's machine: Creating and using images in the brain.* New York: W. W. Norton.

Kosslyn, S. M. (1994). *Image and brain: The resolution of the imagery debate.* Cambridge, MA: MIT Press.

Kosslyn, S. M., Brunn, J., Cave, K. R., & Wallach, R. W. (1984). Individual differences in mental imagery: A computational analysis. *Cognition*, *18*, 195–243.

Kosslyn, S. M., & Pomerantz, J. R. (1977). Imagery, propositions, and the form of internal representations. *Cognitive Psychology*, *9*, 52–76.

Kosslyn, S. M., Thompson, W. L., & Ganis, G. (2006). *The case for mental imagery.* New York: Oxford University Press.

Kozhevnikov, M., Motes, M. A., Rasch, B., & Blajenkova, O. (2006). Perspective-taking vs. mental rotation and how they predict spatial navigation performance. *Applied Cognitive Psychology*, *20*, 397–417.

Langston, W., Kramer, D. C., & Glenberg, A. M. (1998). The representation of space in mental models derived from text. *Memory and Cognition*, *26*, 247–262.

Levelt, W. J. M. (1982). Linearization in describing spatial networks. In S. Peters & E. Saarinen (Eds.), *Processes, beliefs, and questions* (pp. 199–220). Dordrecht, The Netherlands: Reidel.

Levelt, W. J. M. (1989). *Speaking: From intention to articulation.* Cambridge, MA: MIT Press.

Levinson, S. C. (2003). *Space in language and cognition: Explorations in cognitive diversity.* Cambridge, UK: Cambridge University Press.

Linde, C., & Labov, W. (1975). Spatial networks as a site for the study of language and thought. *Language, 51,* 924–939.

Logie, R. H. (1986). Visuo-spatial processing in working memory. *Quarterly Journal of Experimental Psychology, 38A,* 229–247.

Logie, R. H. (1995). *Visuo-spatial working memory.* Hove, UK: Lawrence Erlbaum Associates.

Logie, R. H., Della Sala, S., Beschin, N., & Denis, M. (2005). Dissociating mental transformations and visuo-spatial storage in working memory: Evidence from representational neglect. *Memory, 13,* 430–434.

Logie, R. H., & Pearson, D. G. (1997). The inner eye and the inner scribe of visuo-spatial working memory: Evidence from developmental fractionation. *European Journal of Cognitive Psychology, 9,* 241–257.

Logie, R. H., & Salway, A. F. S. (1990). Working memory and modes of thinking: A secondary task approach. In K. J. Gilhooly, M. T. Keane, R. H. Logie, & G. E. Erdos (Eds.), *Lines of thinking: Reflections on the psychology of thought* (Vol. 2, pp. 99–113). Chichester, UK: Wiley.

Logie, R. H., & van der Meulen, M. (2009). Fragmenting and integrating visuospatial working memory. In J. R. Brockmole (Ed.), *The visual world in memory* (pp. 1–32). Hove, UK: Psychology Press.

Loomis, J. M., Klatzky, R. L., Golledge, R. G., Cicinelli, J. G., Pellegrino, J. W., & Fry, P. A. (1993). Nonvisual navigation by blind and sighted: Assessment of path integration ability. *Journal of Experimental Psychology: General, 122,* 73–91.

Loomis, J. M., Lippa, Y., Klatzky, R. L., & Golledge, R. G. (2002). Spatial updating of locations specified by 3-D sound and spatial language. *Journal of Experimental Psychology: Learning, Memory, and Cognition, 28,* 335–345.

Mammarella, I. C., Pazzaglia, F., & Cornoldi, C. (2006). The assessment of imagery and visuo-spatial working memory functions in children and adults. In T. Vecchi & G. Bottini (Eds.), *Imagery and spatial cognition: Methods, models and cognitive assessment* (pp. 15–38). Amsterdam: John Benjamins.

Marmor, G. S., & Zaback, L. A. (1976). Mental rotation by the blind: Does mental rotation depend on visual imagery? *Journal of Experimental Psychology: Human Perception and Performance, 2,* 515–521.

Meilinger, T., Knauff, M., & Bülthoff, H. H. (2008). Working memory in wayfinding: A dual task experiment in a virtual city. *Cognitive Science, 32,* 755–770.

Mellet, E., Bricogne, S., Crivello, F., Mazoyer, B., Denis, M., & Tzourio-Mazoyer, N. (2002). Neural basis of mental scanning of a topographic representation built from a text. *Cerebral Cortex, 12,* 1322–1330.

Mellet, E., Bricogne, S., Tzourio-Mazoyer, N., Ghaëm, O., Petit, L., Zago, L., et al. (2000). Neural correlates of topographic mental exploration: The impact of route versus survey perspective learning. *NeuroImage, 12,* 588–600.

Mellet, E., Tzourio, N., Denis, M., & Mazoyer, B. (1995). A positron emission tomography study of visual and mental spatial exploration. *Journal of Cognitive Neuroscience, 7,* 433–445.

Mellet, E., Tzourio-Mazoyer, N., Bricogne, S., Mazoyer, B., Kosslyn, S. M., & Denis, M. (2000). Functional anatomy of high-resolution visual mental imagery. *Journal of Cognitive Neuroscience, 12,* 98–109.

Meneghetti, C., Gyselinck, V., Pazzaglia, F., & De Beni, R. (2009). Individual differences in spatial text processing: High spatial ability can compensate for spatial working memory interference. *Learning and Individual Differences*, *19*, 577–589.

Millar, S. (1994). *Understanding and representing space: Theory and evidence from studies with blind and sighted children*. Oxford, UK: Clarendon Press.

Montello, D. G. (1993). Scale and multiple psychologies of space. In A. U. Frank & I. Campari (Eds.), *Spatial information theory: A theoretical basis for GIS* (pp. 312–321). Berlin: Springer.

Montello, D. G. (2009). A conceptual model of the cognitive processing of environmental distance information. In K. Stewart Hornsby, C. Claramunt, M. Denis, & G. Ligozat (Eds.), *Spatial information theory* (pp. 1–17). Berlin: Springer.

Morrow, D. G., Bower, G. H., & Greenspan, S. L. (1989). Updating situation models during comprehension. *Journal of Memory and Language*, *28*, 292–312.

Morrow, D. G., Greenspan, S. L., & Bower, G. H. (1987). Accessibility and situation models in narrative comprehension. *Journal of Memory and Language*, *26*, 165–187.

Noordzij, M. L., & Postma, A. (2005). Categorical and metric distance information in mental representations derived from route and survey descriptions. *Psychological Research*, *69*, 221–232.

Noordzij, M. L., Zuidhoek, S., & Postma, A. (2006). The influence of visual experience on the ability to form spatial mental models based on route and survey descriptions. *Cognition*, *100*, 321–342.

O'Keefe, J., & Nadel, L. (1978). *The hippocampus as a cognitive map*. Oxford, UK: Oxford University Press.

Paivio, A. (1969). Mental imagery in associative learning and memory. *Psychological Review*, *76*, 241–263.

Paivio, A. (1971). *Imagery and verbal processes*. New York: Holt, Rinehart and Winston.

Paivio, A. (1975). Neomentalism. *Canadian Journal of Psychology*, *29*, 263–291.

Paivio, A. (2007). *Mind and its evolution: A dual coding theoretical approach*. Mahwah, NJ: Lawrence Erlbaum Associates.

Paivio, A., & Okovita, H. W. (1971). Word imagery modalities and associative learning in blind and sighted subjects. *Journal of Verbal Learning and Verbal Behavior*, *10*, 506–510.

Pazzaglia, F., & Cornoldi, C. (1999). The role of distinct components of visuo-spatial working memory in the processing of texts. *Memory*, *7*, 19–41.

Pazzaglia, F., Meneghetti, C., De Beni, R., & Gyselinck, V. (2010). Working memory components in survey and route spatial text processing. *Cognitive Processing*, *11*, 359–369.

Pearson, D. G., De Beni, R., & Cornoldi, C. (2001). The generation, maintenance, and transformation of visuo-spatial mental images. In M. Denis, R. H. Logie, C. Cornoldi, M. de Vega, & J. Engelkamp (Eds.), *Imagery, language and visuo-spatial thinking* (pp. 1–27). Hove, UK: Psychology Press.

Pearson, D. G., Logie, R. H., & Gilhooly, K. J. (1999). Verbal representations and spatial manipulation during mental synthesis. *European Journal of Cognitive Psychology*, *11*, 295–314.

Pearson, D. G., Logie, R. H., & Green, C. (1996). Mental manipulation, visual working memory, and executive processes. *Psychologische Beiträge*, *38*, 324–342.

Perrig, W., & Kintsch, W. (1985). Propositional and situational representations of text. *Journal of Memory and Language*, *24*, 503–518.

Péruch, P., Chabanne, V., Nesa, M.-P., Thinus-Blanc, C., & Denis, M. (2006). Comparing distances in mental images constructed from visual experience or verbal descriptions: The impact of survey versus route perspective. *Quarterly Journal of Experimental Psychology, 59*, 1950–1967.

Portugali, J. (Ed.) (1996). *The construction of cognitive maps*. Dordrecht, The Netherlands: Kluwer.

Postma, A., & Barsalou, L. W. (2009). Spatial working memory and imagery: From eye movements to grounded cognition. *Acta Psychologica, 132*, 103–105.

Pylyshyn, Z. W. (1973). What the mind's eye tells the mind's brain: A critique of mental imagery. *Psychological Bulletin, 80*, 1–24.

Pylyshyn, Z. W. (2003). *Seeing and visualizing: It's not what you think*. Cambridge, MA: MIT Press.

Quinn, J. G., & McConnell, J. (1999). Manipulation of interference in the passive visual store. *European Journal of Cognitive Psychology, 11*, 373–389.

Richardson, J. T. E. (1999). *Imagery*. Hove, UK: Psychology Press.

Rieser, J. J., Guth, D. A., & Hill, E. W. (1986). Sensitivity to perspective structure while walking without vision. *Perception, 15*, 173–188.

Rinck, M., & Denis, M. (2004). The metrics of spatial distance traversed during mental imagery. *Journal of Experimental Psychology: Learning, Memory, and Cognition, 30*, 1211–1218.

Rinck, M., Hähnel, A., Bower, G. H., & Glowalla, U. (1997). The metrics of spatial situation models. *Journal of Experimental Psychology: Learning, Memory, and Cognition, 23*, 622–637.

Rinck, M., Williams, P., Bower, G. H., & Becker, E. S. (1996). Spatial situation models and narrative understanding: Some generalizations and extensions. *Discourse Processes, 21*, 23–55.

Robin, F., & Denis, M. (1991). Description of perceived or imagined spatial networks. In R. H. Logie & M. Denis (Eds.), *Mental images in human cognition* (pp. 141–152). Amsterdam: North-Holland.

Röder, B., & Rösler, F. (1998). Visual input does not facilitate the scanning of spatial images. *Journal of Mental Imagery, 22*(3–4), 165–181.

Rodrigo, M. J., de Vega, M., & Castaneda, J. (1992). Updating mental models in predictive reasoning. *European Journal of Cognitive* Psychology, *4*, 141–157.

Shanon, B. (1984). Room descriptions. *Discourse Processes, 7*, 225–255.

Shaver, P., Pierson, L., & Lang, S. (1975). Converging evidence for the functional significance of imagery in problem solving. *Cognition, 3*, 359–375.

Shepard, R. N. (1978). The mental image. *American Psychologist, 33*, 125–137.

Struiksma, M. E., Noordzij, M. L., & Postma, A. (2009). What is the link between language and spatial images? Behavioral and neural findings in blind and sighted individuals. *Acta Psychologica, 132*, 145–156.

Taylor, H. A., & Tversky, B. (1992). Spatial mental models derived from survey and route descriptions. *Journal of Memory and Language, 31*, 261–292.

Thinus-Blanc, C., & Gaunet, F. (1997). Representation of space in blind persons: Vision as a spatial sense? *Psychological Bulletin, 121*, 20–42.

Tinti, C., Adenzato, M., Tamietto, M., & Cornoldi, C. (2006). Visual experience is not necessary for efficient survey spatial cognition: Evidence from blindness. *Quarterly Journal of Experimental Psychology, 59*, 1306–1328.

Tolman, E. C. (1948). Cognitive maps in rats and men. *Psychological Review, 55*, 189–208.

Tom, A., & Denis, M. (2003). Referring to landmark or street information in route directions: What difference does it make? In W. Kuhn, M. F. Worboys, & S. Timpf (Eds.), *Spatial information theory: Foundations of geographic information science* (pp. 384–397). Berlin: Springer.

Tversky, B. (1991). Spatial mental models. In G. H. Bower (Ed.), *The psychology of learning and motivation: Advances in research and theory* (Vol. 27, pp. 109–145). New York: Academic Press.

Tversky, B. (1993). Cognitive maps, cognitive collages, and spatial mental models. In A. U. Frank & I. Campari (Eds.), *Spatial information theory: A theoretical basis for GIS* (pp. 14–24). Berlin: Springer.

Tversky, B. (2003). Structures on mental spaces: How people think about space. *Environment and Behavior, 35,* 66–80.

Tversky, B. (2009). Spatial cognition: Embodied and situated. In P. Robbins & M. Aydede (Eds.), *The Cambridge handbook of situated cognition* (pp. 201–216). Cambridge, UK: Cambridge University Press.

Tversky, B., & Lee, P. U. (1998). How space structures language. In C. Freksa, C. Habel, & K. F. Wender (Eds.), *Spatial cognition: An interdisciplinary approach to representing and processing spatial knowledge* (pp. 157–175). Berlin: Springer.

Tversky, B., & Lee, P. U. (1999). Pictorial and verbal tools for conveying routes. In C. Freksa & D. M. Mark (Eds.), *Spatial information theory: Cognitive and computational foundations of geographic information science* (pp. 51–64). Berlin: Springer.

Tversky, B., Morrison, J. B., Franklin, N., & Bryant, D. J. (1999). Three spaces of spatial cognition. *Professional Geographer, 51,* 516–524.

Ungar, S. (2000). Cognitive mapping without visual experience. In R. Kitchin & S. Freundschuh (Eds.), *Cognitive mapping: Past, present and future* (pp. 221–248). London: Routledge.

van Dijk, T. A., & Kintsch, W. (1983). *Strategies of discourse comprehension.* New York: Academic Press.

Vanetti, E. J., & Allen, G. L. (1988). Communicating environmental knowledge: The impact of verbal and spatial abilities on the production and comprehension of route directions. *Environment and Behavior, 20,* 667–682.

Vecchi, T. (1998). Visuo-spatial limitations in congenitally totally blind people. *Memory, 6,* 91–102.

Vecchi, T., & Bottini, G. (Eds.) (2006). *Imagery and spatial cognition: Methods, models and cognitive assessment.* Amsterdam: John Benjamins.

Veraart, C., & Wanet-Defalque, M.-C. (1987). Representation of locomotor space by the blind. *Perception and Psychophysics, 42,* 132–139.

Waller, D., & Greenauer, N. (2007). The role of body-based sensory information in the acquisition of enduring spatial representations. *Psychological Research, 71,* 322–332.

Watson, J. B. (1924). *Behaviorism.* New York: People's Institute Publishing Company.

Zimler, J., & Keenan, J. M. (1983). Imagery in the congenitally blind: How visual are visual images? *Journal of Experimental Psychology: Learning, Memory, and Cognition, 9,* 269–282.

Zwaan, R. A., & Taylor, L. J. (2006). Seeing, acting, understanding: Motor resonance in language comprehension. *Journal of Experimental Psychology: General, 135,* 1–11.

Name Index

Abbott, V. 11
Abrams, R. A. 115
Addis, D. R. 51
Adenzato, M. 236, 237
Afonso, A. 238–41
Agrawala, M. 6–8
Aguirre, G. K. 47
Alcetti, A. 152
Allamano, N. 94
Allen, G. L. 146, 222, 229
Allen, R. 119
Alloway, T. P. 78
Alpert, N. M. 20, 21, 47, 52, 64, 67
Alsop, D. C. 47
Altieri, P. 132
Anderson, J. R. 23, 78, 194, 205
Andrade, J. 110, 112, 117, 210
Andres, P. 113
Andrews-Hanna, J. R. 50, 52
Ang, S. Y. 95, 96
Annett, J. 113
Arbib, M. A. 188, 190
Arditi, A. 235
Atkinson, R. C. 77
Avons, S. E. 24, 110, 112
Avraamides, M. N. 134, 169, 227, 232
Awh, E. 115
Aziz-Zadeh, L. 52, 183, 188

Baars, B. J. 77
Bachoud-Levi, A. C. 21
Baddeley, A. D. 77–86, 88, 90–6, 107,
    108, 110–14, 117–20, 136, 145, 209–11
Ball, L. J. 168, 169
Ball, T. M. 22, 45, 54
Baraldi, P. 47
Barbey, A. K. 45, 166
Barker, R. G. 11
Barrouillet, P. 88–95, 119

Barsalou, L. W. 45, 166, 189, 193, 194, 245
Bartlett, F. 77
Bartolomeo, P. 21
Basso, A. 20
Bayer, R. H. 169
Bayliss, D. M. 83, 84, 86, 95, 96
Beall, A. C. 222
Beck, S. 146
Becker, S. 61, 67, 112, 218
Behrmann, M. 5, 21
Bekkering, H. 185
Benjamins, J. S. 112
Berman, J. V. F. 136
Bernardin, S. 89, 119
Berthoz, A. 20, 207
Bertolo, L. 3, 5, 150, 230
Beschin, N. 107, 213, 214
Bestelmeyer, P. 94, 98
Biasutti, E. 187
Binkofski, V. 179
Bisiach, E. 20
Black, J. H. 11
Blajenkova, O. 227
Bleckley, M. K. 80
Bloom, P. 224
Blum, A. 238–41
Bonino, D. 164
Borella, E. 151
Borreggine, K. L. 178
Borst, G. 19–39, 54, 55, 195, 208, 209,
    238–241
Bosch, V. 167
Bosco, A. 134, 142, 146
Bosker, W. M. 168
Bothell, D. 78
Bottini, G. 222
Boulenger, V. 187
Bower, G. H. 23, 45, 132–5, 170, 205, 215,
    216, 218, 220

Boyer, P. 229
Brandimonte, M. A. 195
Brereton, N. 79, 82, 83
Bresman, J. 10, 13
Brett, M. 47
Brewer, G. A. 82, 96
Bricogne, S. (or Briscogne, S.? both appear in Google) 20, 207, 208
Broadbent, D. E. 81, 94
Broadbent, M. H. P. 94
Broadway, J. M. 84, 85, 95
Brockmole, J. R. 97
Brooks, L. R. 113, 114, 136, 139
Broussolle, E. 187
Brown, G. D. A. 89, 91
Brown, L. A. 113
Brugieres, P. 21
Brunn, J. 206, 210
Brunyé, T. T. 134, 141–3, 154, 170, 171, 227
Bryant, D. J. 132, 223
Bryden, M. P. 146
Buccino, G. 179
Buckner, R. L. 46, 50, 51, 52
Buëchel, C. 183
Bülthoff, H. H. 224
Bunting, M. F. 79, 93
Burgess, N. 59, 61, 67
Burin, D. I. 112, 116, 118
Byrne, M. D. 78
Byrne, P. 61, 67
Byrne, R. M. J. 215

Calvanio, R. 20
Camos, V. 88–95, 119
Camposano, S. 64, 66
Caplan, D. 79, 82, 95
Cappa, S. 183, 188
Caramazza, A. 186, 191
Carfantan, M. 205, 245
Carité, L. 229
Carlson, L. A. 162, 166
Carlson-Radvansky, L. A. 149, 162
Carpenter, P. A. 79, 84, 166
Case, R. 88
Castaneda, J. 215
Castillo, M. D. 179, 180, 192
Castner, J. E. 187
Cattaneo, Z. 164
Cave, K. R. 206, 210
Cettolo, V. 47
Chabanne, V. 143, 237
Chabris, C. F. 64
Chalmers, P. 87, 96

Chan, A. W. 20
Chance, S. S. 222
Chase, W. G. 166
Chechile, N. A. 142
Chen, W. 64
Chenery, H. J. 187
Chilton, P. 225
Choate, P. A. 23
Chokron, S. 233
Christie, D. F. M. 94
Chrysler, S. T. 129
Church, J. A. 59
Cicinelli, J. G. 236
Clark, H. H. 166
Clark, J. M. 131
Cocchini, G. 78, 88, 107
Cocude, M. 56, 132, 145, 169, 195, 206, 208, 225
Collins, A. F. 168
Compton, B. J. 162
Conway, A. R. A. 79, 80, 81, 93, 95, 96
Coon, V. 132
Cooper, L. A. 20, 55, 88
Copeland, D. E. 151
Cornoldi, C. 3, 5, 95, 107, 116–19, 127–54, 164, 165, 170, 195, 206, 212, 220–24, 230, 234, 236, 237, 242
Cortesi, A. 234
Coupe, P. 38
Cowan, N. 78, 79, 81, 119
Coyne, T. J. 187
Craighero, L. 189
Craik, K. 214
Cramer, S. C. 183
Craver-Lemley, C. 20
Creem, S. H. 59
Crescentini, C. 187
Crivello, F. 20, 58, 208
Curiel, J. M. 151
Cusack, R. 50, 64

Dagnall, N. 109, 112
Dale, A. M. 24, 64
Dalla Barba, G. 21
Damasio, A. 45, 52, 167, 190
Daneman, M. 79, 82, 84
Daniel, M.-P. 7, 127, 177, 185, 229, 232
Darken, R. 149
Daselaar, S. M. 48, 49, 50, 66
Dasen, P. R. 224
Davidson, R. J. 182
De Beni, R. 127–54, 206, 212, 220, 221, 227, 234
De Gelder, B. 21

de Oliveira-Souza, R. 191
De Valois, R. L. 24, 64
de Vega, M. 58, 130, 145, 146, 164,
    177–95, 215, 217, 218, 220, 226,
    242, 245
Dean, G. M. 108, 110, 112
Dean, R. S. 131
Decety, J. 47, 195
Dechent, P. 47
Della Sala, S. 78, 87, 88, 90, 94, 96, 98,
    107, 113, 114, 183, 188, 213, 214
Denes, G. 21
Denhière, G. 132, 134, 225
Denis, M., *passim*
Dent, K. 108, 110, 112
D'Esposito, M. 47, 77, 97
Detre, J. A. 47
Dettmers, C. 183
Dewhurst, S. A. 108, 110, 112
Deyzac, E. 78, 143, 227, 228
Diamond, M. E. 47
Dijkstra, K. 151
Dobson, S. H. 146
Dodds, C. M. 20
Donchin, E. 78
Douglass, S. 78
Downing, P. E. 20
Downs, J. H. 59
Downs, T. H. 59, 117
Dubois, J. 65, 137, 138
Duff, S. C. 79, 82, 83, 85, 86, 88, 91, 95,
    96
Dulin, D. 233
Duncan, J. 50, 64
Dupree, D. 149

Edwards, G. 229
Egan, G. F. 47
Ehrich, V. 225
Ehrlich, K. 129, 133, 137, 138
Ehrsson, H. 183
Eisenberger, N. I. 191
Eisner, W. 10
Ekstrom, R. B. 146
Elford, G. 113
Emerson, M. J. 78
Engel, G. R. 26
Engelkamp, J. 211, 242
Engle, R. W. 79, 80, 81, 84–7, 92, 93,
    95, 96
Engquist, G. 11, 12
Erdelyi, M. H. 112
Ernest, C. H. 233
Evans, G. W. 149, 225

Fadiga, L. 189
Falini, A. 183, 188
Fangmeier, T. 217
Farah, M. J. 20, 24, 210, 211
Farmer, E. W. 136
Fastame M. C. 115
Felician, O. 64, 66
Fendrich, R. 115
Ferguson, E. L. 132
Fernandez, G. 230
Feynman, R. 13
Fields, A. W. 127, 146
Filomena, S. 142, 146
Fincham, J. M. 78
Finke, R. A. 20, 23, 24, 31, 39, 53, 54, 55,
    57, 210, 211
Finklestein, S. P. 183
Fisher, M. H. 187, 188, 192
Fitzimmons, C. 132
Flandin, G. 65
Fleming, P. 168
Fletcher, Y. L. 129, 136, 164
Fodor, A. 63
Foley, M. 183
Fontaine, S. 127, 177, 229
Forbes, D. 113
Forssberg, H. 183
Frahm, J. 47
Fraisse, P. 144
Francescato, M. P. 47
Francis, G. 24
Franklin, N. 131, 132, 157, 215, 223, 233
Freeman, D. K. 47
Freksa, C. 225
French, J. W. 146
Friederici, A. D. 167
Friedman, N. P. 78, 92, 93, 95, 96, 149
Friston, K. J. 47
Fry, P. A. 236
Furey, M. L. 20
Fusella, V. 20

Gallese, G. 179, 188
Ganis, G. 20–2, 25, 43, 45, 46, 48, 53, 54,
    58, 61, 62, 64, 67, 68, 106, 206, 212
Garden, S. 224
Gärdenfors, P. 225
Garnham, A. 129, 215
Garrett, M. F. 224
Garrod, S. 190
Garsoffky, B. 12
Gathercole, S. E. 78, 80, 95, 117
Gaunet, F. 165, 171, 222
Gennari, S. P. 184, 185, 188

Gentner, D. 215
Gernsbacher, M. A. 146, 218
Ghaëm, O. 20, 207
Giesen, C. 144
Gilhooly, K. J. 78, 211
Gitti, F. 152
Giusberti, F. 150, 206, 238
Glaser, W. R. 193
Glauche, V. 183
Glavanov, D. 129
Glenberg, A. M. 132, 135, 136, 178, 181,
    182, 189, 191, 192, 215, 216, 218, 245
Glover, S. 184, 192
Glowalla, U. 134, 170, 218, 220
Gobbini, M. I. 20
Goebel, R. 47
Goetz, E. T. 131
Goldberg, J. 88
Goldenberg, G. 21
Goldreich, D. 166
Goldston, D. B. 63
Golledge, R. G. 134, 169, 222, 233, 235,
    236
Gomez, C. 152
Gonçalves, M.-R. 208
Gountouna, E. 98
Grabowski, T. J. 167
Graesser, A. C. 191, 245
Grasso, I. 151
Gray, J. M. 94, 113, 115
Gray-Wilson, S. 132, 133
Green, C. 211
Greenauer, N. 222
Greenspan, S. L. 132, 133, 218
Grèzes, J. 47
Grill-Spector, K. 68
Grimoldi, M. 95, 117
Groensteen, T. 13
Grothe, J. 47
Guariglia, C. 21
Gunn, D. M. 83, 84, 86, 95, 96
Guth, D. A. 235
Gutowski, K. A. 182
Gyselinck, V. 127–54, 216, 220, 221, 227,
    242

Haber, L. R. 235
Haber, R. N. 235
Habib, R. 46
Hacker, H. 47
Hadjikani, N. K. 24
Hadjikhani, N. K. 64
Haenggi, D. 146, 218
Hahnel, A. 134

Hähnel, A. 170, 218, 220
Hakala, M. 134
Hall, D. L. 149
Hall, L. E. 152
Hall, M. 95, 117
Halpern, A. R. 47
Halpin, J. A. 134
Hambrick, D. Z. 79, 81, 84, 92, 93, 95, 96
Hamilton, C. 115
Hamilton, S. L. 64
Hamzei, F. 183
Haney, K. H. 170
Hannon, B. 79, 82
Hanrahan, P. 6–8
Hard, B. M. 4, 11, 12
Hardy, J. K. 134
Harman, H. H. 146
Harnad, S. 177
Harrington, G. S. 59
Hasher, L. 79
Hatwell, Y. 233
Hauk, O. 182, 184
Havas, D. A. 181, 182
Haxby, J. V. 20, 21, 47
Haygood, R. C. 131
Haymaker, J. 7
Healey, M. K. 81, 95, 96
Hebb, D. O. 188
Hegarty, M. 92, 95, 96, 132, 146, 223, 224
Heiser, J. 6–10
Heitz, R. P. 79, 84, 85, 95
Herriman, G. 13
Herrnberger, B. 47
Hichwa, R. D. 167
Hickmann, M. 225
Hill, E. W. 235
Hillyard, S. A. 166
Hinrichs, J. V. 63
Hitch, G. I. 77–9, 87, 88, 107, 110,
    117–20, 136, 209
Hoenig, K. 47
Holcomb, P. 193, 194
Hollins, M. 235
Hollyfield, R. 235
Holt, R. 203
Holtzman, J. D. 235
Howerter, A. 78
Hughes, R. W. 107
Huijbers, W. 48–50, 66
Hume, D. 77, 98
Humphries, T. 152
Hund, A. M. 170
Hunt, E. B. 166
Hutton, U. 87, 88

Iachini, T. 238, 240
Iacoboni, M. 183, 188
Idzikowski, C. 114
Ilmoniemi, R. J. 180, 182, 184
Inati, S. 59
Intons-Peterson, M. J. 23, 164, 226
Irrazabal, N. 112, 116, 118
Irwin, D. E. 149, 162
Ishai, A. 20, 21, 47
Ishikawa, T. 146, 223, 224
Iyer, G. 11

Jackendoff, R. 167
Jacobsen, R. 163
Jager, G. 169
James, W. 77, 80, 81
Janzen, G. 222, 227
Jarrold, C. 83, 84, 86, 95, 96
Jeannerod, M. 187, 195
Jenmalm, P. 183
Johnson, J. D. 46
Johnson, M. 180
Johnson-Laird, P. N. 128–30, 133, 164,
    166, 214–18, 226
Johnson, W. 97
Jolesz, F. A. 47
Joliot, M. 58
Jones, D. 107
Jonides, J. 115
Just, M. A. 7, 11, 12, 79, 166, 190

Kallai, J. 150
Kane, M. J. 79, 80, 81, 84, 92, 93, 95, 96
Kanics, I. M. 166
Kanwisher, N. 20, 47
Kappers, A. M. 166, 171
Kaschak, M. P. 178, 189, 192
Kaski, D. 164, 233
Kastner, S. 67
Kato, T. 64
Katz, B. F. G. 238–41
Kaufmann, G. 195
Keaton, B. 10, 242–3
Keenan, J. M. 234
Keenan, J. P. 64, 66
Kellenbach, M. L. 47
Keller, T. A. 79
Kelly, J. W. 227
Kemmerer, D. 167, 168
Kemps, E. 110, 112, 115, 117
Kerr, N. H. 234, 238
Keysers, C. 188
Kherif, F. 65
Khorram-Sefat, D. 47

Kiefer, M. 47
Kim, I. J. 64
Kintsch, W. 128, 129, 134, 142, 146, 166,
    186, 214, 215, 218
Kirasic, K. C. 146
Kitchin, R. 163
Klatzky, R. L. 134, 169, 222, 232, 233,
    235, 236
Klauer, K. C. 92
Klein, I. 65
Klein, J. D. 131
Klein, W. 228
Klingner, J. 7
Klug, J. L. 133
Knauff, M. 217, 224
Kosslyn, S. M. 3, 19–39, 43–8, 51–5,
    58–62, 64–9, 106, 107, 111, 112, 118,
    119, 169, 195, 204–6, 208–13, 218, 235,
    237, 245
Koster, C. 225
Kounios, J. 193, 194
Kourtzi, Z. 47
Kozhevnikov, M. 24, 227
Kramer, D. C. 135, 218
Kruley, P. 136
Kulhavy, R. W. 131
Kurland, D. M. 88
Kuse, A. R. 7, 146, 149

Labov, W. 225
Lagner, P. 89, 90, 91
Laiacona, M. 87, 96
Lakoff, G. 180
Lalonde, F. M. 47
Lamme, H. 26
Landau, B. 167
Lanfranchi, S. 117
Lang, S. 217
Langston, W. 135, 216, 218
La Pointe, L. B. 86, 87, 95
Larsen, J. 78
Larsson, M. 150
Lassonde, M. 166
Laughlin, J. E. 80, 96
Law, A. S. 78, 90
Lawrence, B. M. 115
Lawton, C. A. 149, 150
Lebiere, C. 78
Lee, K. 95, 96
Lee, P. U. 5, 6, 8, 9, 142, 229
Lehnert, G. 59, 60
Lehto, J. 119
Leirer, V. 132
León, I. 185, 186

Lepore, F. 166
Lessard, N. 166
Léveillé, M. 144
Levelt, W. J. M. 225
Levin, C. A. 235
Levine, D. N. 20, 24
Levinson, S. C. 225
Lewandowsky, S. 89, 91
Lewis, V. J. 78
Lieberman, K. 114, 210
Lieberman, M. D. 191
Likert, R. 146
Linde, C. 225
Lindem, K. 132, 215
Linn, M. C. 146
Lippa, Y. 169, 233
Lloyd, S. A. 95, 117
Lobley, K. J. 80
Locke, J. 77, 81, 98
Logan, G. D. 162, 166
Logie, R. H. 48, 77–98, 106–8, 110–15, 117, 119, 120, 143, 154, 195, 210–14, 224, 227, 228, 242
Long, R. G. 146
Longoni, A. M. 134, 142, 146
Loomis, J. M. 134, 169, 222, 232, 233, 235, 236
Lovelace, K. 146, 223, 224
Lovett, B. J. 96
Lozano, S. 10
Lucarelli, M. J. 182
Luzzatti, C. 20

McCarthy III, J. J. 47
McCloud, S. 10, 12
McConnell, J. 108, 112, 113, 143, 212
McGeoch, J. A. 88, 98
McGonigle, D. 98
McIntosh, A. R. 46
Macken, W. J. 107
MacKenzie, R. 10
Mackin, P. 115
MacLeod, C. M. 166
McNamara, D. S. 87, 95, 132–4, 143, 169, 170
MacPherson, S. 88
Madden, C. J. 151, 193
Magnussen, S. 150
Mahon, B. Z. 186, 191
Mainwaring, S. D. 4
Malach, R. 68
Maljkovic, V. 64
Mammarella, I. C. 95, 117, 152, 164, 223
Mane, A. 78

Manenti, R. 183, 188
Manghi, E. 232
Mangin, J.-F. 65
Mani, K. 129, 133
Marks, D. F. 149
Marmor, G. S. 234
Marrett, S. 24, 64
Mars, R. B. 112
Marschark, M. 131, 164, 218, 226
Martin, A. 47
Martinez, A. 54, 67
Mathews, N. N. 166
Maybery, M. T. 113
Mazoyer, B. 20, 39, 47, 55, 58, 206–8
McKay, W. 13
Mechelli, A. 47
Mechtouff, L. 187
Mecklinger, A. 167
Meier, B. P. 191
Meilinger, T. 224
Mellet, E. 20, 39, 47, 55, 58, 169, 206–8
Melli, F. 179
Memmi, D. 208
Mendola, J. D. 24, 64
Meneghetti, C. 139, 140, 143, 145, 147–52, 154, 220, 221, 227
Merboldt, K.-D. 47
Metzler, J. 45, 55
Meyer, K. 45, 132, 215
Millar, S. 166, 171, 235, 237
Milner, B. 147
Mishkin, M. 24
Mishra, R. C. 225
Mitchell, D. B. 23
Miyake, A. 78, 81, 87, 88, 91–3, 95, 96
Moè, A. 144, 220
Mogel, J. A. 96
Moll, J. 191
Mondolo, F. 187
Mondoloni, A. 145, 220, 227
Montello, D. R. 146, 223–5
Moody, C. L. 184, 188
Moreno, V. 179, 180, 185, 186, 192
Mores Dibo-Cohen, C. 229
Morita, A. 90
Morrison, J. 10, 223
Morrow, D. G. 132, 133, 135, 215, 216, 218
Moscovitch, M. 21
Motes, M. A. 227
Moulton, S. T. 48, 51–3, 62
Mouly, F. 10
Moyer, R. S. 169
Muckli, L. 47
Myerson, J. 115

Nadel, L. 5, 222, 224
Narimoto, T. 115–17
Naylor, S. J. 142
Nazir, T. A. 187
Neggers, S. F. W. 167, 168
Nelles, G. 183
Nesa, M.-P. 237
Neville, H. J. 166
Newcombe, N. 225
Newtson, D. 11, 12
Nichelli, P. 152
Nikulin, V. 182, 184
Nimmo-Smith, I. 79, 82, 83
Niven, E. H. 77–98
Noordzij, M. L. 134, 143, 144, 162–73,
    227, 233, 237
Nori, R. 150
Nyberg, L. 46

Oberauer, K. 89, 91
O'Craven, K. M. 20, 47
Ogawa, S. 64
Ohgishi, M. 4
O'Keefe, J. 5, 222
Okovita, H. W. 233
Olson, S. 152
Orlov, T. 172
Ormerod, T. C. 168
Osaka, N. 77, 97

Padovani, A. 21
Paivio, A. 19, 20, 45, 131, 144, 166, 193,
    194, 203, 204, 206, 210, 212, 233, 242,
    244, 245
Pani, J. R. 149
Pantano, P. 21
Pare, M. 166
Park, H. 46
Parker, A. 109, 112
Parmentier, F. B. R. 113
Pascual-Leone, A. 64, 66
Patterson, K. 47
Payne, T. W. 84, 92, 93, 95, 96, 112
Pazzaglia, F. 3, 5, 95, 117, 127–54, 177,
    220, 221, 223, 227, 230, 242
Pearson, D. G. 48, 94, 95, 111, 115,
    211, 212
Pearson, N. A. 114
Pearson, P. M. 21
Peeck, J. 144
Peelen, M. V. 20
Pellegrino, J. W. 236
Pendleton, R. A. 114
Pennartz, C. M. A. 48, 49, 50, 66

Perani, D. 183, 188
Perky, C. 20
Perrig, W. 129, 134, 142, 215
Péruch, P. 143, 237
Petersen, A. C. 146
Petersen, S. E. 46
Peterson, B. 149
Peterson, M. A. 224
Peterson, S. E. 131
Petit, L. 20, 55, 207
Phan, D. 6–8
Phillips, L. H. 78
Phillips, W. A. 24, 94
Piccardi, L. 150
Pickering, M. J. 190
Pickering, S. J. 95, 117
Pierson, L. 217
Pietrini, P. 20
Pineda, J. 185
Pinker, S. 22, 23, 24, 31, 39, 54, 57, 211
Pitzalis, S. 54, 67
Pizzamiglio, L. 21
Podgorny, P. 20
Podzebenko, K. 47
Poline, J.-B. 65
Pomerantz, J. R. 205
Ponto, L. L. B. 167
Poole, B. J. 79
Porat, Y. 48–50, 66
Porro, C. A. 47
Portrat, S. 89
Portugali, J. 222
Postle, B. R. 114
Postma, A. 134, 143, 144, 162–73, 227,
    233, 237, 245
Preti, D. 234
Price, C. J. 47
Pridemore, D. R. 131
Proffitt, D. R. 59
Pulvermüller, F. 180, 182, 184, 188
Pundak, G. 172
Pylyshyn, Z. W. 23, 25, 44, 63, 69, 98,
    204, 206, 233

Qin, Y. 78
Quasha, W. H. 146
Quinn, G. 115–17, 120
Quinn, J. G. 106–20, 143, 212

Radvansky, G. A. 134, 151, 160, 170
Ramsey, N. F. 168
Rapp, D. N. 133, 142, 170
Rasch, B. 227
Raz, N. 172

Reddy, L. 51, 64, 66
Redick, T. S. 84, 85, 95
Reeves, A. 20
Regier, T. 162
Reisberg, D. 195
Reiser, B. J. 22, 45, 54, 169
Rettinger, D. A. 92, 95, 96
Reuter-Lorenz, P. A. 115
Reznick, J. S. 23
Ricciardi, E. 164
Richardson, J. T. E. 45, 146, 195, 207, 223, 224
Richman, C. L. 23, 63
Rieser, J. J. 235
Riggio, G. 179
Rigoni, F. 152
Rijntjes, M. 183
Rinck, M. 132–35, 170, 181, 192, 218–20
Rittschof, K. A. 131
Rizzolatti, G. 179, 188, 190
Robert, S. 225
Robertson, B. 21
Robertson, D. A. 192
Robin, F. 226
Robinson, M. D. 191
Röder, B. 166, 238
Rodrigo M. J. 145, 215
Roediger, H. L. 112
Ronnberg, J. 150
Rosen, B. R. 183
Rösler, F. 166, 238
Rourke, B. P. 152
Roy, D. 190
Rudkin, S. J. 95
Ruff, C. C. 217
Rugg, M. D. 46
Ruggiero, G. 240

Sadler, D. D. 162
Sadoski, M. 131
Sahraie, A. 115
Saito, S. 87, 88, 90, 107
Salamé, P. 107
Salway, A. F. S. 115, 120, 211
Sanford, A. J. 192
Santana, E. 180, 181, 191
Santos, A. 189, 193, 194
Sardone, L. 134, 142, 146
Savenye, W. 131
Scalisi, T. G. 134, 142, 146
Schacter, D. L. 19, 46, 50, 51, 52
Schaechter, J. D. 183
Schiano, D. J. 4
Schie, H. T. 112, 185

Schmalhofer, F. 129
Schmitz, C. 183
Schouten, J. L. 20
Schwan, S. 12
Sciama S. C. 136
Scott, J. L. 87, 95
Seanor, B. D. 170
Searle, J. R. 177
Segal, S. J. 20
Seidler, B. 113
Sereno, M. I. 54, 67
Serre, T. 51, 64, 66
Sestieri, C. 110, 112
Shah, P. 91, 92, 95, 96
Shallice, T. 78, 187
Shanon, B. 225
Shapiro, L. 177
Shaver, P. 217
Shelton A. L. 127, 143, 146, 170
Shepard, R. N. 20, 45, 53, 55, 210
Shephard, J. M. 24, 59
Sheptak, R. 78
Shiffrin, R. M. 77
Shtyrov, Y. 180
Siegel, A. W. 149, 153
Silburn, P. A. 187
Silver, M. A. 67
Silverman, M. S. 24, 64
Sim, E.-J. 47
Simmons, W. K. 45, 166, 189, 193, 194
Sinclair, F. 187
Singer, W. 47
Sliwinski, M. J. 96
Slotnick, S. D. 46, 65, 67
Smith, E. E. 11
Smith, E. R. 187
Smyth, M. M. 114
Sommerville, J. A. 195
Speiser, H. R. 113
Spekreijse, H. 26
Sperling, G. 24
Spiegelman, A. 10
Spillers, G. J. 82, 96
Stallcup, M. 47
Stawski, R. S. 96
Sterr, A. 166
Stevens, A. 38, 215
Stoccoet, A. 78
Stock, W. A. 131
Stokes, M. 50, 64
Stolte, C. 8
Stoltzfus, E. R. 79
Stout, G. 77
Stowe, L. A. 112

Striem, E. 172
Struiksma, M. E. 164–6, 168, 233
Sukel, K. E. 64, 67
Super, H. 26
Switkes, E. 24, 64
Szmalec, A. 110, 112, 115, 117

Talmy, L. 191
Tamietto, M. 236, 237
Tank, D. W. 64
Tannock, R. 152
Tardieu, H. 129, 216
Tarroux, P. 238–41
Taylor, H. A. 4, 5, 55, 129, 132–4, 141–3,
    154, 170–2, 215, 226, 227
Taylor, L. J. 178, 179, 187, 188, 245
Teder-Salejarvi, W. 166
Tettamanti, M. 183, 188
Thinus-Blanc, C. 143, 165, 171,
    222, 237
Thirion, B. 50
Thobois, S. 187
Thomas, K. 172
Thompson, R. 50, 64
Thompson, W. L. 20–2, 25, 43, 45–8, 52–4,
    58, 61, 62, 64–8, 106, 115, 206, 212
Tinti, C. 236, 237
Tipper, S. P. 5
Tippet, L. J. 47
Tolman, E. C. 127, 221
Tom, A. 5, 6, 232
Tootell, R. B. 24, 64
Torrens, L. 98
Toso, C. 95, 117
Towse, J. N. 87, 88
Tranel, D. 152, 167
Tranel, N. N. 152
Trawley, S. 78
Treisman, A. M. 119
Tsuchiya, N. 51, 64, 66
Tuholski, S. W. 79, 80, 84, 92, 93, 95, 96
Tulving, E. 46
Turley-Ames, K. J. 87, 95
Turner, M. L. 79, 84, 86, 87, 95
Tversky, B. 3–13, 55, 129, 131, 132, 141,
    142, 170, 172, 215, 221, 223, 226, 229,
    233, 242, 245
Tzourio, N. 20, 39, 47, 55, 58, 207
Tzourio-Mazoyer, N. 20, 207, 208

Ugurbil, K. 64
Uncapher, M. R. 46
Ungar, S. 236
Ungerleider, L. G. 20, 21, 24, 47

Unsworth, N. 79–82, 84–7, 95, 96
Urrutia, M. 180, 184, 185, 193

Vallar, G. 78
van der Lubbe, R. H. J. 143, 167
van der Meulen, M. 48, 78, 91, 94, 98, 212
van Dijk, T. A. 128, 129, 166, 214
van Elk, M. 185
van Oostendorp, H. 132, 133
van Turennout, M. 222
Vandenberg, S. G. 7, 146, 149
Vandierendonck, A. 115
Vanetti, E. J. 229
Vecchi, T. 107, 116–19, 139, 146, 154,
    164, 165, 168, 170, 212, 222, 234
Venneri, A. 152
Veraart, C. 235
Verdi, M. P. 131
Vergauwe, E. 91–5
Vianello, R. 117
Vio, C. 95, 117
Voyer, D. 146
Voyer, S. 146

Wagensveld, B. 222
Wager, T. D. 78
Wallach, R. W. 206, 210
Waller, D. 222
Wanet-Defalque, M.-C. 235
Warach, J. 24
Warren, D. H. 163
Waters, G. S. 79, 82, 95
Watson, J. B. 19, 243
Watson, J. D. G. 47
Wechsler, D. 147
Wede, J. 24
Weiller, C. 183
Weise, S. B. 64
Weisskoff, R. M. 183
Welsch, D. 129
Werniers, Y. 110, 112, 117
West, W. 57, 171, 194
Wheeler, M. E. 46, 119
White, S. H. 149, 153
Whitfield, M. M. 87, 95
Whittaker, A. 108, 110, 112
Wiemer-Hastings, K. 193
Wiesner, D. 13
Wiggs, C. L. 47
Wijers, A. A. 112
Wilhelm, O. 84, 92, 93, 95, 96
Williams, K. D. 6, 191, 218
Wilson, C. D. 45, 166, 189, 193, 194
Wilson, L. 94, 113

Wilson, S. M. 183, 188
Winocur, G. 21
Witzki, A. H. 78
Wolff, P. 191
Wölfl, S. 225
Woodard, K. A. 131
Worling, D. E. 152
Wraga, M. 52, 59
Wright, H. F. 11
Wynn, V. 78, 87, 90, 96

Yaxley, R. H. 151
Yoo, S. S. 47
Young, A. H. 115
Yovel, G. 20

Zaback, L. A. 234
Zacks, J. 9, 11, 12

Zacks, R. T. 79
Zago, L. 20, 207
Zatorre, R. J. 47
Zeman, A. 98
Zhao, Z. 92
Zhu, X. H. 64
Zimler, J. 234
Zimmer, H. D. 43–69, 113,
    145, 168, 169, 171, 206,
    208, 211
Zimny, S. 129
Zohary, E. 172
Zucco, G. 114
Zuiani, C. 47
Zuidhoek, S. 166, 170–2, 237
Zwaan, R. A. 132–4, 151, 166,
    170, 178, 179, 185, 187, 188,
    192, 245

Subject Index

abstract words 109, 191, 193, 194
achromatia 21
action language 178, 182, 186, 188;
  behavioral studies on 178–82;
  neuroscientific studies on 182–7
adventitious blindness 234, 236, 240
affordance(s) 187, 189, 190; meshing of
  187; motor 190
ageing: cognitive 88; and spatial text
  processing 151–2
agnosia 21
alexia 21
alliteration 13
alpha band rhythms 185
Alzheimer disease 78, 154
amodal conceptual representation 164
amygdala 190
analogue spatial mental rotation 54
analogue spatial representations 45
analogy 13, 64, 69, 216, 220
AoU: see area of uncertainty
architectural features and route directions 5
area of uncertainty (AoU) 29–38;
  principles of construction of 29, 34
arithmetic 79, 89; mental 78; verification
  83
array theory of imagery 44
articulation 83, 88, 90, 216
articulatory suppression (AS) 80, 85, 86,
  88–90, 115, 117, 136, 139, 141, 143,
  145, 147–9, 221
artificial intelligence 225
AS: see articulatory suppression
assembly 6–8; visual explanations for 11
Associationism 203
associative auditory cortex 47
associative relations 6
attention: control of, working memory as
  78–95; controlled 77, 79, 81; executive

79, 81; as rehearsal mechanism for
  visual working memory 114–18
attentional capture 79
attentional refreshing mechanism 89
auditory imagery 48–50
auditory localization 166
auditory perception 49, 50

behaviorists 19
blindness 163, 164, 170, 233–5, 244;
  adventitious 234, 236, 240; cognitive
  impact of, on mental imagery processes
  233; congenital 164, 168, 172, 233–6,
  238–41; and perspective and complex
  spatial descriptions 170–71
blind people 144, 233–41; cognition in
  209; and sighted people, spatial
  language use by 162–73; spatial
  representations by 163–6; and use of
  visual imagery 233–5
block diagrams 110, 112
botox 182
brain: imaging 44, 98, 206; lesions 21,
  167; motor 180, 184, 186, 187, 194;
  patterns of activation in 20; structures,
  modality-specific 46–8; visual imagery
  in 43–69
breakpoints 11, 12
brightness judgments 143
Broca's area 183, 184, 187, 188, 194
Brooks test 114
buffer, visual 44–6, 48, 53, 58, 61–7, 106,
  111–13, 119, 206, 209, 210, 212

card rotation test (CRT) 146
categorical judgments 179
categorical spatial information 169
CCT: see cube comparison test
CE: see central executive

central executive (CE) 78, 79, 85, 90, 94, 110, 111, 209, 211, 212
charts 9
Chinese characters 112
CL: *see* cognitive load
cognate concepts 209
cognition: architecture of 98, 210; embodied 177–95; higher order 80, 84–7, 96, 245; on-line 77, 78, 98; spatial 3, 127, 131, 146, 149, 153, 154, 209, 215, 221, 222, 227, 232, 233, 235, 244; visual 206, 211, 213
cognitive ability 79, 82, 85, 87, 97, 146
cognitive ageing 88
cognitive architecture 204, 228; visual imagery as component of 210
cognitive decline 151
cognitive design principles 6–8; for effective visual directions 6
cognitive ergonomics 225
cognitive load (CL) 4, 86, 89, 93, 94
cognitive map(s) 3–5, 56, 127, 221, 233, 238; of larger spaces 235–7
cognitive mechanisms in spatial text processing 135–45
cognitive phenomena, analytic approaches to 206
cognitive psychology 3, 127, 191, 203, 209, 213, 242, 244
cognitive research 242
cognitive science 182, 203
cognitive style 146, 150, 153
comics/graphic novels 9–13
communication as primary function of language 190
compensatory view of blindness 166
complex span: decay and interference in 86–91; performance 80, 82–9, 91–7 [within multiple-component model 85–6]; recall 86, 87, 89, 91; task(s) 80–2, 85–7, 91, 95, 96, 98; and visuospatial resources 91–5
complex spatial descriptions and imagery 168–70
comprehension 215; of discourse 216; language 79, 86, 128–35, 180, 182, 184, 192, 194, 195, 210, 218; narrative 220
computational theory 209, 212
computer graphics 7
conceptual representation 162; amodal 164
concrete words 109, 112, 191, 193, 194
concurrent task(s) 139, 140, 143, 148, 149, 154, 192, 210, 211, 221, 227; verbal 141, 220
Conference on Spatial Information Theory (COSIT) 244
configurational scanning 240
congenital blindness 164, 168, 172, 233–6, 238–41
construction–integration theory 186
Corsi block task 113, 114, 115, 147
COSIT: *see* Conference on Spatial Information Theory
counterfactuals 180, 184, 193
counting span 87, 88
CRT: *see* card rotation test
cube comparison test (CCT) 146

DCT: *see* dual-coding theory
deductive reasoning 216, 217
depictions of events 11
depictive representations 22, 37, 38, 54, 58, 62, 64, 65
diagrams 7, 9, 10, 110, 112, 151, 164
dichotic listening task 79
difference theory 164
digit span 79, 98, 147
direction, sense of 127, 150
discourse: comprehension of 216; representation of, levels of 128–9
dissociation 21, 113, 213
domain specificity 91
dot localization task 20
Downs syndrome individuals 117
dual-coding theory (DCT) 45, 131, 144, 193, 210, 212, 233
dual-task paradigm 136, 137, 144, 145, 153
DVN: *see* dynamic visual noise
dynamic models 216
dynamic visual noise (DVN) 106, 108–12, 116, 143, 212

egocentric representation 59, 61, 166
electroencephalography (EEG) 167, 184, 185, 189
embodied cognition 166, 177–95
embodied meaning 178, 187–91, 194; advantages of 189–90; as interface with physical world 189–90; theories 187–9
embodiment theory(ies) 177, 191, 192
emulative simulation, imagery as 52, 53
episodes, segmentation of 11
episodic buffer 90, 136, 145
ER: *see* error rate
ERP: *see* event-related potential

error rate (ER) 32, 35–7
Euclidean distance 218, 219, 220
Euclidean forms of representation 218
Euclidean metrics 44, 62, 233
European Workshop on Imagery and
  Cognition (EWIC) 244
event-related fMRI study 48, 184
event-related potential (ERP) 112,
  167, 194
events, depictions of 11
EWIC: *see* European Workshop on
  Imagery and Cognition
executive processes 85, 110, 111, 113,
  115–19, 154
experimental psychology 109
extrastriate cortex 51, 65
eye movement control 114

features, representation of 61; and neural
  structures 61–8
FfA: *see* fusiform face area
figural space 223, 225
film 10–11
fMRI: *see* functional magnetic resonance
  imaging
force dynamics 191
forgetting, interference-based 89
formal logic 215
frames of reference, intrinsic and extrinsic
  149
frontal gyrus, left inferior 183
frontal lobes 21
functional magnetic resonance imaging
  (fMRI) 20, 48, 64, 67, 168, 182–4, 188
functional space 45, 64, 223
fusiform cortex 46, 48
fusiform face area (FfA) 21, 47, 51

general fluid (Gf) intelligence 80, 84, 85
geographic features and route directions 5
geometric patterns 112
glyphs 8–10
grammatical words 192
granularity 191
graphemic representation 128
graphic novels/comics 10, 11
graphs 9

haptic tasks 166, 171
Hebbian assemblies 187, 188
Hebbian circuitry 188
Hebbian neuronal mechanism 188
hemispace 213
high imagers 221, 226

higher order cognition 80, 84–7, 96, 245
hippocampus 55, 58, 59, 207, 223
human–machine interactions 225

iconic image(s) (II) 17, 19, 24–33,
  35–7; scanning task 28; of spatial
  resolution 27
iconic representations 217
II: *see* iconic image(s)
image(s) (*passim*) 216; formation 242;
  iconic: *see* iconic image(s); maintenance
  212; mental, in mental model theory
  215–17; modality specificity of 46–8;
  retinal 44; scanning 19, 22–4, 26, 28,
  38, 206–8, 212, 220, 237–40 [brain
  mechanisms underlying 38; mental
  23, 24; paradigms 19, 22, 23];
  transformation 53, 212; visual 43, 44,
  52, 66, 108, 109, 110, 111, 117, 225
imagers: high 221, 226; low 221,
  226, 230
imagery (*passim*) 209; array theory of 44;
  and complex spatial descriptions 168–70;
  instructions 45, 109, 144, 145, 149, 221,
  234; and like-modality perception,
  functional equivalence between 20–1;
  mental, cognitive neuroscience of 206; as
  modality-specific process within
  modality-specific brain structures 46–54;
  modality specificity of 44; motor 195;
  and perception 20–2, 24–7, 48, 50, 51,
  210; representations 22–3; research 3,
  210, 240–5 [history of 45–6, 203–9; and
  working memory 213]; spatial 24, 32,
  54, 55, 59, 61, 67, 168; and spatial
  cognition 221–33; strategies 128, 134,
  149, 153 [in memorization of spatial
  texts 144–5]; underlying representations
  used in 38; without visual experience
  233–40; visual 43, 46–51, 62, 64, 65,
  109–11, 167, 210, 213, 214, 217,
  218, 221, 233–7; visuospatial 23,
  211, 218, 224; and working memory
  209–14
imagination 43, 223
inferior/middle occipital gyrus 50
inferior temporal gyrus 21
inner scribe 106, 107, 110, 116, 211;
  function of 113–14
interference-based forgetting 89
interhemispheric sulcus 183
International Union of Psychological
  Sciences 3
irrelevant pictures task 116, 118

kinematic models 216
kinesthesis 222
kinesthetic scanning 232, 234, 240

language (*passim*): abstract 178, 186,
    191–4; action: *see* action language;
    communication as primary function
    of 190; comprehension 79, 86,
    128–35, 180, 182, 184, 192, 194, 195,
    210, 218
lateral fusiform gyrus 20
lateral occipital cortex (LOC) 48, 49, 51,
    67
left inferior frontal gyrus 183
left and right ventral parietal cortex 49
letter rotation task 91
lexical decision 179
like-modality perception 19, 20; and
    imagery, functional equivalence
    between 20–1
limited-capacity attentional control 97
linguistic markers 192
linguistic meaning 177, 178, 186, 191
linguistic system 194
linguistics 127, 224
LOC: *see* lateral occipital cortex (LOC)
localization, auditory 166
location, memory for 127
locomotor tasks 166, 171
logic, formal 215
long-term memory (LTM) 19, 23, 26, 27,
    45, 61, 77–9, 82, 95, 96, 98, 136, 145,
    154, 210, 213
low imagers 221, 226, 230

MAD magazine 10
magnetoencephalography (MEG) 184
map(s) 5, 9, 12, 55, 56, 57, 127, 169, 172,
    221, 233, 238; cognitive, of larger
    spaces 235–7; information 216; learning
    195; -like mental representations 232;
    mental 3, 4, 78; route 5, 8, 11, 229;
    tactile 163
matrix symmetry judgment 95
meaning, embodied: *see* embodied
    meaning
meaning–action interaction 178, 192
medial fusiform gyrus 20
medial prefrontal cortex 49
medial temporal lobes 61, 223
MEG: *see* magnetoencephalography
memorization 131, 139, 148–50, 168, 224,
    226; of spatial texts, imagery strategies
    in 144–5

memory: long-term (LTM) 19, 23, 26, 27,
    45, 61, 77–9, 82, 95, 96, 98, 136, 145,
    154, 210, 213; pictorial, traces 45;
    primary 77, 80, 81, 98; secondary 81,
    98; span 79, 83, 88; spatial 61, 84, 94,
    107, 117, 222, 227; temporary 77, 86;
    trace 52, 87, 88; verbal 115; visual 47,
    106, 109, 110, 113, 115, 117–19, 210;
    visuospatial 84, 107, 115, 117, 119;
    working: *see* working memory
mental arithmetic 78
mental image (MI) 28–33, 36, 37, 43–5,
    54–6, 58, 62, 130, 132, 166, 167, 169,
    195; generation of 221; in mental model
    theory 215–17; scanning 22–4; spatial
    19, 25–8, 30, 32, 33, 35, 37, 38 [spatial
    resolution of 19, 27–38]; visual 19–39,
    44, 145, 149, 166, 167, 169, 235
mental imagery 19–38, 45, 46, 48, 51, 61,
    64, 65, 69, 144, 195, 204–6, 208–12,
    215–17, 219–22, 227, 229, 232, 242,
    243; cognitive neuroscience of 206; as
    perceptual information is accessed from
    memory 43; processes, cognitive impact
    of blindness on 233; spatial 19, 24,
    27–9, 31, 34, 36–8, 55; visual 20–4, 54,
    208, 225; visuospatial 24
mental maps 3, 4, 78
mental model(s) (passim): conceptual 216;
    conceptualization of 215; construction
    of 217 [from spatial description 135];
    generating 56–8; physical 216;
    reasoning with 217–18; spatial 4, 139,
    145, 146, 151, 153, 154, 170, 171, 217–
    20, 236, 237]; theory 128, 166, 209, 215
    [mental images in 215–17]; and working
    memory 220–21
mental representation(s) (*passim*): abstract
    ("supramodal") 233; map-like 232; of
    space 209, 235; spatial 57, 142, 145,
    148, 232, 236 [construction of 232] ;
    text, spatial, and visual mental images
    145; and text perspective 142
mental rotation 45, 53–5, 63, 67, 127, 132,
    153, 206, 211–13, 223, 224, 234; ability/
    skills 7; spatial, analogue 54; test (MRT)
    146–9, 154, 221
mental scanning 54, 56, 57, 63, 67, 169,
    195, 206, 220, 238, 240; neurocognitive
    signature of 208
mental simulation 45, 51, 166, 178, 182,
    192, 245
mental synthesis 110, 211
MEP: *see* motor evoked potentials

meshing of affordances 187
metaphor(s)/metaphorical meaning 13, 43, 191, 192, 233; orientational 180, 181; visual 222
metric distances, representation of 220
metric spatial information 169
MI: *see* mental image
mimicry 53
minimal effort, principle of 225
Minnesota paper form board (MPFB) 146, 147
mirror neurons 187–9, 195
mnemonic, pegword 108, 110, 112, 118
modality-specific brain structures 46, 47, 48; imagery as modality-specific process within 46–54
modality-specific neural structures 50; early, contribution to imagery by 48–51; shared 50
modality-specific processing 48
modality-specific representations 46, 52; shared 51
modality specificity 46, 51, 117, 119; of images 44 [processing 51–4]
motor affordance(s) 190
motor brain 180, 184, 186, 187, 194
motor coordination, poor 152
motor cortex 59, 178, 180, 186, 187, 188, 189, 192, 195
motor evoked potentials (MEP) 179
motor imagery 195
motor involvement 154
motor resonance 185–90, 194
MPFB: *see* Minnesota paper form board
MRT: *see* mental rotation test
mu rhythms 184–6, 189
multiple-component model 90, 92, 94; complex span performance within 85–6
multivoxel pattern analysis 51

narrative(s), visual 9–13
narrative comprehension 220
navigational performance 232; and visuospatial abilities 224
negation 192, 193
neural overload 180
neural resonances 195
neural structures 44, 46–8, 50, 58, 69; representing features of 61–8; spatial structure, functionality of 66–8
neurobiological research 213
neurocognitive signature of mental scanning 208

neuroimaging 167, 184, 187, 194, 208; research 213
neurons 66, 180, 183, 187–90, 195
neuropsychological research 213
neuropsychology 98, 119, 213
neuroscience 5, 23, 69, 178, 180, 182, 186–8, 191, 195, 206
NLD: *see* nonverbal learning disability
nonspatial inferences verification task 134
nonverbal learning disability (NLD) 146; children with, and spatial ability 152–4

occipital cortex 46, 49, 51, 54, 64, 67
occipital and temporal lobes 21
on-line cognition 77, 78, 98
operation span 81, 84, 87
orientational metaphors 180, 181
orienteering 150
Orsay Hospital 206

paper folding test (PFT) 38, 146
paper form board test 38
parahippocampal gyri 20
parahippocampal place area (PPA) 21, 47, 51
parietal cortex 46, 55, 68, 183, 187, 192; posterior 54, 59, 67; and spatial imagery 58–61; ventral, left and right 49
parietal lobe 21, 188; left inferior 184, 185
Parkinson disease 187
pars triangularis 183, 188
PAS: *see* pattern activation system
patterns of activation in brain 20
pattern activation system (PAS) 111–13, 119
pegword mnemonic 108, 110, 112, 118
perception (*passim*): and imagery 20–2, 24–7, 48, 50, 51, 210; as information is registered directly from the senses 43; like-modality 19, 20; visual 19–24, 47, 50, 210, 213, 214
perceptual neglect 213
perceptual representation 162
perceptual symbols 187
perspective and blindness, and complex spatial descriptions 170–1
PET: *see* positron emission tomography
PFT: *see* paper folding test
phoneme–grapheme matching 152
phonemic representation 128
phonological loop 85, 86, 90, 91, 136–8, 209; domain-specific 80
pictorial memory traces 45

positron emission tomography (PET) 64, 206–8
posterior cingulate 49
posterior parietal cortex 54, 59, 67
posterior superior temporal gyrus (STG) 49
PPA: *see* parahippocampal place area (PPA)
premotor cortex 47, 182, 183, 187, 188
primary memory 77, 80, 81, 98
primary visual cortex (V1) 26, 27, 46, 48–51, 64–8, 164
principle of minimal effort 225
processing: spatial 56–9, 68, 84, 93, 113, 114; visual 24, 44, 46, 48–50, 66, 90, 93, 106, 108, 112, 113, 119, 162
propositional representation(s) 44, 128–30, 132, 170
propositional text-base 128, 129
proprioception 222
prosopagnosia 21
psychological space, scales of 223
psychology: cognitive 3, 127, 191, 203, 209, 213, 242, 244; scientific 3
psychometric tests 223, 224

random number generation (RNG) 117; task 116
Raven's Advanced Progressive Matrices 38
reading span 84, 87, 91, 92
reasoning 215; deductive 216, 217
reference, frames of, intrinsic and extrinsic 149
reinstatement hypothesis 46
relational models, simple 216
repetition: instructions 145, 221; priming, reciprocal 47
representation(s): depictive 22, 37, 38, 54, 58, 62, 64, 65; of discourse, levels of 128–9; egocentric 59, 61, 166; imagery 22–3; mental: see mental representation(s); of neural structures 61–8; propositional 44, 128, 129, 130, 132, 170; sequential 166; visual imagery 44
representational neglect 213
representational space 22
representational system 228; and analogy 216
response paradigm 179
retinal image 44
retinotopically organized early brain structures 50

retrosplenial cortex 49, 61
right-hemisphere dysfunction 152
RNG: *see* random number generation
rote verbal learning 152
route: description(s) 5, 134, 143, 145, 154, 162, 171, 172, 177, 189, 227–9, 232, 237 [task 177]; directions 5–11, 149, 150 [production and comprehension of 227–32]; instructions 5, 220, 229; map(s) 5, 8, 11, 229; perspective 4, 170, 227, 232, 237; -text processing 143, 144, 153 [interference effect on 143]

SAT scores 91, 92
scanning: image 19, 22–6, 28, 38, 206–8, 212, 220, 237–40; rate of, and speed–accuracy trade-off 35; task(s) 25–8, 32, 33, 36, 37, 39, 56, 207, 238
scientific psychology 3
secondary memory 81, 98
segmentation: of episodes 11; of events 11 [in visual narratives by frames 12]; of routes 11; of space 11; of time 11
semantic judgment 179
semantic task 179
sense of direction 127, 150
sensibility judgments 179
sentence: –picture verification task 166; verification 83, 139, 141, 145, 151, 153, 154, 167, 218, 221
sequential representation 166
sequentiality 154
short-term memory (STM) 60, 77, 79, 80, 95, 96, 111, 225; spatial 92; verbal 78, 92
sighted people 144, 233–41; and blind people, spatial language use by 162–73; blindfolded 234, 236, 238, 240
simple relational models 216
simple span recall 91
simple span tasks 81, 86, 87
simulation(s) 45, 50–3, 55, 63, 166, 178, 180, 182, 184, 190, 192–5, 245; emulative, imagery as 52, 53; language-based 192; mental 45, 51, 166, 178, 182, 192, 245
simulators 187, 194
situation model(s) 128, 129, 214
size comparisons 212
SMG: *see* supramarginal gyrus
somatosensory cortical areas 47
space: coding of, by blind people 166; mental representation of 209, 235;

psychological, scales of 223–4; representational 22

span task: complex 83–8, 93, 94; simple 80, 81, 84

spatial ability 7, 91, 92, 146–9, 153, 154, 223, 224; in children with nonverbal learning disability (NLD) 152–4; and spatial text processing 146–8

spatial attention 115, 119

spatial behavior 221

spatial cognition 3, 127, 131, 146, 149, 153, 154, 209, 215, 235, 244; and imagery 221–33

spatial communication 162, 163, 172

spatial competencies 152

spatial concurrent task(s) 139, 220

spatial descriptions, complex: and blindness and perspective 170–1; and imagery 168–70

spatial discourse 229, 232

spatial effects 56, 57, 67, 68; while processing visual images 54–5

spatial environments, verbal descriptions of 224–7

spatial imagery 24, 32, 54, 55, 67, 168; and parietal cortex 58–61

spatial images 55, 58, 61, 67, 68, 163–6, 168, 171, 172, 233, 240

spatial information 26, 27, 29, 30, 32, 53–5, 58, 59, 67, 68, 96, 107, 133, 134, 136, 146, 147, 151, 153, 154, 163, 166, 170–2, 211, 222, 225, 232, 236, 238, 240; categorical 169; metric 169; representation of 127

spatial interference 148, 149, 221

spatial knowledge 55, 209, 221, 224, 236, representation of, amodal forms of 209

spatial language 141, 150, 153, 224; processing and use of 225 [by blind and sighted individuals 162–73]

spatial learning 171, 222

spatial memory 61, 84, 94, 107, 117, 222, 227

spatial mental image(s)/imagery 19, 24–38, 55; scanning task 28; spatial resolution of 19, 38

spatial mental model(s) 4, 55, 131, 137, 139, 144–7, 151–4, 170, 171, 217, 218, 221, 233, 236, 237; early studies 132–3; generating 56–8; nature of 133–5

spatial mental representation(s) 57, 142, 145, 148, 232, 236

spatial mental rotation, analogue 54

spatial model(s) 57, 58, 128, 132–5, 145, 153, 216, 218, 233

spatial neglect, unilateral 213

spatial perspectives 127, 170; capacity to reason about 127

spatial processing 56–9, 68, 84, 93, 113, 114

spatial quality of visual images 44

spatial relations 44, 55–8, 62, 64, 66, 67, 133, 135, 139, 168, 169, 216, 220, 237; implicit, automatic awareness of 135

spatial representation(s) 24, 30, 38, 59, 61, 63, 64, 67, 68, 134, 135, 144, 146, 153, 154, 170, 171, 220, 224, 232, 235, 236, 239–41; ability to construct 127; analogue 45; of blind individuals 163–66; cognitive styles in, and spatial text comprehension 149–51; intrinsic (or egocentric) and extrinsic (or allocentric) frames of reference in 149

spatial resolution: of iconic images 27; of mental images 27–38

spatial retention 114

spatial sequential task 117, 119

spatial simultaneous task 117, 119

spatial storage 84, 93, 95

spatial structure 6, 26, 27, 32, 35, 36, 38, 44, 46, 216; neural 66 [functionality of 66–8]; visual buffer as 61–4

spatial tapping (ST) 116, 136, 139, 141, 143, 145, 147–9, 154, 211, 221

spatial tasks 58, 59, 67, 144, 150, 153, 163, 223

spatial text(s) 138, 139, 141, 143, 169, 171, 220; comprehension 135, 136, 145–7, 149, 153, 154 [and cognitive styles in spatial representation 149–51]; memorization 148, 149 [imagery strategies in 144–5]; mental representation, spatial [and visual mental images 145]; processing 127, 128, 131, 135, 136, 139 [and aging 151–2; individual differences in 127–54; from different perspectives 141–4; and individual differences in imagery and working memory 145–53; and spatial ability 146–8; and working memory 136–41]

spatial updating 59, 221, 222

spatial vision 24

spatial visualization 146, 153

speech balloons 13

speed–accuracy trade-off and rate of scanning 35

ST: *see* spatial tapping
static matrix forms 117
STG: *see* posterior superior temporal gyrus
STM: *see* short-term memory
Stroop task 80
subvocal rehearsal 78, 80, 85, 95
superior temporal cortex 46
supramarginal gyrus (SMG) 168, 183, 184; left 167
survey perspective 4, 143, 151, 171, 227, 231, 232, 237
Sylvian fissure 183
symbolic language: external 177; internal 177
symbolism 177, 189, 191
symbolist theory(ies) 177, 189
synthesis, mental 110, 211

tactile acuity 166
tactile maps 163
tapping task 115, 116, 138, 148, 221
target localization 134
task(s): ball span task 95; concurrent verbal 220; Corsi block task 113–15, 147; dichotic listening 79; dot localization 20; haptic 166, 171; iconic image scanning 28; irrelevant pictures 116, 118; letter rotation 91; locomotor 166, 171; nonspatial inferences verification 134; random number generation (RNG) 116; route description 177; scanning 25–8, 32, 33, 36, 37, 39, 56, 207, 238; semantic 179; sentence–picture verification 166; simple span 81, 86, 87; span [complex 80, 83–5, 87, 88, 93, 94; simple 80, 81, 84]; spatial tasks 58, 59, 67, 144, 150, 153, 163, 223 [concurrent 139, 220; mental image scanning 28; simultaneous 117, 119; sequential 117, 119]; Stroop 80; tapping 115, 116, 138, 148, 221; Vandenberg mental rotations 7; verbal 139 [suppression 86]; visual noise (VN) 116; *see also*: complex span task(s), concurrent task(s)
TBRS model: *see* time-based resource-sharing model
temporal lobes 21, 61, 223; medial 61, 223
temporal models 216
temporary memory 77, 86
test(s): Brooks 114; card rotation (CRT) 146; cube comparison (CCT) 146; mental rotation (MRT) 146–9, 154, 221; paper folding (PFT) 38, 146; paper form

board 38; psychometric tests 223, 224; visual patterns (VPT) 113, 115
text(s): comprehension 127–37, 145–9, 152–4, 220; perspective 142, 143, 151, 152, 154, 163, 172 [and mental representation 142]; spatial: *see* spatial text(s)
time-based resource-sharing (TBRS) model 89, 90, 91, 92, 93
TMS: *see* transcranial magnetic stimulation
topographical disorientation 152, 154
transcranial magnetic stimulation (TMS) 66; single-pulse 179

unilateral spatial neglect 213

V1: *see* primary visual cortex
Vandenberg mental rotations task 7
Venice 3, 150, 230, 231, 232
ventral parietal cortex, left and right 49
ventral temporal cortex 51
ventrotemporal cortex 20
verbal abilities 152
verbal classification 152
verbal descriptions of spatial environments 224–7
verbal encoding 45, 83, 212
verbal memory 115
verbal skills 152
verbal tasks 139; suppression 86
verbal working memory (VWM) 107, 108, 113, 114, 136, 145, 151, 153, 221
verbal working model 107
verbatim memory 168
vestibular system 222
virtual reality 9, 13
vista space 223
visual association cortex 47, 49
visual attention 119, 162; control of 114
visual buffer 44–6, 48, 58, 67, 106, 111–13, 119, 206, 209, 210, 212; as physical space at neural level 64–5; as spatial structure 61–4; spatially organized 53, 63
visual cache 48, 106, 107, 111–13, 119, 211, 212
visual cognition 206, 211, 213
visual experience, imagery without 233–40
visual explanations 8, 9, 11
visual image(s) 43, 47, 49, 58, 62, 66, 68, 78, 108–11, 117, 149, 187, 206, 210, 212, 217, 221, 225, 226, 231–3, 236, 237, 240; mental 19–9, 44, 145, 149,

166, 167, 169, 235; processing [and
spatial effects 54–5; modality specificity
of 51–4]; spatial quality of 44
visual imagery 43, 109–11, 167, 210, 213,
214, 217, 218, 221, 236–37; blind
people's use of 233–5; in brain 43–69;
mental 20–4, 54, 208, 225;
representation(s) 44
visual knowledge, retrieval of 48
visual memory 47, 106, 109, 110, 113,
115, 117–19, 210
visual metaphor 222
visual narrative(s) 8–13
visual noise (VN) 106, 108, 143, 212; task
116
visual patterns test (VPT) 113, 115
visual perception 19–24, 47, 50, 210, 213,
214
visual poetry 13
visual processing 24, 48, 49, 66, 90, 93,
106, 108, 112, 113, 119, 162; domains,
spatial structure of at neural level,
functional role of 44; regions 50;
structures 46
visual representations, classes of 23–4;
mental 43
visual storage 93, 94
visual storytelling 11
visual working memory 48, 54, 106, 107,
108; attention as rehearsal mechanism
for 114–18
visualization 146, 153, 217
visuospatial abilities and navigational
performance 224
visuospatial cognition 194, 195, 213, 233,
235
visuospatial complex span performance 86
visuospatial imagery 23, 211, 218, 224;
mental 24

visuospatial memory 84, 107, 115, 117, 119
visuospatial processes/processing 113,
139; and executive processes 116
visuospatial representations 230
visuospatial resources 91; and complex
span 91–5
visuospatial sketchpad (VSSP) 136, 139,
209–12
visuospatial tracking 210
visuospatial working memory (VSWM)
106–20, 128, 135–9, 141, 143, 145–8,
153, 211–13, 220–4, 227; direct access
to 108–11; measures of 224
VN: *see* visual noise
VPT: *see* visual patterns test
VSSP: *see* visuospatial sketchpad
VSWM: *see* visuospatial working memory
VWM: *see* verbal working memory

Wernicke's area 187
WMC: *see* working memory capacity
word(s): abstract 109, 191, 193, 194;
concrete 109, 112, 191, 193, 194;
grammatical 192; span 79
working memory (WM) (*passim*): as
contemplation 77; as control of attention
78–95; and imagery 209–21 [research
213]; and mental models 220–1; as
multiple domain-specific resources
77–8; spatial 107, 108, 114, 115, 117,
139, 144, 224; and spatial text
processing 136–41; system, visual,
access into 106; verbal 107, 108, 113,
114, 221; verbal and spatial components
of 139, 220; visuospatial (VSWM): *see*
visuospatial working memory
working memory capacity (WMC) 77,
79–82, 84, 86, 88, 92; spatial 92;
verbal 92